DRUGS AND CRIME
DEVIANT PATHWAYS

To our families

Drugs and Crime
Deviant Pathways

Edited by

SERGE BROCHU
International Centre for Comparative Criminology,
University of Montreal, Canada

CANDIDO DA AGRA
Centre of Deviant Behaviour Sciences,
University of Oporto, Portugal

MARIE-MARTHE COUSINEAU
International Centre for Comparative Criminology,
University of Montreal, Canada

ASHGATE

Published by
Ashgate Publishing Limited
Gower House
Croft Road
Aldershot
Hampshire GU11 3HR
England

Ashgate Publishing Company
131 Main Street
Burlington, VT 05401-5600 USA

Ashgate website: http//www.ashgate.com

British Library Cataloguing in Publication Data
Drugs and crime deviant pathways
   1. Deviant behaviour 2. Drug abuse and crime 3. Criminal psychology
   I. Brochu, Serge II. Agra, Candido da III. Cousineau, Marie-Marthe
   364.3

Library of Congress Cataloging-in-Publication Data
Drugs and crime deviant pathways / edited by Serge Brochu, Candido da Agra, and Marie-Marthe Cousineau.
     p. cm.
   Includes bibliographical references.
   ISBN 0-7546-3023-4
    1. Drug abuse and crime. 2. Criminal behaviour. I. Brochu, Serge.
  II. Agra, Candido da. III. Cousineau, Marie-Marthe.

HV5801 .D742 2002
364.2'4-dc21
                                               2002018202
ISBN 0 7546 3023 4

Typeset by Martingraphix
Printed and bound in Great Britain by MPG Books Ltd, Bodmin, Cornwall.

Contents

List of Figures

List of Tables

Foreword

Kai Pernanen

The explanation of human behaviour is a multidisciplinary task. Nowhere is this more evident than in the case of behaviour which is linked to the use of psychoactive substances. Whether it is behaviour under the influence of a drug or behaviour that is in some degree determined by dependence on drugs, it is clear that this chemical–biological component ought to be integrated into explanations using different types of psychological and environmental components.

Multidisciplinary determination means that theoretical integration is needed. However, finding a suitable conceptual and theoretical framework for this purpose is not easy, and attempts that are too ambitious can easily fail. This is nevertheless a goal that should be kept in mind while we pursue the more mundane task of describing and explaining deviant behaviour, whether or not it is linked to the use or abuse of drugs.

Looking at human behaviour as it evolves over extended periods of time introduces yet another dimension of complexity to the description and explanation of behaviour, interactions and relationships. The human organism develops and matures, environments change from school and dependence on parents to the contexts of work and other forms of intimate relationships. Structural factors change over time according to their own logics (or lack of such). In the lives of young people who are not protected by a healthy family life the orderly developmental progression is often disrupted and structural and environmental factors such as economic conditions and the policies of social authorities can have more profound consequences.

Despite the complexities of studying the development of life courses and the factors that influence aspects of these courses, the task is intuitively appealing even to the non-scientist. People do structure their lives in terms of pathways; they recognize, especially in hindsight, significant life events and junctions where decisions were made that had far-reaching consequences for the course of one's life (sometimes without realizing the significance of the decision or the occurrence at the time). People are known to muse over the course that their own and other people's lives have taken or could have taken: 'where did I go wrong', 'if it hadn't been for ...'. Individuals who are at high risk of deviating from central societal norms are no different in many of the types of influences that affect them and their attempts to make sense of these occurrences and their own reactions, although their plans and objective prospects are often restricted by both environmental and individual psychological factors.

Charting and explaining the course of a life or segments of lives is therefore something that comes naturally. Surprisingly, this preoccupation has not found a systematic and prominent counterpart in the study of deviant behaviour (nor in studies of human behaviour generally). The framework of *deviant pathways* promises to become a significant aid in this systematization. It promises to bring together disparate elements of theory, method and empirical findings.

Drug use is strongly associated with other forms of deviance in many cultures. An important challenge for pathway analysis is to lay bare the processes by which this occurs. There will no doubt be somewhat different answers for different countries and jurisdictions. Some of these answers may surprise us.

Societal occurrences outside the reach of individual determination can have a tremendous effect on human pathways. At times hardly anyone can escape the consequences of such events even with the protection provided by a positive intimate life sphere. A large segment of the older generation in Europe and other continents still live with the effects of World War II. More recently, many Americans and their families were traumatized and had their lives take a new course because of the war in Vietnam. The wars and atrocities in the former Yugoslavia and in Rwanda and Burundi are even more recent examples of events that can shatter and dramatically redirect individual pathways. In many cases, such occurrences influence the life course of several generations. This is also true of the effects of moving from one country and cultural sphere to another, and it is of course well known that children of immigrants are at relatively high risk of deviant behaviour.

In modern societies, determinative influences in individual deviant pathways often include the introduction to drug use and the beginning of habitual use of these substances. Still, even as a separate phenomenon, we have insufficient knowledge about the extended processes that are involved when drugs become determinative for other forms of deviance, most importantly for serious criminality. How much of these processes and their phenomenological salience for the individual can be explained by biological and psychological predilections, by environmental influences such as the peers that they associate with and the interactions that they experience with them or by the very structure of situations, the risks and opportunities imposed by restrictive or lax drug policies? The task of charting deviant pathways is daunting, but this framework is necessary if we are ever going to comprehend the factors and processes that determine how deviance is initiated, sustained and abandoned within the course of the lives of individuals.

It is evident that linear one-directional causality does not suffice for the task at hand. It does not even suffice for the accounting of physical developments. Already during the first few milliseconds of the Big Bang the world became a system of interacting parts, and then, very quickly, evolved into a vast system of interacting systems by far exceeding the modelling capabilities of even the most powerful computers. The world's climate and the interaction between meteorological systems that determine the development of weather from one moment to the next are good examples of complexities that can only be represented in a systemic approach. It is perhaps encouraging that they can, with the necessary macro-level simplifications of the processes involved, be so summarized and represented.

However, this exposition of complexities keeps us too close to the physical world. The cognitive capabilities, interpretations and conscious and subconscious adjustments that characterize human behaviour naturally introduce new explanatory elements. In the explanation of human behaviour we must find ways to subsume the semiotic, the symbolically interpretive, aspects of the determination of human behaviour, and the emergent qualities of social systems that exert their influence on human lives.

For integration attempts to succeed, we need a perspective that is common to most important forms of influence on deviant pathways and that can also encompass the methods and conceptualizations represented in this volume. We need a framework that will allow a translation of as many as possible of the approaches to one common language. At the present time it seems that the most inclusive language is to be found in the phenomenological approach (and other wider systems of representation that incorporate phenomenological processes, such as the autopoietic). It is in the phenomenological experience that significant childhood experiences, salient life-events, trends and relationships found in aggregate analyses, the effects of policy changes on individual lives and so on, are all translated by the actor into a basis for individual action.

Perhaps what we need to do as one of the initial steps is to study how the different explanatory factors each in turn and all together get translated into the phenomenologically relevant states of mind and body that either increase or decrease the likelihood of deviant behaviour of a kind that society finds undesirable.

Is it possible to find recurring patterns of influence in the seemingly infinite variety of idiosyncracies and environmental influences that characterize human lives? The phenomenological consequences of disparate elements found in the course of human pathways can be very similar. Being neglected or abandoned in childhood, being subjected to inconsistent parental rearing patterns or being bullied at school have phenomenological consequences that are sufficiently similar to allow success in treatment which addresses them as a total complex, although they have little in common at the surface level. This indicates that they are largely equivalent at the phenomenological level. In addition, negative factors or occurrences in one stage of an individual pathway can be neutralized by later occurrences that are totally different when described as objective occurrences. The significant event or link can only be found on the level where new mental structurings emerge which change the apprehension of the self and its place in the world.

We should not lose sight of the fact that deviance in one form or another shapes the world in ways that are more profound than does conformity. Deviance is in part adjustment to special prevailing conditions facing an individual, but it is also action and reaction in spite of the reality faced by the individual. Deviance can be an adjustment to external conditions and to changes in these conditions, but it can also be a creative initiative independent of environmental factors. Examples of positive deviance are well known in scientific progress. Freud was a deviant in terms of the theories that he exposed, and Einstein was a non-conformist who initially was met with ridicule by a great portion of the scientific community. Going back further, we encounter names like Socrates and Galileo among those who had to pay a high price for their nonconformity. Can we turn destructive innovative deviance into creative positive deviance? If we are to do so, and we know that it is possible in some cases, we need a holistic, dynamic, integrative framework for our endeavours.

The deviant pathway perspective acknowledges that we need more than a listing of 'causal factors', more than a listing and measurement of 'relationships', but even those have a place in the scientific endeavour. The strength of the deviant pathways approach as presented in this volume is its inclusiveness; attesting to the legitimacy of very varied approaches in trying to explain, predict and prevent deviant behaviour, and the stress on the longitudinal that is implicit in the very concept of a pathway. It is evident that, in addition to a rich variety of empirical studies, we also need philosophical analysis in order to secure a stable foundation for an integrative pathway analysis.

While trying to find integrative solutions for the analyses of deviant pathways, we do well to approach the empirical study of deviant pathways with an open mind and with an inclusive attitude towards the types of research questions asked and methodologies used. The different approaches used by the contributors to this volume all exemplify the factors and processes that link drug use with other forms of deviance. They have a natural place in an integrated accounting of deviant pathways. Perhaps two of the most important contributions of the Deviant Pathways seminars arranged thus far is that they stress the value of contributions from different approaches while prominently displaying the goal of integration.

Acknowledgments

This book is the result of the first and the second Deviant Pathways seminars held in Montreal and Oporto. We would like to thank people who collaborated in the organization of these conferences. Of special importance for the success of the meetings was the fine work of Isabelle Parent and Maria Manuela Santos.

Two institutions played a key role in supporting this event: the International Centre for Comparative Criminology (University of Montreal) and the Centro de Ciências do Comportamento Desviante (University of Oporto) who provided valuable logistic and administrative assistance. In addition, the Social Sciences and Humanities Research Council of Canada (SSHRC) and the Fundação Calouste Gulbenkian provided financial support for the conferences as well as for the publication of this book.

This book meant a lot of work for the authors as well as for the editors. The original papers were completed during the time that has elapsed since the seminars. The editors greatly appreciate the precious collaboration and the patience shown by the authors. They would like to give special thanks to Nicole Pinsonneault whose painstaking work in preparing the final copy from all kinds of original work has been priceless.

Finally, thanks to Ashgate Publishing for believing in and supporting the production of this manuscript. We hope that this collection of texts will give inspiring insights in the study of drugs and crime deviant pathways.

The Editors

List of Contributors

Sophie Alarie is a researcher at the Douglas Hospital Research Centre, Verdun, Quebec, Canada.

Michel Born is a professor in Psychology and Head of the Department of Criminology at the University of Liège, Belgium.

Serge Brochu is a professor at the School of Criminology and Director of the International Centre for Comparative Criminology of the University of Montreal, Quebec, Canada.

Natacha Brunelle is a professor in the Department of Psycho Education at the Université du Québec à Trois-Rivières and associate researcher at the International Centre for Comparative Criminology of the University of Montreal, Quebec, Canada.

Jennifer Butters is a research associate at the Centre for Addiction and Mental Health, Ontario, Canada.

René Carbonneau is an assistant Professor in the School of Criminology of the University of Montreal, a member of the Research Unit on Children's Psychosocial Maladjustment of the Centre de Recherche Fernand Seguin, and of the Research Unit on Prevention and Treatment of Substance Abuse, Montreal, Quebec, Canada.

Marie-Marthe Cousineau is a professor in the School of Criminology and a researcher at the International Centre for Comparative Criminology of the University of Montreal, Quebec, Canada.

Candido da Agra is Dean of the Faculty of Law, Head of the Centro de Ciências do Comportamento Desviante, University of Oporto, Oporto, Portugal.

Eloise Dunlap is Principal Investigator at the National Development and Research Institutes, New York, United States.

Patricia G. Erickson is Senior Scientist at the Centre for Addiction and Mental Health and Adjunct Professor at the Department of Sociology, University of Toronto, Ontario, Canada.

Françoise Facy is Project Leader at the Institut national de la santé et de la recherche médicale, Paris, France.

Claude Faugeron is Research Director at the Centre national de la recherche scientifique, Paris, France.

Theodore Ferdinand is a professor emeritus at the Southern Illinois University, Carbondale, Illinois, United States.

Luís Fernandes is a professor in the Faculty of Psychology and Education Sciences and Senior Researcher at the Centro de Ciências do Comportamento Desviante of the University of Oporto, and at the Observatório Permanente de Segurança do Porto, Oporto, Portugal.

Claire Gavray is a sociologist, assistant researcher and PhD candidate in the School of Criminology of the University of Liège, Belgium.

Beric German is an AIDS Outreach Educator, at Street Health, Toronto, Ontario, Canada.

Bruce D. Johnson is Director of the Institute for Special Populations Research at the National Development and Research Institutes, New York, United States.

Michel Kokoreff is a lecturer at the University of Lille I and a member of the Centre lillois d'études et de recherches de sociologie et d'économie and of the Groupement de Recherche Psychotropes, Politique, Société, Paris, France.

Helmut Kury is a professor at the University of Freiburg, and Senior Researcher at the Max Planck Institut for Foreign and International Criminal Law, Freiburg, Germany.

Lisa Maher is a consultant at the National Development and Research Institutes, and research fellow in the National Drug and Alcohol Research Centre at the University of New South Wales, Sydney, Australia.

Celina Manita is an assistant professor in the Faculty of Psychology and Education Sciences and Senior Researcher at the faculty's Centro de Ciências do Comportamento Desviante of the University of Oporto, and a researcher and member of the Administrative Council of the Observatório Permanente de Segurança do Porto, Oporto, Portugal.

Céline Mercier is an associate professor in the Department of Psychiatry at McGill University and Researcher at Douglas Hospital Research Centre, Montreal, Quebec, Canada.

Tiago Neves is a lecturer at the Universidade Lusófona, Lisbon, guest lecturer at the Faculty of Psychology and Education Sciences of the University of Oporto, and researcher at the Observatório Permanente de Segurança do Porto, Oporto, Portugal.

Joachim Obergfell-Fuchs is a psychologist and researcher at the Max Planck Institut, Freiburg, Germany.

Isabelle Parent is a PhD candidate in the School of Criminology of the University of Montreal, Quebec, Canada.

Myriam Rabaud is a research engineer at the Institut national de la santé et de la recherche médicale, Paris, France.

Daniel Ruffin is a statistician at the Institut national de la santé et de la recherche médicale, Paris, France.

Introduction

Serge Brochu, Candido da Agra and Marie-Marthe Cousineau

In 1998, the Social Sciences and Humanities Research Council (SSHRC) of Canada and the Calouste Gulbenkian Foundation of Portugal provided funding for international research meetings of deviant pathway experts to discuss the most recent advances in the field. The meetings were held in Montreal in May 1999, and in Oporto in January 2000. On both occasions, experts from eight countries (Belgium, Canada, France, Italy, Germany, Portugal, Norway and the United States) met for two days. The chapters in this book are taken from the best research papers about deviant drug- and crime-related pathways in different cultural contexts presented at these meetings.

DEVIANCE: FROM SIN TO A PATHWAY PERSPECTIVE

The initial moral perception of deviance as a sin necessitating the imposition of external controls was rapidly replaced in criminological theories by sociopsychological perspectives in which certain behaviours were seen to be psychological problems (Eysenck, 1977), social pathologies (Shaw and McKay, 1942) or norms violations (Durkheim, 1956; Erikson, 1966). Since these perspectives continued to associate deviance with behaviours labelled as 'bad', as opposed to pre-established and well-accepted norms considered to be 'good' (Brochu, 1995), deviance could be defined as the antithesis of conformism. However, the consensus over social norms was challenged by authors such as Parsons (1951) and Becker (1963), who considered deviance to be a social construct, the consequence of the application of the norms developed by a dominant culture.

Like Matza (1969), we believe that the term 'deviance' still has the potential to be useful if separated from its moralistic or Manichean connotations and used in conjunction with the social actor perspective (Debuyst, 1989). Given that deviance does not belong to a sociopathological perspective, but should instead be associated with a differentiation perspective, we should not endorse a corrective view in studying deviance but rather adopt the point of view of an observer concerned with acquiring a better understanding of reality (Brochu and Brunelle, 1997).

THE DEVIANT PATHWAY PERSPECTIVE

The concept of deviant pathways, as explored in this book, was determined by a number of epistemic conditions. First, given its general and abstract nature, the concept of deviance covers a wide range of social problems, some of which are defined as such by social, health or judicial systems. The concept of deviance makes

1

it possible to study social problems scientifically without referring to such normative systems.

Secondly, it was necessary to introduce notions of time and interaction into the explanation of deviance. Causal explanations were replaced by explanations based on interactive and evolutive processes. Interactionist and developmental perspectives grew out of the same epistemic background, the dynamic perspective. The notion of *pathway* conveys this dynamic dimension of the deviant phenomenon. The pathway is a trajectory adopted by a system in movement. Thus the concept implies a relationship between that system and other systems, and the evolution of the system as a succession of points or states over time.

However, there is still a risk that the notion of pathway may be understood in mechanistic terms. The principal danger is that of mechanistic determinism, which assumes that deviant behaviour is determined by a system external to the individual; the determining power of external forces is considered to be so strong as to make behavioural pathways invariable and predictable, like the curve or orbit described by a body's gravitational centre, or a missile's trajectory. It would therefore be possible to reduce the explanation of pathway to a formal mathematical equation. A second danger is that of continuism, or the perspective according to which the behaviour dynamic over time brings nothing new: what is now is what was and what evermore will be. Discontinuity and transformation are out of the question in the continuist perspective. We have therefore rejected the mechanistic concept of pathway.

Instead, we have adopted a phenomenological concept according to which the pathway dynamic implies self-organization through discontinuity. Under its surface continuity, the line formed by behaviour consists of a series of discontinuous segments, each with its own direction. The concept of the deviant subject as autopoietic subject (da Agra, 1990) already contains a phenomenological definition of the deviant pathway. From the autopoiese's perspective, the deviant subject's pathway implies a trajectory that includes segments made up of both wide and narrow roads, of established footpaths and of trails opened up by the subject himself. The deviant pathway is not the trajectory of a body in space, but that of a subject who has availed himself of spatial and temporal segments.

In short, in this perspective, the term 'deviant pathways' refers to (a) the constitution of, involvement in, and withdrawal from, various forms of deviant life, (b) a system of existential segments linked to one another, (c) a movement of determinism and indeterminism that generates meaning and (d) a set of interactions established between individual behaviour and the systems of social control (da Agra, 1997).

THE BOOK

The chapters in this book represent various theoretical perspectives and methodological orientations used to depict *deviant drug and crime-related pathways*. This, in our view, constitutes one of the book's principal strengths.

The book has been divided into four parts. The first part, 'Deviance, set and setting', discusses a new basis for the understanding of deviant pathways. The second part, 'Youth, drug and delinquency pathways', presents empirical studies adopting various approaches or methodologies in order to understand the drug–crime relationship. The third part discusses 'Adult, drug and crime pathways' adopted by drug users, 'flexers', traders or dealers, and traffickers, again using various approaches or methodologies. Finally, the fourth part, 'Ways out' of deviant pathways, explores possible ways of controlling drug use and criminality socially or individually, with or without legal intervention or formal help, and thus of abandoning deviant pathways. In short, this book, like the discussions at the expert seminar meetings, presents an overview of the most advanced research in the field of deviant drug- and crime-related pathways.

Part I: deviance, set and setting

In order to understand deviant behaviour, one must take into account both the actor (his personality, perceptions and behaviour) and the context in which the actor evolves. Thus this first part of the book is devoted to defining the basic concepts upon which to build interdisciplinary research programmes.

In Chapter 1, Candido da Agra presents a research programme conducted at the Centro de Ciências do Comportamento Desviante (Centre of Deviant Behaviour Sciences) of the University of Oporto, Portugal, a programme specifically designed to explore the relationship between drugs and crime. The primary aim of the research programme is to analyse the scientific models traditionally used to explain the drug–crime connection. The author presents the logical basis, frame of reference and methodology adopted, as well as the empirical data collected by the interdisciplinary programme as a whole, returning to theoretical analysis again so as to build a comprehensive system from the empirical data, resulting in the theory of the autopoietic subject.

In Chapter 2, Celina Manita and Candido da Agra explain the application of the theory of the autopoietic subject (da Agra, Chapter 1) to deviant drug- and crime-related pathways. The biogram method was developed in order to explore the temporal nature of the drug–crime pathways. To do so, the authors analysed the life histories of individuals with both drug- and crime-related pathways. The instrument has also been applied to other forms of deviant behaviour, as well as in the treatment of drug addicts and victims of post-traumatic stress.

In Chapter 3, Michel Kokoreff and Claude Faugeron examine the theoretical implications of the notions of *trajectories* and *careers*, when used in conjunction with the notion of deviant *pathways* and, more precisely, in the explanation of the drug–crime relationship in an individual life course. The discussion includes an examination of the relationship between user careers and drug-dealing careers, based on data drawn from research Kokoreff conducted in association with Duprez in poor neighbourhoods in France.

In Chapter 4, Luis Fernandes and Tiago Neves discuss the results of an ethnographic study conducted in an inner city council estate in Oporto generally considered to be a 'dangerous place'. The ethnographic method leads to the comprehension of the evolution of an urban community in terms of norms and control.

Part II: youth, drug and delinquency pathways

This second part of the book examines the pathways of youths involved in both drugs and delinquency. Thus it explores both the risk and protection factors likely to lead to or prevent the adoption of deviant pathways as well as how our understanding of the phenomenon can be furthered by studying the meaning youths themselves attribute to the development of their own pathways. In all instances, data are analysed with a view to discovering means of preventing the adoption of deviant pathways or, if need be, halting its development.

In Chapter 5, René Carbonneau presents the results of the MLES, a longitudinal experimental study conducted in Montreal, Canada, examining the development of delinquency and substance use in boys from socioeconomically disadvantaged families. Subjects were followed from kindergarten to adolescence. From the developmental perspective adopted in this study, the greatest risk factor in the development of delinquency and drug and alcohol use would appear to be the continued demonstration throughout elementary school years of a tendency to externalize problems. Environmental factors, such as family and parenting difficulties, especially in terms of parental supervision, punishment and support, also contribute to the development of deviant behaviour.

In Chapter 6, Michel Born and Claire Gavray identify factors contributing to the continuation or termination of delinquent youth pathways, viewed more specifically in terms of drug use and delinquent behaviour. By following 139 youths, first questioned at the age of 16 and then at the age of 21, the authors have been able to conclude that drug use plays a role in the continuation of deviant pathways. However, other factors, such as family, social relationships and employment status, also play an important role in the continuation or abandonment of the pathway.

In Chapter 7, Natacha Brunelle, Marie-Marthe Cousineau and Serge Brochu adopt a phenomenological stance aimed at revealing the meanings youths themselves attribute to the relationship between drugs and delinquency in their pathway. Using a qualitative research approach, the authors examine autobiographical accounts from 38 young drug users and delinquents between the ages of 16 and 18 (22 boys and 16 girls). In order to provide a phenomenological understanding of the young people's pathways, essentially characterized by alcohol and drug consumption and delinquency, they trace the evolution of deviant youth pathways as expressed in the young people's own words.

Part III: adult, drug and crime pathways

Part III focuses primarily on the drug–crime pathway as it manifests itself in adulthood. This part first explores the stages of the progression of the drug–crime relationship as experienced by a group of cocaine users, then the methods used by the middlemen of the crack trade (the flexers) to deal drugs in an open drug scene (on the street). Finally, it examines the influence of exposure to an underground economy (linked to drug trafficking and prostitution) and early involvement in street life, in a context in which the social and cultural capital of the dominant class is inaccessible to the individual, on the development of deviant pathways. Two studies examine male pathways while the final one explores female deviant pathways.

In Chapter 8, Isabelle Parent and Serge Brochu describe the pathways of 42 adult cocaine users, introducing the concept of a *deviant lifestyle*. Their analysis reveals three stages in the development of such a lifestyle: the initial, exploratory stage (when drug use is occasional), the mutual reinforcement stage, and the compulsive, economic stage (when a person has developed a dependency on psychoactive substances). Analysis of these three stages provides a better understanding of the dynamic relationship between drugs and crime on a pathway that is neither linear nor one-dimensional.

In Chapter 9, Patricia Erickson, Jennifer Butters and Beric German describe pathways resulting in the adoption of the role of crack cocaine dealer. Drawing on interviews with 17 male crack dealers in Toronto, the authors explore ways in which cumulative disadvantages in numerous aspects of dealers' lives result in the adoption of this highly deviant lifestyle. Various factors which influence the decision to adopt such a lifestyle are identified, such as involvement in other forms of drug use, the individual's criminal history, typical use of the individual's time on the streets, crack-related violence and positive aspects associated with the action and excitement of street life. Finally, the authors explore how the lack of social resources perpetuates the downward spiral of deviance.

In Chapter 10, Lisa Maher, Eloise Dunlap and Bruce D. Johnson adopt an ethnographic approach to document pathways leading to regular involvement by African women in the sale and use of crack. These pathways included the presence of limited options while growing up, involvement of family members in criminality, and participation in street life during adolescence. As young adults, these women, who had either limited or no formal work experience, engaged in prostitution as a means of generating income, enjoyed partying and had little or no possibility of becoming involved in lawful activities. Structural neighbourhood conditions played a key role in the women's past and current involvement in deviant pathways.

Part IV: ways out

Ultimately, in the minds of decision makers, citizens and numerous researchers, the aim of drawing an accurate portrait of drug–crime pathways and their ins and outs should be to make it possible to intervene, collectively or individually, in such a way so that individuals abandon such pathways.

In Chapter 11, Helmut Kury, Joachim Obergfell-Fuchs and Theodore Ferdinand begin by underlining how, in earlier years, the problem of drug abuse, especially among juveniles, drew a great deal of attention not only to illegal drugs such as cocaine and marijuana, but also to such legal addictive substances as alcohol, cigarettes and prescription drugs. Normative attitudes played an important role here, too. Still, the notion that criminalizing drug consumption might play a preventive role with the general population and encourage addicts to seek treatment became increasingly popular, at the same time as support for the view that criminalizing drugs undermined treatment techniques also grew. As a result, many European countries, such as Germany, adopted a policy of tolerating small-time drug dealers while punishing major drug traffickers.

In Chapter 12, Françoise Facy, Myriam Rabaud and Daniel Ruffin analyse the pathways of addicts and the latter's response to institutional intervention (at a drug and alcohol treatment centre or in prison). Instead of a comparative assessment of subject evolution according to the type of institutional intervention, descriptive studies of different subgroups demonstrate the impact of judicial difficulties, outlining typical pathway profiles. The authors observed that, although the pathways of subjects with longer periods of addiction are marked by repeated judicial intervention, there are a variety of profiles.

In Chapter 13, Céline Mercier and Sophie Alarie discuss the results of a study conducted in Montreal, Canada, to permit the development and improvement of services for homeless persons with substance abuse problems. The study pursued two main goals: to document the rehabilitation process as described by the people who had experienced it and to identify those factors perceived by service users to be progress and stabilization indicators. In the interviews, the respondents revealed that they considered substance abuse rather than homelessness to be their main problem. They referred to most of the common outcome dimensions (substance abuse, living and financial conditions, social relationships, mental health) encountered in the literature, but suggested new indicators within these dimensions as well as new potential indicators such as changes in communication behaviours and attitudes and access to citizenship.

REFERENCES

Becker, H.S. (1963), *Outsiders: Studies in the Sociology of Deviance*, New York: Free Press.
Brochu, S. (1995), *Drogue et criminalité: une relation complexe*, Collection perspectives criminologiques, Montreal: Presses de l'Université de Montréal.
Brochu, S. and Brunelle, N. (1997), 'Toxicomanie et délinquance. Une question de style de vie?', *Psychotropes: Revue internationale des toxicomanies*, **3** (4), 107–25.
da Agra, C. (1990), 'Sujet autopoiétique et transgression', in *Acteur social et délinquance – hommage à Christian Debuyst*, Brussels: Pierre Mardaga Ed., pp.415–27.
da Agra, C. (1997), 'A Experiência Portuguesa: Programmea de Estudos e Resultados', in C. da Agra, *Projecto Droga e Crime: Estudos Interdisciplinares* vol. I, Lisbon: G.P.C.C.D–Ministério da Justiça.
Debuyst, C. (1989), *Acteur social et délinquance*, Brussels: Pierre Mardaga Ed.
Durkheim, E. (1956), *Les règles de la méthode sociologique*, Paris: Presses universitaires de France.
Erikson, K. (1966), *Wayward Puritains*, New York: Wiley.
Eysenck, H.J. (1977), *Crime and Personality*, London: Routledge & Kegan Paul.
Matza, D. (1969), *Becoming Deviant*, Englewood Cliffs, New Jersey: Prentice-Hall.
Parsons, T. (1951), *The Social System*, London: Routledge and Kegan Paul.
Shaw, C.R. and McKay, H.D. (1942), *Juvenile Delinquency and Urban Areas*, Chicago: University of Chicago Press.

Part I
DEVIANCE, SET
AND SETTING

Chapter 1

The Complex Structures, Processes and Meanings of the Drug/Crime Relationship

This chapter presents, in four sections, the programme of studies on the relationship between drugs and crime carried out at the Centro de Ciências do Comportamento Desviante (Centre of Deviant Behaviour Sciences) of the University of Oporto, Portugal, between 1991 and 1996. Under our scientific direction, 14 researchers developed a set of articulated studies, in which different empirical research methods were applied to approximately 1000 subjects.

The first section presents the results of theoretical research on the models of scientific research and its application to the explanation of the drugs/crime connection. The second section presents the logic, the frame of reference and the method of the research programme. The third section presents the results of the empirical research. The aim, the method and the results of each of the main studies are presented in this section. Finally, the fourth section goes back to the theoretical analysis, in order to build a comprehensive system from the empirical data.

THE SCIENTIFIC EXPLANATION AND THE EXPLANATION OF THE RELATIONSHIP BETWEEN DRUGS AND CRIME

The scientific explanation

The question of what is a scientific explanation is one of the most difficult issues in epistemology. Supported mostly by the work of Kuhn (1971, 1977), we have come to conclude that there are three types of scientific explanation: causal, structural and processual (da Agra, 1996).

Causal explanations predict direct relationships between two different phenomena of the type: A causes B. According to the physics epistemologist Bunge (1971), a relationship between two phenomena can only be called causal if it obeys a number of conditions: (a) that the relationship implies two different systems, one being the determinant and the other the determined; (b) that the reaction of the determined system on the determinant system is considerably weaker than the action suffered (feedback negligible); and (c) that there are no spontaneous effects on the determined system. Bunge thus states that very few systems are causally connected. Referring to causal explanation in physics, Kuhn claims that its significance declined in the

9

nineteenth century and has almost disappeared in the present day. Considering that this kind of elementary explanation has been abandoned in the sciences that deal with natural phenomena, how can we accept its use in the sciences that study much less deterministic phenomena, such as human behaviour?

The structural explanation is one of the most fruitful kinds of scientific explanation. It consists in reducing a phenomenon's surface appearance to its deep structure and in explaining global and macroscopic properties through properties found at a microscopic level. In other words, in metaphorical language, the visible appearance of things is explained by invisible structures.

The processual explanation defines the succession of a phenomenon's conditions over a period of time, and the rule according to which such conditions are articulated. It demands that two conditions are fulfilled: the change of condition in a system and the rule or law that expresses the connections between the different conditions over time.

Scientific explanations demand, on the other hand, an epistemological stance towards determinism and indeterminism. Superficial analyses place the question in dichotomic terms: phenomena are either determinate or indeterminate. However, more serious epistemological analyses reveal a tremendous complexity of intermediate points between pure determinism (which is an abstraction) and pure indeterminism (also an abstraction). These are the degrees of determinism/ indeterminism: causal determinism, dynamic determinism (knowledge of the phenomenon's 'initial conditions' and their predictability), legal determinism (description of the laws that rule the phenomena), statistical determinism (description of the system's state in global and indirect terms, through statistical distribution), statistical indeterminism (which supposes 'free' laws besides the 'necessary' laws characteristic of determinism) and contingency. The concept of self-organization and autopoiesis supposes this ensemble of explanatory possibilities to be located between determinism and indeterminism.

The explanation of the drugs/crime relationship

Let us apply the basic modes of scientific explanation to the scientific literature dealing with the relationship between drugs and crime. All of the vast amount of literature produced since the 1960's can be split into three models: causal explanation, structural explanation and processual explanation.

Explaining through causal determinism

The small scientific community in this field usually identifies three causal explanatory schemes: (a) *the psychopharmacological model* (anti-social behaviour is a consequence of the psychopharmacological properties of the substances); (b) *the economical–compulsive model* (when in need of drugs that he/she cannot afford to buy, the drug addict is forced to resort to illegal means to obtain them); and (c) the *systemic model* which explains drug-related criminality in terms of the violence intrinsic to illegal drugs traffic markets.

Brochu (1995) adds two more models to the causal type of explanation:

Goldstein's tripartite model and the *inverse causality model*. Goldstein (1985) advanced his tripartite model in a paradigmatic paper titled 'The drugs/violence nexus: a tripartite conceptual framework'. The reason why Goldstein calls his model 'tripartite' is that it aims at integrating, in a theoretical system, the three models of simple causality that had been developed until then: the psychopharmacological, the economical–compulsive and the systemic. The inverse causality model, based on empirical evidence, shows that the consumption of drugs also proceeds from criminal activity (the determination of the two phenomena is now inverted; that is, crime is now seen as causing drug taking).

The debate about the causal model

The issue of causality has joined authors around two different tendencies: those who while rejecting causal relationships, suggest that there is a spurious relationship, a co-occurrence model; and those who claim that there is a causal relationship. This debate on causality sinks into deep epistemological incoherence, for it confounds causal determinism with statistical determinism or co-occurrence and spurious relationship with the absence of determinism.

Clayton and Tuchfeld (1982) are among the few authors who point their finger at this serious problem in the debate about causality. They accuse those who argue that there is a spurious relationship of ignoring what they are defending, namely of ignoring the existence of intermediate variables between drugs and crime. Supported by Hirschi and Selvin's definition of causality, they argue that there is empirical evidence supporting a causal relationship between drugs and crime; it is claimed that statistical and probabilistic relationships are found between both phenomena. However, like the authors they criticize, these authors also reveal a frail conceptualization of causality. In fact, if we speak about statistical and probabilistic relationships we are prevented from speaking about causality in a strict sense (as defined above). The alternative to the spurious relationship is not necessarily causality.

The notion of 'inverse causality' is also frail and deceptive. The empirical evidence supporting it, (that criminality precedes drug taking), works only to deny the causal relationship between drugs and crime; it does not contribute to the emergence of an opposite value causality. The fact is this: if drugs cause crime but crime also causes drug taking with an identical weight of determinism, we no longer have a phenomenon that determines and a phenomenon that is determined, and that is, as we pointed out above, a crucial condition for a relationship to be called causal. If drugs cause crime and crime causes drug taking, all we can say is that there is a reciprocal or complex causality or, to put it more simply, there is no causality in a strict sense.

The emergence of a will to complexity

A will to explain the drugs/crime relationship in complex terms has been surfacing since 1985. The complex explanation model refuses both the simple direct causal relationship and the spurious relationship.

We find signs of that will to complexity in Goldstein (1985), Watters *et al.* (1985), Inciardi (1985) and Faupel (1989). Goldstein's tripartite model is a transition model between simple causal models and complex models. In fact, while it still has a deterministic basis, it is no longer – contrary to Brochu's suggestion – a causal model. Because it is an explanatory model that integrates three major factors with different explanatory weights (the nature of the substances, the economical – compulsive factor and the situational factor), then by definition it rejects simple and direct explanations and admits, even if not explicitly, complex relations. It is our belief that in his integrative model, Goldstein transfers the 'law of the effect' to the drugs/crime relationship (according to this law, the effect of drugs cannot be explained without taking into consideration three major factors: the substances, the individuals and the contexts).

Similarly, in a paper also published in 1985, titled 'Causality, context and contingency: relationships between drug abuse and delinquency', Watters *et al.* argue that the relationship is not direct but complex, more contingent than causal.

As we understand it, the complex explanation of the drugs/crime relationship has been developed in two models: structural explanation and processual explanation.

Structural deviance: from macroscopy to microscopy of the drugs/crime relationship

As we move from the surface towards the structures underlying the drugs/crime behavioural complex, we find elements of structural explanation in five major domains, among which are the 'correlational models' (Brochu, 1995). In short, they are as follows.

Structural statistics Here we find the statistical studies by Anglin and Speckart 1986. Using 'structural equation modelling', they manipulate a latent variable and a manifest variable. The authors show that variables such as lifestyle, social background and personality structure interfere in the drugs/crime relationship, thereby preventing a given behaviour from being predicted on the basis of an analysis of the other element. They also show that early deviance is related to a future association between drug taking and criminality.

'Deviance syndrome' This kind of explanation is usually fitted into the 'correlational models' category because, when understood as a syndrome, deviance encompasses a series of different behaviours brought together by a common characteristic: antisociality or transgression (taking drugs, committing offences, running away from and being undisciplined at school, acts of vandalism, early sexual experiences, and so on). The deviance syndrome is regarded as being associated with psychosocial 'structural marginality' (Brochu, 1995).

Psychopathological explanation This is also part of the 'correlational models' which, according to Brochu, explain the drugs/crime relationship by 'common causes'. Some personality traits, identified by instruments of psychological diagnoses, are taken to explain simultaneously addictive and criminal behaviour.

Psychiatric and ethnopsychiatric explanations Personalities with structural functioning difficulties associated with problems in the resolution of the Oedipal conflict are responsible, with latent structures, for deviant behaviour such as drug taking, criminality, suicide and so on (Mendel, 1969; Bergeret, 1980). In his turn, Devereux, following his studies in ethnopsychiatry, prefers the concept of 'social negativism' to that of antisocial personality for the explanation of the psychopathology of deviant behaviour. According to Devereux, deviant behaviour, criminal or not, is always symptomatic: it expresses an anguish resolution strategy. However, where does this anguish come from? From the incoherent and contradictory nature of complex societies, according to Devereux (1977).

The social–cognitive explanation By 'social–cognitive' we mean the theoretical strategy that explains the drugs/crime relationship either as a neutralization technique or as a labelling process. In this perspective, the drugs/crime relationship is not natural but artificial, constructed by social interaction and cognitive and affection factors. Apart from Becker's (1963), there are few studies on the social–cognitive processes. However, since the beginning of the 1990s, authors such as Fagan, Elliot and Huizinga have opened up some research trends in this perspective.

The deviant process

The processual explanation locates the drugs/crime relationship in time, in the time of the actors of drugs and crime. As we see it, there are four major approaches in this general perspective.

From structural explanation to processual explanation – biopsychological processes and the general deviance hypothesis An example of this approach is the important study carried out by Newcomb and McGee (1991). The authors research the relationship between what they call 'sensation seeking' and general deviance, and its behavioural expressions (drug taking, delinquency, criminality, sexual experiences, and so on). These variables are studied in a developmental perspective. Newcomb and McGee confirm the deviance syndrome theory; they show, however, that the constellation of problematic behaviours changes in the transition from adolescence to youth. On the other hand, they verify the existence of a relationship between sensation seeking in adolescence and specific deviant behaviours in adult youth.

The process as psychosocial development: deviant behaviour in adolescence Le Blanc's empirical studies constitute the paradigm of empirical research supporting the thesis according to which adolescent deviant behaviour is an epiphenomenon of that stage of human development. This does not mean that there is no specialization or aggravation later. The authors define three crucial stages in the development of a deviant lifestyle: activation, aggravation and giving up (there are sub-stages in each stage). Applying the developmental construct to the drugs/crime relationship, both behaviours emerge as the effect of a common determinant (adolescence) and evolve in the individual's history in a sequence of stages. This sequence can be lived right to the end or be confined to the initial stage, in which deviant behaviour (drug-taking, delinquent acts, and so on) is a normal state.

The social–cultural process: the 'career paradigm' In his beautiful preface to Faupel's *Shooting Dope*, Inciardi identifies quite clearly Faupel's epistemological stance, calling it a 'career paradigm'. 'Career' is defined as a 'series of meaningfully related statuses, roles, and activities around which an individual organizes some aspects of his or her life' (Faupel, 1989: 24). This definition of 'career' expresses the processual kind of explanation: it assumes the idea of a series of phases that follow in time articulating different interrelated events. In Faupel's theory, there are four phases or types of heroin consumption, and they follow according to a logic or regularity determined by two 'career contingencies': 'drug availability' and 'life structure'. From their joint interaction results a 'typology of heroin-user career phases'. These are 'the stable addict', 'the occasional user', 'the free-wheeling addict' and 'the street junkie' (ibid.: 47).

The phenomenological–existential process: the deviant lifestyle This approach gives special consideration issues to subjectivity and intent in deviant lifestyles. The drugs/crime deviant lifestyle is explained neither by the power of the substances nor by environmental and social contexts.

This is the empirically based epistemological stance of Grapendaal *et al.* (1995). Referring to their research about drug users in Amsterdam, they argue that 'They are extremely active, they make choices, and sometimes they do the unexpected'. The authors define types of deviant lifestyles so as to organize different existential trajectories (their beginning, usual course and continuity) in which crime and drugs are involved. It is thus the lifestyle that brings sense to drug taking and delinquency.

In Canada, Serge Brochu has been developing an integrative theoretical model which, as we understand it, tries to articulate Faupel's model with the approach of Grapendaal, Leuw and Nelen.

THE LOGICS OF A SCIENTIFIC RESEARCH PROGRAMME ON THE DRUGS/CRIME RELATIONSHIP AS A DEVIANT COMPLEX

A critique of the research on the drugs/crime relationship

In his introduction to the collective work *Drugs and Crime*, Tonry (1990) defines research in this field as follows: 'drugs and crime is a minor scholarly activity and it is poorly funded. The literature is scant, much of it is fragmented, and too much of the research is poor in quality and weak in design'.

The knowledge created by this fragmented and unstable small scientific community can be summarized, in generic terms, in a set of dispersed data on behaviours. It is consensual that there is a relationship between drugs and crime; that minors under tutelage take more drugs than those who are socially integrated; that people in jail take more psychoactive substances than those who are not in jail; and that the deviant use of drugs (heroin) have grown tremendously among the European lower classes since the mid-1980s. In spite of the creation of the European Monitoring Center for Drugs and Drug Addiction (EMCDDA) by the European Union, we do not currently have at our disposal an accurate description of the dimension and characteristics of drug-related criminality. If there is a serious lack as regards the description of the phenomenon, the lack is even greater as regards its explanation.

Drugs and criminal issues are a domain in which scientific research starts off with enormous obstacles and epistemological contradictions: while it is an interdisciplinary domain (it relates two different phenomena, drugs and crime), the interdisciplinary method is almost absent; being a pluridimensional object, it is reduced to a simple behavioural dimension; demanding complex explanations, it is reduced to simplistic schemes abandoned in other scientific domains, even in the behavioural sciences.

We speak of a general tendency. Fortunately, this tendency is opposed by a different perspective that announces a true 'epistemological rupture' (from the point of view of Bachelard's epistemology, or a 'scientific revolution' according to Kuhn). This rupture or revolution translates as the abandon of simple explanations in favour of complex explanations, characterized by their openness to structural and processual explanations as described above.

However, these explanations of the structural and the processual kind are *latent* in the diversity and multiplicity of empirical data and theoretical hypotheses. They are latent in the sense of an epistemic unconscious or an *unthought thought*. In fact, the *thinking thought* of the complexity in the drugs/crime relationship is extremely rare, even when it is causal and simple models that are proposed or criticized. Manifestations of openness to structural and processual thought are still far from *consciously* and *actively* sharing a paradigm that solves the problem of methodological and explanatory reference frameworks.

Reference frameworks

Epistemological analyses have shown a serious lack of theoretical frameworks able to support interdisciplinary empirical research designs. The reference framework we present is a result of our theoretical work; it is what we have used for developing empirical research (the results of which will be presented in the third section of this chapter). It is aimed at overcoming some of the epistemological flaws and obstacles identified in the critical analysis of international research.

Analytical levels

The first step scientifically researching a given object or problem consists in transforming its holistic appearance into a system made up of several elements which require different levels of analysis. Three main levels of research were identified: macroscopic, mesoscopic and microscopic (da Agra, 1996). For each of these levels we developed several studies.

The macroscopic level Not being a given, natural phenomenon, the drugs/crime deviant complex is historically and socially constructed. The analysis of the larger historical processes that lead to labelling and criminalizing drugs seems indispensable. At this level, then, there are two types of interrelated research: the study of the primary criminalization of drugs (the emergence and transformation of laws) and the study of secondary criminalization (law enforcement).

The mesoscopic level This refers to research aiming at establishing the dimension of the drugs/crime phenomenon, issues of incidence and prevalence, and the relationship between types of drugs and types of crime. These are fundamentally epidemiological studies, not only of consumption behaviours in youths and adults involved in the criminal justice system and in minors under tutelage, but also in the population outside those institutions.

The microscopic level This kind of research deserves special attention. Paradoxically, in spite of the fact that it is crucial for explaining the relationship between drugs and crime, it is quite rare. To fill in the existing emptiness as regards structural–processual microscopic-level knowledge, three kinds of research seem fundamental: the first focused on the individual, the second on his/her ecosocial contexts, and the third on his/her existential trajectory. In other words, research must consider the *individual*, his *space* and his *time*:

1   the individual level: taking it as a hierarchical system, this series of studies deals with the central nervous system, the body, emotions, cognitions, personality and action, and existential meanings;
2   the individual and his space: deviant life systems in their relation to the city;
3   the individual and his time: the phases in the deviant trajectory and the regularity articulating those phases or states in biographic time.

The explanatory model: determination, structure and process

Explanations of a complex kind do not allow reductions to any of the elementary schemes of scientific explanation. Therefore our explanatory model aims at articulating the issues of determinism and contingency, the reduction of visible manifestations to deep structures and the definition of trajectories understood as a succession of phases of a given life system through time.

Confining ourselves to the issues of determinism and contingency, we would explain both the determination and the contingency relationships between drugs and crime that can be detected in some circumstances. However, we would do that leaving aside individual variables, as well as the structures and processes underlying behaviour (for example, in the economical–compulsive model).

On the other hand, when confined to the structures of the drugs/crime deviant complex, we find factors common to both behaviours but we miss what is specific to each of them; we can only detect that if we resort to heterogeneous (deterministic) explanation and to processual explanation.

Finally, processual analysis (deviant trajectories) establishes facts related to the phases in the evolution of the drugs/crime relationship in different lifestyles. However, it denies access to the factors related to the architecture of the psychological system. In short, a research programme aimed at explaining deviant complexes such as that of drugs/crime cannot leave aside the three-faced explanation model: determination–contingency, structure and process.

The hermeneutical model

Human behaviour is not only an object of description and explanation. It is also, and perhaps most crucially, an object of interpretations. The interpretive method (hermeneutics) explores finalities and meanings. Hermeneutical analysis of the drugs/crime complex is for that reason indispensable and must associate itself with structural and evolutionary (processual) analyses. In fact, in complex systems such as human behaviour systems, finality dominates the functional, evolutionary and structural economy of the system.

Therefore, supported by systems theory and phenomenology, we have been elaborating a theoretical system (da Agra 1986, 1990, 1991, 1996) called 'auto-poietic subject'. Its systemic–phenomenological nature tries to articulate structures, processes, and meanings of human behaviour. This theory establishes four major realms of existential meaning which simultaneously represent a typology and an ensemble of states in life systems differentiated between themselves by their degree of autopoiese and self-organization (a property of complex systems which emerges from the interplay between determinism and contingency). What follows is a brief description of those realms.

The first realm of meaning (ethological realm) is characterized by a strong determinism of the life system by systems which are external to it. In this realm, the system has a low degree of autopoiese and is governed by external and short-term finalities.

In the second realm (ethological–ethical realm), the system, determined more by its exterior than by its interior, discovers the external normative conditions of its behaviour. The system aspires to normativity: conventional, deviant or both.

The third realm creates a critical distance in relation to external normativity (the ethical–ethological realm). In this critical realm, the system shows a high degree of autopoiese, and creates its own normativity, a self-normativeness. The system's economy of structure and evolution is governed by finalities decided by the system. A will to power and knowledge about itself emerges in this realm.

The fourth realm (ethical realm) is characterized by a stance towards existential meaning in which the system not only organizes itself in terms of its private finalities, but places its own self-organizing (autopoietic) power at the service of the finalities of collective systems. In this way, it takes part in the creation of an intersubjectivity that truly thinks, acts and has power. Participation in historical intersubjectivity takes the form of a *communication contract* established in medium- and long-term social-historical processes.

Our research on drugs, crime, the drugs/crime complex and deviant and normative behaviours generically speaking has been developed in this general reference framework.

Method

Of course, in a reference framework concerned with the production, in the same research programme, of knowledge about behaviours, structures, processes and meanings, in a reference framework concerned with the collection of epidemiological data, with the study of psychological, ecosocial and biographic variables, there is no room for the sterile qualitative/quantitative, innovative/classical methods debate. Here we agree with Feyerabend's anarchist methodology: all methods are good. Thus in an interdisciplinary and pluridisciplinary spirit, the production of knowledge on the drugs/crime complex requires everything from lab methods to ethnomethodology, including psychometric, clinical, comparative and longitudinal methods.

The research programme about the Portuguese situation included methodological contributions from psychophysiology, experimental psychology, clinical psychology, social psychology, statistics, epidemiology, ethnography and history.

The method and the results of every study are presented in the next section. The aim is to find invariancies in the data through variations in the methods used. This is a specific way of trying to give life to Popper's principles of falsifiability and corroboration. In other words, should a hypothesis about a given aspect of reality remain unchanged after several and diverse methodological tests, the better guaranteed is the theory supporting it. Our hypotheses were thus 'attacked' by different methods.

EMPIRICAL STUDIES

The emergence of criminal laws and their application

A study was carried out on the history of 'primary criminalization' of drugs in Portugal from the beginning of the twentieth century up to 1994 (the year of introduction of the most recent law). The aim of this study was to characterize the different legislative periods to contribute to the understanding of the main reasoning behind the creation of these laws.

This genealogical analysis (inspired by Foucault) reveals four legislative periods. The first one, from 1914 to 1970, is characterized by a fiscal and commercial paradigm. In this period, drug use was not yet considered an illness. On the other hand, Portugal showed some resistance towards International Conventions, while in Macau the use of opium was allowed. The second period, from 1970 to 1974, differs from the former in terms of social–political and sanitary concerns. The 1970s law was strongly influenced by the 1961 international convention. The third period, after the 1974 revolution, is characterized by the emergence of mechanisms of political, criminal, sociomoral and medical–psychological concerns. The fourth period, from 1983 to 1994, reveals a new legislative paradigm: drug addiction is considered an illness, not a delinquency. The delinquency of the drug addict is a consequence of his/her addiction, understood as a pathological condition.

Epidemiological data

The research at this level implied two studies: of drug use among prisoners, and of licit and illicit drug use among minors living in juvenile houses. Two surveys were conducted in 1993 in the most important Portuguese prisons and in three juvenile houses (n = 450).

The first study (Negreiros, 1997) reveals that 71 per cent of the respondent inmates had used drugs in the four months preceding their imprisonment. There was no connection between any drug and any crime: the connection between heroin and acquisitive crimes and traffic prevails; two main predictors were found: precocity in beginning deviant lifestyle and having lived in juvenile houses.

The aim of the supplementary study was to show clearly the extent of drug use among minors (aged 14–17) living in juvenile houses in Lisbon. Results: (a) 47 per cent of the cases were revealed to use both licit and illicit drugs; (b) deviant use of drugs was related to other kinds of precocious deviant behaviour (Rodrigues *et al.*, 1997).

The individual: structures, functions and meanings

Individual and psychological issues have lain outside the scope of the current empirical research on drugs/crime connection. The structures, functions and meanings underlying drugs/crime deviant behaviour are rarely studied. Our research programme at this level aimed to fill this gap.

The following variables were studied: central nervous system (CNS) activity, corporal sensations, emotions, cognitions, personality and existential meaning. These variables were studied comparatively in three target groups: drug addicts without a criminal record; criminals without drug addiction; and individuals who are both drug addicts and criminals. We forged the concept of a *drugs/crime complex* referring to this last target group.

Central nervous system activity

The vast majority of studies on drugs and crime neglect an important variable that may contribute to the explanation of this deviant complex. An experimental study carried out in the psychophysiology laboratory of the University of Oporto applying the rules of the classical experimental method led to the following results: (a) no structural psychophysiological 'gaps' were found in either drug users or delinquents; (b) the drugs/crime complex presents functional problems such as inflexibility, uniformity and simplicity when reacting to different situations; (c) delinquents without drug addiction present the same reaction pattern (Teixeira, 1997).

Experiencing bodily sensations

A scale of somatic sensations was constructed and applied in order to measure physiological sensations, such as cold, heat, sweat and muscular tension (Queirós, 1997). The analysis revealed that the drugs/crime complex and criminals without addiction present the same reaction patterns, and that the somatic reaction patterns of addicted subjects (without criminal record) when compared with the other experimental groups suggest that addict behaviour becomes indifferent to experiencing normal sensations.

Emotions

The same psychophysiological instrument, the ECSS (emotions and corporal sensations' scale) (Queirós, 1997) was applied to the same sample: the experimental group (50 criminals, 50 addicts, 50 drugs/crime complex group) and the control group (50 students and industrial workers without crime or addiction records). The data analysis reveals a deep emotional negativism in experimental groups when compared to the control group.

Emotions and cognitions

Drugs/crime complex and addicts' cognition processes present an important level of emotional determinism. These individuals show difficulties in organizing the information based on behavioural settings. On the other hand, criminals' cognition processes present a normal pattern. In spite of non-complex cognitions, this deviant style is oriented towards reality.

In summary, when compared to the other deviant lifestyles, the drugs/crime complex reveals the worst psychophysiological, emotional and cognitive functioning structure.

Personality and action

The main functional structures of the psychological system were assessed through a projective test (Exner Rorschach's Comprehensive System) (Manita, 1997) and two inventories: problem solving and self-concept (V. Serra). The sample included three groups: criminals (n = 35), addicts (n = 21) and drugs/crime complex (n = 34). The thesis of the 'criminal personality' or 'addict personality' was not confirmed. However, there were significant statistical differences in the three groups concerning the psychic system and interactions with behaviour settings.

The results have shown that in the drugs/crime complex the related psychological processes are not the consequence of the combination of the different characteristics usually connected with drug use or crime. There is evidence of other, new processes. Drug addicts present some cognitive–affective disorders underlying a distorted construction of reality. Nevertheless, this functional problem does not imply any behavioural disorder. In fact, behavioural inhibition is a typical feature of drug addiction. Therefore social negativism was not found in drug addicts.

Delinquents present opposite personality characteristics. They develop more realistic coping strategies than drug addicts do. On the other hand, their social negativism implies a reduced conventionality.

The drugs/crime complex presents the following specific features: cognitive rigidity and affective–cognitive disorders (negative self-concept, lack of concern for interpersonal relationship) and ambiguity towards the environment and everyday situations.

Existential meaning

Drug addiction, criminality and the drugs/crime complex present psychophysiological emotional cognitive and personality differences. Do they present existential differences too? Do they react in different ways to existential problems such as AIDS? A study was carried out in two groups to try to answer these questions. The first group was formed by HIV-positive inmates with drug addiction (n = 23). The second group was formed by HIV-positive drug addicts following a treatment programme in a rehabilitation centre (n = 22) (Guerra and da Agra, 1997). Two variables, self-actualization and social support, made the self-organization concept and the psychological autopoiesis concept effective (da Agra, 1990). By dealing with their seropositiveness, individuals construct different meanings about existential conditions.

The drugs/crime complex reveals a low level of self-organization and autopoiesis. The individual's interpretation of their existential condition is fatalistic: they can do nothing against their own destiny. An existential negativism influences the meaning of life from a psychological point of view. Moreover, social and emotional non-adjustment are typical 'gaps' of the drugs/crime complex lifestyle.

HIV-positive drug addicts without criminal record following a treatment programme in a rehabilitation centre embrace a higher existential meaning. Although they accept their limited condition, they react conventionally or creatively to their circumstances; they express a certain level of psychological autopoiesis by developing self-actualization skills.

Determinism, 'autopoiesis' and meaning

In order to explore further the individual psychological power, responsibility and meaning, another study was carried out in the most important Portuguese prisons (Manita *et al.*, 1997). The specific aim of this study was to establish levels of determination for deviant drugs/crime behaviour between two poles: 'hetero' and 'auto' determinism of action related to plans of existential meaning of the actors of the drugs world. In all, 334 inmates were interviewed about their own life story of drugs and crime. A categorical analysis of content and a statistical analysis led to the conclusion that the inmates' experiences on drugs and crimes are broadly organized into three main realms of existential meaning. We now specify this generic conclusion: the first plan organizes the drugs/crime experience in a fatalistic and deterministic sense. The large majority of prisoners explain their deviant behaviour as having an external cause. Moreover, they report that drug use and criminal behaviour are linked in a causal way: drug use leads to crime.

The second realm organizes the drugs/crime experience in a moderate sense of determinism. Far fewer prisoners adopt this attitude. Some explain their beginning drug use and crime by both internal and external factors. Some bring a certain relativism to the drugs/crime connection.

The third realm recognizes the role of the individual in the drugs/crime experience. Self-organization and psychopoiesis are the emergent properties of this plan of existential meaning. Only a few prisoners have such a point of view, specifically when they explain initial deviant drug use.

This study provides enough evidence to support the 'techniques of neutralization' argument theorized by Sykes and Matza (1957). In fact, the economical–compulsive model (the notion that drug use leads to crime) works as a device that aims to rationalize crime and deviant behaviour.

Ecological and social settings

Inspired by the tradition of the Chicago School, Fernandes has developed, since 1985, ethnomethodological studies on inner city areas of Oporto. The aim of these studies is to research the 'natural' dimension of the drug phenomenon and related lifestyles. In 'Territórios Psicotrópicos' (Psychotropic Territories) (Fernandes, 1997), the ethnographic research has established empirical evidence on the following items: substances, drug markets, deviant behaviour associated with drug use and drug markets, actors of the drugs world and their lifestyles, and deviant behaviour learning.

Substances

Heroin is still the most used drug, followed by cocaine, in Portugal. Cannabis presents some gaps in the distribution system. The synthetic drug, 'ecstasy' (MDMA) has gained an increasing importance. The diversity of available substances in the illicit market proves that the phenomenon is far from being controlled.

Drug market

The 'territorial' drug market shows three main characteristics: self-organization, permanence and resistance. The first characteristic is associated with ecological characteristics and lifestyles of a certain city. These areas form specific and characteristic systems of individual and collective behaviours with self-organization features, within the normative city.

The second characteristic emerges from the drugs market actors' ability to develop somehow paradoxical interstices: simultaneously visible and invisible. The retail market persists because of this visibility/invisibility game. The third characteristic, resistance, shows clearly the processes by which the drug market survives its fluctuations and how it resists controlling interventions aimed at 'psychotropic territories'.

Deviant behaviours associated with drug use and market

Violent behaviour appears associated only with the buying and selling system (systemic violence, according to Goldstein, 1985), and is not related to use. Concealment of stolen goods, drug possession and small trafficking are the most common offences integrated in the underground micro-economy logic of an economically disadvantaged population.

The drugs world actors and their lifestyle

There are several actors in the drugs world in deviant subcultures: dealers, occasional users, regular users and junkies. The drug use and market tend to expand in two directions: youths between 10 and 11 years old and individuals over 30. The drug subculture is characterized by a set of commercial, economical, relational, organizational, ethical, behavioural and territorial elements. This set of elements characterizes real lifestyles.

The dealer lifestyle

This ethnomethodological study was focused only on the small dealer, the last link of the distribution chain, the one who provides the street meeting with the client. His lifestyle implies several elements: (a) dominance of a given territory where he develops commercial activity; (b) diversified sets of relationships and business connections managed under hypervigilance (homeless adolescents, older people, users, prostitutes); (c) communication channels between the underground economy and the surrounding economy; (d) personal estate: money obtained through his personal enterprise that allows access to socially desired goods (housing, furniture, car, trademark clothes); (e) the desire to reconcile conventional and deviant lifestyles; and (f) a self-image (sometimes hero, sometimes victim) associated with strategies of neutralization and self-excuse.

The junkie lifestyle

The junkie lifestyle in council neighbourhoods is characterized by the following elements: (a) the use of psychotropic substances is the organizing principle of daily life; (b) a set of dependencies – physical, psychological and economical; (c) unlike the 'ancient' junkies, the modern ones do not have either thought-organizing or discussion-organizing subjects or topics; (d) the relationship established with other people is instrumental, dependent and utilitarian; (e) being ambivalent towards their economical–compulsive delinquency, they neutralize their moral decadence, using social stereotypes (for example the responsibility is always of the individuals of no scruples: traffickers).

Deviant behaviour learning

One of the main findings established by the ethnographic studies in Oporto is the precocious learning of deviant lifestyles in drug-related behavioural settings. Children and adolescents, through their active participation in the life of the neighbourhood, where drugs have become normal, structure their behaviour according to specific norms of deviant lifestyles.

Deviant pathways: typology of the drugs/crime complex

The ethnographic studies address the drugs/crime connection from a spatial point of view. The study presented here (da Agra and Matos, 1997) addresses the drugs/crime connection from a temporal point of view, the existential pathway of individuals with a long background in drug use and criminal activity. The method applied has allowed us to establish typologies of pathways and cycles. The typology found in this study is presented here. The cycles will be described in the system of theoretical integration (next section of this chapter).

Deviant pathways can only be studied from a longitudinal perspective either through individual follow-up during a certain period of one's life or, retrospectively, through the reconstruction of one's life history. This study has applied the method of reconstructed biography. This method consists in the reconstruction of the individual's story, based on heterobiographic data (facts) recorded in the available files of the justice system (probation officer teams working in prisons, prison records and criminal courts) and on autobiographic data collected through interviews with the sample.

Heterobiography and autobiography are graphically translated into the biogram, a tool created in the scope of this study to allow a clear and objective visualization of the subjects' existential pathways at several levels: familial, scholastic, professional, intervention of the criminal system, deviant and delinquent pathways and drug use (see chapter 2).

Although the specificity of studies on deviant pathways and careers requires basically a qualitative approach based on biographic methods, the design of data collection methods for this study considered the possibility of a subsequent quantitative treatment of the information in order to articulate qualitative and quantitative analyses. Therefore an exploratory quantitative study was also carried out, based on the outcomes of the qualitative analysis.

The sample was composed of 100 biographies of non-first offenders, with drug addiction, who had using hard drugs for over five years. The analysis of the biographies has shown the general characteristics of the sample and has revealed the presence of three types of deviant pathways, taking into account the way in which the drugs/crime connection is construed during the life of these individuals.

General characteristics of the sample

Our sample is composed mainly of individuals aged between 25 and 39, living in urban and suburban areas. They belong to large households of the lower or middle–lower class. About half of these households show a familial dynamic disturbed by structural changes (relationship breakdowns, divorces, bereavement of a parent, migration and so on). More than a third of the sample have never set up a family and approximately a third do not have children.

Three quarters of the population studied have an irregular school record that is expressed in failures and more or less systematic absenteeism. School leaving generally occurs before the completion of the ninth grade (14–15 years old). For almost the entire population, the beginning of professional life occurs before the legal age, immediately after leaving school. They are mainly non-qualified building workers, workers in the services sector and sales assistants. They have a professional pathway where irregularity and lack of specificity tends to increase during their working lives (approximately half of the subjects were unemployed in the period preceding their last detention).

Almost all the subjects begin their criminal activity before the age of 22, especially with a robbery and/or theft.

More than half of the subjects begin their soft drugs use between the ages of 11 and 16 and their first contact with hard drugs occurs, for the most part, before the age of 19. Approximately half of the subjects underwent 'clinical' intervention (rehabilitation centres for drug addicts, private doctors and clinics) to carry out detoxifications in outpatient or inpatient programmes.

Approximately half of the subjects were sentenced to custodial and non-custodial sentences by criminal courts before the age of 20.

Typology

Based on how the drugs/crime connection began, the analysis of biographies has revealed the presence of three distinct groups: group I – *delinquency and drug addiction*, with pre-delinquent activity (systematic school absenteeism, playing truant, idleness, petty thefts) and/or delinquency prior to becoming a drug user; group II – *drugs/crime specialists* whose delinquent activity emerges between the use of soft and hard drugs; and group III – *drug addiction/delinquency*, that is characterized by the use of both soft and hard drugs prior to delinquent activity.

Group I (delinquency/drug addiction) This is the major group, comprising more than half of the population studied. The individuals that comprise this group present, from an early age, a poor social attachment. Their households are large (more than six people), the intrafamilial relationship is disturbed by relational problems (an alcoholic parent, manifest aggressiveness and so on) and by high occurrence of structural changes (such as relationship breakdowns and divorces). The family breakdown generally occurs before the individual has reached the age of 16. These breakdowns are caused either by voluntary neglect of the family or by admission to juvenile houses. The creation of autonomous households generally occurs after the first contacts with formal control instances; these households are unstable and of short duration. However, it must be pointed out that most of these subjects have never married. Their schooling trajectory is irregular from the beginning and they generally quit after the completion of fourth grade (9–10 years old). Their professional life begins immediately after their leaving school, mainly as building workers. Their professional performance is irregular.

Deviant activity (surfacing at about the age of 11) is a continuous sequence that begins with school absenteeism and ends up in pre-delinquent behaviour, predictors of precocious criminal activity. Pre-delinquent behaviour (petty thefts) is related to survival and to deviant activities of their social peers.

Their first contacts with soft drugs occur mainly before the age of 16, with their involvement in the delinquent and pre-delinquent subculture. The use of such substances is a further component of deviant lifestyle in the general activity of the group. Hard drugs use is principally caused by peer pressure and curiosity, and the first experiences are generally assessed negatively.

Social reaction to pre-delinquent behaviours is precociously applied through sentences of admission to juvenile houses (experienced by more than a quarter of the population) by juvenile courts. The system of criminal jurisdiction intercepts the deviant pathways of these subjects before the age of 20, applying custodial and non-custodial sentences.

Group II (drugs/crime specialists) This group includes approximately a quarter of the population studied. Belonging to large households, most of the subjects show a more structured familial framing than the preceding group. The voluntary breakdowns with their original households are especially due to a wish for autonomy and to the need to leave a disturbed familial relationship. However, most of the subjects composing this group reveal a tendency to (re)establish familial links that is expressed by the creation of several households that they tend to maintain during their lives. Showing, generally, adjustment strategies to structured and normative environments, approximately half of the subjects reveal a regular school course. In the rest of the sample, school absenteeism and failure emerge during just the initial period of school attendance or occur shortly before leaving school. Most of the subjects manage to finish fourth and sixth grade (11–12 years old). Their professional lives begin before the age of 16, working in the construction or in the services sector, and tend to present an increasing irregularity. Their first contacts with soft drugs occur mainly before the age of 17, with more or less frequent contacts with the delinquent subculture and/or drug users. Hard drug use appears at about the age of 22, in the game of relationships and settings of delinquent activity (basically defined by narcotic traffic practice).

Delinquent behaviour emerges between the ages of 17 and 19 through theft or robbery, which are precursors of narcotic traffic practice. These activities are basically related to economical and/or social status improvement issues. Before the age of 24, almost all subjects had been convicted by criminal courts.

Group III (drug addiction/delinquency) Belonging to smaller, and socially, economically and structurally more stable, households, these individuals present a strong link to their original household. They stay with them until they create their own households. Their school life lasts generally until the age of 15 or 16, and approximately half of the subjects successfully attend high school. Some of them succeed in finishing high school studies. They reveal behaviours of non-adjustment to school (absenteeism, failures) that appear from the initial period or the period immediately prior to leaving school.

Their professional life begins immediately after leaving school, as non-qualified service workers and sales assistants. Almost all the subjects regularly perform these activities until about the age of 20. Their first contact with soft drugs occurs mainly between the ages of 14 and 16, and their hard drug use begins usually before the age of 19. The use of these substances derives from their integration into the drug subculture. Offences (theft/robbery or trafficking) emerge after the use of hard drugs and are justified by the need to take drugs.

For most of them, social control is applied through 'clinical' interventions (with detoxifications carried out mainly in residential programmes) and only after this do criminal courts intervene, applying custodial and short prison sentences.

AN INTEGRATIVE SYSTEM: A PHENOMENOLOGICAL–EMPIRICAL MODEL

We have applied a set of methodologies, organized and determined by a given framework, to study the phenomena of drug consumption, crime and the drugs/crime complex. This framework is constituted by an explanatory and a hermeneutical model. The explanatory model involves three kinds of analysis: determination–contingency, structural analysis and processual analysis. The hermeneutical model interprets existential meanings, the experience of deviant ways of living. A problem arises at this point: how do we articulate the data produced by the analyses developed in the two models?

What follows is an attempt to provide an answer to this question. The attempt is grounded on systems theory and phenomenology, and it is oriented by the concept of the teleological system.

Explanatory analysis

Deviant structures and systems: general and differential deviance

The empirical studies have rendered visible two types of structural deviance: general and differential.

General deviance Common features were found in the diversity of deviant behaviours studied. There seems to exist, then, a structural or latent deviance which has a general and undifferentiated character. Metaphorically, we called it a 'transgressive magma' of biopsychosocial nature. Adolescence is the most evident expression of this structural latent deviance. Our studies do corroborate the notion that there is a factor common to drug use, crime and other deviant behaviours.

Considered in terms of its duration in time, general and structural deviance presents an ensemble of elements located at the following levels:

1   the internal environment is characterized by anguish and negativity. In their turn, the neuronal, emotional, cognitive and behavioural subsystems present deficient interrelations which point to problems in the subject's internal organization;
2   the external environment is characterized by a precarious 'normal' social bond, and by adherence to deviant life systems;
3   the interaction between the internal and the external environment constitutes the process whereby differential deviance is structured.

Differential deviance Besides the common factor, our studies have also revealed specific aspects. These differential factors produce different transformations in the general deviance background. The different developments of such transformations in general deviance constitute deviant systems. Such systems differ from each other by the teleological association of specific characteristics at three levels: individual, ecosocial and biographical.

First, the drug-addict life system presents the following general characteristics: the internal environment is overdetermined by a suffering emotional state associated with disorganization of thought; the relationship with the environment is developed from the interior to the exterior; biographical traits indicate existential rather than social negativity.

Second, the delinquent life system presents the following general characteristics: primary emotional processes and simplistic thought; the relationship with the environment is determined more by the exterior than by the interior; biographical traits reveal systematic attitudes of social negativity.

Thirdly, there is the drugs/crime life system: the drugs/crime complex. We use the concept of 'drugs/crime complex' to translate the notion, confirmed by several studies in our research programme, according to which drug use and delinquency, when associated, constitute a specific system, different from both the drug-addict life system and the delinquent life system. These are its main features: the internal environment does not orient itself towards the interior or the exterior – it is profoundly ambiguous; the relations with the environment are characterized by unpredictability, uncertainty and ambivalence; biographical analysis shows early initiation in and continuity of different deviant behaviours leading to the creation of heterogeneous behavioural constellations or complexes.

The deviant process in the drugs/crime complex: between contingency and necessity

A system of variables can be found underlying behaviours associated with both drugs and crime: the individual, his/her internal environment (biopsychological and existential variables), his/her external environment (context and social and economic conditions), his/her history (biographical trajectory) and his/her general deviance. Thus the relationship between drugs and crime is neither purely contingent nor necessary or deterministic. It must be understood as a *process* implying different degrees of self-organization. Such degrees define stages that follow during the time of the drugs/crime life system. The facts established by our longitudinal research allow us to conceptualize four major stages in the system:

1   *expression:* here the subject's system 'chooses' drug taking and delinquency as ways of manifesting deviant behaviour that expresses latent deviance or a general tendency to transgress the norms of conventional life. In this stage, drugs and crime express, signify and make real (latent deviance);

2   *occlusion:* the drugs/crime complex emerges here as a life system. The subject's system is closed by circular relationships between the internal environment, the external environment, general deviance and differential deviance. Dominated by the drugs/crime complex, the life system closes upon itself;

3   *fusion:* the internal differentiation of the subject's subsystems and their integration in order to mediate his/her relationship with the context disappears under the influence of psychoactive substances. The specificity of both drug taking and delinquency merge into an undifferentiated mass. The system's internal and external environments are also merged and undifferentiated;

4   *implosion:* at this stage it is the structure of the drugs/crime complex itself that dissipates. The transformations taking place are equivalent to the collapsing of the system: the power of the substances irrupts inside a life system reduced to a behavioural mechanics. Drugs and crime are an aimless deviant behaviour, without logics, efficiency or style.

Hermeneutical analysis

The drugs/crime complex as a realm that dissipates existence: an ethology of the behaviour

Economical dissipation is just the visible part of an existential style that tends towards dissipation (the drugs/crime complex). Space, time and the body dissipate as drug taking and delinquency converge, interact, integrate and become undifferentiated. The drugs/crime system of life is structured around four principles: non-investment, instability, 'one aim only' and closed evolution (or involvement).

1   *The non-investment principle:* psychological, relational, social–environmental and economical resources are not invested, despite all difficulties, in higher or even conventional realms of existential meaning. The project of the drugs/crime complex does not make long-term investments in life; it prefers, just like many other existential realms in modern societies, to consume life immediately.
2   *The instability principle:* the system's functioning adaptation is dominated through an external process rather than by internal processes. Strongly determined by the exterior, the drugs/crime system of life develops in an erratic trajectory. Such a life trajectory floats with the fluctuations of the external environment: the illicit drugs market, economic resources, delinquency, consumption, arrest, consumption again, delinquency one more time...
3   *The 'one aim only' principle:* drug taking and acquisitive criminality, dominating the system's aims, block up the game of multiple life chances, the game feeding adaptation and the evolution towards higher existential realms.
4   *The closed evolution or involvement principle:* oriented only to one aim, the drugs/crime life system presents a trajectory opposed to that of development understood as creation and innovation. The drugs/crime complex brings to life a latent deviance that is differentiated in three major subsystems: delinquency v. drug addiction; drug addiction v. delinquency; drug-taking v. delinquent act. The deviant process begins by differentiating them, but ends up homogenizing and rendering them undifferentiated. This homogenization is determined by the very serious involvement in the consumption of psychotropic substances. It represents the zero degree in the invention of oneself, or autopoiesis.

From the ethical to the ethological

The above analysis interprets data referring to the drugs/crime complex in a given time and space (Portugal, 1991–96). It would be misleading to produce generalizations on the assumption that drug taking is inevitably inscribed in this basic level of existential meaningfulness.

As we interpret it, the relationship between drugs and crime represents a life system which, in successive stages, was reduced to a behavioural ethology. However, drug taking can be reconciled with other realms of existential meaning. What realms are these? The ones discussed in the second section of this chapter (the theoretical framework). These realms, hierarchically organized, suppose a diversity of autopoiesis and self-organization degrees. Let us interpret drug use located in the realms beyond the one we have considered (the ethological realm, or the realm that dissipates existence).

Drugs in the ethical existential meaning realm: the invention of oneself and of the world This kind of drug taking is inscribed in life systems opposed to that of the ethological existential meaning realm. Here, drug use is integrated in a system dominated by universal type values and long temporal processes. The complexity of the internal world and the consumer's individual and collective existential projects resist well the 'power' of the substances. Consumption of drugs does not prevent the subject from inventing him/herself and the world.

Drugs as a subject's show and the use of pleasures The universalist ethics is transformed into an individualist and expressive ethics. In this realm of existential meaning, drug use is inscribed into a life system oriented towards criticism of social conventions. This happens not so much because it really clashes with them, but more as an expression of an alternative lifestyle guided by two fundamental principles: the show of oneself and the use of pleasures (sex, drugs, and so on). This *expressive and aesthetical ethology* of behaviour involves, because it is also a show, a sort of deviant communication ethics, given that it interacts with the values of conventional society.

Drugs: the pleasure in consumption Here, drug taking is inscribed in a life system ruled by conventional values, namely consumption as a value. What we find here is the consumer lifestyle, characterized by intensity rather than intentionality, opening itself up to psychotropic substances. The consumption of drugs becomes instrumental. In the life economy characterized by pleasure in consumption, drug use becomes dominant in individuals whose internal and external environments present some vulnerability, leading them to drug addiction.

Drugs: physical–chemical fusion Drug taking inscribes itself in the ethological realm while projects tend to dissipate an existence in which drugs are the only value.

CONCLUSION

There is no causal relationship between drug use and crime. There is a complex system of connections between drugs and crime: the drugs/crime complex. In fact, the programme of studies has clearly shown a diversity of structural and evolutionary variables, characteristic of individuals whose lifestyles include drug use and criminal activities. Thus the drugs/crime complex is irreducible both to drug addiction and to delinquent lifestyle. It is a differential delinquent lifestyle, the structure and processes of which are specific in what concerns drug addiction and delinquency.

BIBLIOGRAPHY

Anglin, M.D. and Speckart, G. (1986), 'Narcotic Use, Property Crime, and Dealing: Structural Differences Across the Addiction Cases, *Journal of Quantatative Criminology*, (4), 355–75.

Becker, H.S. (1963), *Outsiders: Studies on the Sociology of Deviance*, New York: Free Press.

Bergeret, J. (ed.) (1980), *Le toxicomane et ses environnements*, Paris: Recherche INSERM, Presses Universitaires de France.

Brochu, S. (1995), *Drogue et criminalité, une relation complexe*, Montreal: Les Presses de l'Université de Montréal.

Brochu, S. (1997), 'O Estado da Investigação Científica na América do Norte', in C. da Agra (ed.), *Projecto Droga e Crime: Estudos Interdisciplinares*, vol. II, Lisbon: G.P.C.C.D.– Ministério da Justiça.

Bunge, M. (1973), *Philosophy of Physics*, Dordrecht, Holland: D. Reidel Publishing.

Clayton, R.R. and Tuchfeld, B.S. (1982), 'The drugs/crime debate: Obstacles to understanding the relationship', *Journal of Drug Issues*, **12** (2), 153–67.

Collins, J.J. (1990), 'Summary Thoughts about Drugs and Violence: Causes, Correlates and Consequences'. in *Drugs and Violence: Causes, Correlates and Consequences*, NIDA Research Monograph 103, Rockville: National Institute on Drug Abuse, pp.265–73.

da Agra, C. (1986), 'Projeco de psicologia transdisciplinar do comportamento desriante e auto-organizado', *Análise Psicológica*, **3/4** (IV), 311–18.

da Agra, C. (1990), 'Sujet autopoiétique et transgression', in *Acteur social et délinquance – hommage à Christian Debuyst*, Brussels: Pierre Mardaga Ed, pp.415–27.

da Agra, C. (1991), 'La Recherche anthropologique sur la toxicomanie au Portugal', *Rétrovirus*, **IV** (9), 33–4.

da Agra, C. (1994), 'Science de l'éthique et droit pénal', in *Ethique, démocratie et droit pénal. Carrefour, Revue de réflexion interdisciplinaire*, Département de Philosophie, Université d'Ottawa, **16** (12), 108–29.

da Agra, C. (1996), 'Drugs/crime connection: The Portuguese experience', paper presented at a Scientific Meeting in the University of Gent.

da Agra, C. (1997), 'A Experiência Portuguesa: Programmea de Estudos e Resultados', in C. da Agra (ed.), *Projecto Droga e Crime: Estudos Interdisciplinares*, vol. I, Lisbon: G.P.C.C.D– Ministério da Justiça.

da Agra, C. and Matos, A.P. (1997), 'Trajectórias Desviantes', in C. da Agra (ed.), *Projecto Droga e Crime: Estudos Interdisciplinares*, vol. II, Lisbon: G.P.C.C.D.– Ministério da Justiça.

da Agra, C., Poiares, C., Fonseca, E.P. and Quintas, J. (1997), 'A Criminalização da Droga: da Emergência à Aplicação da Lei', in C. da Agra (ed.), *Projecto Droga e Crime: Estudos Interdisciplinares*, vol. III, Lisbon: G.P.C.C.– Ministério da Justiça.

De la Rosa, M., Lambert, E.J. and Gropper, B. (1990), 'Exploring the Substance Abuse–Violence Connection', in *Drugs and Violence: Causes, Correlates and Consequences*, NIDA Research Monograph 103, Rockville: National Institute on Drug Abuse.

Devereux, G. (1977), *Essai d'ethnopsychiatrie générale*, Paris: Gallimard.

Fagan, J. (1990), 'Intoxication and Aggression', in M. Tonry and J.Q. Wilson (eds), *Drug and Crime*, Chicago: University of Chicago Press, pp.241–320.

Faupel, Ch. E. (1989), *Shooting Dope: Career Patterns of Hard-Core Heroin Users*, Gainesville: University of Florida Press.

Fernandes, L. (1997), 'Etnografia Urbana das Drogas e do Crime', in C. da Agra (ed.), *Projecto Droga e Crime: Estudos Interdisciplinares*, vol. X, Lisbon: G.P.C.C.D.– Ministério da Justiça.

Goldstein, P.J. (1985), 'The drugs/violence nexus: A tripartite conceptual framework', *Journal of Drugs Issues*, **15** (4), 493–505.

Grapendaal, M., Leuw, E. and Nelen, H. (1995), *A World of Opportunities: Lifestyle and Economic Behaviour of Heroin Addicts in Amsterdam*, New York: State University of New York Press.

Guerra, M.P. and da Agra, C. (1997), 'Planos existenciais, droga e crime', in C. da Agra (ed.), *Drogra-Crime: estudos interdisciplinares*, Gabinete de Planeamento e de Coordenação do Combate à Droga.

Heer, Y., Chih-Ping, C. and Anglin, M.D. (1990), 'The criminality of female narcotic addicts: a causal modeling approach', *Journal of Quantitative Criminology*, **6** (2), 207–28.

Inciardi, J.A. (1985), *The War on Drugs*, Palo Alto: Mayfield Press.

Kuhn, Th.S. (1970), *The Structure of Scientific Revolutions*, Chicago: University of Chicago Press.

LeBlanc, M. (1994), 'La conduite des adolescents et ses facteurs explicatifs', in D. Szabo and M. LeBlanc (eds), *Traité de criminologie empirique*, Montreal: Les Presses de l'Université de Montréal, pp.49–90.

Manita, C. (1997), 'Personalidade e Acção em Consumidores de Droga e Delinquentes', in C. da Agra (ed.), *Projecto Droga e Crime: Estudos Interdisciplinares*, vol. VIII, Lisbon: G.P.C.C.D.– Ministério da Justiça.

Manita, C., Negreiros, J., Guerra, M.P. and da Agra, C. (1997), 'Planos Existenciais, Droga e Crime', in C. da Agra (ed.), *Projecto Droga e Crime: Estudos Interdisciplinares*, vol. IX, Lisbon: G.P.C.C.D.– Ministério da Justiça.

Matza, D. (1969), *Becoming Deviant*, New Jersey: Prentice-Hall.

Mendel, G. (1969), *La crise des Générations – études sociopsychanalytique*, Paris: Payot.

Negreiros, J. (1997), 'Consumo de Drogas nas Prisıes Portuguesas', in C. da Agra (ed.), *Projecto Droga e Crime: Estudos Interdisciplinares*, vol. IV, Lisbon: G.P.C.C.D.– Ministério da Justiça.

Newcomb, M.D. and McGee, L. (1991), 'Influence of sensation seeking on general deviance and specific problem behaviours from adolescence to young adulthood', *Journal of Personality and Social Psychology*, **61** (4), 614–28.

Queirós, C. (1997), 'Emoções, Cognições em Consumidores de Droga e Delinquentes', in C. da Agra (ed.), *Projecto Droga e Crime: Estudos Interdisciplinares*, vol. VII, Lisbon: G.P.C.C.D.– Ministério da Justiça.

Reuchelin, M. (1995), *Totalités, éléments, structures en psychologie*, Paris: Presses universitaires de France.

Rodrigues, L.M., Antunes, C. and Mendes, Z. (1997), 'Padrões de Consumo e Desviância em Menores sob Tutela', in C. da Agra (ed.), *Projecto Droga e Crime: Estudos Interdisciplinares*, vol. V, Lisbon: G.P.C.C.D.– Ministério da Justiça.

Schneeberger, P. (1994), 'Évolution des théories explicatives de la relation drogue–crime', unpublished MSc thesis, Université de Montréal.

Speckart, G. and Auglin, M.D. (1986), 'Narcotics and crime: A casual modeling approach', *Journal of Quantitative Criminology*, **2** (1), 3–28.

Sykes, G. and Matza, D. (1957), 'Techniques of Neutralisation, a theory of delinquency', *American Sociological Revue*, 22, 664–70.

Teixeira, J.M. (1997), 'Processos Psicofisiológicos em Consumidores de Droga e Delinquentes', in C. da Agra (ed.), *Projecto Droga e Crime: Estudos Interdisciplinares*, vol. VI, Lisbon: G.P.C.C.D.– Ministério da Justiça.

Tonry, I.M. and Wilson, J.Q. (eds) (1990), *Drugs and Crime*, Chicago: University of Chicago Press.

Watters, J.K., Reinarman, C. and Fagan, J. (1985), 'Causality, context and contingency: Relationships between drug abuse and delinquency', *Contemporary Drug Problems*, **12**, 351–73.

Chapter 2

The Study of Psychological Self-organization Processes in Deviant Pathways: Contributions of the Biogram Method

Celina Manita and Candido da Agra

For decades, research into crime, the use of drugs and the drug/crime relationship focused on causal and structural dimensions and placed less importance on, or completely ignored, procedure and meaning dimensions. In the same way, qualitative methodologies capable of showing regularities, but above all, capable of revealing singularities, subjectivities and meanings, apart from the temporal evolution of behaviour phenomena and their procedural dimensions, were almost entirely absent from the heart of this research.

The present return to methodologies that had been (almost) abandoned for decades – for instance narratives and life histories – together with the development of new biographical methods (such as the biogram method), the concern with the integration of quantitative and qualitative methodologies and the growing number of studies on deviant pathways can be considered indicators of the evolution in this field of knowledge in the last few decades.

In this context, and guided by an epistemological position, theory and methodology based on constructivism[1] – which rejects the traditional quantitative–qualitative, nomothetic–idiographic, objective–subjective and explanatory–comprehensive dichotomies – we have developed (Manita, 1996, 1997, 1998; Manita et al., 1997) a series of theoretical and empirical studies. The main aim of these studies, as pointed out in the preceding chapter, has been to analyse psychological self-organization processes associated with transgressive actions, in particular the practice of crimes and drug consumption, analysed in the interrelation between the personality system, the action system and the meaning system of the individual, in light of the theory of the autopoietic subject (da Agra, 1990, 1991).

These studies were structured into three parts: first, *disclosure*, or the analysis of the *conditions of possibility*, emergence and development of three concepts (and of the different theories based upon them) that, until a few years ago, were fundamental in the study of the criminal: risk, dangerousness and criminal personality; second, systematization and critical analysis of the main psychological theories of crime, ranging from the theories derived from the Italian anthropological school (such as Garofalo and Di Tullio) to the factorialistic theories of the criminal personality (for example Pinatel and Eysenck); thirdly, concluding the other two, critical

33

deconstruction of the concept and theories of *criminal personality* (a concept that we found to be inadequate for characterizing the personality system of the criminal and for understanding his action) and a contribution to the development of an alternative approach, based on the theory of the autopoietic subject (da Agra, 1990, 1991).

In order to analyse and deconstruct the concept of and theories on criminal personality, we performed (Manita, 1998) an analytical exercise inspired by the archaeology and genealogy of Foucault. It included: (a) analyses of the way the concept and the main theories of criminal personality emerged and developed; (b) alternative suggestions and comments that have been produced over the years; (c) present conditions of production of knowledge and the unsuitability of the concept in this context; and (d) presentation of the aforementioned alternative theoretical model. At the same time, different empirical studies were also carried out within the framework of the autopoietic subject theory. This is a complex model that seeks to address the issues of determinism and contingency, of the structure, organization and functioning of the systems, of the procedural evolution and the course of the life system.

PERSONALITY, ACTION AND MEANING: THE THEORY OF THE AUTOPOIETIC SUBJECT IN THE STUDY OF TRANSGRESSION

Having analysed and compared some of the most important modern theoretical views (for example cognitive, developmental, constructivist, phenomenological, of the social actor, narrative), we chose the theory of the autopoietic subject (da Agra, 1986, 1990, 1991, 1994) as the guiding model for our research, since it allows us to analyse the subject's relation with norms/normativeness and transgression; to apply ethics to the subject's action; to make an integrated study – rather than an isolated one, which has become a rule in criminology – of personality, of action and of meanings; to develop the study of the logics and senses of transgression, and, more specifically in our study, of the practice of crime, the use of drugs and their relationship (Manita, 1998).

Very briefly, the theory of the autopoietic subject conceptualizes the system of the individual as a complex, self-organized system, with the property of autopoiesis, consisting of three subsystems, which are also complex and self-organized: the *personality system*, the *action system* or *etho-ethical* system and the *meaning system*.

Seven strata are considered in the personality system. They are hierarchically organized and maintain service and mutual interference relations among each other, proceeding by progressive integrations. They evolve from the neuro, psychological to the political stratum, passing through the psychosensorial, expressive, affective, cognitive and experiential strata. The political stratum deals with the management and the final, complex integration of the system. The personality system is a matrix of the psychological system, whose central function is to give a psychological destination/meaning to the biological substratum and the sociocultural superstratum. It is form and not content, a matrix of possibility (it produces the possibility conditions) of the action system (da Agra, 1986, 1990). In its turn, the action system, or etho-ethical system, constitutes a pragmatic subsystem (to guide the action) of the psychic system, which also consists of different strata-sets of actions (psychobiological, affective, cognitive and so on), so that the interrelation between the strata gives rise to emerging properties: emergence of the ethical and emergence of the psychic. Da Agra defines four stages of the action system – ethological, ethological–ethical, ethical–ethological and ethical – related to different strata of the personality system and corresponding to different levels of autopoiesis or self-organization.

The personality system is the production matrix of the action system and defines the conditions of its possibility, while the action system is the materialization process of the personality system and defines the conditions of its operationality. Its interrelation (form–content relation) produces sense(s) and the individual's meaning system emerges from this (da Agra, 1990). There are four basic levels of meaning defined by the author, corresponding to the levels of the action system and governed by different strata of the personality system: ontological, deontological, logical and teleological. In applying this grid to the study of transgression, we also obtain four *positions of transgressive meaning: substantive* (of biological or psychobiological *fatalism*), *cooperative* (of social determinism, of hetero-normativeness), *solitary* (of psychological self-determination, of self-determination of the existential meanings, of knowledge of acts) and *projective* (of action on circumstances, of projection and transcendence of individuality, of full biopsychosocial integration).

From the operationalization of these positions it is possible to agree upon the different logics and meanings of transgression and to define the dominant position of each subject, or group of subjects, in relation to the transgressive action.

FROM CRIMINAL PERSONALITY TO PSYCHOLOGICAL PROCESSES INVOLVED IN THE CONSTRUCTION OF DEVIANT PATHWAYS: RESULTS OF A SERIES OF EMPIRICAL STUDIES

Within the framework of the theory of the autopoietic subject, we developed three empirical studies that sought to include the three systems that form the psychological subject and his interrelations. The first study focused on the personality system and its relation to action. The second analysed the determinations and meanings of transgressive action, more specifically the practice of crimes and the use of drugs. The third worked on developing an instrument and a methodology to analyse and integrate the different processes that occur at the level of these three subsystems (personality, action and meaning), considered within the framework of the subject's life history, in particular his deviant pathway.[2]

In order to do this, we had to use a multiple, composite methodology, capable of dealing with the complexity of the object and the concepts under study, linking quantitative and qualitative methods and grids. Thus, in the first study, different instruments of psychological assessment were used (for example, the Rorschach Test according to the Exner system and the Vaz Serra Inventory of Problem Resolution), which sought to gain access to the processes of functioning and of psychological (self-) organization of criminal individuals and/or drug users. In particular, they sought to deal with the structure and organization of the personality system, the foremost psychological processes, the ways in which individuals perceive and organize the different elements of their environment, build a given *vision* or *version of reality*, give it a given sense and, in view of these aspects, implement certain modes of action.

The second study aimed to analyse the determinations and meanings of the actions – crime, drug use and the relationship between the two – and of the individuals' deviant pathways. This implied operationalization of the concepts of the guiding theoretical model followed by characterization of the sample in relation to these elements.[3] This study involved collecting short narratives, using a standardized, semi-structured interview (Patton, 1988). The narratives were submitted to a content analysis using independent judges both in the operationalization phase and in the phase of analysis of determinations and senses of the subjects' action.

The third study sought to develop a grid and a method to make an integrated and integrating analysis of the different dimensions studied, considered within the context of each subject's life history. With this in mind, we chose to work from the 'biogram method' (da Agra and Matos, 1997) – a method of collection and graphical representation of biographies – and use this to form an interpretative–phenomenological grid that would enable not only graphic representation of the areas and the fundamental moments in the individuals' lives, but also analysis of the psychological processes involved and of the meanings of the action and of the (deviant) existence that the subjects formed – in other words, we seek to gather the different experiences of their deviant ways of life.[4]

In terms of the first study, the results obtained at the level that we could consider psychological *invariables* did not reveal any basic personality structure (or any specific organization of 'psychological traits') determining crime and/or drug use that could differentiate these individuals from non-criminal individuals or non-drug addicts (Manita, 1997, 1998). In general, no relevant deficiencies or pathology were identified at the perceptive level, or at the level of perceptive–cognitive mediation, of integration and information processing, of the processes of integration and construction of reality, cognitive–ideative processes, affective processes and basic interpersonal relationships, an observation that would contradict most of the available bibliographical data. In other words, the features normally mentioned as characteristic of *criminal personality*[5] were not found in these individuals.

However, at the level of the functional organization in the upper levels of the personality system some characteristic regularities were found for each of the sample's subgroups (delinquents with no drug use, drug addicts with no criminal activity, criminal drug addicts) that could be at the root of modalities and processes of psychological self-organization associated with the emergence of problematic behaviour. These processes are predominantly related to what we could call 'cognitive integration and complexity' and 'modalities of relationship with the environment and with others'.[6]

On the basis of the results obtained, we can say that the transgressive behaviour of these individuals does not come from an incapacity to act in another way or from a structural determination to (only) act in this way, but is related to the superior processes of significant construction of reality and the ways of relating to it. This leads them to construct a given version of reality (and a given view of themselves and their existence), to give it a determined sense and, in view of personal and environmental characteristics and of the meanings constructed throughout their personal history, it leads them to act. Their psychic system, a place par excellence for the creation of themselves and of the world, and a place of creative escape from the biological and social conditions and determinism, will mediate between all these elements, sustaining the construction of these different 'versions of reality', seeking to make sense of them and to preserve a coherent and viable (narrative) identity in the course of existence[7] within a changing environment. Once they have been identified, it is therefore important to know the way in which the different processes of the construction of reality are organized into existentialist positions, into ways of dealing with the world and into *positions of meaning* for the action.[8]

This was one of the aims that led to the planning and realization of a second study into the levels and types of auto-hetero-determination of crime and drug use, as well as the subjects' positions of transgressive meaning, bearing in mind that each individual, social actor and autopoietic subject is called to construct his course in life in his own particular context, occupying a given social position in space and time that provide support for the constructions of the reality he lives. It is within this context and this time (individual life and historic time), in the game of the relation with himself and the interrelations with others that he is called upon to be a social actor, an active constructor of himself and his existential paths (Touraine, 1984; Debuyst, 1960, 1985, 1990a, 1990b).

This second study clearly showed the mediating role and the importance of the action's meanings and of the positions of existential and transgressive meaning, as well as the type of narrative organization of the senses, above all at the level of determinations of the action (Manita, 1998). At this level, we should point out immediately that although we found different determinations and different possible meanings, both for the practice of crimes and for the consumption of drugs, we also found that the drug/crime relationship was greatly strengthened both at the level of determinations and at the level of meanings. In other words, both criminal activities and drug use assume different meanings for the subjects, linked to different types and degrees of self-hetero-determination of this action, integrated in different positions of transgressive meaning. This variability is greater in the case of drug use, especially when consumption first begins, a moment at which this behaviour presents a wide spectrum of meanings and determinations, much wider than the spectrum that occurs in terms of the practice of crime(s), both in the first act and in recidives. When a relationship is established between the two behaviours, the range of variability practically disappears, and the individual's action is focused almost exclusively on the ontological significant/determinat drugs, more specifically the drug addiction[9] (Manita *et al.*, 1997; Manita, 1997, 1998).

Basically, three levels of meaning were identified. Firstly, there is a deterministic level, in which the perpetrators of the crime consider their deviant behaviour to be determined by external and uncontrollable causes, particularly drug consumption (which would be the cause of the crime). Secondly, there is a moderate deterministic level, linking external and internal factors, causality, contingence and indetermination. A third level stresses the active and self-determinate role of the subject in his deviant experience, from the game of his capacities of self-organization (da Agra, 1998; Manita, 1998). By analysing the links between meanings, determinations and ways of action, made possible through the statistical method of factorial analysis of multiple correspondences, this second study also clearly showed the fundamental role that meanings play in mediating the action, in the development of different deviant pathways, in the construction of different ways of relating to the world and in the organization of different positions of transgressive meaning.

This integrated analysis of the different dimensions studied showed some subgroups among the subjects, characterized by different groups of psychological processes, determinations and meanings, linked to different types of action and drug/crime relations, as well as non-relations (Manita *et al.*, 1997; Manita, 1998). In fact, in contrast to what 'implicit theories' on the phenomenon have construed to be true, the drug/crime relationship is not direct or linear. Different forms of determination and self-management of consumption are linked to different forms of determination of the criminal activity (and vice versa). Different meanings for consumption (as well as for the drug/crime relationship) are linked to different modes of determination, to different meanings of criminal activity and to different patterns of evolution over time.[10] In summary, determinations and meanings will function as mediators of the individual's relation with the action, of the individual's relation with the world and, together with determined processes of psychological self-organization, they will be at the basis of different transgressive pathways and different positions of transgressive meaning.

As these are processes, events and changes, seen at different times in the transgressive pathway, their integration into the subject's life history would allow us to understand more fully their sense and the impact they have on the bearings and paths the subject takes in life. The third study enabled us to work on the development of an instrument initially designed by da Agra (da Agra and Matos, 1997) which proved to be triply effective: as a research instrument into deviant pathways, as a theoretical reading grid of the processes that sustain them and as an instrument for psychological counselling.

CONTRIBUTIONS FOR DEVELOPING A METHODOLOGY OF ANALYSIS AND UNDERSTANDING OF DEVIANT PROCESSES AND PATHWAYS: THE BIOGRAM METHOD IN THE LIGHT OF THE AUTOPOIETIC SUBJECT THEORY

Once the notion of criminal personality had been deconstructed in the series of theoretical and empirical studies performed (Manita, 1996, 1997, 1998), another grid had to be developed with which to read criminal behaviour and, more generically, transgressive phenomena. New research and assessment instruments also had to be made that would be able to sustain a hermeneutic and procedural approach to these phenomena. The *biogram method*, developed by da Agra and Matos (1997), or rather, a modified version of it, proved the most suitable option. We therefore chose to use the nucleus of the biographical methodologies, which is highly qualitative in nature, but did not ignore the potential of linking and integrating it with analyses of a quantitative nature. In fact, there are many authors and studies that demonstrate the advantages of this integration (Ingold and Ingold, 1988, Guba and Lincoln, 1985, 1989; da Agra, 1997, 1998; Manita, 1997, 1998).

After being caught up in the whirlpool of experimentalism and quantitativism and being forgotten for decades, the 1980s saw a progressive return to biographical methods, namely to life histories or biographies, as well as other forms of narrative. This return followed the failure of the extremist positivist, quantitativist positions, which was particularly visible in the study of complex human action and even more so in the interstitial phenomena[11] that are alien to the dominant logics and visibilities, as are criminality and drug use. Another important factor was the incapacity of positivist models to gain access to the dimensions of subjectivity, of experience, of meanings and, generically, all the procedural dimensions (they only deal with the resultant visible behaviour and not the underlying processes). There was also the will (and the need) to reach fairly inaccessible populations, normally excluded from the dominant language and systems, and the realization that life histories constitute privileged raw material for a 'transdisciplinary social science' (Legrand, 1992, 1993; Poirier, Clapier-Valladon and Raybaut, 1983; Ferrarotti, 1980, 1983; Fernandes, 1989, 1996).

Because of the individual's own nature the term 'biography', is highly ambiguous, but fecund. The biography 'is the life of a single individual, understood in its temporal and historical course, but it is also – immediately, if we pause at its etymology – the writing on this life, its narrative reconstruction, its *récit*' (Legrand, 1993: 11). It is therefore method and object and it is in this dual role that we use it. Just as in the work of Legrand, and other authors (Bertaux, 1980a, 1980b, 1981; Ferrarotti, 1980, 1983; Clapier-Valladon, 1983; Pineau, 1980; Pineau and Legrand, 1993; Fernandes, 1989, 1996), we assume this duplicity and adopt the biographies not only as an instrument of research, but also as an object for analysis: the life history approach through narration of this history, in an effort to reach individuality as an object in itself, to reach narrative and experiential organization[12] of the processes that have happened and of the projects constructed during each individual's transgressive pathway.

We therefore share the need felt by Legrand (1992, 1993) to uncover what must be one of the strangest 'oversights' of psychology: the work of Politzer and the way this author perceived a 'science of biographies' in developing the theory of the psychological subject in its concrete and dramatic singularity. Effectively, this author defended the view that the object of psychology must be the series of unique events that unfold between birth and death, in other words, the drama of human existence just as a unique history unfolds, a concrete life, the drama of existence. He maintained that the appropriate method for the study of this existential drama would be the *récit*, the existential narrative, the life history, the biography, narrated by the author of the drama itself.

The project begun by Politzer in 1929 was incomplete and today there is a resurgence in the wish to create a theoretical, epistemological and methodological device for life histories.[13] At this level, the work of Legrand (1992, 1993) stands out, in which he strives to form a psychology of a biographical order. This is not a psychobiography in the strictest sense of the word (a way to reach the mental processes through biographies), but something much wider and more complex. It is a psychology of the uniqueness of existence, of life, of the individual human history that never ceases to be formed in and through its narration.[14]

This issue refers us to the work of Ferrarotti (1983) and to the need, defended by the author, to eliminate the distinction between general and particular, between nomothetic and idiographic, since the individual is the synthetic praxis of the social reality. He does not reflect the real, he appropriates it, filters it, retransforms it into psychological structures and projects it into a social world, through his individuality and subjectivity. In other words, he builds it. At the same time, the differences found in the various *récits* indicate the organization of the subject's personality. They are raw materials in his explosive subjectivity. In this way, they allow us to incorporate in the method what, until a very short time ago, had been seen as an epistemological obstacle: subjectivity. 'Objectivising subjectivity and giving it status in the document instead of discarding it as waste is like restoring to the field of knowledge the meanings that the actors attribute to social life and recognising in the subjects exactly what makes them psychological subjects: their individuality and their subjectivity' (Fernandes, 1996: 148).[15]

The histories are always narrative rearrangements of the realities and the text's author is a (re)construction of self. They are strategies that strive to capture the singularity of a pathway, the identity of a life, treating the subject as a living body in a world of meanings, integrating what has been lived and experienced, linking lived life, experienced life and recounted or narrated life, linking path and project. Consequently, they give us access to the psychological material itself: among other aspects, access to the content of the psychic life and to its relation with the world, access to self-perceptions and to the determinations of the action, obtained through the self that speaks in them. 'This constant move from the self to the world, this general mix of the subjective with events, which characterises all life history is a familiar level of analysis to the psychologist. (...) However, a general theory is missing on the relations between the person and the event. Psychology clarifies almost nothing in terms of relations between the moments of existence, events and the environment' (Clapier-Valladon, 1983: 721).

The life history may contribute precisely towards filling this void, since it is located on the edge and in the link between the subject and the social, and 'it is this link between the levels of existence – that human sciences have tried to avoid or deny to ease research and simplify theory – that we find again here' (ibid.). Men never cease to recount (the story of) their life and, through this narrative process, to form it. Psychological subject and social actor re-encounter themselves and are thus reunited, at the wider level of analysis of the life histories – method and object.[16]

More specifically, life histories allow us to reach the different ways of relating to norms and values and, by the same way, transgression and ethics. They allow us to understand how the subject is located in relation to the social conditions in which he lives, they allow us to approach the subject as a moral and ethical subject, capable of distancing himself and of reflecting, capable of transcending the daily routine in which he is so deeply involved, by reference to projects. In other words, life histories show us ways of *life management*, and are excellent ways in which to gain access to processes, theories and behavioural and existentialist meanings (Debuyst, 1960, 1985; Digneffe, 1989).

These were some of the reasons that led us to think of the life history as a privileged instrument for the study of relations and integration between the action system, the personality system and the meaning system, based on the methodological proposal we present here: the biograms (of an interpretative nature). We therefore returned to the biogram method created by da Agra and Matos (1997), on which we have worked over the last two years. In short, this is:

a methodology of biographic reconstitution or *reconstructed biographic method*, which consists of linking *hetero-biographical* data (significant facts in the subjects' existential course, collected and recorded by others) and *auto-biographical* data (collected through interviews with the same subjects). The *reconstructed biography* (consisting of the *hetero-* and *auto-biography*) is portrayed graphically in the *biogram*, an instrument designed as part of this study, which enables us to visualise and link clearly and objectively the individual existential course at the following levels: family, school, professional, judicial–penal intervention, deviant course, delinquency and drug consumption. (da Agra and Matos, 1997: 35)[17]

Based, as we have said, on the biogram, the theoretical and methodological instrument we have developed has, like the biogram, a dual potential: firstly, to study transgression and deviant pathways (at the individual level, by going deeper into a given life history, or at the level of 'types' of trajectories, through combined analysis of different courses and detection of their procedural and/or behavioural invariables), from an alternative conceptual model (in our case, linking the theory of the autopoietic subject with the theories of narrativity, within the framework of the theories of self-organization); secondly, to obtain from the subjects a narrative of their existential course, which is easily assimilated through the use of graphs, both at its points of continuity and at those of branching, reordering, impasse, development, transition and so on. Psychological intervention from biograms proves to be a true process of narrative (re)organization of the most significant events in the subject's life, as well as the course of his existence. In other words, it is a (significant) reorganization of the *existential drama* made by the subjects themselves, by confronting the different moments and characteristics of their personal pathway.[18]

By adapting the biogram to this research, we are able to make a graphic summary, not only in the area of the individuals' lives (which happened in the original version) but also – bearing in mind the operationalizations of the *general theory of the autopoietic subject* done in the meantime – a graphic summary of the dominant modes and levels of operation of the personality system, of the plans of meaning, of the modalities and degrees of auto-heterodetermination of the action and, also, of the position of transgressive meaning that guides the subject's action at the different times he indicates as critical points in the course of his deviant pathway (cf. Figure 2.1).

In constructing and reading Figure 2.1, each row corresponds to one of the dimensions studied, while columns are marked with the moments and/or events that the individuals gave as crucial points in the evolution of their pathways (divided by the subject into 'phases', 'cycles' or 'periods' which they have named). Where the two lines intercept, there are coloured squares in which each colour corresponds to the classifications of the dimensions analysed[19] (cf. Figures 2.1 and 2.2).

Though they are not visible in Figure 2.1 (because of difficulties of graphic representation that can easily be resolved by using superimposed transparent sheets), the areas of life (cf. Figure 2.2) underlie the first biogram and sustain it, portraying the subject's life at different levels of analysis. In other words, the two methods are not incompatible nor do they exclude one another. On the contrary, they cannot be disassociated (the second cannot exist without the first), they complement each other and converge towards a deeper and more complex knowledge of the transgressive behaviour of each subject and the dynamic and transgressive processes that sustain them, in view of the real hermeneutic of transgression.

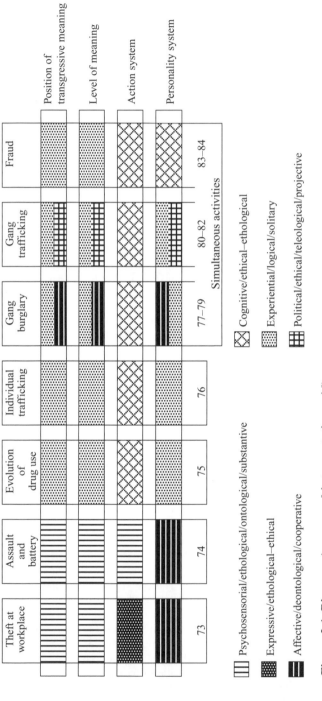

Figure 2.1 Biogram (processual interpretation grid)

Unlike the original biogram (da Agra and Matos, 1997), whose first version is filled in from collected heterobiographic data, we begin by collecting the necessary autobiographical data from the subject to complete the biogram, followed by a second phase, its graphic organization on the biogram sheet.[20] In a third phase, entirely like the one originally proposed by da Agra and Matos, the subject is shown the graphic result and the aspects it presents are checked with him to ensure nothing is missing, or that it is not necessary to change, remove or add any elements. When the subject agrees that the fundamental elements and moments in his behaviour (criminal activity, drug use, victimization and so on) are represented there, another method is used: the subject is asked to divide 'his life' into different phases, which are marked on the graph. One change that was gradually introduced into the biogram's application is the fact that the subjects were asked, after identifying the different phases or cycles in their life, to give them a name or label (and later to explain them) – the moment that focuses most on the existential meanings and senses. At the end, a 'summarized narrative' is made of the subject's life history.

In the version of the biogram with which we worked, apart from these phases, a theoretical reading grid is also used resulting from the theory of the autopoietic subject and the operationalizations of the model developed until now (Manita, 1997, 1998). For each action or group of actions, and for each time and/or period identified by the subjects, we analyse what the dominant modes and levels of auto-heterodetermination of the action and the psychological self-organization processes are, the levels of the system of action in which they are located, the levels or strata of the personality system that governs them and the positions of transgressive meaning that guided their action in that period/moment.[21] Applying this instrument to different concrete cases (which will not be mentioned here, since that is not the aim of this chapter) has already proved to be useful and productive.

THE OPEN FUTURE

With the autopoietic subject theory and the biogram method – mentioned here in a necessarily brief and incomplete way – and, above all with the link between the two, the subject reassumes, theoretically and empirically, the place that was denied him for decades in much scientific research. The individual who transgresses reassumes the role of social actor, autopoietic subject capable of defining and creating himself, in the game of determinations and indeterminations; a transgressor who on the one hand is free-will and on the other hand is subject to unavoidable determinisms. Obviously, we cannot exclude the importance of several factors: biological, psychological and ecosocial characteristics, the society and culture in which he is immersed, the economic and political conditions and system of which he is part, the social position he holds, his gender, the opportunities that result from this series of positions and roles, the contexts in which he lives, the relationships he forms, the experiences that form his life and his personal course. In fact, with reference to J.P. Sartre, we can say that we analyse what the subject is capable of *doing* with what all these factors and events *have done* or *are doing to him*.

The notion of (deviant) career or pathway emerges in this context as a point of convergence or link between the individual's behaviour, the different dimensions or

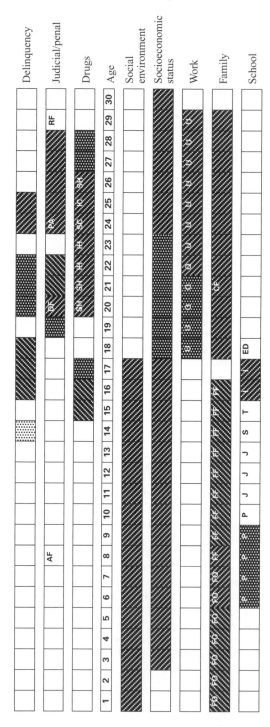

Figure 2.2 Example of a biogram

(In da Agra and Matos, 1997. Adapted with authors' agreement)

Work

regular
irregular
U | unqualified
Q | qualified

Drugs

alcohol, amphetamines
cannabis, grass
heroin, cocaine
medical treatment
IH | injected heroin
SH | smoked heroin
IC | injected cocaine
SC | smoked cocaine

Social environment

urban environment
suburban environment
RE | rural environment

School

regular
difficulties, absences
indiscipline
P | primary school
J | junior school
S | secondary school
T | technical–professional
U | university
ED | abandoned studies due to economic difficulties

Socioeconomic status

low socioeconomic level
middle socioeconomic level
upper socioeconomic level
RE | rural environment

Judicial/penal

prison sentence
suspended sentence
remand
RA | released through amnesty
DF | definitive freedom
PA | parole
MR | minors' institutions, regular
MI | minors' institutions, irregular
AF | alternative family, court order

Family

stable
unstable
FO | family of origin
FF | foster family
CF | constituted family

Delinquency

vagrancy, runaways, prostitution
trafficking
crimes against others
theft
consumption

areas in which his life unfolds, the fundamental events that mark it and the underlying psychological and psychosocial processes. Through the collection and graphic representation of a life history on the biogram, and its theoretical analysis and interpretation in the light of the theory of the autopoietic subject, we believe that it could be easier to understand how different processes, at different levels of the system, affect the results of what they produce at each turning point in the history. Doing so we have to recognize and understand to what extent and in what way each subject was actor and acted, determined and was determined, was a product and producer of his life circumstances, following a given life course that culminates in the formation of a given existential meaning, and in the attribution of a given sense to his actions, specifically the transgressive ones.

NOTES

1   We can consider it constructivist at different levels: to begin with, at the level of what we could call 'constructivist epistemology', or, more correctly, 'epistemological constructivism', which is also a methodological constructivism, based on the thinking of Foucault; and also at the level of explanatory and/or comprehensive theories of the criminal's action closest to that from which we proceed – apart from the theory of the autopoietic subject, which guided us in this research, the theories of the social actor, developmental theories and constructivist theories (which go back to principles of symbolic interactionism and Piaget-like thinking, among other aspects); and, finally, also at the level of the empirical research methodologies used, or, more generically, at the level of the paradigm of research into which we fit: the so-called 'constructivist, interpretative' or 'hermeneutic' paradigm (Guba and Lincoln, 1985, 1989).

2   In the context of this last study we also developed a first exercise of operationalization of the theory of the autopoietic subject, from the notion of self-organization and autopoiesis – a notion that enables us to go from interpretation to explanation and its empirical translation (da Agra, 1997, 1998) – applying it to the study of crime, drugs and drug/crime relationships.

3   Different levels of analysis were considered in this study: the determinations of the action – in terms of the type of determinant, mode and levels of (auto-hetero-) determination and their fluctuations during the subject's deviant pathway; the meanings of the action; the positions of transgressive meaning and their changes throughout the subject's history.

4   The notion of deviant pathway or career is central here, considered as a series or sequence of positions, roles and social status, actions, events and deviant activities that are significantly related to each other, around which the individual organizes parts of his life (in the sense that Faupel refers to it).

5   Not even an 'addictive personality' or 'criminal drug-addictive personality'.

6   The results obtained at this level will not be developed here, since this is not part of the aims of this text. Those interested should refer to Manita (1997, 1998).

7   A more detailed characterization of the results obtained at the level of the different subgroups in the study (criminals, drug addicts, criminal drug addicts), and the different types of crime analysed (acquisitive crimes, violent crimes and drug-related crimes), can be found in Manita (1997, 1998) and Manita *et al.* (1997).

8   There is here a first point of convergence between the results of the analysis and theoretical reflection and the results of the empirical studies developed (Manita, 1998): the first analyses pointed out the need to deconstruct and abandon the idea of criminal personality. This first study does not empirically find the criminal personality and indicates other directions of research that later studies reinforce.

9   Here, we may, in part, be dealing with the effects of a *sampling bias*. In contrast to the first study, and for reasons we will not comment on here, this second study was developed with a sample group consisting exclusively of inmates, most of whom were drug users.

10   Even to different types of criminality (for example, the link between heroin dependency and burglary, between excessive alcohol consumption and rape, between moderate and controlled consumption of benzodiazepines and fraud). Crime and consumption may also exist at the same time, without the criminals drawing any relation between the two.

11   We refer to this concept in the sense given to it by Cohen.

12   The level of meanings now doubled and felt by the subject. In other words, a level of expressive, affective, cognitive, experiential and political integration (according to the theory of the autopoietic subject), that each individual makes of the different constitutive elements and processes of his identity and personality, of the environmental elements on which he acts and that act upon him, of the sociodemographic conditions and the social position he holds, which give him different levels of power at which to act.

13 Seeing that the biography or life history assumes a component of intuitive comprehension or, according to Bourdieu (1997), is one of those commonsense concepts that penetrated the scientific world, the question remains as to whether we will be able to go beyond this intuitive dimension and the analyses of common sense and construct a true 'science of biography'. The works of Poirier *et al.* (1983), Clapier-Valladon (1983), Ferrarotti (1983), Digneffe (1989), Denzin (1989, 1990), Legrand (1992, 1993), da Agra and Matos (1997) and Fernandes (1989, 1996), among others, lead us to believe that it is possible.

14 Legrand (1993) returns to the ideas of authors such as L. Séve, C. Castoriadis and J.P. Sartre.

15 This is why its study implies hermeneutics and phenomenology. In fact, the analysis of life history reveals more of hermeneutics in the broad sense of the word than a scientific explanation in the more traditional and limited sense of the concept (Clapier-Valladon, 1983) and, by calling on interpretation, realizes a possible complementarity between explanation and comprehension (Ricoeur, 1976, 1977, 1986).

16 Linking the study of biographies to the theories of narrativity, it will be possible to reach what Ricoeur calls 'narrative identities', the elements that allow us to structure our experiences coherently in relation to the world, throughout time and space, elements that compose the existential paths that we make and follow. The histories we tell about our lives enable us to understand how we deal with sense, coherence, uniqueness and identity, but also with illusion, difference, variability, incoherence and the contradictory. According to Ricoeur all the *récit* configures what will mediate between concordance (group arrangement, organization of the diverse and heterogeneous) and discordance (breaks, deviations, the unexpected). The *heterogeneous synthesis* is a discordant concordance, characteristic of all narrative composition. The histories also enable us to understand how we deal with the sociocultural dimensions that define our own identity, such as gender, class, status and social group to which we belong (Denzin, 1989).

17 In our case, we do not work with *reconstructed biographies* from autobiographical and heterobiographical data, but just from autobiographical data collected from direct contact with the subjects.

18 Different exploratory studies have been made in the last two years that have used the biogram method, in addicts support centres, with inmates of different prisons and at a Victims' Psychological Consulting Service. In all these studies the biogram revealed surprising effects at the level of psychotherapeutic intervention with the subjects, making its future development as a method of psychological intervention possible, as well as that of a research instrument.

19 Each area is filled in according to the results of a content analysis of the narratives collected, arranged in the categories obtained in previous studies (Manita, 1997, 1998), from the theory of the autopoietic subject. This version of the biogram thus represents the main areas of life, and an analysis of *theoretical* dimensions, or rather, an 'interpretation' of the processes involved in the criminal activity (and consumption) from the subject's own verbal account.

20 Some subjects can be responsible for filling in the various fields of the biogram themselves. The fields of the biogram may vary in view of the object of study or the intervention situation at stake.

21 By doing so, we will be able to understand better its effect at the level of options that the individual takes step by step and which define different deviant courses, linked to certain types of action, to certain positions in view of the crime, to the use of drugs and to the constitution or not of a deviant identity, throughout the existential path.

REFERENCES

Bertaux, D. (1980a), *Histoires de vie ou récits de pratiques. Méthodologie de l'approche biographique en sociologie*, Paris: CORDES.

Bertaux, D. (1980b), 'L'approche biographique: Sa validité méthodologique, ses potentialités', *Cahiers internationaux de sociologie*, **69**, 197–225.

Bertaux, D. (1981), *Biography and Society: The Life History Approach in the Social Sciences*, Beverly Hills, CA: Sage.

Bourdieu, P. (1997), *Razões práticas. Sobre a teoria da acção*, Lisbon: Ed. Celta.

Clapier-Valladon, S. (1983), 'Le récit de vie, une nouvelle orientation de la recherche en sciences humaines. Pour une contribution de la psychologie', *Bulletin de Psychologie*, **XXXVI** (361), 717–22.

da Agra, C. (1986), 'Adolescência, comportamento desviante e auto-organizado: Modelo de psicologia epistemanalítica', *Cadernos de Consulta Psicológica*, **2**, 81–7.

da Agra, C. (1990), 'Sujet autopoiétique et transgression', in *Acteur social et délinquance – Hommage à Christian Debuyst*, Brussels: Pierre Mardaga, Ed, pp.415–27.

da Agra, C. (1991) 'Sujet autopoiétique et toxicodépendance', paper presented at the Centre international de criminologie comparée of the University of Montreal.

da Agra, C. (1994), 'Science de l'éthique et droit pénal', *Carrefour*, **16** (2), 108–29.

da Agra, C. (1997), 'A Experiência Portuguesa: Programa de Estudos e Resultados', in C. da Agra (ed.), *Projecto Droga e Crime: Estudos Interdisciplinares*, vol. I, Lisbon: G.P.C.C.D– Ministério da Justiça.

da Agra, C. (1998), *Entre droga e crime*, Lisbon: Ed. Notícias.

da Agra, C. and Matos, P. (1997), 'Trajectórias Desviantes', in C. da Agra (ed.), *Projecto Droga e Crime: Estudos Interdisciplinares*, vol. II, Lisbon: G.P.C.C.D– Ministério da Justiça.

Debuyst, Ch. (1960), *Criminels et valeurs vécues: étude clinique d'un groupe de jeunes criminels*, Louvain: Publications Universitaires.

Debuyst, Ch. (1985), *Modèle éthologique et criminologie*, Brussels: Pierre Mardaga Ed.

Debuyst, Ch. (1990a), 'Présentation et justification du thème', in *Acteur social et délinquance – Hommage à Christian Debuyst*, Brussels: Pierre Mardaga Ed., pp.21–36.

Debuyst, Ch. (1990b), 'Remarques conclusives', in *Acteur social et délinquance – Hommage à Christian Debuyst*, Brussels: Pierre Mardaga Ed., pp.46–7.

Denzin, N.K. (1989), *Interpretative biography*, Qualitative Research Methods Series, vol. 17, California: Sage.

Denzin, N.K. (1990), *Interpretive interactionism*, Applied Social Research Methods Series, vol. 16, California: Sage.

Digneffe, F. (1989), *Éthique et délinquance. La délinquance comme gestion de sa vie*, Geneva: Ed. Médecine et hygiène.

Fernandes, J.L. (1989), 'Estratégias qualitativas de investigação do uso de drogas e da toxicodependência', *Análise Psicológica*, **1–2–3**, 329–38.

Fernandes, J.L. (1996), 'Actores e territórios psicotrópicos. Etnografia das drogas numa periferia urbana', unpublished PhD thesis, FPCEUP, Oporto.

Ferrarotti, F. (1980), 'Les biographies comme instrument analytique et interprétatif', *Cahiers internationaux de sociologie*, **LXIX**, 227–48.

Ferrarotti, F. (1983), *Histoire et histoires de vie*, Paris: Librairie des Méridiens.

Guba, E.G. and Lincoln, Y.S. (1985), *Naturalistic Inquiry*, California: Sage.

Guba, E.G. and Lincoln, Y.S. (1989), *Fourth Generation Evaluation*, California: Sage.

Ingold, S. and Ingold, F.R. (1988), 'Complémentarité méthodologique des approches quantitatives et qualitatives de la recherche dans le champ de la toxicomanie', *Bulletin de méthodologie sociologique*, **20**, 33–48.

Legrand, M. (1992), 'L'approche biographique: théorie, méthode, pratiques', *Análise Psicológica*, **X** (4), 499–514.

Legrand, M. (1993), *L'approche biographique*, Marseilles: Hommes et Perspectives, ÉPI.

Manita, C. (1996), 'Y-a-t-il une "personnalité criminelle"? – une étude d'évaluation dans le domaine de la criminalité', *Revue internationale de criminologie et de police technique*, **1**, 105–13.

Manita, C. (1997), 'Personalidade e Acção em Consumidores de Drogas e Delinquentes', in C. da Agra (ed.), *Projecto Droga e Crime: Estudos Interdisciplinares*, vol. VIII, Lisbon: G.P.C.C.D– Ministério da Justiça.

Manita, C. (1998), 'Auto-organização psicológica e transgressão. Análise empirico-crítica de duas figuras do comportamento desviante: criminosos e consumidores de drogas', unpublished PhD thesis, FPCEUP, Oporto.

Manita, C., Negreiros, J. and da Agra, C. (1997), 'Planos de Vida, droga e Crime', in C. da Agra (ed.), *Projecto Droga e Crime: Estudos Interdisciplinares*, vol. IX, Lisbon: G.P.C.C.D– Ministério da Justiça.

Patton, M. (1988), *How to Use Qualitative Methods in Evaluation*, Beverly Hills: Sage.

Pineau, G. (1980), *Vies des histoires de vie*, Montreal: Les Presses de l'Université de Montréal.

Pineau, G. and Legrand, J.L. (1993), *Les histoires de vie*, Paris: Presses universitaires de France.

Poirier, J., Clapier-Valladon, S. and Raybaut, P. (1983), *Les récits de vie. Théorie et pratique*, Paris: Presses universitaires de France.

Politzer, G. (1973), *Crítica dos fundamentos da Psicologia*, Lisbon: Ed. Presença (1st edn 1929).

Ricoeur, P. (1976), *Interpretation Theory: Discourse and the Surplus of Meaning*, Fort Worth: Texas Christian University Press.

Ricoeur, P. (1977), 'Expliquer et comprendre', *Revue philosophique de Louvain*, **75**, 126–47.

Ricoeur, P. (1986), *Du texte à l'action. Essais d'herméneutique,* vol. 2, Paris: Ed. Seuil.

Touraine, A. (1984), *Le retour de l'acteur. Essai de sociologie*, Paris: Ed. Fayard.

Chapter 3

Drug Addiction and Drug Dealing – from Trajectories to Careers: the Status of the Question in Social Sciences in France

Michel Kokoreff and Claude Faugeron

The current status of social science research in France concerning deviant trajectories is likely to be rather disappointing. This research topic tends to be studied in the framework of anamneses undertaken in clinical approaches. In the course of the 1970s, social science research took some interest in this area, in the context of social control theory. One of the most recent studies done from this perspective is that on delinquent minors by Léomant and Sotteau-Léomant (1987). As this theory fell out of favour, and above all because few researchers were involved in this type of work, it was not until the beginning of the 1990s that researchers became interested in deviant trajectories again.

It is worthwhile to spend a few moments on the theoretical and institutional framework that has fostered this revived interest. The transformations seen in contemporary sociology (Ansart, 1990) were particularly profound in the 1980s and 1990s, and constitute a key feature. Highly heated arguments developed around the issue of social totality, taken either in its determinations, in its dynamism or in its openness to the strategies of agents. At the same time the question of the place of individuals in the social fabric arises, whether they are defined as 'agents' or 'actors', 'strategists' or 'atoms'. While these conceptual preferences are less related to fashionable trends than to significant theoretical differences, there is no avoiding the observation that a 'turning point' in description took place, seen in greater attention paid to the singular, the local and the biographical context. The 'return of the actor' – a work published by Alain Touraine in 1984 – has in this respect value as both symbol and programme. It clearly expresses the reintegration of actors in the construction of the models in French research, after a period marked by the 'major discourses' (Marxism and its variants, structuralism, Foucauldism and so on). At the same time this formula also reveals the political and ideological implications of research. The rhetoric of 'destiny' is replaced by the figure of the individual, invited to choose and to be the actor of his or her own life. At this point we witnessed a powerful resurgence of interactionisms. Not only symbolic interactionism, but also microsociology, ethnomethodology, ethnography of communication and so on.

This was reinforced by the social and political context that prevailed in France in the early 1990s. The major phenomenon was what was so often called the 'crisis of

51

the suburbs' in ministries and administrative offices as well as in newsrooms. The urban disorder in so-called 'tough' neighbourhoods, the non-functional nature of traditional instruments for assisting poverty-stricken populations, the extension of the use and commerce of illegal substances, spurred a return to approaches initiated by the Chicago School in the United States. This school of thought had clear applications in the work commissioned in the 1980s and 1990s in neighbourhoods deemed to be 'sensitive' (Collectif, 1997).

The research dynamic that emerged in other specialized fields should also be mentioned, although it lies beyond the scope of this chapter. For the low level of interest in the temporal dimensions of deviant conduct is in strong contrast to the popularity of sociobiographical analyses that were developed in the 1980s, most particularly in the sociology of education and urban sociology.[1] The shift in focus from 'life histories' to 'life stories', according to this expression introduced in 1976 by D. Bertaux and expanded in many surveys (Bertaux, 1997); the renewal of analyses of socialization of youths no longer seen as a 'category of behavior in which class, sex or ethnic origins constitute indicators of sociocultural differentiation', but taken as a 'temporal category, a stage in a life cycle in ongoing change' (Blöss and Féroni, 1991: 5); the interest shown in the construction of and the relationships between different generational categories, and lastly the far-reaching reflection undertaken by authors such as J.C. Passeron, F. Godard, F. de Conninck and C. Dubar – all these phenomena constitute a capital of knowledge and know-how that can be tested in relation to other social processes. This is all the more true in that this work and thinking on temporal analysis has continued up to the present day, taking as its subjects job insertion (Demazière and Dubar, 1997), youths' careers in precariousness (Roulleau-Berger, 1999) and flexibility in life stages (Bessin, 1993), among others.

In parallel came the translation of fundamental American works, such as Anderson's *Hobo* in 1993, a collection of articles by E. Hughes solidly supported by collective work done around J.-M. Chapoulie in 1996, *The Polish Peasant* by Thomas and Znaniecki in 1998, and discussion of 'Grounded Theory' by Glaser and Strauss (1967). This led – in any event this is a possible hypothesis – to a rereading between the 'first' and the 'second' Chicago Schools, linking them in a continuum.

It is from the junction of these phenomena that the revival of work on deviant trajectories should be understood. In this chapter we will start with some reminders of the theoretical stakes involved in the notions of trajectories and careers, before presenting the main research work done on the social practices of illicit drugs. This outline will continue with a viewpoint encompassing the articulation between users' careers and careers in drug dealing, based on investigation in poor neighbourhoods carried out by Duprez and Kokoreff (2000).

TRAJECTORIES, CAREERS, BIOGRAPHICAL LINES: THE CONSTRUCTION OF CONCEPTS

Dissipating the foggiest notions

It is one thing to focus on the temporal dimension of social phenomena – in this case drug use and dealing – and another to clear up the persistent confusion that is the result of (too often) indiscriminate use of the notions employed in these accounts. In this set of concerns, three forms may be distinguished conceptually and methodologically: first of all, analysis of social trajectories, socially determined, that can also be approached as a set of trajectories (residential, familial, educational, migratory); then approaches in terms of 'life histories' or 'life stories', 'biographies' or 'life lines', which have often been developed in reaction to any and all forms of 'social determinism'; lastly, analyses in terms of 'careers' in a perspective melding institutional dimensions (penal, delinquent careers) and biographical aspects (deviant careers, itineraries).

But where are the dividing lines? Between a determinist macrosociological reading of a 'trajectory' updating a *habitus* and an *interactionist* outline of a 'career'? Unless an attempt is made to think out their dialectical articulation? This corresponds to J.-C. Passeron's position (1989: 20):

> The concept of career, when its use fulfils the promise of its theoretical content, allows us to grasp, by a description both interpretative and explanatory, the indissociably subjective and objective meaning that a succession of actions – reactive, defensive, tactical, anticipatory, etc. – takes on ex post facto as a career (for the sociologist, but also in the hindsight of the subject), actions that the subject has chosen in his/her own name as a way to handle his/her relationships with the restrictive power of a structure that has anonymously imposed its predetermined scale of sanctions or rewards corresponding to these chosen responses (or lack thereof).

This articulation that could be operated by social theory nonetheless remains problematic. The definition given is questionable, in particular for the scope granted to this 'restrictive power of a structure' in relation to other dimensions. And methodologically the issue is unresolved. How can this succession of actions be observed, from what point of view, using what data?

Another hypothesis can be submitted: the hypothesis that life stories, trajectories and careers have as targets 'different levels of organization of temporal experience' (Leclerc-Olive, 1997). To what extent is the retrospective aspect a factor of differentiation between these different terms? Whatever the answer, the different forms of causality perceived in sociobiographical studies by de Conninck and Godard (1989) could be used to characterize these levels and think about their articulation: *archaeological* (a deed generating others), *processive* (successions of events) and *structural* (the relation between external temporalities).

The construction of the concept of career

'The word "career" has a career of its own', remarked H. Hughes (1996). While one of the fundamental works of the Chicago School was devoted to life histories of Polish peasants, inspiring much work in the 1930s, notably in the area of juvenile delinquency by Clifford Shaw, author of a renowned biography (*The Jack Roller*), analysis in terms of 'careers' developed somewhat later. Compared to the earlier formulations by Tarde and Manheim, Hughes reintroduced a broad and non-instrumental conception of this notion in the 1950s at the University of Chicago (Ogien, 1996). For him the succession of events is less important than the moments of transition. The issue is finding out how the passage from one phase to another occurs in a career in which the typical stages are institutionalized, but where 'there are many uncertainties and unforeseen irregularities' (Hughes, 1996: 176) as well. The study of careers is aimed specifically at this dialectic.

Hughes thus starts from the idea that a career cannot be reduced to a model regulated by a bureaucratic or any other type of organization. It is not a synonym for 'success'. He underscores the mobility of positions, by distinguishing between 'central activity' and 'secondary activity', and between 'work system' and 'related systems'. This reference to the sociology of professions should be emphasized for the innovative nature of its transposition to the sociology of deviant trajectories. This is tantamount to considering narcotics dealing in terms of work, skills and socialization (Letkermann, 1973; Bachman and Coppel, 1989; Duprez and Kokoreff, 1999).

> Some trades exist in systems that offer numerous openings towards other related systems and towards the public at large; when someone comes to the end of his/her career, he/she may be transferred to a position in one of the related systems. It may also be that a work system unrelated to the original trade happens to offer a favorable terrain or using the talents and characteristics acquired in the original trade. (Hughes, 1996: 182)

Howard Becker (1985) has put this conception to its fullest use. He extends the notion of career to a class of individuals possessing ambition and will-power. The notion is broached in *Outsiders*, where an approach other than the multivariate approach of deviance is opposed to the etiological approach of 'evil': this is an approach via a model that takes into account the development of behavioural modes according to an ordered sequence. The aim is to differentiate between 'a succession of phases, changes in behaviour and outlook of the individual' (p.46), the cause of each phase being only one element of the final behaviour. Thus Becker proposes the concept of 'deviant careers', extended in its objective and subjective dimensions so as to account for factors of mobility from one position to another.

To the question of the intentionality of deviance and the motivation thereof, Becker suggests a response via an analysis of the process of *commitment* or the adoption of certain lines of conduct. This implies a long period of study of the author of deviant conduct who has made it a 'way of life'. A fundamental – and controversial, as we will see – mechanism by which a durable taste for these activities is constituted is *apprenticeship* to an organized subculture. In the famous chapter on marijuana smokers, the analysis is built upon the process of apprenticeship, various forms of which are described: apprenticeship of technique, of the perception of effects, of liking for the effects.

> In short, he [the smoker] has learned to answer 'yes' to the question: 'Is this pleasurable?' The later course of his usage of the drug depends on his capacity to continue to answer this question affirmatively, as well as on his capacity to respond positively to other questions that arise when he becomes aware of society's condemnation of his practice: 'Is this prudent, is this moral?' (...) The practice becomes impossible only when certain experiences with the drug engender a change in the smoker's conception thereof, making him lose the capacity to find pleasure in the sensation of 'being high'. (Becker, 1985: 81)

Although Becker's sequential model clearly continues to have a strong explanatory capacity for describing the typical path of a marijuana smoker, and particularly the conditions of the smoker's apprenticeship and commitment to a deviant career, a double criticism can be made. For one, the model has an all-encompassing nature that assumes a oneness in careers, regardless of the substance and how it is used, whereas other studies have shown that acquiring a liking does not always lead to regular use (Hirsch *et al.*, 1990). Secondly, this model does not look at careers in dealing, and questions arise as to its capacity to give an account of this aspect, owing to the fact that the universe being explored refers back to a world made up of socially acquired positions and dispositions (Fagan, 1995; Duprez and Kokoreff, 2000).

The same tendency to gloss over simple events and focus on durable changes is found in Goffman. According to this author, it is the very ambiguity of the concept of career that is significant in this back-and-forth movement that it allows, moving between intimate personal meaning and the individual's official situation, from the ego to the social context, without being limited to the individual's self-image. Thus the following from Goffman's essay in *Asylums:* 'It will focus primarily on the moral aspects of the career, i.e. on the cycle of personality changes that occur as a result of this career and on the modifications of the system of representations by which an individual becomes aware of himself and apprehends others' (Goffman, 1961: 189–90).

Psychiatric hospitalization constitutes the single inductive event that transforms an individual into someone who is mentally ill. Consequently, it is the institutional sanction that constitutes the inaugural phase of his/her career as seen through the distinction between two phases: 'pre-hospitalization' and 'hospitalization'. This approach is now contested in light of the analysis of contemporary changes in the field of psychiatric intervention (Ogien, 1989). The notion of moral career is out of kilter with the conception of mental patient implicit in the functioning of *total institutions* analysed by Goffman, and with the development of the paradigm of work in an 'open environment'. Faced with this problem, the notion of career can be reduced in scope to make it analogous to the notion of trajectory, by retaining only a succession of events recorded by social control authorities. But we can also go back to Goffman's fundamental distinction between a person who is following psychiatric treatment and a person who is categorized as mentally ill, to adopt a more dynamic conception of the mentally ill.

This is the direction proposed by Ogien, in substituting the notion of *biographical line* for the equivocal – because unitary and essentialist – notion of identity. Ogien's aim is to decry a linear, homogenous and definitive approach to the history of an individual, and understand the designation of the individual only in a pertinent domain and his/her acts in a specific context of action, without feedback.

Two analytical concepts can therefore be used to give an account of the fluctuation of an individual's implication in his/her relationship to psychiatric intervention: the concept of biographical line (that denotes that the social life of an actor may be only in part interpreted with reference to mental illness), and the concept of the status of mental patient (which indicates that the social world of an actor is almost exclusively organized within the institutional universe of psychiatry) (...). This is to say that these two concepts are not employed to the end of reconstructing, ex post facto, the stages of the transformation of the social identity of an individual categorized as mentally ill, the way the concept of moral career is used, but instead they aim to describe a form of practical experience – (Ogien, 1989: 81–2).

RESEARCH ON DELINQUENT TRAJECTORIES

Research work on deviant trajectories reflects the difficulty of organizing research in this field and, more broadly, the weaknesses of French criminology (Faugeron, 1991). Statistical work is well represented, but work on trajectories is far less common, particularly for minors. This is in large part due to the non-renewal of researchers who might potentially study these topics (particularly since the closing of the Vaucresson centre), and to the low level of interest manifested by public decision makers for this area of study.

Consequently, we will focus primarily on two groups of recent research. One group is unfortunately represented by only one piece of research, by Le Moigne (1999). The other group includes work devoted more specifically to drug addiction and drug dealing, having received a boost from several tenders in the early 1990s (Faugeron, 1999).

Repeat-offender minors

A recent piece of research (Le Moigne, 1999), studies minors who have been repeatedly taken into supervised education and penal programmes. This research is grounded in an interactionist perspective. It shows how multiple interventions, repeated with, in many instances, new workers who pick up the case in mid-stream, wind up ensconcing the youth in a 'tough guy' or 'hero' status, which is legitimized by the glorification of certain features of their history, and which ends in a prison sentence. In such cases the trajectory takes on the appearance of a destiny, whereas the problem is found in the multiplicity of interventions which ultimately outline this destiny.

This work is based on analysis of the legal records of youths dubbed repeat offenders. It does not seek to describe the succession of events, but rather the way in which the intervention, first of supervised education, then of penal measures, outlines a space delimited by judicial standards: 'the collective organization engendered by legal procedures qualifies not only the actors, it also constructs their position and provides the framework of their exchange within the confines of its space. Even so, it is not entirely closed, nor its borders definitively set'. All is not set within this space either. The actors possess a freedom of movement and delinquent behaviour is far from exhausting the full range of possible intervention. This research thus breaks with a strictly deterministic outlook. Nonetheless, Castel's lesson (1989) to not underestimate the 'order of determinations' is not forgotten. But this order is established progressively, and is only the outcome of repeated intervention that is the result of the protagonists' resistance to obeying orders; resistance which stems more from incomprehension, or inadequate measures, than from revolt. In this context, the repeat offences appear as 'a specific form of social competence' acquired in what Castel calls the 'order of interactions'.

Trajectories of users and small dealers

The other research direction we have cited is more turned towards work that attempts to situate behaviours in social pathways and contexts, in an economy of daily life where relationships with families are at play as well as those with peers and institutions. We are thinking of the collective research undertaking directed by Castel on the 'ways out of substance abuse'; there is also the particularly significant work of this type by Bouhnik on heroin addicts, AIDS and prison (Bouhnik, 1994; Bouhnik and Touzé, 1996) and a whole series of recent inquiries into the underground economies of low-income housing estates (Joubert *et al.*, 1996; Duprez *et al.*, 1995a, 1996; Kokoreff, 1997; Aquatias *et al.*, 1997; Tarrius, 1997; Tarrius and Missaoui, 1998).

Bouhnik, like Castel, is more specifically interested in the trajectories of heroin users. Most heroin users encounter the penal justice system and prison in the course of their lives, but these encounters, or indeed the behaviours that lead to these encounters, enter only tangentially into the course of the research. For the first author, the research subject is to shed light on life systems. For the second, the aim is to understand the processes involved in long interruptions (at least two years) in drug use practices. As for the work done with Dominique Duprez in the north of France and in the Paris area, these studies are centred upon the place held by a narcotics economy within the economy of housing estates and neighbourhoods deemed 'sensitive', in the drug users' life systems. These researchers recruited a sizeable proportion of the respondents queried in prison or via penal records, and another set in the neighbourhoods under observation. It is therefore not surprising to find more delinquent careers in these last two pieces of research; all the more so because one of the prime research focuses was on the way small-time drug dealing is organized. Even so, in all cases the authors point out the frequency of repeated prison stays among these populations, either for acquisition offences, for possession of illicit substances or for petty dealing.

A common factor found in all this research is the epistemological position of the researchers vis-à-vis the subjects of their analyses: they are considered to be actors of their own story, and not objects. They construct their social identities through the relations that they maintain with their surroundings. Even when they come from very underprivileged social situations, when they belong to 'disaffiliated' categories, to use Castel's expression (1995), or when they are highly dependent on a substance, they nonetheless remain social actors capable of managing their poverty or their addiction.

One of the problems encountered in this research is identifying the effects of social structure and classifying these biographies, by singling out factors that contribute to homogeneity (Bourgois, 1997). This research uses typological tools based on Weberian classifications to class individuals in biographical configurations in order to relate them to economic resources and activities.

Getting out of drug addiction

The GRASS research was carried out between 1989 and 1991, and has recently been reissued (Castel, 1998). Its orientation leads to a reversed analytical perspective:

comprehending substance abuse, not as a pathology, but as a way of life; looking, not at the reasons for getting into drugs, but at how one gets off them. Defining drug addiction as a way of life is to make a break with medical categories and the narrow focus on health and legal issues.

> Delinquents too live in society, and they often form micro societies that have their own laws and rules of proper conduct. By analogy, before or beyond general considerations on the place of drugs in modern society that are more metaphysical than sociological, it should be possible to analyze the specific nature of the drug consumer's behavior in relation to money and not working, to sexuality, to the family, the neighbors, in short all the elements that make up a way of life. (Castel, 1998: 19)

Looking at the ways out of drug addiction is to question the dominant representation that makes downfall and death the fate of drug addicts. For the junkie as fiend is someone at the end of the road, who has multiple social handicaps or stigma. We know that drug use is a matter of age group: it is relatively rare after the age of 35, as epidemiological studies show, and this despite a clear trend to ageing among drug addicts. Most addicts get 'unhooked', albeit in a number of different ways. In short, the situation is reversible, contrary to popular wisdom. Following Castel, this observation amounts to making the hypothesis that 'drug addiction is a pathway, or rather follows various pathways, that should be analyzed in their inflections, taking into account all the variables – psychological, medical and social – that affect the addict's career' (ibid., 22)

In practice, even while being an addict and presenting oneself as such – which is a sign of the force of the institutional marking of his or her social identity – the individual also has a social life that brings him into contact with universes other than that of drugs and leads him or her into other 'role playing'. In this sense, we can 'represent the life of an individual as organized along a few main lines of personal investment': family background, schooling, professional itinerary, love life, even political commitment.

> These lines fit more or less well together, there may be some halo effects or reinforcement, but 'normally' each direction is relatively independent, and imposes its own type of requirements (a personal crisis is often a short-circuit between two directions such as when a love affair disturbs relationships at work, or vice versa). An 'inveterate addict' is one whose relationship with the substance, and all that it implies in terms of organization of daily existence, becomes the dominant biographical line, polluting the other lines of the individual's trajectory and upsetting the balance. This situation may have variants and degrees. (Ibid 26–27).

It is not enough to retrace the person's path in drugs, without taking into consideration the variables that refer back to his or her social status and to the various types of capital or resources that he or she can call upon. Sketching in the contours of the irregularities that ruffle the rectilinear or homogeneous features of the biographical line is to map the various elements that crystallize along this line, to look at the breaks in the line that translate, not so much into a cycle of recoveries/relapses, that is, 'failures', as into false steps along a pathway (Castel, 1994).

What sets this research apart is that it looks at exit models from an original perspective. 'Getting out' of drug addiction can be *a dominant biographical line*, which comes down to accepting the following postulate, diametrically opposed to the legal/healthcare model of abstinence: getting out/off is a way of producing an acceptable reordering of the biographical lines that make up an existence, of accomplishing a *reconceptualization of existence*, taken as a form of rationality, of which some procedures are analysed using the explanations put forth in interviews. In other words, getting out is extracting oneself from a world, reorganizing a lifestyle, getting rid of a system of obligations.

This analysis induces a response distinguishing between 'other-controlled' and 'self-controlled' settings. The first type of case refers to a model of 'assisted recovery' with institutional support, medical or non medical; the second type refers to a model of 'voluntary recovery' without institutional support but which depends on the quality and quantity of other forms of support. The question posed is how they interact, and it is not a theoretical one, but a highly practical matter. Indeed, 'the different forms of control – repressive, healthcare, social – seem to be effective only when they occur at "the right time", i.e. in circumstances allowing them to articulate different levels of reality' (Castel, 1992: 234). Unfortunately, and probably for methodological reasons, the snowball method shows its limitations; the author was unable to establish clear relationships between the cultural and social resources (the capital) of the respondents and their ways of getting out of drug addiction.

Differentiation of trajectories and life system

This research also reveals a high degree of diversity between trajectories, as well as within a single trajectory. These life stories are, according to Bouhnik, made up of breaks, ruptures and rising and falling phases. Understanding the conditions of such a process involves reconstituting what she calls a *life system*. A certain number of components enable and give support to drug addiction practices: a mass vulnerabilization of youth in low-income housing neighbourhoods; a social environment constituted by networks of informal relationships as the basis for illicit practices and markets; the dynamics of these practices that point to material and social survival tactics; the whole being consolidated by 'processes of anchoring and taking root grounded in the dynamics of interdependence' (Bouhnik and Touzé, 1996). But such a life system does not imply that we can designate a family of trajectories that could be called the world of drug addiction. Thus, according to Bouhnik, the notion of career is inappropriate, given the significance of discontinuity that predominates in the experience of hard drug users, breaking points that are more important than the apprenticeship (Bouhnik, 1994). What constitutes a break? Hashish less than heroin, AIDS less than the effects of physical deterioration. As for the notion of 'dominant biographical line', even if it does indeed designate a moment in the person's history, it cannot summarize this history. A series of sequences preceded it and there are many ways out.

In light of the differentiation of histories, how can we talk about trajectories? This question is addressed by a model in which typical cases are cross-referenced with the differentiated positions of users in the life system. To build up this model, Bouhnik starts with the notion of biography in order to distinguish biographies grounded in a continuity where taking substances is inscribed in a lifestyle or family history of addiction; biographies marked by break-ups where addiction is found within a fragile family framework; and unorganized biographies where there is extreme dependence. The specific features of each pathway depend on the position in the life system, in relation to the degree of involvement in the drugs market, in the practices and networks of petty delinquency, or whether the subjects define themselves as simply users in a situation of disaffiliation. The crossing of these two axes reveals areas of existence or passage of a trajectory: areas of structured practices, areas of displacement and adaptation, areas of destructuration (see Table 3.1). In this way this analysis offers, among other perspectives, a way to 'retrace the play of the processes and intermeshing, locate these areas in the biographies and attach them to a social and territorial situation that is responsible for the new arrivals and conversions in a social world centered around heroin consumption' (Bouhnik, 1996).

Table 3.1 Pathways in relation to the position in the life system and involvement in drugs

	A	B	C
Drug addiction lifestyle	Structured practices	Adaptive practices	Unstructured practices
Involvement in market	Dealer, drug addict contacts	Reselling, petty dealing taking	Indebtedness, risk
Delinquency	Gang, organized crime, professionalization	Petty delinquency and dealing	Shoplifting, breaking and entering, robbery
Management of consumption	Alcohol, drug abuse integrated	Drug abuse relatively well managed	Day-to-day basis

Source: (after Bouhnik 1996).

We will not comment at length on column A, which corresponds to users who are integrated and professionalized in delinquent activity, and sometimes had been so even before becoming addicts, and who will be delinquent regardless of the substance involved. To a certain extent their insertion in delinquent activity protects them from destructuration, allows them to stay within the confines of a controlled addiction. Column B is more precarious. If some incident (familial or legal) throws them off balance, these users can fall into the unstructured C type of system. It would be fairly easy to formulate the hypothesis that users of this type are those most likely to turn to institutions for care.

This sort of classification always appears rather stilted. It can only indicate dominant features. Nonetheless, the type C in Bouhnik's typology is reminiscent of what Castel wrote in *Les métamorphoses de la question sociale* (1995: 469): 'One could see in the ideal typical example of a young drug addict from the suburbs the homologue of the form of disaffiliation incarnated by the vagabond in pre-industrial society. This figure is completely individualized and overexposed by the absence of ties and support with reference to work, familial transmission, the possibility of building a future'. It is not surprising that it is this figure that inspires fear, and who repeatedly winds up in prison. This is also the individual who will not be able even to find the way to a treatment centre, despite being more often than not in very poor health.[2]

For our part, we have analysed the diversity of ways into these careers, distinguishing three types of itinerary. One appears with reference to a major biographical event that symbolizes a turning point in the individual's existence and the encounter with the world of drugs. This can be called the *rupture* type. Inversely, a second type lies in a progressive entry into the career, punctuated by a series of micro events more or less separated over time. The sum of these events is synonymous with domination, that is, being 'caught' in a process that is perceived as ineluctable. Again using a category from heroin users, we will call this the *mechanism* type. But a third type can be distinguished, which, while it has some features of chance circumstances, encounters and opportunities, also manifests the power of the neighborhood in the unfolding of these different phases. Here, even more than an apprenticeship, there is a process of socialization via life in neighbourhoods or housing estates. For lack of a better term we will call this the *socialization* type (Duprez and Kokoreff, 2000).

Within these types thresholds have been identified, 'moments which symbolize a change in status and identity, of the relationship to oneself and to others', for instance going from sniffing to injecting.

It should be emphasized that these three types do not exhaust the range of empirically observable situations. Furthermore, they can very well be superimposed, or follow different sequences. For instance, the 'mechanism' can be imagined and recounted as an accumulation of breaks. Ultimately, they do not function as the 'causes' of behaviours, but rather as 'modalities' adopted by the careers, even as their dominant tone.

There remains the question of the linking of sequences. We have proposed the notion of 'biographical segments', relatively homogeneous in nature, with points of radical shift (Kokoreff, 1997). An example will clarify this point. Take the case of Mokhtar, seen in a treatment facility, residing in the township of Asnières (a municipality with a population of close to 80 000, in the suburbs just west of Paris). One of nine children, who came to France from Algeria in the early 1970s, he shares with many others what is euphemistically called a 'difficult childhood' marked by his father's death, and was in addition taken into the care of the state at the age of eight and spent his adolescence in a group home in the city of Limoges. At the age of 17, when he 'got out' as he says, as if talking about a disciplinary or prison establishment, he moved to Asnières. There, through his older brother, he met youths in neighbouring housing estates; he began to smoke hashish ('le shit'). But the singular aspect of his career comes in the following segment: while working day and night he began to 'run on coke'; in the information technology company where he worked his way up little by little he set up a system with colleagues for buying drugs directly from Holland. Then, too 'deep in', he was fired. At this point he fell back into the typical itinerary of a 'downward spiral', from coke to heroine, from sniffing to injecting; but he also followed an itinerary of 'stopping' (kicking the habit, recovery) and 'relapses', up to the time he started on Skenan and entered a substitution programme when he was 33. There are thus four biographical segments, two of which are strongly tied to taking 'hard drugs', and the last one constituting a phase of rebuilding experience outside the world of drugs.

USERS' CAREERS AND CAREERS IN DRUG DEALING IN FRENCH SUBURBS

Heroin consumption in French suburbs can be seen as endemic, linked to living conditions. It is the drug for forgetting, a way of forgetting the harsh realities of life in a neighbourhood branded with a bad reputation, awash in unemployment. Heroin use is in no way tied to specific cultural practices in the sectors in this study, as is the case with the relationship found between ecstasy and house music, for example. Drug dealing is an easy way to make money, a substitute for other forms of delinquent activity. Dealers are often first thieves and robbers. Not all are drug users, but in the Lille metropolitan area, for instance, where dealing by 'ants' (drudges, drones) is dominant because of the proximity of supply sources (mainly Rotterdam), most networks are composed of user/resellers.

The legal case files clearly reveal career identities. Groups of youths who are subject to the same modes of socialization (school, community facilities and so on) start smoking cannabis together around the age of 17 or 18, then very quickly start reselling the product to finance their own consumption, before taking up heroin a few years later. The boys are more exposed to group emulation (challenge, lure of gains, theft and so on), whereas the entry ways for girls are more highly correlated to biographical breaks (separation, birth of the first child and so on). In the same way correspondences are seen at work between periods of activity and inactivity, on one hand, and phases of abstinence, moderate consumption or excess on the other. We must not, however, hide the methodological 'biases' induced by this type of input. As Cicourel saw in studies more than 30 years ago,[3] the effects of the institutional construction of 'reality' that operate in different procedures (citation, court appearance, medical and psychological testing, and so on) tend to highlight certain data for the sake of furthering the legal proceedings. In terms of temporal analysis, it is a matter of emphasizing trajectories in a ballistic sense, for their determining characteristics (failure at school, family problems, prior encounters with the law), to the detriment of careers or types of itinerary, taken for the singular biographical aspects they manifest.

The interviews with drug addicts in jail (Chantraine, 1998) or recently released give dramatic relief to this tension between career identity and biographical singularity (Kokoreff, 1997). While these accounts support the hypothesis that drug addiction is a process that requires temporal analysis, and therefore is something that individuals get out of, they also bring into play a range of relationships to time that deserve further investigation. We have mentioned the time of forgetting and absence that corresponds to the active phase of heroin consumption. But there is also a time of living that is more complicated to understand: a discontinuous time line in which a multitude of situations follow each other, often redundant, going back and forth, that nonetheless constitute a regulated, almost coded pathway, perceived as oriented by fatality and destiny. Far from being played out in a single act, these careers are the outcome of multiple phases or stages that group themselves into recognizable sequences. There are 'beginnings': the first needle or 'a little smoke', then the craving, the start of stealing, the first time in jail, then a relapse after getting out, despite programmes, returning home to parents, resolve, because, living in such a neighbourhood, 'falling in again' is inevitable. Then it may be dealing that starts, a second jail sentence, more or less long, release and then, after a few months, another relapse, despite work that helps.

So, it was, it started in, in...Well, I was living in a neighborhood, uh, what they call a tough neighborhood, like. So I had some acquaintances like, we had a group of ten–fifteen people, we went out to night-clubs pretty regularly, we were always in a hallway like, we were, we were always around, like, when we got out of school we got together, we hung out. So well there were the nights out on Saturdays like, so it was always alcohol like, because, ok I was, I was 15, it was in the early 1980s.

Then little by little in the neighborhood there were the, well there were people who began to sniff cleaning fluid, you know trichlo. Well, for us in our group it was, that didn't get us. That didn't appeal to us. But there was hashish that did, that also came along at about the same time, so that was in the early 80s in the neighborhood. (...)

So I tried it once like, and it didn't work at all, like, I was really sick, so I didn't ever try again, even cigarettes like, I didn't smoke, I had tried cigarettes and I had been sick too, like. So I couldn't take it, either cigarettes or hashish. So that was that, what, so it was just alcohol in clubs. And when I was, in 84 what, I was about 18, there were two or three people from outside of the neighborhood who came into the group, what, and they did heroin and... So little by little in the group, like, we found out, and there were some who decided to find out, to try and, to taste it, like. Well I was one of those people and well it was ok a little, and then it was there, one thing led to another like.

It can be seen that the 'entry' into consumption is regulated by a set of conditions. It does not happen all at once. First of all, it is the apprenticeship of the effects of addiction that marks a threshold, almost as much as the first contact with the substance. In the accounts given by heroin users, craving the fix has a central position: it is not only pain and suffering that is involved (although that too), but also the question of resources to pay for consumption that has rapidly become a daily matter, and ways to get them (stealing, dealing, fencing stolen goods, expedients and so on). If there is an 'entry' it is characterized by the decisive role of the peer group and entourage. We can speak of intragenerational and intergenerational socialization, because the acquisition of knowledge and know-how is so firmly rooted in the succession of generations.

Between uses and trafficking, passageways in the world of illicitness

We feel it is essential to articulate users' careers with careers in drug dealing. This articulation is the result of the central nature of supply and solvability in the context of poor neighbourhoods.

What explanation can we give for the passage from one to the other? The explanation of paying for one's own consumption by resale of the product constitutes part of the answer, that corresponds to a certain social reality. Particularly in the case of cannabis, in this view the spread of cannabis use in housing estates has gone hand-in-hand with widespread reselling. But this is not systematically so. A number of circumstances have to be envisioned: users who are not sellers, users–sellers, sellers who are not users, but also networks of 'small' and 'big' consumers... Other explanations hold that repression 'galvanizes' the drug economy, and they emphasize the elasticity of demand. But economic analysis must not obscure the context of poor neighbourhoods. As is underscored by Sylvain Aquatias: 'The problem, in these specific areas where vulnerable populations are concentrated, with little access to income from legal work, is not the elasticity of demand, but indeed the possible ways of procuring money' (Aquatias *et al.*, 1997: 88–9). In this context, the resources offered by selling drugs compensate for the lack of access to the job market and the precariousness of employment. However, the level of income ensured by dealing can be extremely variable. It depends simultaneously on the types of points of sale and their mutual competition, the position in the trafficking hierarchy, the duration and intensity of sales, insertion in networks of sociability and possibilities for expanding the clientele. (On the uncertainty of local dealers' income, see Joubert *et al.*, 1996: 42.)

The interview quoted above gives a good illustration of the impact that territorial dynamics have on careers. In neighbourhoods on the outskirts of Paris and Lille, a strong tie is observed between the massive arrival of heroin in socially disqualified spaces (the dynamics of supply) and individuals embarking on careers as users and/or as sellers of hard drugs (the dynamics of demand). This process is made possible by a transformation of social relationships: deficient societal controls, on the part of 'big brothers' in particular, deterioration of living conditions with rising unemployment and precarious situations, serial incarceration of cannabis dealers, leaving the way open for the sale of other, more lucrative, products.

But it is also the gradual specialization of local markets that leads to divergence in the itineraries of individuals involved in dealing at a given time. Career and not trajectory, for the systems of values, interactions, the relationship to the surroundings and institutions, the social, physical and cultural leanings of individuals, must all be taken into consideration. Some keep on selling, with declining income due to the banalization of cannabis, others convert to heroin without becoming users of the product, still others feel they are 'tough' enough to avoid 'falling' but are caught in the trap of chance and depression (Duprez and Kokoreff, 2000).

Overall, in housing estates – unlike other places, such as high schools[4] – the market shift from cannabis to opiates provides the explanation for the change in dealers' careers; from hashish they move on to heroin or cocaine, which yield bigger profits. Small cannabis dealing networks are all the more subject to this movement in that their members have often become heroin users and their financial needs have soared. While hashish allowed them to live comfortably (clothes, restaurants, cars), with a lifestyle close to that of the middle class, the discovery of heroin forces them to sell the product, and/or steal.

Career accounts

In conclusion, on the methodological plane, we must underscore that the situation and the time of the interview are not without incidence on the content recorded, and the analysis that can be made in terms of careers. Other than mechanisms of adaptation and rationalization of the speaker's discourse, the effects of institutional treatment on the subjects' purely narrative abilities can be seen. By this we mean the fact that having been inside institutions and the system of actors (police officers, judges, probation officers, judicial oversight officials, specialized teachers and so on) seems to interfere with their enunciation of the different moments and aspects of careers in drug addiction – which does not mean, however, that there is reduction or simplification, but rather that the minimum conditions for a distancing from oneself and from the illicit setting are prescribed. For contrary to what one might think, these individuals who are sometimes heavily involved, do 'talk'. In comparison, interviews done in the context of other research with young cannabis users, more or less involved in small local dealing, attest to the difficulties – as well as reticence – of giving recent experience verbal expression. These remarks give force to the methodological need for longitudinal analysis of these activities, in order to conduct interviews at different times in the careers.

It remains however, that the breadth and richness of the material gathered, the mobilization of our respondents not only as actors but also as field informants of a well known type for ethnographical work, and the cross-insemination that occurs between accounts, are arguments in favour of this method. The examples cited in this discussion of the status of the issue are in any event convincing evidence. This material gives precedence to knowledge of this world from the inside, from the actor's point of view.

BY WAY OF CONCLUSION

Countering summary representations of the field of drug addiction is a sociological approach that postulates 'capacity of choice' in users taken as actors. Describing their career thus links the career to the events that punctuate it and give it meaning: actions, reactions, tactics and decisions.

But many issues are at stake. Are the sequences or phases continuous or discontinuous? How can we avoid losing our way among the discontinuities? The strong point of the writings of Hughes, Becker, even Goffman, and those who have been inspired by them in France, is to reject a linear, homogeneous and irreversible approach to an individual's history. But how far can we go in speaking of 'committing' to a career? Is there not a contradiction between stressing careers and a sequential model, as Becker does, while insisting on the importance of judgement in action? In essence, should we or should we not represent the life of a drug addict as existing independently of people who take drugs?

To give an account of these discontinuities without getting lost in multiple details, Ogien (1996: 121) has forged a tool: the biographical line 'which aims to qualify the series of events that can be assimilated to one of the forms of commitment that an individual contracts along the windings of his/her social existence. This notion rejects the idea of oneness in biography, in admitting this postulate: the life of an individual can rarely be comprehended as a linear, homogeneous and definitive history'. We can then understand that, in situations of strong constraints (hospital, prison, or even dependence on a product like alcohol or opiates), the adaptation to these constraints can dominate in the biography of individuals, and disappear when the constraints no longer exist. This notion only extends the Goffmanian idea of primary and secondary adaptations to situations outside closed institutions, and in this way allows structural effects to be reintroduced in the analysis (Passeron, 1989): effects that reveal, for example, the role of societal support mechanisms in the biographies, or the acquisition of skills even during a deviant or delinquent career. This is stressed by Castel (1998: 235): 'The fact of taking drugs would then be just one marker among others of a situation of social deprivation that is the real element to be taken into consideration in order to try and understand what "being a drug addict" means for these youths. Inversely, an entirely different analysis might be valid for other settings.' The consequences of strong constraints cannot thus be assessed in the same way, depending on the societal support mechanism (or in other words the social and cultural capital) available to the individuals. This is reminiscent of the research on social costs done by Blankevoort, Landreville and Pirès in Montreal.

As underscored by Passeron (1989) and de Conninck and Godard (1989), the basic issue in biographical approaches in social sciences is successfully to restore social intelligibility through life histories marked by the seal of the individual story, subject to the unpredictableness of daily life. De Conninck and Godard recommend integration of what they call 'archaeological' variables, that is the effects of social structure and its normative modalities, with 'processive' variables – the way in which the events of a biography unfold – in order to associate them in what we can then call a career, and no longer just a biography that is still too individualized and without social meaning. In the tension between these two sets of variables sociologists will undertake work on social theory.

NOTES

1   One may wonder about the role played here by representations of 'drugs' strongly coloured by ideological and moral considerations; whether indeed setting out to study this social problem was not 'in each discipline, marginal, polluting, disqualifying' (Ogien, 1994: 9).
2   Heroin distribution programmes in Switzerland and Amsterdam are designed for this type of person.
3   A. Cicourel, *The Social Organization of Juvenile Justice*, New York: Wiley, 1968.
4   In contrast, in schools there has recently been an observable shift from cannabis to synthetic drugs like ecstasy.

BIBLIOGRAPHY

Anderson, N. (1993), *Le Hobo. Sociologie du sans abri*, Paris: Nathan-Recherches (1st edn 1923).
Ansart, P. (1990), *Les sociologies contemporaines*, Paris: Edition du Seuil.
Aquatias, S., Genfoud, K., Khedim, H. and Murard, N. (1997), *L'usage dur des drogues douces. Recherche sur la consommation de cannabis dans la banlieue parisienne*, Paris: GRASS.

Bachman, C. and Coppel, A. (1989), *Le dragon domestique: deux siècles de relations étranges entre l'occident et la drogue*, Paris: Albin Michel.

Becker, H.S. (1985), *Outsiders. Études de sociologie de la déviance*, Paris : Métailié (1st edn The Free Press of Glencoe, 1963).

Bertaux, D. (1997), *Les récits de vie*, Paris: Nathan-Université.

Bessin, M. (1993), 'Cours de vie et flexibilité temporelle', unpublished PhD thesis, Université de Paris VIII.

Blöss, T. and Feroni, I. (1991). 'La socialisation de la jeunesse', *Cahiers du CRECOM*, 6.

Bouhnik, P. (1994), 'Le monde social des usagers de drogues dures en milieu urbain défavorisé', unpublished PhD thesis, Université de Paris VIII.

Bouhnik, P. (1996), Système de vie et trajectoires des consommateurs d'héroïne en milieu urbain défavorisé, *Communications*, **62**, 241–56.

Bouhnik, P. and Touzé, S. (1996), *Héroïne, sida, prison. Trajectoires, système de vie et rapports aux risques des usagers d'héroïne incarcérés*, Paris: RESSCOM-ANRS.

Bourgois, P. (1997), 'Résistance et autodestruction dans l'apartheid américain', *Actes de la recherche en sciences sociales*, **120**, Décember, 60–68.

Castel, R. (1989), 'Institutions totales et configurations ponctuelles', *Le parlé frais d'Erving Goffman*, Paris: Edition de Minuit.

Castel, R. (1992), *The Regulation of Madness*, Oxford: Polity Press.

Castel, R. (1994), 'Les sorties de la toxicomanie', in P. Mignon and A. Ogien (eds), *La demande sociale de drogues*, Paris: La Documentation Française, pp.23–30.

Castel, R. (1995), *Les métamorphoses de la question sociale. Chronique du salariat*, Paris: Fayard.

Castel, R. (1998), *Les sorties de la toxicomanie*, Fribourg: Editions universitaires de Fribourg, coll. Res Socialis (1st edn, 1992).

Chantraine, G. (1998), *De la sortie au retour. Caractéristiques socio-économiques et trajectoires des récidivistes de la maison d'arrêt de Loos-lez-Lille*, Lille: IFRESI.

Cicourel, A. (1968), *The Social Organization of Juvenile Justice*, New York: J. Wiley.

Collectif (1997), *En marge de la ville, au cœur de la société. Ces quartiers dont on parle*, La Tour d'Aigues: Edition de l'Aube.

Coppel, A. (1996), 'Toxicomanie, sida et réduction des risques', *Communications*, **62**, 75–108.

de Conninck, F. and Godard, F. (1989), 'L'approche biographique à l'épreuve de l'interprétation', *Revue Française de sociologie*, **XXXI**, 23–53.

Demazière, D. and Dubar, C. (1997), *Analyser les entretiens biographiques. L'exemple des récits d'insertion*, Paris: Nathan.

Duprez, D. and Kokoreff, M. (1999), 'La drogue comme travail. Des carrières illicites dans les territoires de la désaffiliations', in C. Faugeron (ed.), *Les drogues en France*, Genève: Georg édition.

Duprez, D. and Kokoreff, M. (2000), *Les mondes de la drogue. Usages et trafics dans les quartiers*, Paris: Odile Jacob.

Duprez, D., Kokoreff, M. and Verbeke, A. (1995a), *Des produits aux carrières. Contribution à une sociologie du trafic de stupéfiants*, Lille: Lastree-Ifresi.

Duprez, D., Kokoreff, M. and Verbeke, A. (1995b), *Contribution à l'analyse des carrières délinquantes. Les récidivistes de la maison d'arrêt de Loos-lez-Lille*, Lille: LASTREE-IFRESI.

Duprez, D., Kokoreff, M., Joubert, M. and Weinberger, M. (1996), *Le Traitement institutionnel des affaires liées à l'usage de drogues*, Lille, Paris: IFRESI-GRASS.

Fagan, J. (1995), *Women's careers in drug use and drug selling. Current Perspectives on Aging and the Life Cycle*, Greenwich, CT: JAI Press.

Faugeron, C. (1991), 'La production de l'ordre et le contrôle pénal. Bilan de la recherche en France depuis 1980 (sociologie, science politique, économie, ethnologie, anthropologie, histoire)', *Déviance et Société*, **XV** (1), 51–91.

Faugeron, C. (ed.) (1999), *Les drogues dans la société française*, Geneva: Georg Editeur.

Glaser, B.G. and Strauss, A.L. (1967). *The Discovery of Grounded Theory. Strategies for Qualitative Research*, Chicago: Aldine.

Goffman, E. (1961), *Asiles. Etudes sur la condition sociale des malades mentaux et autres reclus*, Paris: Édition de Minuit (1st edn Anchor Books Doubleday and Compagny, New York, 1961).

Hirsch, M.L., Conforti, R.W. and Graney, C.J. (1990), 'The use of marijuana for pleasure: replication of Howard's Becker study of marijuana use', *Journal of Social Behaviour and Personality*, **5** (4).

Hughes, E.C. (1996), *Le regard sociologique. Essais choisis* (présenté par J.-M Chapoulie), Paris: Editions de l'École des hautes études en sciences sociales.

Joubert, M. (1999), 'Politiques locales et nouveaux dispositifs d'action dans le domaine des toxicomanies', *Déviance et société*, **23** (2), 165–88.

Joubert, M., Weinberger, M. and Alfonsi, G. (1996), *Les toxicomanies dans la ville. Contribution socio-ethnologique à l'analyse des logiques sociales et économiques des réseaux et rapports sociaux de trafic*, Paris: GRASS.

Kokoreff, M. (1997), *De la défonce à l'économie informelle. Processus pénal, carrières déviantes et actions de prévention liés à l'usage de drogues dans les quartiers réputés 'sensibles'*, Lille: IFRESI.

Kokoreff, M. (1998), 'L'économie de la drogue: des modes d'organisation aux espaces de trafic', *Les annales de la recherche urbaine*, **78**, 114–24.

Leclerc-Olive, M. (1997), *Le dire de l'événement (biographique)*, Lille: Edition du Septentrion.

Le Moigne, Ph. (1999), *Le traitement des intraitables*, Louvain: De Boeck.

Léomant, Ch. and Sotteau-Léomant, N. (1987), 'Itinéraires de vie et trajectoires institutionnelles de jeunes délinquants', in Acteurs en justice. Stratégies et rôles professionnels, *Annales de Vaucresson*, **26**, 199–222.

Letkermann, P. (1973), *Crime as work*, Englewood Cliffs, NJ: Prentice-Hall.

Mauger, G. (1984), 'L'apparition et la diffusion des drogues en France, Bruxelles', *Contradictions*, **40**, 131–48.

Ogien, A. (1989), *Le raisonnement psychiatrique*, Paris: Méridiens-Klinckeck.

Ogien, A. (1991), 'Courte bibliographie raisonnée', in A. Ehrenberg (ed.), *Individus sous influence*, Paris: Edition Esprit.

Ogien, A. (1994), 'L'usage de drogues peut-il être un objef de recherche?' in A. Ogien and P. Mignon, *La demande sociale de drogue*, Paris: La Documentation française, 7–12.

Ogien, A. (1996), *Sociologie de la déviance*, Paris: Armand Colin.

Passeron, J.-C. (1989), 'Biographies, flux, itinéraires, trajectoires', *Revue française de sociologie*, **XXXI**, 3–22.

Peraldi, M. (1996), 'Drogues visibles, drogues invisibles: l'économie du trafic de drogues et son imaginaire', in O. Romani and A. Tarrius (eds), *La ville, l'argent, la mort*, Perpignan: Edition Trabucaïre.

Preble, E. and Casey, J. (1969), 'Taking care of business: The heroin life users in the street', *International Journal of Addictions*, **4**, 1–24.

Reuter, P., Mac Coun, R. and Murphy, P. (1991), *Money from crime. A Study of the Economics of Drug Dealing in Washington DC*, Santa Monica: Rand Corporation.

Roulleau-Berger, L. (1999), *Le travail en friche. Les mondes de la 'petite' production urbaine*, Paris: Edition de l'Aube.

Shaw, C.R. (1930), *The Jack Roller*, Chicago: University of Chicago Press.

Tarrius, A. (1997), *Fin de siècle incertaine à Perpignan. Drogues, pauvreté, communautés d'étrangers, jeunes sans emplois, et renouveau des civilités dans une ville française moyenne*, Perpignan: Edition Trabucaire Perpignan.

Tarrius, A. and Missaoui, L. (1998), *Héroïne et cocaïne de Barcelone à Perpignan: des économies souterraines ethniques de survie à la généralisation des trafics transfrontaliers de proximité*, Paris: OFDT.

Thomas, W.I. and Znaniecki, F., *Polish Peasant in Europe and America*, vols. 1 and 2, Chicago: University of Chicago Press, 1918; vols. 3 to 5, Boston: Badger Press, 1920 (partly in French: *Le paysan polonais en Europe et en Amérique. Récit de vie d'un migrant*, Paris: Essais et Recherches, Nathan, 1998),

Touraine, A. (1984), *Le retour de l'acteur: essai de sociologie*, Paris: Fayard.

Chapter 4

Ethnographic Space–Time: Culture of Resistance in a 'Dangerous Place'

Luís Fernandes and Tiago Neves

This text presents a summary of the results of ethnographic studies undertaken in an inner city council estate in Oporto labelled by the town's collective rumour as a 'dangerous place'. This kind of approach offers the researcher a style of research whose vocation lays precisely in an intimate relationship with a given place.

The figure of the *flâneur* is a good example of such vocation: 'The *flâneur* elects the street as the wondrous place where, sometimes under the appearance of mild routine, sometimes as explosions of circumstances, the scenery is constantly changing. The street hides and reveals, conceals and exposes, it seems made of sounds and speech is its noise. [And in the words of João do Rio:] "To embark on a *flânerie* is to be a vagabond and to reflect (...) it is to have the virus of observation linked with the virus of roaming"' (Fernandes, 2001: 11).[1]

The study of a social setting implies access to the processes whereby its memory is built and the images of interaction with the surrounding city are created, and also to the succession of happenings that grant it a biographical dimension that can be translated as the 'history of the place'. Ethnography is therefore a research style that manifests its comprehensive vocation not only in relation to a space, but also in relation to time, what we trace along these pages is the social-cultural trajectory of a community living in an area labelled a 'dangerous place'.

The notion of *culture of resistance*, developed within the theories of cultural production and reproduction, namely by Willis (1977) and Bourgois (1996), is the analytical frame used to draw upon the ethnographic data generated. We believe that this notion, grounded in a critique and complexification of Oscar Lewis's concept *of culture of poverty*, and in an appropriation of Pierre Bourdieu's works, will enable us to produce a fertile reading of the fieldwork material.

THE ETHNOGRAPHIC METHOD

'Ethnography' means a research activity that consists in sharing, for a significant period of time, a part of the life of the research subjects and the research setting. It requires, then, that the researcher accept the premise of interaction with the individuals and groups in the situations that occur; this eventually implies socialization in context. In ethnography, the researcher is the main research instrument, for he/she is the 'source of data (through participant observation and interaction), instrument of its gathering (through listening, questioning and registering) and its treatment' (Fernandes, 1998: 28). It is a naturalistic method, centred on naturally occurring phenomena. Its origins can be found in ethnology and cultural anthropology, but the Chicago School was a landmark in its application to the study of deviant urban contexts. The object's specificity, its special characteristics – deviant worlds are by definition worlds of suspicion and clandestinity – justify the option for special empirical research strategies (Weppner, 1977; Adler, 1985).

The data presented and analysed here are the result of research conducted in a council estate in the periphery of Oporto. This estate, with a population of about 5000, is considered one of the town's major drug-selling venues and is a frequent target of police intervention.

THE CULTURE OF RESISTANCE

First, it is important to make clear what we understand by culture of resistance: who are its actors, where it is located, how it is expressed and who or what are its targets.

The notion

By culture of resistance we mean a historically located and permanent (re)production set of symbols and beliefs, fashions of relationship with oneself, others and the material world which diverge from dominant values and norms in a given social–economical–spatial formation. A conflictive relationship of symbolic and material opposition to a diversity of exclusions generated by mainstream culture and economy is thus produced, and it is expressed both in words and in actions: exclusion, for example, from the labour and the housing markets and from the school world. However, this opposition, this resistance is at the same time a constitutive element of such exclusions. How does that happen?

Firstly, it happens because the relationship between the one who excludes and the one who is excluded is always dialectical, mutually constitutive. Secondly, and in the kind of contexts we are dealing with here, this relationship takes on peculiar characteristics. Both Bourgois (1996) and Willis (1977) have shown that, in western democratic capitalist societies, there is a certain degree of self-condemnation in the taking of subordinate roles; paradoxically, such taking of subordinate roles is experienced and perceived as learning and resistance (Bourgois, 1996). As they mediate the relationship between the individual and the larger structures, locally produced cultural practices create what Willis (1977) points out to be the support basis of capitalist societies, namely that a non-free condition may be the object of a free choice. According to Willis, the explanation for this phenomenon lies in the fact that the option for manual labour is understood, in the moment of making the choice, as a rejection of and liberation from the principles ruling the capitalist world; however, in the final instance, such choice ends up determining a specific and subordinate position in that very world.

Willis is therefore calling our attention to a paradox that needs to be taken into account: the paradox between the promise of future freedom, to be acquired through resistance to mainstream rules, and the present reality of exclusion and oppression which, contradictorily, creates serious obstacles to the transformation of both individuals and communities, closing them in a world-vision that concurs with the reproduction of their condition. We recall La Boétie who, in the mid-sixteenth century, in the ferocious attack on feudalism he developed in his *Speech on Voluntary Servitude*, tells us:

> Truly amazing, although quite common, and as painful as impressive, is to see millions of men serving, miserably bent by the burden of oppression, crushed not by a very strong force, but apparently dominated and enchanted by the name of a single man whose power should not frighten them, for he is only one, and whose qualities they should not appreciate for he treats them cruelly and inhumanely. (La Boétie, 1986)

If La Boétie advised the servants to take their destiny into their own hands, some years before, in his advice to the Prince, Machiavelli (1976) also presented a clearly profane speech, refusing interferences or external limitations on the prince's behaviour. This negation of transcendence can be found, in its most developed form, in capitalist management. Aiming at the accumulation of abstract richness – the 'value' – resulting from the split between exchange value and use value, this kind of social organization 'is applied to the construction of an axiomatic, a normality (...) that finalizes behaviours making them enter an economy where there is no place for fruition or waste' (Gandra, 1978: 48). Not only the ones who are dominated, but also the ones who are dominant, are now subjugated to a global, penetrating reality: the accumulation rationality. Gandra (ibid.) quotes Deleuze and Guattari about the present state of capitalism: 'There are no masters anymore, just slaves commanding other slaves; there is no more need to carry the animal, it can now carry itself.' This lack of an easily identifiable target (the 'animal' is everywhere) probably helps in accounting for the fact that resistance is largely disorganized in political terms; in fact, few are the occasions on which its own actors grant it a conscious content.

As we shall see further ahead in the text, resistance is characterized by the creation of a parallel social life and a more or less intense rejection of the mainstream game rules, including the political game, which could work as an arena for a possible constructive transformation of exclusion situations from within. Bourgois (1996) argues that this culture of resistance consists in a 'spontaneous set of rebellious practices that in the long term have emerged as an oppositional style'. He adds that it is the search for personal dignity implied in those rebellious practices that opens the way to a destructive impetus that ends up, unlike what was desired and predicted, by leading to personal and community decadence.

There is, then, a complex web of paradoxes to be considered in order to understand the workings of the culture of resistance: resistance/self-destruction; present/future; normative social lives/parallel social lives; oppositional practices/ oppositional politics.

Actors and space

The actors of the culture of resistance we approach here live in a council estate where there is a strong presence of the drugs business. This estate has characteristics that allow us to frame it within the notion of *psychotropic territory*, as defined by

Fernandes (1998: 167): 'an attractor of individuals who share interests in drugs, and present a behavioural programme oriented to the instrumental aspects related to a lifestyle in which drugs play a major role; its communicational characteristic is minimal interaction and it is structured as interstice of space and time'. Places where the final stage of the drugs distribution circuit takes place – selling to the consumer – they are the most visible face of the drugs world. Inasmuch as they harass the normative citizen's insecurity imaginary, they are harassed by social intervention technicians, in their constant search for problems and corresponding solutions, and the mass media, in their constant search for the extraordinary and the subnormal, usually presented in a stereotypical fashion against a background of excessive, merely idealized normality (Young, 1972).

Territories on the margin, even when they are located in the middle of an urban environment are marginal because of their architecture, access routes, spatial and temporal organization, sound landscape or interactional style among residents. We cannot help noticing the curious fact that one of the major threats to the big city, technically organized, rational and predictable, comes from spatial clusterings that frequently remind us of village-like territories... Most of the time placed in the estates owing to the urban dynamics, it can be said that the resistance of those who live in the estates begins right here. It expresses itself in their lack of involvement with the neighbourhood, sometimes with their own lodging, and in a feeling of impotence and victimization in face of the course of happenings; all this, and the decrease in self-esteem, produces exclusion. The council estate where we conducted the research, built in the mid-1960s, was used both to provide lodging for those who came from the 'ilhas'[2] and to work as a 'punishment estate' for those opposing Estado Novo.[3] Relationships with municipal agents and PIDE[4] officers were complicated, as one can imagine, and that fact contributed to the internalization of a hostile and negative attitude towards external control entities.

People who live in this kind of estate tend to feel that the space in which they live is different from the rest of the town, and to feel themselves different from the other citizens. We can therefore understand why many of the older inhabitants of the estate built in the mid-1960s structure their narratives about the history of the estate in terms of a succession of deviant activities, of which the drugs business is simply the present stage. As Clarke and Jefferson argued (1973), representations are part of the world they describe and thus tend, in the course of time, to acquire a material substance. In this same estate, painted in the doorway of one of the buildings, visible from the street, the graffiti 'Welcome to the Jungle' (written in English) – a truly ecological metaphor – institutes a split between the estate and the rest of the town: it is interpreted as either a warning, a threat, cultural affirmation or simply a welcome sign (Neves, 1997).

Dimensions and expressions of the culture of resistance

We shall proceed by analysing three dimensions in which the culture of resistance manifests itself, and in which we can signal important elements of the deviant socialization processes at work in these territories. What we are going to do, then, is to describe and analyse some ethnographic data in the light of the notion of culture of resistance as developed earlier.

The educational realm

For a period of time during the research, one of the authors had the opportunity to work and do research in the estate's leisure activities. This was part of a community centre that also had a kindergarten. It was, therefore, a place where children up to 13/14 years old would come to play, learn and eat. It proved to be an excellent location for observation, more manoeuvrable than the streets, the other place where children spend a good deal of their daily life.

The children's interactive style is markedly aggressive: both in terms of verbal expression, given that much communication takes place in the form of shouts and not conversation, and physical expression, for the usual way of solving disagreements is by pushing, hitting or kicking. 'This communicational style is a constitutive element of the urban periphery habitus; it is as if in hard territories (...) language were equally hard; or even as if, in places "where daily life is itself a struggle" (Delarue, 1991) the act of talking is a translation of that fighting attitude' (Fernandes, 1998: 199). Sometimes, the staff at the community centre are the target of this aggressive style. Let us resort here to the field notes written on the first day at work in the community centre, referring to a moment when we were at the back of the stage where children aged six to 13 were preparing an activity:

> At first, I leaned on the door, with my hands in my pockets, trying to understand what was going on, but I soon realised – not because I was feeling watched but because I was feeling ridiculous – that I had to change place and posture. I sat on a table by the door, where two kids were already sitting. Later, I came to know that they're Nélson and Ricardo, both seven years old.

> I sat down and said nothing; I preferred to let them start the interaction, and I was pretty sure that they would do it quite soon... A minute later, Ricardo – who was wearing black boots, black jeans and a black t-shirt – stands up in front of me and tries to slap me; I manage to avoid his hand. I grab his arm and ask him: 'What was that, mate?' and laugh about the situation. As I grab his arm I show him I'm stronger than him, and he and Nélson end up introducing themselves, and tell me they're best friends (...).

A slap in the face was the way chosen to start conversation with an adult stranger; agonistic was his definition of himself. In the same fashion, just a while afterwards, 'Ricardo, who just the minute before had put his arm around me, gets up from the table, grabs a plastic golf cue and hits me hard on the knee. I show him I'm angry and we didn't talk much more.' Children usually measure the limits to their behaviour in a relationship with someone they are not yet acquainted with. The level of aggressiveness placed on the measurement was, however, a surprise.

Regarding the relationship with the centre's staff, we can stress the following aspects: orders and requests from the staff are rarely taken into prompt consideration, if at all. Prompt obedience is regarded as a synonym of being 'fearful' or 'chicken-hearted'. It also happens that punishment or quitting an activity is preferred to apologizing for not carrying out an order or for infringing a rule of the community centre. Consider, for example, the option of a 13-year-old boy:

Filipe's culture of resistance surfaced a couple of times: when Alzira (a member of the auxiliary staff) told him to behave, at the beginning of the gym game, he stopped playing for a while. At teatime, there were two cakes available because it was Cátia's birthday. Filipe refused to eat any of it because he had initially said that he did not want cake in reaction to some criticism a staff member had made about something he had done. Filipe continued to refuse to eat the cake even though he frequently won the contest for extra cake slices (for example, completing proverbs, finding the solution to riddles, etc.) and even though it was quite clear that he wanted to eat it.

On the same day, later in the afternoon, the author who was working at the community centre went to a private, middle-upper-class music school with a friend who taught there

> to listen to an audition of children playing flute, guitar and piano. The contrast between the two settings is striking: here, nine and ten-year-olds hold their mothers by the hand; there is no shouting (...); obedience rules. My friend said that Ismael, an 11-year-old boy from the Community Centre with whom I got on particularly well, looks 15 years older than these children.

The contrast between this extract from the field notes and the previous one is quite clear with regard to socialization rules of the dominant class. We can recall the differences between the groups of *lads* and *ear'oles* Willis (1977) studied: representatives of counter-school culture, the lads (group constituted by working-class youngsters) are fundamentally characterized by their opposition to authority, by the rejection of the idea of teacher, by the defence of a kind of knowledge grounded more in experience and in practice than in the theoretical contents transmitted by the school. The lads are also characterized by their contempt for the ear'oles, the ones who listen and obey to everything figures of authority in the school context tell them; they regard ear'oles as passive, ignorant and inexperienced. The director of a preparatory school located on the edge of the estate told us that she sometimes tells the children, in an attempt to modify their behaviour or to 'make them see' how things ought to be that: 'This is not the estate – this is the school!'

The relationship with forms of authority and control, not just the school, is frequently difficult. The three following field notes excerpts refer to the relationship with the police.

> In a visit to the kindergarten:

> Vítor, a blond 3- or 4-year-old in a green pinafore and a red hat, whose parents are involved in the drug business and have already been arrested, sometimes says: 'When I'm big I'm gonna kill those men [the police] who go to my home and take my mother away.'

> Also, on the first day at the Community Centre, I was introduced to some youngsters: Meanwhile, in the playground, I met Luís, who was introduced to me by G. [a staff member] as 'the dealer' [his parents are important cocaine suppliers in the estate]. The kid reacts looking down when I look at him and asks: 'What's that [being a dealer]? Some kid asks what am I doing there and suddenly someone asks if I am a cop. I turn to Luís, because it seemed that it was he who had asked that, and say: 'Do you reckon I look like a cop?' and add, 'What do I look like?' 'You look like a teacher,' Luis answered, after thinking for a while.

In the estate, I watch a five-a-side football match between kids who go to the Community Centre and some kids who don't. (...) I took some photos of the match and, after it was over, I photographed the 'Morte aos Bófias [Kill the Cops]' graffiti painted on a wall of the pitch. Ismael notices me taking the photo and asks: 'Are you going to order the arrest of the people who painted that?' – he said that after a month of me being there, of knowing who I am, of wanting to be with me all the time...

Episodes such as these make us wonder about what leads these children to regard an unknown man, dressed as a civilian, in their community centre as a police officer. Upon closer watch, it becomes clear that the fact that 'Ismael knows who I am' needs to be understood; such understanding reveals, on the one hand, the possibility of the police's omnipresence and, on the other hand, the precariousness of identities and interpersonal relationships. The fear of the police's omnipresence is presented together with a lack of consideration about its capacities: just as Ismael said on another occasion, 'The police are really stupid. They never catch anything because they [dealers and junkies] can always hide the drugs away. The police don't seem to know.'

In the same fashion, the relationship between what could be regarded as lack of education or aggressiveness and caring for someone takes on a complex shape:

as I say goodbye to Sílvia [a 13-year-old] she turns to me and shouts: 'go away, *chavalito*' [slang word for 'little kid']. One of the youth workers listens to Sílvia and replies: 'You're treating him like that, but the other day you asked if he wasn't coming anymore and told me you had even cried for him not being here...'

A 36-year-old junkie describes his relationship with his adolescent daughter like this: I've got a great relationship with my daughter. When she gets fucking irritating I punch her in the face. I really trust her (...).

The labour realm

The way the culture of resistance is expressed in this realm was summarized in this fashion by a social worker who has worked for many years in the estate considered here:

People here are almost always aggressive, tense, which can be explained because they live difficult lives, don't they? Most women do not work, nor can they keep a job for a long time whenever they get one. They are not used to dealing with timetables – and they have difficulties in jobs in which they have to remain in a building for hours. (...) They live for just today and are unable to think in terms of the future. In a job, for instance, as soon as they have a problem with the boss or a work colleague, they quit, they don't show up the next morning, etc. They can't overcome this kind of problem (...) They just live for today.

The fact that the income received from the participation in the mechanisms of the formal economy is usually scarce and frequently irregular makes it more difficult to control the future, and herein lies one of the explanations for the option of living just for today. The relationship established with the formal economy does not allow the construction of ambitious projects for the future: the low academic qualifications of the previous generations, the present high rates of school abandonment and the high unemployment rates create serious obstacles to the absorption of the rationality of accumulation of abstract value through labour in the formal economy. Therefore the exclusionary processes taking place within the labour realm are not restricted to the economic dimension: they clearly involve a cultural dimension.

The relationship between the labour realm and the culture of resistance presents a crucial analytical axis: that of the relationship between formal and underground economies. In this kind of estate, economical activities escaping the state's control are fundamental complements to the income earned in the legal economy: for example, car and electrical repairs, electricity theft, cleaning services, baby-sitting and the organization of raffles.

> Armindo, for example, told us: 'I work at home. I have a small workshop for electronic repairs. I do some services for the neighbours and there are also some shops that send me devices that are not working properly. I had an electronics course at Philips, and another one while I was in the army.'

However, none of these activities offers the chance of both income and career offered by the drugs business. In 1969, Preble and Casey had already shown the potential of the parallel economy – specifically of the heroin business – in the production of cultural adaptations by the socially excluded. Arguing that there is a similarity between the entrepeneur-like character of the heroin business and that of any other private initiatives in the legal economy, they also signalled the active and adventurous character of the heroin user career. Preble and Casey suggested that the addiction is due more to the career than to the product (heroin) itself, and that the use of heroin is therefore grounded on the search for a meaningful life, on an escape from the boredom imposed by social constraints, and on revenge upon a society that is understood as unfair and victimizer. The same authors were already arguing that the solution to the heroin problem lies in the creation of legitimate opportunities for a meaningful life for all those who wish it.

More recently, Pearson (1987) analysed the relationships between unemployment and heroin, not establishing a causality relationship but suggesting that the absence of a worker status makes it more difficult to abandon the drugs lifestyle; the effects of drug use thus become more devastating. Pearson develops Preble and Casey's culturalist thesis, arguing that unemployment may lead to heroin use as it constitutes a challenge to self-control; the drug business may also provide some status for those who have none in the labour market and it can also contribute to the creation of temporal structures for those who live in the daily bleakness generated by unemployment.

> Just like Mr. A. said: 'There is a lot of unemployment, and that makes it easier to get into drugs and harder to get out.'

Pearson also develops a geographical–economical analysis, presenting reasons for the fact that excluded neighbourhoods are frequently the locus of drugs distribution networks. Most individuals living in these estates have urgent needs and few options available to fulfil them; in other words, those areas bring together a number of social problems due to housing policies that keep reproducing social stratification. This is how what Pearson (1987) calls *clusters of social problems* arise; in these clusters, it is very difficult to develop and implement effective strategies against drug use and the drug business.

It is perhaps useful to quote Fernandes (1998: 148): 'Every "socially excluded" area is (...) capable of creating a spontaneous social life which is not very similar to exclusion. We are not saying anything new: the old Chicago School monographs had already called our attention to the social life of the interstitial spaces and the "deviant worlds".' Excluded areas are not empty spaces, easily shaped by moral and technical orthopaedics; they are spaces where a full, entire life, a life of resistance, is lived.

Resistance and opposition to authority, as discussed in the previous section, can also be found in the adult work realm. Recent changes in urban economy, namely the decrease in factory jobs, have been taking place more rapidly than the cultural transformations that try to accompany them; therefore they cause not only economical but also cultural disturbances in these contexts. If in the factory context confrontation with the hierarchy is part of the normal functioning of the production unit, in the growing services sector – where contacts with clients are frequently part of the job (and 'the client is always right') – such confrontation disturbs employees' performances quite drastically and puts their job at risk. We can appreciate here how issues related to the interactive style influence the material realm (Bourgois, 1995). We can also recall Willis (1977) when he argued that, at school, deference and good manners are, more than a consequence, a precondition and a price to be paid for the acquisition of academic qualifications. The close relationship between the educational and the labour realms is thus made clear.

The drug business

The centrality of drugs in the reinforcement of the parallel economy and in the structuring of cultural resistance movements was signalled in the previous section. We now develop that analysis.

In these kinds of estates, where the residents are 'exposed to dust', a 'banality of drugs' sets in as a result of the proximity and the daily character of the contacts with the drugs world (Fernandes, 1998). The banality of drugs is an important element in the socialization processes taking place in psychotropic territories.

For each home living off the drugs business there are a number of individuals – kin, friends and neighbours – that take indirect economical profit from the situation. In this way are created bonds of economic dependence that reinforce cultural bonds of solidarity and loyalty. How can you earn money when you do not participate directly in the drugs business? For example, by keeping the product or the scales used to weigh it; by receiving money to 'keep your mouth shut'; in the case of women, by cleaning dealers' houses or taking care of their children; by accepting small offers of money or goods in times of hardship; by 'lending one's home to death', that is, by renting it for drugs users to come and take the drugs. Dense networks of mutual complicities and benefits are created, reinforcing the split between the Others (the normative city) and Us (the ones who live on the estate) and embodying the culture of resistance (Neves, 1997).[5]

As it is hard to control things effectively through police intervention owing to the fact that, in the drugs world, it triggers rapid replacement and dislocation processes of the product itself, of sales points and storage places, and of traders themselves (Dorn *et al.*, 1992), the insistence on this kind of intervention brings about situations that frequently, more than solving problems, worsen them. We may stress the family destructuration caused by the arrest of parents, uncles and grandparents: that is, of the ones who could, one way or the other, support the children and the infants in the family. Children and infants may end up replacing their older relatives in the drugs business. In the situation we report next, the uncle's attitude may have avoided the arrest of the three adult members in the family:

> then S [an 8-year-old girl] and her sister showed up (...) and they began talking with me, L [an educator] and another kid by the fence. S was barefoot, and wore tight cotton shorts and a dirty t-shirt; her sister wore sneakers, socks with holes, shorts and t-shirt. [S described a police assault on her home that led to the arrest of her mother, her grandmother and her uncle.] S told us that undercover cops came into the flat and caught her mother and her uncle counting money in the bedroom. 'They had been selling drugs,' S explains. Grandmother was also at home at the time, in another room. Her mother and her grandmother were in prison in Tires, but they were released after the trial because the uncle took all blame for himself.

Luís, the 13-year-old son of dealers we have already referred to, always acts as a commander, both with the other boys and girls and with adult junkies. However, our key informant, a 38-year-old junkie, describes the situation in this manner:

> That will all go down in an instant if the police go to his home and arrest his mother and his father. Afterwards, the kid will be alone, and although there is always someone who can take care of him during the first times, who will have the patience enough to continue?

Solidarities and mutual complicities do not seem to go that far. Also in this way, the search for better life conditions through entrepreneurship in the underground economy leads, in the last instance, to the degradation of community life, namely through the destructuring of families.

Furthermore, the drug culture has been undergoing some changes in these territories, becoming progressively instrumental and hard, and losing its symbolic, expressive elements. Resistance tends to lose its reflexively organized contents, while at the same time it acquires a previously unthought of material potential. The dimension in which resistance has a more political flavour is in the representation of police work:

> M and F, two drug-users, discuss police raids on cafés. F says: 'In the café they select people (...) they already have people filed.' M adds: 'The café has usual customers, and they already know who they are.' F says: 'But they took Carlos, who has got nothing to do with it' [the drugs-business. When I ask what Carlos looks like, F answers], 'he's a kind of freak: long hair, ponytail, tight trousers...'.[6]

> M says: 'The more unfavoured [meaning the drug users from the lower classes] are usually taken [to the police station]. You know... that's what happens to the lads here... the ones who are poor...'

CONCLUSION

'Biographical methodologies frame a given problematic behaviour in the whole of the happenings of the actor's life' (da Agra and Matos, 1997). The reconstruction of the space-time of an urban community, either from its actors' memories or from social practices as observed by the researcher, translates into a collective dimension the same work biographical methodologies apply on the individual scale.

The organization of data around the concept of culture of resistance enabled the introduction of the processual dimension in our analysis. In its anthropological definition, *culture* contains the dynamic element that grants time the labour of sedimentation and reproduction of the collective; *resistance*, while a visible manifestation of a local identity built in opposition to the normative city, confers a meaning on the process dimension: resistance is a social logic, a way of understanding the world that was forged around the processes that produce social exclusion.

NOTES

1   See also Jenks and Neves (2000). This research is a part of the studies conducted by the Observatono Permanent de Segurança do Porto, an organization directed by Professor Candido da Agra and financed by the Ministerio da Administração Interna and Camora Municipal do Porto.
2   'Ilhas' are underclass residential areas corresponding, in general and in architectural terms, to a 'yard or a street surrounded by small houses' (Seixas, 1997) frequently hidden behind bourgeois houses the façades of which face the main street.
3   Estado Novo is the period (1926–74) in Portuguese history during which a right-wing dictatorship ruled the country. Another estate in Oporto, the São João de Deus estate, fulfilled the same functions in an even clearer fashion: even nowadays it is called 'Tarrafal' by many people, and Tarrafal was the name of a concentration camp in the former Portuguese colony of Cape Verde.
4   PIDE was Estado Novo's political police.
5   See Neves (1997) for an analysis of the dimension of the underground economy in one of the estates considered here.
6   See Harvey Sacks, 'Notes on police assessment of moral character'.

REFERENCES

Adler, P. (1985), *Wheeling and Dealing*, New York: Columbia University Press.
Bourgois, P. (1995), 'The political economy of resistance and self-destruction in the crack economy: An ethnographic perspective', *Annals of the New York Academy of Sciences*, **749**, 97–118.
Bourgois, P. (1996), *In Search of Respect – selling crack in El Barrio*, Cambridge: Cambridge University Press.
Clarke, J. and Jefferson, T. (1973), 'Working-class youth cultures', stencilled occasional paper, Centre for Contemporary Cultural Studies, University of Birmingham.
da Agra, C. and Matos, A.P. (1997), 'Trajectórias Desviantes', in C. da Agra (ed.), *Projecto Droga e Crime: Estudos Interdisciplinares*, vol. 11, Lisbon: G.P.C.C.D–Ministério da Justiça.

Drugs and Crime Deviant Pathways

Delarue, J.-M. (1991) *Banlieues en Difficultés – la relegation*, Paris: Syros/Alternatives.

Dorn, N., Murji, K. andSouth, N. (1992), *Traffickers – drug markets and law enforcement*, London and New York: Routledge.

Fernandes, L. (1998), *O Sítio das Drogas*, Lisbon: Ed. Notícias.

Fernandes, L. (2001), *Pelo Rio Abaixo – crónica duma cidade insegura*, Lisbon: Ed. Notícias.

Gandra, F. (1978), *Para Uma Arqueologia do Discurso Imperial*, Lisbon: A Regra do Jogo.

Jenks, C. and Neves, T. (2000), 'A walk on the wild side: Urban ethnography meets the flâneur', *Cultural Values*, **4** (1), January, 1–17.

La Boétie (1986), *Discurso sobre a Servidão Voluntária*, Lisbon: Antígona.

Machiavelli, N. (1976) *O Príncipe*, Lisbon: Publicações Europa-América.

Neves, T. (1997), 'Lives of resistance – the drug-business, underground economies and policing', unpublished MA thesis, Goldsmiths' College, University of London.

Pearson, G. (1987), 'Social deprivation, unemployment and patterns of heroin use', in N. Dorn and N. South, (eds), *A Land Fit for Heroin? Drug Policies, Prevention and Practice*, London: Macmillan Education.

Preble, E. and Casey, J. (1969), 'Taking care of business – The heroin user's life on the street', *International Journal of the Addictions*, **4** (1), March, 1–24.

Sacks, H. (1978), 'Notes on police assessment of moral character' in P.K. Manning and J. Van Maanen (eds), *Policing: A View from the Street*, Santa Monica: Goodyear.

Seixas, P.C. (1997), 'Identidades de uma cidade: as ilhas e o Porto', in V.O. Jorge and R. Iturra (eds), *Recuperar o Espanto: o olhar da antropologia*, Porto: Edições Afrontamento.

Weppner, R. (ed.) (1977), *Street Ethnography*, Beverly Hills: Sage.

Willis, P. (1977), *Learning to Labour: How Working Class Kids Get Working Class Jobs*, Westmead: Saxon House.

Young, J. (1972), *The Drugtakers: The Social Meaning of Drug Use*, London: Paladin.

Part II
YOUTH, DRUG AND
DELINQUENCY PATHWAYS

Chapter 5

Developmental Trajectories Leading to Delinquency and Substance Use in Adolescence: Results from Quebec Studies

René Carbonneau

Longitudinal studies around the world have shown that children's problem behaviour is one of the best predictors of adolescent and adult antisocial behaviour (Farrington, 1994; Huesman *et al.*, 1984; Stattin and Magnusson, 1989; Tremblay *et al.*, 1994; White *et al.*, 1990). Efforts to examine specific types of conduct problems have suggested different trajectories, or pathways, leading, for instance, to overt delinquency (such as aggression) and covert delinquency (theft, vandalism and so on) (Loeber, 1996). Others have examined the trajectories of antisocial behaviour through the concepts of onset and persistence (LeBlanc and Fréchette, 1989; Moffit, 1993). Finally, many studies have underlined the importance of comorbid conditions, including substance use/abuse (Hawkins *et al.*, 1992; Van Kammen *et al.*, 1991) and internalizing problems (Fergusson *et al.*, 1996).

Yet, despite the importance of these findings, there is still a need for empirical validation of specific pathways of individual behaviour leading to different forms of antisocial behaviour and to the evolution of such behaviour through adolescence and adulthood. Moreover, considering that most longitudinal studies have started when children were already at a relatively advanced stage in their development (for example from the middle of elementary school onward), the identification of trajectories starting at an early age is still needed. Finally, while a number of environmental factors have been associated with the onset and the development of conduct problems (Loeber and Stouthamer-Loeber, 1986), research is still needed to identify which of these factors contribute to specific developmental trajectories leading to different forms of antisocial behaviour and to the persistence of such behaviour over time.

In recent years, a number of studies pertaining to the development of antisocial behaviour have been conducted in the province of Québec. The following pages describe results from the Montreal Longitudinal–Experimental Study (MLES), related to the development of delinquency and substance use in boys. Studies reported here have in common a developmental perspective and a quantitative methodology in examining the phenomenon of delinquency and substance use from early childhood to late adolescence. More specifically, such development is investigated by identifying trajectories of individual behaviour over time leading to these adjustment problems.

Thus the present chapter first examines separately individual factors defining trajectories of behaviours leading to delinquency and substance use in boys, and secondly, environmental factors related to such trajectories. Finally, current research from the MLES is described and possible directions for future research are discussed.

THE MONTREAL LONGITUDINAL–EXPERIMENTAL STUDY (MLES)

The MLES is based on a population of boys from low socioeconomic status (SES) families in Montreal, Quebec, followed up from kindergarten to early adulthood (Tremblay *et al.*, 1994). In the spring of 1984, kindergarten teachers in schools of low socioeconomic areas in the Montreal French school board were asked to rate the behaviour of each boy in their classroom. An 87 per cent response rate was obtained from the teachers, and 1161 boys from 53 schools were assessed. In order to control for cultural effects, boys were then included in the study only if both parents were born in Canada and were French-speaking. This created a homogeneous sample of 1037 French-speaking, non-immigrant boys, living in low SES areas of a large urban city. The majority of these boys (67 per cent) lived with both parents, 24 per cent lived only with their mother, and 5 per cent with their mother and a man who was not their father. The other 4 per cent of the sample lived in different family arrangements (for example with grandparents or father and stepmother). Mothers' mean age at birth of their son was 25.4 years (SD, 4.8 years), with a range of 15 to 45 years, and fathers' mean age at birth of their son was 28.4 years (SD, 5.6 years), with a range of 16 to 56 years. Mothers had completed, on average, 10.5 years (SD, 2.8 years) of school, and fathers, 10.7 years (SD, 3.2 years). Most parents were unskilled workers. Data collected when the boys were 10 years old indicated that the mean and the median family income were between $25 000 and $30 000 (Canadian dollars), compared with a median income of $44 000 for Canadian couples with children in 1987 (Tremblay *et al.*, 1994). Boys participating in the MLES were assessed every year between kindergarten and late adolescence. Information was collected on a variety of individual characteristics (for example, behaviour problems, 'prosociality', internalizing problems, cognitive abilities, school adjustment and substance use) as well as environmental dimensions (such as parents' behaviour and psychopathology, parenting, parent–child interactions and peers' characteristics).

DELINQUENCY AND ANTISOCIAL BEHAVIOUR

Individual factors

Different strategies were used to examine developmental trajectories of individual behaviour related to antisocial problems and delinquency. First, the stability of antisocial behaviour from kindergarten to the end of elementary school was established (Carbonneau *et al.*, 1998; Haapasalo and Tremblay, 1994), supporting results from previous longitudinal studies around the world. Aggressive behaviour, in particular, appeared to be stable between the ages of six and 12 years, for boys who showed initially a high level of aggression. Haapasalo and Tremblay (1994) also showed that boys with a profile of stable aggressive behaviour, based on teachers' reports, between the ages of six and 12 years, were more delinquent, according to self-report, across the ages of 10 to 14.

Another research strategy consisted of creating behaviour profiles, a 'person approach' (Magnusson and Bergman, 1988), rather than a 'variable approach' based on the association between different measures, to study the development of antisocial behaviour. Tremblay and Haapasalo (1998) used cluster analysis to create behaviour patterns based on kindergarten measures to predict delinquency between the ages of 10 and 13. This method showed that among aggressive boys two subgroups were especially at risk of later delinquency: the *Bullies*, those who were also rated by their teacher as non-'prosocial' and hyperactive, and who showed a low level of anxiety and inattention; and those labeled '*Multiproblem*', who scored high on anxiety, inattention, hyperactivity and non-'prosociality'. Compared to the *Normal* group, the boys who scored low on all deviant behaviours, boys from the above two groups were about five times more likely to be stable delinquents, based on self-report, between the ages of 10 and 13 (odds ratio (OR) = 5.06, p < 0.01 for *Bullies*, and OR = 5.13, p < 0.001 for *Multiproblem* boys).

A similar approach, using kindergarten measures to define personality dimensions in order to predict stable delinquency between the ages of 10 and 13, was proposed by Tremblay *et al.* (1994). Their results showed that boys who were rated by their teacher as high on impulsivity, low in anxiety and low in reward dependence (a dimension similar to 'prosociality') – the antisocial personality category based on Cloninger's model (Cloninger, 1987) – were more at risk for stable delinquent involvement in early adolescence. Interestingly, boys who were high on impulsivity, low in anxiety but high on reward dependence were much less at risk for delinquency, suggesting that this dimension of personality may act as a protective factor against antisocial behaviour. Finally, differences in delinquent behaviour among these different personality categories were stable from ages 11 to 13.

In another effort to identify protective factors against delinquency, Kerr *et al.* (1997) used peer-rated inhibition, withdrawal and disruptiveness at age 10 to 12 years to predict delinquency between the ages of 13 and 15. Their results showed that disruptive boys who were non-inhibited in pre-adolescence were more likely to be delinquent in early adolescence, while disruptive boys who were inhibited were not. Additionally, non-disruptive boys who were inhibited were much less at risk of becoming delinquent than their peers. Interestingly, disruptive-withdrawn boys were at the greatest risk for delinquency, indicating that social withdrawal and inhibition, although behaviourally similar, represented different risk for later delinquency.

Environmental factors

A number of environmental factors have been examined in association with trajectories of antisocial behaviour in the MLES. In the study by Haapasalo and Tremblay (1994), the stable aggressive boys from six to 12 years, who were more delinquent between the ages of 10 to 14, came from families with a higher level of family adversity, as defined with an index based on parental education, parental age at birth of their son, parental occupational status and family structure. These boys also had lower supervision and a higher level of punishment from their parents at age 10, 11 and 12 years. Both family adversity and parenting were significant predictors of delinquency, even when the individual characteristics of the boys (aggressiveness) were taken into account, suggesting that family environment had an influence on boys' delinquency apart from the boys' behavioural profile in pre-adolescence. Tremblay and Haapasalo (1998), in their predictive study based on behaviour patterns, also observed that family adversity when the boys were in kindergarten was a significant predictor of later delinquency, along with the different patterns based on the individual characteristics of the boys.

The association with deviant peers, considered by many sociologists as a necessary step in the development of delinquency (Sutherland, 1939) has also been investigated in the MLES. Tremblay *et al.* (1995), examining peer-rated aggression and likeability, observed that best friends' behavioural characteristics were associated with the boys' own profile between the ages of 10 and 12 years. However, using structural modelling, they found that the main path towards early onset of both covert and overt delinquency (Loeber, 1996) was from kindergarten disruptive behaviour to aggression between the ages of 10 and 12 years, and to delinquency from ages 11 to 13 years. Friends' characteristics did not explain the level of self-reported delinquency when the subjects' own characteristics had been taken into account. However, using a different approach based on group category, Vitaro *et al.* (1997) observed a slightly different picture where highly disruptive and conforming boys' delinquent behaviour at 13 was unaffected by their friends' characteristics at ages 11 and 12, while moderately disruptive boys, according to their teacher, with disturbing friends were more delinquent at age 13 than other groups of moderately disruptive boys. This suggests that peer influence may be more important in boys who do not present an extreme behaviour profile, adapted or not.

In summary, the studies of developmental trajectories leading to delinquency based on the MLES suggest that boys' individual characteristics, especially externalizing problems – disruptiveness, hyperactivity and aggression in particular – represent an early step in the development of later antisocial behaviour. Other boys' characteristics, such as withdrawal and inattention, seem to bring additional risk, while inhibition and anxiety appear to act as protective factors against delinquency. From a developmental perspective, the stability of externalizing problems across elementary school years appears to be the path most at risk of becoming delinquent. Additionally, environmental factors such as family adversity and parenting, especially parental supervision and punishment, and to a lesser degree, peers' characteristics, although linked with the boys' pre-adolescent behaviour, bring a distinct contribution to the development of delinquent behaviour. However, in this latter case, peers' characteristics in the MLES seem to be a social dimension associated with delinquent behaviour more than a cause of delinquency.

SUBSTANCE USE AND ABUSE

Individual factors

In a subsample of 82 families from the MLES, Dobkin *et al.* (1997) examined early behaviour leading to substance use (cigarettes, alcohol and drugs) at age 13. Using data both from kindergarten and from the past year, they found that stable disruptive boys between the ages of six and 13 reported more substance use, when compared to non-disruptive boys. In another study, Dobkin *et al.* (1995) examined the association between boys' behavioural characteristics in kindergarten, and at age 12, and substance abuse (alcohol and/or drug) at age 13. Using structural equation modelling, they found that teacher-rated disruptiveness in kindergarten, defined as a combination of fighting, hyperactivity and oppositional behaviours, leads to peer-rated disruptiveness at age 12, which subsequently leads to substance abuse, defined as having been drunk and/or using drugs at age 13 or younger.

Bringing more support to the importance of individual characteristics in the onset of substance use/abuse, Mâsse and Tremblay (1997) found that personality dimensions measured as early as in kindergarten predicted the onset of substance use in the MLES boys. In this study, Cloninger's (1987) dimensions of personality based on teacher ratings in kindergarten, and when the boys were 10 years old, were independent variables. Both sets of measures were used to predict the onset of substance use (cigarettes, alcohol and other drugs) when the boys were between 10 and 15. Results showed that high novelty seeking and low harm avoidance significantly predict early onset of substance use. Interestingly, the power of prediction was similar between the measurements at ages six and 10 years, suggesting that the individual characteristics eventually influencing the onset of substance use were already present at an early age.

Environmental factors

In their study of stable disruptive boys between the ages of six and 13, Dobkin *et al.* (1997) observed that family characteristics were associated with boys' characteristics as well as with early onset of substance use. Based on observational measures of mother-child interactions, results showed that disruptive boys' mothers were significantly less nurturing and demanded obedience rather than promoted autonomy. When used to predict early-onset substance use, mother's lack of nurturing was a significant predictor even when boys' disruptive behaviour was taken into account. Despite a trend in the results, paternal alcoholism, in this study, was not associated with boys' substance use, possibly because of the extreme nature of boys' characteristics (for example stable disruptive or non-disruptive over seven years).

Adopting a methodology similar to the one proposed by Tremblay *et al.* (1995), Dobkin *et al.* (1995) used structural equation modelling to examine the relative contribution of individual and peers' characteristics to the development of substance abuse. They found that, although peers' characteristics were associated with subjects' characteristics from 10 to 12 years, they did not contribute to the trajectory of deviance observed from teacher-rated disruptiveness in kindergarten, to peer-rated disruptiveness at age 10 to 12 or to substance abuse at age 13. Results were replicated using peer-rated disruptiveness at ages 10, 11, and 12 with three subsamples of the original sample.

Thus, similarly to what has been observed for the trajectories leading to delinquency, individual characteristics, more than friends' deviance, appear to be the main factor in the development of substance abuse in boys participating in the

MLES. However, as noted above, family characteristics, especially mother's nurturing behaviour, seemed to have a significant influence, independent of the boys' characteristics.

USING A NEW STRATEGY TO EXAMINE DEVELOPMENTAL TRAJECTORIES

Most longitudinal studies examining antisocial behaviour from childhood to adulthood have used only one or two assessments during childhood. Although this strategy has proved to be useful for predictive research, it represents an important limitation when studying developmental trajectories. Making the best of the yearly measures of the MLES, Nagin and Tremblay (1999) have used a method proposed by Nagin and Land (Land and Nagin, 1996; Nagin and Land, 1993) to establish developmental trajectories of aggression, opposition and hyperactivity on the path to juvenile delinquency. This method uses a semi-parametric mixture model designed to identify distinctive groups of developmental trajectories within the population.

Using teacher ratings made at ages six, 10, 11, 12, 13, 14 and 15 years, four trajectories were identified for each of the externalizing problem behaviours. Trajectories were as follows: a group of boys called 'nevers', who never displayed the problem behaviour significantly, which comprises 15 per cent to 25 per cent of the sampled population; a second group called 'low-level desisters', who manifested at six years of age a low level of the problem behaviour, but who desisted by age 10 to 12, which accounted for about 50 per cent of the sample; a third group called 'high-level near desisters', who scored relatively high on externalizing behaviours when they were six years old but scored much lower by age 15, and accounted for 20 to 30 per cent of the population, and finally, a fourth group called 'chronics', who scored high on the problem behaviour throughout the observation period, comprising about 5 per cent of the sample.

Interestingly, although a certain correspondence was observed between the different groups for the three problem behaviours, boys who followed a given trajectory for a given dimension did not necessarily follow the same trajectory for the other behaviours. Indeed, less than half (46.7 per cent) of the chronic aggressive boys were also chronic oppositional, and only 13.3 per cent were chronic hyperactive. Among chronic oppositional boys, only 23.1 per cent were also chronic hyperactive.

After computing the developmental trajectories of aggression, opposition and hyperactivity, Nagin and Tremblay (1999) examined the delinquent outcomes of the different groups for each externalizing behaviour. Their results indicated that the boys from the chronic group for the three problem behaviours had clearly engaged in more delinquent acts by age 17. At that time, the average number of events of physical violence, serious delinquency (such as breaking and entering, arson and destroying property) and theft were respectively 3.6, 2.0 and 6.1 for the chronic group defined by physical aggression, 2.4, 1.2 and 4.3 for the chronic group of opposition, and 2.4, 0.9 and 3.3 for the chronic group of hyperactivity. In comparison, the average number of events of physical violence, serious delinquency and theft by age 17 for the boys who never manifested the behaviour problems were respectively 0.72, 0.28, and 1.36 for the non-aggressive boys, 0.60, 0.15, and 1.20

for the non-oppositional boys, and 0.98, 0.10, and 0.97 for the non-hyperactive boys. Overall, the average cumulative number of infractions by age 18 was 7.17 for the chronic aggressive group, 6.38 for the chronic oppositional group and 2.34 for the chronic hyperactivity group. In comparison, at the same age, the boys categorized as 'nevers' for physical aggression, opposition and hyperactivity reported an average cumulative number of infractions of 0.06, 0.01 and 0.33, respectively. Examining the different groups for the same behaviour dimension also showed important differences. Based on Nagin and Tremblay's results, figure 5.1 shows the average number of infractions by age 18 for the four trajectories of aggressive behaviour. Clearly, the chronic aggressive boys had been much more involved in delinquent acts than boys from the other trajectories, with an average of 7.17 infractions, compared to 2.21 for the high-level near-desisters, 0.50 for the low-level desisters and 0.06 for boys of the 'never' group.

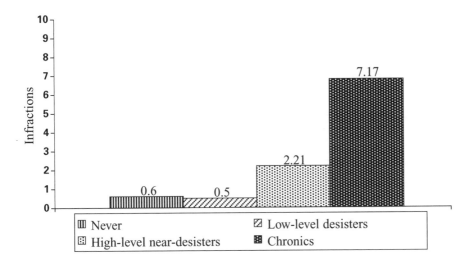

Source: Adapted from Nagin and Tremblay (1999).

Figure 5.1 Cumulative juvenile infractions (average number of infractions) up to 18th birthday

CURRENT RESEARCH AND FUTURE DIRECTIONS: SUBSTANCE USE IN ADOLESCENCE AND FAMILY CONTEXT RELATED TO BOYS' TRAJECTORIES OF AGGRESSION

While previous reports from the MLES underscored the importance of boys' individual characteristics, especially externalizing behaviour, and of the stability of behaviour problems over time in predicting delinquency, Nagin and Tremblay's (1999) results showed that different trajectories of behaviour can be identified between kindergarten and adolescence, and that these trajectories are clearly associated with the development of delinquent behaviour. Building on this recent work, current research aims at examining the outcomes of these developmental trajectories for substance use/abuse, and identifying environmental factors associated with the development of these trajectories.

Figure 5.2 shows the proportion of boys from each trajectory of aggression, using drugs several times or often during the last year, for the ages of 11, 12, 13, 14 and 15. Drug use was defined as either having been drunk or using marijuana or hard drugs. A stable pattern can be observed where more chronic aggressive boys start abusing drugs as early as age 11, and keep showing a higher consumption throughout adolescence, when compared to the other trajectories. About 10 per cent of these boys already reported using drugs several times or often at age 11, and 81 per cent by age 15. Boys who had never been aggressive between the ages of six and 15 years started abusing drugs later and showed the lowest consumption from 11 to 15. None of these boys reported using drugs several times or often at age 11, and only 29.2 per cent at age 15, a tremendous difference from boys from the chronic group. Low-level desisters appeared to be at low risk of substance abuse as well. However, high-level near-desisters also started to consume early, although less than chronic aggressive boys, but from 11 to 15, a substantial proportion of these boys (53.9 per cent by age 15) reported abusing drugs compared to the 'nevers' and the 'low-level desisters', suggesting that this group might also be at risk. Overall, results supported the idea that boys showing a trajectory of stable aggressive behaviour throughout elementary school and early adolescence were much more at risk of abusing drugs during adolescence.

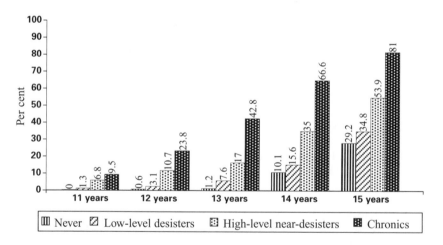

Figure 5.2 Substance use several times or often over the last year

Considering that some dimensions of the family environment were predictors of juvenile delinquency and substance use in previous work from the MLES, we next examined the extent to which family context and parent–child interactions were associated with developmental trajectories of aggression. First, an index of *family adversity* was computed based on the following variables: mother's and father's age at birth of their first child, mother's and father's education, mother's and father's occupational SES (based on Blishen and McRoberts' index, 1976) and family structure (intact or non-intact). Simply put, families under the 30th percentile on the first six variables (indicating either early parenting, a low level of education or occupational SES) were given one point of family adversity, as well as non-intact families, creating a 0–7 point scale, standardized into a 0–1 point scale for analyses. For the present chapter, we examined the information collected when the boys were 10 years old, thus, about half-way through the observational period considered for the definition of trajectories. Results indicated that the level of family adversity (FA) was higher in the families of the chronic aggressive boys (FA = 0.56), followed by the high level near desisters (FA = 0.40), the low level desisters (FA = 0.31) and the families of the never aggressive boys (FA = 0.23). The differences between each group were statistically significant (F(3669) = 21.99, p < 0.001).

Two dimensions of parent–child interactions were also examined when the boys were 10 years old: parental authority and parental pleasure in contacts with their son. Figure 5.3 shows the average score on a scale of 'authority' for the different groups. This dimension assesses how much parents have to use authority in their relationship with their son. Results indicated that parents had to use authority nearly twice as much (mean = 10.4) with the chronic aggressive boys than with the never aggressive group (mean = 6.0). A clear pattern of increase in using authority with their son can in fact be observed from the never aggressive boys to the chronically aggressive.

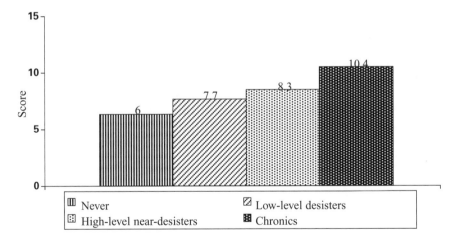

Figure 5.3 Average score on parental authority scale

Figure 5.4 shows the results for the other dimension of parent–child interactions, the pleasure experience by the parents in their contacts with their son. A reverse pattern from the one found for authority was observed: Parents of never aggressive boys reported more pleasure in their interactions with their son than parents of chronic aggressive boys. Again, a trend can be observed across the different groups, this time a decrease in parents' pleasure in interacting with the boy from the never aggressive group to the chronically aggressive group.

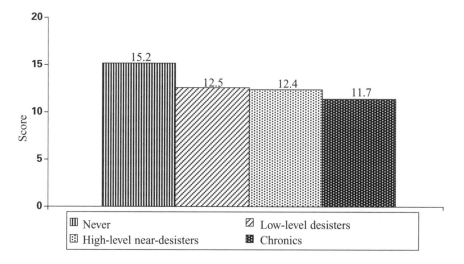

Figure 5.4 Average score on parental pleasure scale

The above results regarding the association between some dimensions of family environment and boys' trajectories based on aggressive behaviour suggest that different courses of individual behaviour take place in different environmental contexts as well. Specifically, the observations based on family context as well as parent–child interactions indicated that boys following a trajectory of aggressive behaviour from kindergarten to adolescence grew up in a family with a higher level of adversity (as previously defined) and experimented more negative and fewer positive interactions with their parents than boys who were not chronically aggressive.

Future research will try to substantiate boys' behaviour profiles leading across time to different types of delinquent behaviour (for example violent and non-violent) and to delinquency with specific comorbid conditions (for example substance use and internalizing problems). In that respect, the convergence (or divergence) between developmental trajectories based on different problem behaviours over time and its relationship to juvenile delinquency and substance use in adolescence has to be investigated. The method used by Nagin and Tremblay (1999) to identify developmental trajectories of problem behaviours will also be applied to substance use throughout adolescence. This will enable researchers to identify the behavioural and environmental backgrounds of specific types of substance abusers, based on a developmental perspective, as well as examining the extent to which specific developmental trajectories of behaviour problems, say, between childhood and early adolescence, lead to specific trajectories of substance use/abuse throughout adolescence.

Methods allowing the inclusion of environmental dimensions in larger models explaining the development of delinquency and substance use/abuse also have to be explored. As shown in MLES studies reported in this chapter, developmental trajectories leading to delinquency and substance use can be identified from the course of individual behaviour over time. However, environmental conditions were also clearly associated with these trajectories of individual behaviour. Dynamic models integrating both individual and environmental dimensions are not only an exciting challenge for researchers, but are a necessary step in order to understanding the interplay between an individual's characteristics and his environment, and its impact throughout development. Finally, the continuing assessment of the MLES boys, now in early adulthood, will make it possible to examine the full developmental course of behaviour between pre-school and adult age. This will be an invaluable opportunity to identify the course of behaviour over time, and the related environmental contexts, leading to a variety of adjustment problems in adulthood (for example, criminality, substance abuse, family violence and unemployment). Moreover, a methodology examining the course of behaviour throughout development, as well as related familial and social contextual factors, offers a great opportunity to identify protective factors influencing boys' adaptation to their social world. The identification of trajectories starting as early in development as in kindergarten, and of related risk and protective factors, should be most useful to guide prevention efforts. Although a number of methodological obstacles remain to be overcome, past and current studies based on the MLES open exciting perspectives for future research on developmental trajectories leading to delinquency and substance use in males.

REFERENCES

Blishen, B.R. and McRoberts, H.A. (1976), 'A revised socioeconomic index for occupations in Canada', *Canadian Review of Sociology and Anthropology*, **13**, 71–91.

Carbonneau, R., Tremblay, R.E., Vitaro, F., Saucier, J.-F., Dobkin, P.L. and Pihl, R.O. (1998), 'Paternal alcoholism, paternal absence and the development of problem behaviours in boys from age 6 to 12 years', *Journal of Studies on Alcohol*, **59** (4), 387–98.

Cloninger, C.R. (1987), 'A systematic method for clinical description and classification of personality variants: A proposal', *Archives of General Psychiatry*, **44**, 573–88.

Dobkin, P.L., Tremblay, R.E. and Sacchitelle, C. (1997), 'Predicting boys' early-onset substance abuse from father's alcoholism, son's disruptiveness, and mother's parenting behaviour', *Journal of Consulting and Clinical Psychology*, **65** (10), 86–92.

Dobkin, P.L., Tremblay, R.E., Mâsse, L.C. and Vitaro, F. (1995), 'Individual and peer characteristics in predicting boys' early onset of substance abuse: A seven-year longitudinal study', *Child Development*, **66**, 1198–214.

Farrington, D.P. (1994), 'Childhood, Adolescent, and Adult Features of Violent Males', in L.R. Huesman (ed.), *Aggressive Behaviour: Current Perspectives*, New York: Plenum Press, pp.215–40.

Fergusson, D.M., Lynskey, M.T. and Horwood, L.J. (1996), 'Origins of comorbidity between conduct and affective disorders', *Journal of the American Academy of Child and Adolescent Psychiatry*, **35**, 451–60.

Haapasalo, J. and Tremblay, R.E. (1994), 'Physically aggressive boys from ages 6 to 12: Family background, parenting behaviour, and prediction of delinquency', *Journal of Consulting and Clinical Psychology*, **62** (5), 1044–52.

Hawkins, J.D., Catalano, R.F. and Miller, J.Y. (1992), 'Risk and protective factors for alcohol and other drug problems in adolescence and early adulthood: Implications for substance abuse prevention', *Psychological Bulletin*, **112**, 64–105.

Huesman, L.R., Eron, L.D., Lefkowitz, M.M. and Walder, L.O. (1984), 'Stability of aggression over time and generations', *Developmental Psychology*, **20**, 1120–34.

Kerr, M., Tremblay, R.E., Pagani, L. and Vitaro, F. (1997), 'Boys' behavioural inhibition and the risk of later delinquency', *Archives of General Psychiatry*, **54**, 809–16.

Land, K.C. and Nagin, D. (1996), 'Micro-models of criminal careers: A synthesis of the criminal careers and life course approaches via semiparametric mixed Poisson models with empirical applications', *Journal of Quantitative Criminology*, **12**, 163–91.

LeBlanc, M. and Fréchette, M. (1989), *Male Offending from Latency to Adulthood*, New York: Springer-Verlag.

Loeber, R. (1996), 'Developmental Continuity, Change, and Pathways in Male Juvenile Problem Behaviors and Delinquency', in J.D. Hawkins (ed.), *Delinquency and Crime: Current* Theories, Cambridge: Cambridge University Press, pp. 1–27.

Loeber, R. and Stouthamer-Loeber, M. (1986), 'Family Factors as Correlates and Predictors of Juvenile Conduct Problems and Delinquency', in M. Tonry and N. Morris (eds), *Crime and Justice: Annual Review of Research*, vol. 7, Chicago: University of Chicago Press, pp.29–149.

Magnusson, D. and Bergman, L.R. (1988), 'Individual and Variable-Based Approaches to Longitudinal Research on Early Risk Factors', in M. Rutter (ed.), *Studies of Psychosocial Risk*, Cambridge: Cambridge University Press, pp.45–61.

Mâsse, L.C. and Tremblay, R.E. (1997), 'Behaviour of boys in kindergarten and the onset of substance use during adolescence', *Archives of General Psychiatry*, **54**, 62–8.

Moffit, T.E. (1993), 'Adolescence-limited and life-course persistent antisocial behaviour: A developmental taxonomy', *Psychological Review*, **100** (4), 674–701.

Nagin, D. and Land, K.C. (1993), 'Age, criminal careers and population heterogeneity: Speci-fication and estimation of a nonparametric, mixed poisson model', *Criminology*, **31**, 327–62.

Nagin, D. and Tremblay, R.E. (1999), 'Trajectories of boys' physical aggression, opposition and hyperactivity on the path to physically violent and nonviolent juvenile delinquency', *Child Development*, **70**, 1181–96.

Stattin, H. and Magnusson, D. (1989), 'The role of early aggressive behaviour in the frequency, seriousness, and types of later crime', *Journal of Consulting and Clinical Psychology*, **57**, 710–18.

Sutherland, E. (1939), *Principles of criminology*, Philadelphia: Lippincott.

Tremblay, R.E. and Haapasalo, J. (1998), 'Boy's Behavioural Patterns in Kindergarten Predict Male Delinquency, Withdrawal and School Adjustment', in J. Boros, I. Münnich and M. Szegedi (eds), *Psychology and Criminal Justice: International Review of Theory and Practice*, Berlin: Walter de Gruyter, pp.197–211.

Tremblay, R.E., Mâsse, L.C., Vitaro, F. and Dobkin, P.L. (1995), 'The impact of friends' deviant behaviour on early onset of delinquency: longitudinal data from 6 to 13 years of age', *Development and Psychopathology*, **7**, 649–67.

Tremblay, R.E., Pihl, R.O., Vitaro, F. and Dobkin, P.L. (1994), 'Predicting early onset of male antisocial behaviour from preschool behaviour', *Archives of General Psychiatry*, **51**, 732–9.

Van Kammen, W.B., Loeber, R. and Stouthamer-Loeber, M. (1991), 'Substance use and its relationship to conduct problems and delinquency in young boys', *Journal of Youth and Adolescence*, **20**, 399–413.

Vitaro, F., Tremblay, R.E., Kerr, M., Pagani, L. and Bukowski, W.M. (1997), 'Disruptiveness, friends' characteristics, and delinquency in early adolescence: A test of two competing models of development', *Child Development*, **68** (4), 676–89.

White, J.L., Moffit, T.E., Earls, F., Robins, L. and Silva, P.A. (1990), 'How early can we tell? Predictors of childhood conduct disorder and adolescent delinquency', *Criminology*, **28**, 507–33.

Chapter 6

Deviant Trajectories at the Turning Point between Adolescence and Adulthood

Michel Born and Claire Gavray

This chapter will investigate deviant trajectories in an effort to understand the development of adolescents or adults whose socialization is out of step with the established norms of society. Regardless of whether deviance is defined according to a statistical norm or in terms of the transgression of a coherent group of norms and rules considered to guarantee social order, the deviant is exposed to society's disapproval and reproving looks and, even more specifically, those of the moral entrepreneurs, according to Becker (1985).

Either the transgression remains an occasional act, limited to some behaviours for which society shows a certain tolerance, not endangering the individual's social, cultural and moral integration, or the deviance becomes a way of life, invading social life and relationships over a long period of time.

Research shows that, although hyperspecialized deviant careers exist, they are rare. Usually, one observes a diversification, a spiral and an entanglement of the committed acts: thefts and attacks, but also transgressions linked to the sale and consumption of drugs. All of this is done as part of a life out of step with the conventional social world. In their works, Gottfredson and Hirschi (1990), as well as Jessor and Jessor (1977) come to the same conclusion: some common factors explain strictly deviant trajectories and those associated with delinquency. This way of life does not happen overnight; it is built into a developmental process. Every psychological or psychosocial intervention as well as every inquiry or test in the course of a study comes at a specific moment in the subject's personal trajectory, when he/she commits acts which are more or less deviant, and at a different phase of social maladjustment or exclusion.

In order to tackle the theme of drug use and criminality, it is impossible to neglect the construction hidden behind these words, the social, moral or ideological connotations brought about by these social phenomena.

In examining deviant trajectories, we have to question the issue of convergence between criminal careers and drug-user careers during an individual's development. Even if biases are important and recognized as visible, we can refer to a few informative studies of convergences observed among populations of offenders and drug users.

A study in Hamburg (Schwanke, 1989; see Junger-Tas, 1991) shows that, among the drug users identified as such by the police, 20 per cent were responsible for aggravated theft and 33 per cent for burglary. In Stockholm, identified drug users only represent 2 per cent of the male population but were responsible for 45 per cent of the known crimes (Sarnecki, 1987). In England, a sample with 300 delinquents revealed that 30 per cent of those responsible for aggravated theft and 60 per cent of burglars were drug users (Parker and Newcombe, 1987). In Belgium, statistics from the Liège Police Department indicated (October 1992) that half of the 24 143 registered thefts in 1991 were linked to drug abuse.

Let us look, then, at a few studies about some aspects that do not rely on the identification of drug abuse by police departments themselves (Grapendaal, 1989; see Junger-Tas, 1991). The Netherlands studied the source of incomes of about 150 serious drug users (100 of them under methadone treatment): 40 per cent of their incomes came from delinquency (22 per cent from the classical delinquency plus 18 per cent from drug trafficking) and 18 per cent from 'deviant behaviour' (prostitution). Burr (1987) observed that a group of young adults in the urban South London centre all confessed to a past during which they skipped school and were delinquents and also light drug users. Some of them then evolved towards a way of overcoming a heroin addiction but continued to use hashish and alcohol.

As far as trajectories are concerned, Elliott *et al.* (1985) assume from data of the National Youth Survey, a longitudinal study on 1725 subjects between 1976 and 1986 (in six waves), that some category shifts are more frequent than others. It is more frequent (and hence more probable) to stay in the same category as years go by, in other words:

- stay neither multiple drug user nor delinquent,
- stay multiple drug user and delinquent,
- stay either multiple drug user or delinquent.

In addition, it appears that most of the people who start as multi-drug users and as serious delinquents tend to remain multiple drug users but not necessarily serious delinquents. The most stable category is that of multiple drug use: once in this category, it is highly probable for the individual to stay there and to add delinquent ways of behaving.

It seems that these convergences of behaviours are supported by common factors which are seen as similar predicting elements identified in research on drug use and on delinquency. For example, the list of predictors for drug abuse suggested by Kandel (1987) is clearly comparable to the list of predicting elements for delinquency set up by Leitenberg (1987). See Table 6.1.

These convergences are observable in surveys simultaneously studying delinquency and drug abuse variables among identical subjects.

The covariation of delinquent and drug addiction trajectories relies on a great convergence of risk and predicting factors. More than that, we are led to believe that there is a common ground as far as family, relationships and personal characteristics are concerned which will be expressed in a specific way of discovering drugs for some young people or of having 'exploratory' delinquent behaviours for others. Often when these behaviours tend to persist towards the end of adolescence and at the beginning of adulthood, the behaviour convergence will be fully realized: the drug addict commits crimes and the delinquent encounters drugs either in the places where he/she hangs around or in prison.

It is within this developmental perspective that the results presented here must be viewed. They are based on a research project done in the department of Psychology of Delinquency and Psychosocial Development at the University of Liège (Born *et al.*, 1997; Gavray, 1997). They give a comparative view of the deviant trajectories appearing in a 'run-of-the-mill' population group at the turning point between adolescence and adulthood.

This study concerns the less serious or moderate delinquent career, a reflection of ordinary delinquency and addiction in the general population of which only certain members will be caught and possibly subjected to criminal penalties or even prison.

Table 6.1 List of predictors for drug abuse by Kandel and list of predicting elements for delinquency by Leitenberg

Kandel: drug abuse	Leitenberg: delinquency
alcohol consumption	be a boy
belief in the positive value of	live in a disadvantaged area
some drugs	experience flimsy and/or rejecting
poor relationships with one's parents	family discipline and/or inadequate
depressive feelings	supervision
being associated with drug users	grow up in a family where dissension
desire for independence	and a lack of affection and/or of
feeling of psychological malaise	cohesion rule
weak expectations	be rejected by one's parents
weak school motivation	(and mostly by one's father)
biased, tolerant attitude in favour	be a 'difficult', restless, hyperactive,
of deviant ways of behaving	'aggressive' child
delinquency	experience successive failures at school
	come from an unemployed 'minority'
	have a family or brotherhood with
	delinquent activities
	have a negative self-image
	be in contact with delinquent peers

METHOD

A longitudinal follow-up of a population group at the turning point between adolescence and adulthood can shed light on the dynamics between a deviant trajectory and a trajectory of economic, social, family, normative and cultural integration by youths. The results presented here come from analysis done on data gathered four years apart, from a mixed sample of 139 youths (74 girls and 65 boys) who were interviewed for the first time in 1992 when they were between 16 and 21 years old.

This research relies on self-reported delinquency. Despite the fact that this methodology may be the object of some reservations and criticism because of the way it takes into account a relatively harmless delinquency and only effectively applies to the cases of individual youths, it seems to be the only one apt to detect the real extent of delinquency. This seems even truer if one uses the longitudinal and comparative viewpoint to try to understand the processes at work in the general population rather than to generate statistics.

Subjects came from an initial mixed sample of 618 youths from Liège between 14 and 21 years old in 1992, a sample comprised according to the framework and criteria of research on self-reported delinquency carried out by the International Self-Reported Delinquency Survey (Born and Gavray, 1994). The sample was representative of the Liège population for that age group (sex, nationality, status – student, worker or other status – kind of studies followed or finished, belonging to what type of household or roots). Owing to the desire to study the many aspects of young people's integration, the decision was made in 1996 to recontact as many young people as possible from the original sample, who by then were 21 to 25 years old. Of the 444 subjects corresponding to the age criteria, 139 were found and administered a new questionnaire. The consistency and representativeness of this longitudinal sample's demographic, statutory and behavioural characteristics were ensured. The youths who were questioned again were revealed to be neither more nor less delinquent than in 1992. This subsample did not include very young adolescents in the first round, which could reduce the possibility of bringing to light all the stages of development referred to in the literature and mentioned in the introduction. On the other hand, the follow-up of these persons went beyond the strict limits of adolescence and into adulthood, the period of statutory, professional and demographic transition.

The list of potentially deviant actions over the last 12 months is the standard used by the international study mentioned above. They can be classified into general categories: fraud and offences linked to age and status, theft (shoplifting or purse snatching), violence and aggression against goods or persons, activities linked to drug use, sale and trafficking. Alcohol use has been included in the list of potentially deviant behaviour because it can lead to prejudicial demeanour towards oneself or others. However, sporadic and reasonable drug use during the period being studied did not seem to be a sign of deviance for our reference group.

The desire to observe and classify deviant trajectories required that several artificial variables of the degree of delinquency and its transition be set up. For each wave, one had available the following:

- detailed information according to which the subject had admitted to committing each of the acts considered, over the last 12 months;
- artificial information according to which he/she had committed at least one act on the full list, no matter which one;
- intermediary information about his/her possible participation in the four general categories classified under the key words 'theft, violence, drug, fraud';
- a combination of these kinds of acts (specialization or polymorphism).

Detailed and artificial indicators provided information about the frequency of committing each act or each category of acts.

Finally, a score of general seriousness was attributed to each youth for each of the years under consideration. This score was constructed by adding all of the partial scores concerning each act on the list and keeping in mind three elements:

- Has the subject admitted committing this act during the period under consideration?
- How many times has he/she committed this act during this period?
- What is the frequency of committing this act in the entire sample group?

RESULTS

First wave of investigation: frequency of delinquent and drug related behaviours in adolescence (age 14 to 21 in 1992)

For the total sample of 618, we mainly found practices which, by their repetitive nature and component elements, were of a minority deviant culture. Thus, we might think of the very high frequency of graffiti. In fact, among the 14 per cent who had drawn graffiti, 21 per cent had done it more than 11 times during the year. Carrying a weapon quite easily becomes a habit, since among the 11 per cent of young people who had done this, 44.3 per cent had done it more than 11 times. Drug taking is also highly repetitive: among the 6.5 per cent who had done it in the previous year, 37.2 per cent had done so more than 11 times.

The other acts for which we observed a high frequency were relatively tolerated practices, such as driving without a licence, fare dodging or truancy from school.

Table 6.2 Frequency of delinquent acts committed during 'last year' in 1992 (n = 618)

Type of act	0 time		1–2 times		3–5 times		6–10 times		11–50 times		51 times or more	
	n	%	n	%	n	%	n	%	n	%	n	%
Theft	462	74.2	63	10.2	41	6.6	16	2.6	29	4.7	7	1.1
Violence	450	72.8	42	6.8	30	4.9	26	4.2	34	5.5	36	5.8
Drug use	575	93.0	16	2.6	5	0.8	6	1.0	5	0.8	11	1.8
Cheating	379	61.0	68	11.0	67	10.8	39	6.3	47	7.6	18	2.9

Fortunately, Table 6.2 reveals a rather low frequency of criminal acts classified as serious, which are only committed repeatedly by a few subjects already heavily involved in criminal practices (Born, 1983; Le Blanc, 1996). An analysis of correspondence using the Benzecri method (which is based on covariations between contingency tables) carried out on these cases clearly demonstrated the continuum of seriousness and incidence of criminal acts (see Figure 6.1).

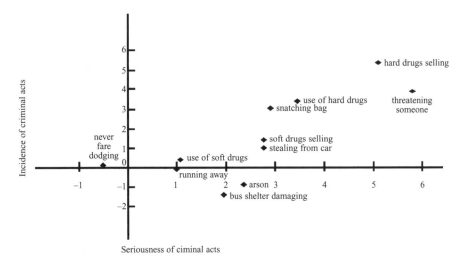

Figure 6.1 Seriousness and incidence of criminal acts

The comparison of replies given by boys and girls to questions about criminality show that wrongdoing is much more common among boys than among girls. The total percentages of young people having committed acts hide the large disparities which exist between young male and female offenders. The more violent, uncommon and risky the act, the greater this disparity becomes (see Table 6.3). For example, theft with violence, participating in fights or injuring others are more often a phenomenon of small, structured groups.

Table 6.3 Comparison of replies given by males and females to questions about criminality

Type	Male		Female	
	n = 285	%	n = 333	%
Property offences	102	35.8	67	20.1
Violent offences	113	39.6	72	21.6
Drug offences	36	12.6	15	4.5
Other youth-related offences	145	50.9	108	32.4
Overall prevalence of delinquency	192	67.4	155	46.5
Without alcohol and problem behaviour				
Problem behaviours without alcohol	110	38.6	80	24.0

Similarities of predicting models for drug use and delinquency

Using logistic regression, we can identify the best model based on the available variables to predict two types (weak and serious) of drug consumption and thefts when compared with those who do not have such behaviours. Among all the variables tested, only those above the 0.05 level of significance in at least one analysis were kept (see Table 6.4).

Table 6.4 Similarities of predicting models for drug use and delinquency

Logistic regression N = 631	Drugs Having taken		Delinquency	
	Cannabis	Heroin, cocaine	Having committed a theft in a store	Having committed a theft in a car
	67 subjects	9 subjects	214 subjects	29 subjects
Sex: boy	S		S	S
Age	S			
Citizenship Belgian EEC Non-EEC			S	
Land of origin: not Belgian				
Does not live with parents	S	S	S	
Lives with the mother alone	S			
Lives with the father alone	S			S
Relationships with the father during childhood			S	
Relationships with the mother during childhood		S		
Relationships with the mother now				S
Confide in the mother				
Parents know where kids are	S	S	S	S
Parents don't know with whom kids go out				S
Stood down a class				S
Do you like school?	S			
Small paid jobs		S	S	

Note: S < 0.05

The similarities, as well as the divergences, of these factors deserve to be taken into account and contradict Hirschi's theory of social bound by showing that the lack of parental control is the only common factor. This is demonstrated by the fact that the youth does not live with his/her parents and does not inform the parents when going out.

Comparison between the two years of the investigation

Despite taking into account some 'exploding' practices such as carrying a weapon or buying stolen goods, the data collected during the two rounds of inquiry indicated that the number of offences admitted to between 1992 and 1996 increased significantly (see Table 6.5). The average score for boys as well as for girls doubled between the two years, but the male score was on average five times higher than that of the girls for the two rounds. An increased prevalence was borne out for every type of deviant act except statutory acts (fraud). This is not really surprising because, in essence, this kind of act is closely tied to the judicial, official and social status of the subject (student, young person less than 18 years old forbidden access to certain places or practices). Vandalism and graffiti were equally revealed to be more 'concentrated' in adolescence.

Table 6.5 Prevalence of delinquent acts

Type of act	1992	(n = 618)	1992	(n = 139)	1996	(n = 139)
	n	%	n	%	n	%
Prevalence of thefts	169	27.3	36	25.9	50	36.0
Prevalence of violent acts	185	29.9	30	21.6	45	32.4
Soft drug use	49	7.9	11	7.9	25	18.0
Hard drug use	6	0.9	–	–	8	5.8
Soft drug sale	10	1.6	3	2.2	4	2.9
Hard drug sale	–	–	–	–	2	1.4
Prevalence of acts linked to drugs	51	8.2	11	7.9	26	18.7

The same trend towards an increase was borne out in the terms of participation in the number of different kinds of acts, confirming the trend towards polymorphism. Nineteen per cent of the sample's subjects (21 per cent of the boys and 16 per cent of the girls) appeared simultaneously in several of the four categories of behaviour in 1992, 33 per cent (43 per cent of the boys but 22 per cent of the girls) in 1996. In fact, the gap between the sexes and between the rounds of inquiry differed according to the type of behaviour. The gap widened when examining acts of violence, that remained the prerogative of the male subjects over the period being studied.

On the other hand, the gap narrowed concerning statutory acts, theft, the presence during a fight or 'symbolically' damaging goods. Surprisingly, a substantial increase in acts linked to drugs for the boys and a decrease for the girls was observed between the two rounds.

In accordance with the developmental approach, one can ask how the development of delinquency follows another rhythm or logic according to gender. It is interesting to note how the subject's age influences the commission of a delinquent act or certain type of offence. The fact that the sample did not include individuals less than 16 years old in the first round does not allow one to look into the precocious stages of the development of delinquency cited above. The sample was divided into three age categories in 1992: the 16–17-year-olds, the 18–19-year-olds and the 20–21-year-olds.

In fact, age was not shown to play a significant role except in statutory acts in the second round, and this in a way one expected: the closer the subject was to 25 years old in 1996, the more likely that he/she had not committed any 'fraud' during the second year. For the rest, no significant link was established between age and the score of delinquency, the propensity to have presented a specific type of act or a different rate of prevalence, whether examining 1992 or 1996. It was the same for young men and young women. Does one have to abandon the developmental path to understand deviant acts? Or does one have to think in a different way to learn valid lessons on the explicative ability of the latter? In fact, the comparison of tendencies between the two rounds did not make it possible to know to what extent it was the same people who continued to be delinquent from one year to another. It is the same when studying unemployment. The rate may be steady, but that does not mean that the same subjects form the group of unemployed people from one year to another. Only a longitudinal type of investigation may allow us to move forward in an analysis in trajectory or transitional terms.

Links in the seriousness of exhibited deviancy between the first and second rounds

Based on existing data, a 'rough' typology of transitions can be constructed according to whether a subject has committed a deviant act:

- neither of the two years = no delinquents
- only the first year = desistents
- only the second year = new delinquents
- both in 1992 and 1996 or, more precisely, within the 12 months preceding each round of investigation = persistents.

Table 6.6 Deviant trajectories according to transitions in/out of delinquency in relation to specific delinquent acts

	Desistents (n = 12) 1992 %	New delinquents (n = 37) 1996 %	Persistents (n = 51) 1992 %	Pesistents (n = 51) 1996 %
Theft	66	40	55	69
Aggression	33	38	60	64
Cheating	66	56	55	61
Use/traffick of drugs	0	22	21	35

The analyses show that between the two years that were studied, a majority of the young people persisted in committing at least one delinquent act. A minority showed up only in the first round with at least one behaviour on the list (see Table 6.6).

What does the very significant correlation between the score of seriousness of deviancy in 1992 and 1996 mean (r = 0.42) (p = 0.001)? Does it attest to persistence, or even getting out-of-control in the delinquency process? This hypothesis seems to be confirmed by the strong correlations that also exist concerning the number of acts and the number of types of acts between 1992 and 1996. When examining how the correlations show up according to age group, only the inter-year correlations concerning acts of violence and drugs were significant in the three age groups. They indicated the getting-out-of-control and the persistence of delinquency. Among the subjects having committed at least one delinquent act, a strong involvement in drug-related incidents in 1992 proved to be predictive of the same kind of act in 1996 (r = 0.46, p < 0.001), no matter which age group was considered. This is also confirmed by the fact that the mean scores of delinquent activities of those who are drug users are higher than those who are non-drug users (see Table 6.7).

Table 6.7 Mean score of delinquency in 1996 according to drug use in 1992

	Mean score of delinquency in 1996
Non-drug users in 1992	0.48
Drug users in 1992	2.69

Note: P = 0.0001.

As expected, if the analysis of correlations between the same kind of acts shown in the first and second rounds is refined by gender, there is still no significant correlation concerning youthful frauds, either for boys or for girls. On the contrary, in the two subgroups, a precocious tendency towards aggression has proved to be a good predictor of the anchoring of this behaviour in adulthood. As for the correlation between the years concerning committed theft, it is true only for the girls. The number of drug-related incidents in 1996 did not remain significantly correlated to the situation in 1992, as was the case with the boys. The complexity of results taken from statistical analysis is noticeable here.

What about the significant correlations between the different types of acts for a specific year and between the years by gender? In general, the 1992/1996 behaviour of boys is more consistent than that of the girls. Only the boys demonstrate a significant and systematic correlation between the number of incidents linked to drug use in 1992 and the behaviour connected to each of the four main categories of deviant acts exhibited in 1996. For them, participation in drug-related incidents show up in the adoption of a marginal lifestyle with statutory acts and 'wanton' defacing at the start of adulthood. No matter which age group is considered, the overall masculine delinquency score in the second round proves to depend very significantly on the degree of involvement in drug-related incidents and violence. On the other hand, in the female group, even if it concerns a rare phenomenon, the only significant correlation observed is that between a serious involvement in theft in 1992 and violent demonstrations four years later.

After we take into account the customary precautions with respect to the small scope of the sample, we can reasonably believe in the worth of such a model that makes a link between the gravity of the deviance of 1996 each time according to the occupied status and the involvement in a drug-related act ($p = 0.0001$ when we take into account the consumption in 1992 and in 1996). See Table 6.8.

Table 6.8 Mean score of deviance in 1996 according to the combination of two factors (social and professional trajectories and possible drug consumption in 1996)

Social and professional trajectory	Drug consumption in 1996	Number of subjects	Gravity and deviance score
Student	no	31	0.20
	yes	10	0.84
Working person	no	48	0.22
	yes	4	3.17
Unemployed who has already worked	no	19	0.50
	yes	7	5.20
Unemployed who has never worked	no	14	0.04
	yes	5	1.15

These results are startling since they show an increase in the number of young drug users between the two surveyed years. This evolution goes far beyond the sole consumption of psychoactive substances and also refers to the needs, practices and group norms among the young users. Our analyses shed light on the links between deviance and difficulties in becoming involved or stable in active life. Yet these links are probably not unilateral. In a dynamic vision of delinquent life, one's behaviour also influences the position and resources of youth in the future.

Early involvement in acts linked to drugs is significantly important for the young adult's later delinquent life. Particular attention will have to be devoted to drug-related practices, including the consumption of soft drugs. Such behaviour increases the probability not only of multiplying participation in all other types of prohibited acts, but also of the confirmation of the delinquent course beyond adolescence. Persistent deviant persons have clearly started a delinquent spiral, inasmuch as they accumulate the type and number of acts and tend proportionally to be more exposed to victimization than other groups.

Comparison between persistent delinquent non-users and persistent delinquent users

When only taking into account the 51 youths who confessed a persistent delinquent way of behaving between 1992 and 1996, 18 admitted having used drugs during the 12 months before the 1996 survey (see Table 6.9). The delinquent drug users (DU) were characterized by a greater likelihood of having committed thefts or violent acts in 1996, but there was no difference as far as statutory acts were concerned: a majority of youths, from both groups committed them (see Table 6.10).

Table 6.9 Characteristics of consumption among delinquent users

18 DU Subjects	Soft drugs (n = 17)	Hard drugs (n = 7)
Usage	2/3 occasional users 1/3 regular users	One used heroin Six used cocaine Five used amphetamines Five used ecstasy Five used cocktails
Sale	4	2

The DU group is characterized – and this comes as no surprise – by the multiplicity of forms the produced delinquency takes (one third of the subjects showed a combination of all types of deviant acts) whereas the delinquent non-user (DNU) group committed acts which were generally more selective and specialized (more than the half of the group committed only one type of act). Hence it seems logical that the delinquency score of the DU group turned out to be on average three times higher than the DNU score in 1992 and seven times higher in 1996. This means that the users' group includes a greater number of delinquents in the two waves. It is even more interesting to observe that, whereas the average DNU delinquency rate remained stable between 1992 and 1996, the DU rate tripled. The use of psychoactive substances seems to play a role in the dynamics and notably in the early use (before the 1992 survey). The DU group is also more likely to be victimised, most often the object of violent acts (more often having been given a beating ($p = 0.03$)). This group eventually becomes more frequently involved in such things as carrying and using a weapon, either in self-defence or to intimidate others.

Table 6.10 Characteristics of delinquency among delinquent non-users and delinquent users

	DNU (%)	DU (%)
More than one theft during the last 12 months	54	94
A violent act	51	77
Against goods	18	44
Against persons	24	61

It is interesting to observe that 17 of the 18 subjects from the DU group who were users in 1996 showed a high level of depression in 1992, compared with 19 among 33 DNU subjects who were non-users at the end. Yet we did not notice in 1992 any significant relationship within the group between drug taking and simultaneous signs of a breakdown, whereas more DNU than DU subjects subjects ended up very depressed in 1996.

We might evoke the hypothesis that low psychological resources coupled with drug use during adolescence is fertile ground for the birth of a serious delinquent process taking various forms, such as increased use of psychoactive substances. This process is not necessarily accompanied by increased symptoms of depression but might allow them to be maintained at a manageable level.

While we did not find any significant difference with respect to age (or indeed sex) between the deviant groups (DU and DNU), we nevertheless found social and family-specific points within both groups. The DU group turned out to come from a more privileged social and cultural background and more often had Belgian citizenship (see Table 6.11). In fact, 25 per cent of the DNU youth (compared to 11 per cent of the DU group) thought their parents did not have any social and professional plans for them in the future (a sign of a lack of parental involvement but also maybe of a lack of social or cultural resources which might allow them to advise or orient their child efficiently).

Youths from the DU group described their original social group as being higher than that of youths in the other group. The former were twice as likely (66 per cent of the DU versus 33 per cent of the DNU) to believe they will have a higher social position than their parents. In fact, this optimism might not be grounded since it relies on their parents' higher financial support. In the first place, 66 per cent of the DU (36 per cent of the DNU) regularly received money from their family. In the second place, 42 per cent of the DU (only 7 per cent of the DNU) were sometimes financially helped by their parents (to settle problems when they arose). Besides this support, we also found greater possibilities of making money among the users: 51 per cent of the DNU and 22 per cent of the DU had official professional incomes; 27 per cent of the DNU and 44 per cent of the DU said they worked or were active on the black market. Moreover, 83 per cent of the DU (36 per cent of the DNU) confessed to taking part in the illegal trafficking of stolen goods (as buyer or retailer).The habitual delinquent users in 1996 had a very close relationship with money and desired goods.

Table 6.11 Nationality and work situation of the father among DNU and DU

	DNU (%)	DU (%)
Belgian citizenship	54	83
Father who works	67	90

It is interesting that, whereas the DNU group had a rather realistic image of themselves and their know-how, users were in two extreme situations. This group (more than the DNU group) simultaneously and proportionally had young people who accorded themselves no know-how and young people who granted themselves maximum know-how. This might be seen as an indicator of a lack of clear-mindedness for these young people with respect to the tools they possess and build upon.

The original social advantages are indeed shaken by lesser quality objective professional and social integration perspectives among the delinquent users. Indeed, we find the smallest number of students among them (16 per cent of the DU, 42 per cent of the DNU) but the highest number of persons without a specific status: neither workers nor students (50 per cent of the DU, 27 per cent of the DNU). There was also a higher proportion of young people who stood down a class (33 per cent of the DU and 18 per cent of the DNU), the highest number of youths who say they experienced serious difficulties at school (42 per cent of the DU compared with 27 per cent of the DNU) and the smallest number of young people who attended remedial classes or extra day or evening school lessons. Whether or not they were still attending school, the highest level of current or completed study was not as good. Half of the young DU did not go beyond a vocational diploma; such is the case for 18 per cent of the DNU. It therefore comes as no surprise that working users had a lower qualified job compared with others. As a follow-up, 34 per cent of the DU (15 per cent of the DNU) said that schoolteachers never understand their students.

As far as family is concerned, the DU group were more likely to express the possibility of their parents' strong disappointment with respect to their professional and training prospects: 27 per cent of them thought their parents were very disappointed by their child compared to only 6 per cent in the other group. Hence relationships with the parents were very different in the two groups, whereas we did not find any significant difference as far as parental control was concerned for the two groups in either wave of the survey.

The difference did not show up in the level of satisfaction with the affection received from parents or on their openness to dialogue, but on the degree of distance established by the young person. Eighty-four per cent of the DU and 66 per cent of the DNU said they never confided in their father (p = 0.06), whereas 36 per cent of the DNU (only 16 per cent of the DU) said they never confided in their mother. The strictly affective relationship with the mother was also deeper in this last group.

Could the slightly higher number of young users who live with their mother alone leading to the youth's feeling of responsibility or remorse be the sole explanation for these results? At least it appears that the young DU were in fact more numerous in comparison to the DNU in wishing to follow family values similar to those of their parents.

As far as values and opinions are concerned, these young users operate in a short term, materialistic and individualistic way. Although 27 per cent of the DU (9 per cent of DNU) proclaimed that it is important to defend one's ideas, they did not look inward for guidance about their lives or to make up their mind. Eleven per cent of the DU (27 per cent of the DNU) insisted on the importance of spirituality, thought, and inner beauty; 44 per cent of the DU (63 per cent of the DNU) said that it is important to give meaning to one's life. Getting into opposition mattered, but this has to happen with the maintaining of the security brought about by the parents' liberalities. A greater proportion of users were looking for a way of having fun than the non-users (56 per cent versus 21 per cent) and increasing a casual love life (33 per cent versus 6 per cent). Yet the DU were less satisfied than the DNU with their love and affective life (6 per cent versus 28 per cent). Not as many wanted to find *the* great love affair (1 per cent versus 33 per cent). On the contrary, they lived surrounded by friends. They would often go out on the town with 'buddies' (almost every day for 78 per cent of the DU and 35 per cent of the DNU and regularly for 69 per cent of the DU versus 33 per cent of the DNU.

The values of 'work' and 'profession' were more widely criticized by the users' group, with 27 per cent of the DU and 58 per cent of the DNU saying that work is very important: they distanced themselves more from the ideas defended by their parents' generation on that matter. Hence users were temporarily or progressively involved in a subculture in conflict or breaking with the societal culture still recognized by the majority as progressive and leading to a higher life standing. Compared to the other group, they were less keen on the virtues of perseverance, respecting societal rules and honesty. What they really valued was being imaginative, curious and being a leader. Thirty-three per cent of the DU and 9 per cent of the DNU said they worked according to their own wishes, saw themselves as being impulsive but tended to think more about the pain an action could cause their family before or after the fact. This confirms the close relationship to family we noted earlier. Compared to the DNU (6 per cent of the DU versus 23 per cent of the DNU), they were less likely to think that stealing from a rich person is a serious crime.

Such an experience and the conception of life which accompany it do not necessarily lead to a happier life, without any problems or tension, since the psychoactive substance users were significantly more likely to say they regularly have black thoughts (28 per cent versus 3 per cent of the DNU), are unable to make a decision (16 per cent versus 3 per cent) and are very easily irritated (34 per cent versus 9 per cent).

Internal and social functioning can thus help reinforce the delinquent and psychoactive substance-using trajectory, which can then induce changes in personality, attitudes and values. The dangers of a social and social-professional disintegration are real. As for the family, nothing tends to indicate that the parents will go on being long-term partners during these evolutions. The familial financial help can turn out to be the best, but also the worst, thing.

Results of the explanatory model used by the PROBIT analysis

The analysis deals with the combination of early factors (adolescence in 1992) and those during adulthood (in 1996) explaining the probability that a persistent delinquent (N = 51 subjects) will end up being a drug user: 18 are in such a situation, 33 are not (see Tables 6.12 and 6.13).

Table 6.12 Regression of 1992 factors on the use of drugs among persistent delinquents

Factors 1992	Intercept P = 0.005	
Be very depressed in 1992	P = 0.007	Estim. 1.91
See one's future in a positive, optimistic way	P = 0.007	Estim. 1.30
Take part in the trafficking of stolen goods, in schemes (small services on the black market)	P = 0.004	Estim. 1.39

Table 6.13 Regression of 1996 factors on the use of drugs among persistent delinquents

Factors 1996	Intercept P = 0.02	
Have conventional values and attitudes	P = 0.02	Estim. −1.12
Have a job or study	P = 0.04	Estim. −1.10
Confide in one's father	P = 0.01	Estim. −1.35
Confide in one's mother	P = 0.04	Estim. 1.05
Behave according to one's instinct and wishes	P = 0.04	Estim. 0.89

According to these analyses, young people who add drug use to their persistent delinquency trajectory are characterized by the following elements. *During their adolescence* (between 16 and 21 years old) they felt ill-at-ease and got involved in small trafficking networks which gave a slightly more optimistic self-image as regards their future. Yet we do not find any relationship to self-assessed parental relationships at the time, to the affirmed values or to particular personality traits. *During adulthood* (between 21 and 25 years old), these same persistent delinquent drug users tend to show clear signs of social and professional disintegration and seem to enter a counter-conventional subculture. They move and progress according to their own wish. The distance from the father has widened, whereas the mother is approached or accepted as an ally.

CONCLUSION

Research tends to show that the predicting elements for persistent delinquency and drug use are similar, since the lack of family ties, school drifting, marginalizing of values and association with deviant peers are always found. In our survey, we have tried to understand which effect drug use could have on the adult trajectory of those who are persistent delinquents. The results are very clear on that level, since delinquency worsens if drug use was present during adolescence. Moreover, we have tried to understand the differences between a persistent delinquent drug user and those who are persistent delinquents but who do not use drugs.

Young adults who add drug use to their persistent delinquency have experienced during adolescence a more intense psychological malaise, have used a whole range of schemes (more or less illegal jobs) which allowed them to believe that their future might offer them various possibilities despite their lack of involvement in school. By the time they were adults, the resources turned out to be insufficient (notably because of relationship problems with the father, who in many cases had stopped providing any financial help, crucial for their continued use). Their sole possibility was then to turn to their living on the fringe and fully participate in this culture. Thus drug use and delinquency tend to be the everyday life conditions of these young adults who have not yet been in touch with the judicial system but who are already strongly involved in a delinquent and drug use trajectory which might continue for many years.

REFERENCES

Becker, H.S. (1985), *Outsiders*, Paris: A.M. Métailié.
Born, M. (1983), *Jeunes déviants ou délinquants juvéniles?*, Liège: Mardaga.
Born, M. and Gavray, C. (1994), 'Self-reported Delinquency in Liège', in J. Junger-Tas, G.J. Terlouw and M.W. Klein (eds), *Delinquent Behavior among Young People in the Western World*, Amsterdam: Kluwer Publications, pp.131–55.
Born, M., Chevalier, V. and Humblet, I. (1997), 'Resilience, desistance and delinquent career of adolescent offenders', *Journal of Adolescence*, **20**, 679–94.
Burr, A. (1987), 'Chasing the dragon: Heroin misuse, delinquency and crime in the context of South London culture', *British Journal of Criminology*, **27** (4).
Elliott, D.S., Huizinga, D. and Ageton, S.S. (1985), *Explaining Delinquency and Drug Use*, Beverly Hills: Sage Publications.
Elliott, D.S., Huizinga, D. and Menard, S. (ed.) (1989), *Multiple Problem Youth, Delinquency, Substance Use and Mental Health Problems*, New York: Springer-Verlag.
Gavray, C. (1997), 'Trajectoire déviante à la lisière entre adolescence et âge adulte', *Déviance et Société*, **21** (3), 273–88.
Gottfredson, M. and Hirschi, T. (1990), *A General Theory of Crime*. Stanford, CA: Stanford University Press.

Hammersley, R., Forsyth, A. and Lavelle, T. (1990), 'The criminality of new drug users in Glasgow', *British Journal of Addiction*, **85** (12), 1583–94.

Jessor, R. and Jessor, S.L. (1977), *Problem Behavior and Psychosocial Development: A Longitudinal Study of Youth*, New York: Academic Press.

Junger-Tas, J. (1991), 'Jeunes adultes délinquants et politique criminelle', Dixième colloque criminologique, Conseil de l'Europe, Strasbourg.

Kandel, D.B. (1987), *Longitudinal Research on Drug Use*, New York: John Wiley.

Le Blanc, M. (1996), 'Changing patterns in the perpetration of offenses over time: Trajectories from early adolescence to the early 30's', *Studies on Crime and Crime Prevention*, **5**, (151), 65.

Leitenberg H. (1987), 'Primary prevention on delinquency', in J.D. Burchard and S.N. Burchard (eds), *Prevention of Delinquent Behavior*, Newburg Park, CA: Sage Publications.

Parker, H. and Newcombe, R. (1987) 'Heroin use and acquisitive crime in an English community', *The British Journal of Sociology*, **38**, (3), 331–50.

Sarnecki, J. (1987), 'The Connection between Drug Abuse and Crime', Conseil de l'Europe, Conférence sur la réduction de l'insécurité urbaine, novembre.

Chapter 7

Deviant Youth Trajectories: Adoption, Progression and Regression of Deviant Lifestyles

Natacha Brunelle, Marie-Marthe Cousineau and Serge Brochu

A large proportion of the adult population in North America (and elsewhere) views adolescence with a great deal of anxiety, fear and indignation. The negative image of adolescence is largely due to the media and the emphasis it places on difficulties exhibited by a certain portion of this population: dropping out of school, drug abuse, delinquency, suicide and so on. Although these difficulties, which we will call forms of deviance, do not reflect the reality of all or even the majority of the juvenile population, they are indeed experienced by many adolescents. We will focus here on delinquency and illicit drug use as two examples of these forms of youth deviance. They are considered to be part of a more or less deviant lifestyle, depending on the individuals and the evolution of their trajectory (Brochu and Brunelle, 1997).

The aim of the present chapter is to present the evolution of deviant youth trajectories in the young people's own words so as to provide a phenomenological understanding of the trajectory in question. We will then demonstrate the importance of the elements of personal perception that the youths associate in their account with different points along their trajectory: childhood environment, adoption of a deviant lifestyle, its progression[1] and regression.[2]

DRUGS AND DELINQUENCY

Many adolescents have a dual problem of drug use and delinquency. Indeed, drug use affects a large percentage of the institutionalized delinquent population, both adult and juvenile (Cloutier et al., 1994; Brochu, 1995; Brochu et al., 1997; Dembo et al., 1997; Loeber et al., 1998). Many drug abusers undergoing treatment, whether adult or adolescent, admit to having previously committed at least one delinquent act (Hubbard et al., 1989; Guyon and Landry, 1993; Le Blanc, 1994b; Brochu, 1995; Byqvist and Olsson, 1998).

In an effort to explain the dual drug-crime problem experienced by many young people, numerous studies carried out over the past decades have focused on risk and protection factors likely to result in or prevent the adoption of behaviours consistent with a deviant lifestyle. A deficient family environment (Hawkins et al., 1992; Tubman, 1993; Petraitis et al., 1995; Patterson et al., 1998); school maladjustment (Tremblay et al., 1992; Farrington, 1994; Grapendaal et al. 1995; Loeber et al.,

1998); association with deviant peers (Brownfield and Thompson, 1991; Normand and Brochu, 1993; Farrington, 1994; Petraitis *et al.*, 1995; Patterson *et al.*, 1998); experiences of victimization (Hammersley *et al.*, 1990; Agnew, 1991; Dembo *et al.*, 1992a, 1992b; Miller and Downs, 1995; Alexander, 1996) and precocity of deviant experiences (White *et al.*, 1990; Windle, 1990; Hawkins *et al.*, 1992; McCord, 1995; Loeber and Farrington, 1998; Patterson *et al.*, 1998) are some of the most frequently mentioned risk factors. On the contrary, close ties to parents, ample time spent as a family, involvement in school, academic and social competency, adoption of social norms and values, positive self-esteem and allocentrism seem to constitute protective factors, which enable young people to resist the influence of risk factors leading notably to delinquency and drug abuse (Hawkins *et al.*, 1992; Cloutier, 1996; Loeber *et al.*, 1998).[3]

While the studies on risk and protection factors are very informative, they fall short of providing an overall understanding of the processes leading to youth deviance.[4] They are usually conducted from a predictive, and thus relatively deterministic, perspective, generally focusing on the collection of factual material, thus restricting our understanding of the phenomenon, while giving insufficient consideration to young people's role as social actors likely to participate in determining their own destiny (Debuyst, 1989). These statistical studies produce essentially soulless, functional analyses (Cousineau and Hamel, forthcoming) and do not highlight the connections made by young people between the various situations and feelings they experience, which would provide us with a better understanding of the personal logic that they develop with regard to their deviant lifestyle.

Like Debuyst (1989), we shall treat the young person as a situated social actor, as a subject capable of taking initiatives, of being creative and rational, of reacting to his or her destiny. From this perspective, delinquent or addicted adolescents are not the victim of a psychoactive substance or of imposed circumstances; instead, young people are seen as interacting with their personal and social environment and organizing their lives according to their own point of view. Young people's behaviour is seen as being less directly tied to past external determining factors than to the meaning they currently attribute to their life experience, which is influenced by, among other things, their perception of past and present life events. Thus this perspective is based on a phenomenological understanding of deviance (Schutz, 1987).

DEVIANT TRAJECTORIES FROM A PHENOMENOLOGICAL PERSPECTIVE

In discussing the juvenile deviance process, we shall use the term 'trajectory' because it permits us to focus on life experiences and their chronological evolution, and can reflect the more phenomenological aspects connected to meaning attributed to these events and the feelings they induce. The use of the term 'trajectory' also makes it possible to reflect the circuitous nature of the subject's evolution.[5]

One of the most highly documented areas on the topic of deviant trajectories is the progression of juvenile delinquency in terms of the nature, diversity and seriousness of the offences committed over the entire course of the delinquent trajectory (Fréchette and Le Blanc, 1987; Le Blanc, 1994a; Kelley *et al.*, 1997). In scientific literature, this criminal progression has often been associated with personality structure and, more recently, related to the psychosocial context in which the progression occurs. Certain longitudinal studies have made such links to the psychosocial context, but in a purely quantitative manner by studying a limited number of dimensions (for example, relationship with family, association with deviant peers, sexual promiscuity), using the verification of research hypotheses as a starting point (deductive process) rather than the young people's own perceptions (inductive process) (Simons *et al.*, 1994; Nagin *et al.*, 1995; Le Blanc and Kaspi, 1998). Thus they pay little attention to young people's underlying account – an account which, when examined, proves to be most revealing (Binet and Sherif, 1992; Piron, 1993, 1996; Billson, 1996; Way, 1998). In the study discussed in this chapter, the young people's point of view serves as the initial point of reference from which the conclusions are drawn (inductive process).

Further, several longitudinal or 'trajectory' studies assume that there is a general tendency among the majority of juvenile delinquents towards consistent or progressive delinquency during the first part of adolescence (12–15 years of age), which continues beyond this point in the case of the (more) active minority (Hirshi and Gottfredson, 1983; Fréchette and Le Blanc, 1987; Le Blanc, 1994a; Lanctôt and Le Blanc, 2000). Horney *et al.* (1995) have shown that adult deviance is marked by short term variations, affected by changes in context such as cohabitation with a spouse, drug use and so on. Similarly, we believe that the deviant trajectories of juveniles are not, in fact, linear. What is of interest here is primarily the elements that, in the young people's own opinion, trigger change in one direction or the other (towards conformism or towards deviance). By using qualitative methodology to deepen our understanding of the processes that direct and dictate deviant juvenile trajectories, we will be able to identify means of intervention that are effective with juveniles because they correspond directly to the young people's own experience.

METHOD

For this study, we adopted the autobiographical account method (Desmarais and Grell, 1986) which, because it allows subjects to speak freely about their life while favouring a chronological discourse structure, permits description of an individual's trajectory from the individual's own perspective. In particular, this means of data collection enables researchers to obtain material that is not strictly factual, which was our objective.

The qualitative principle of empirical saturation was used to establish the sample group: in order to obtain a fair representation of reality, collection of data was terminated when interviews revealed no new or different information, that is, when any additional data proved to be repetitive or essentially anecdotal (Mayer and Ouellet, 1991; Pirès, 1997). The final sample comprised 38 young Montreal adolescents, girls and boys, ages 16 to 18, Francophones of Québécois origin. It was made up of two subgroups: 28 juveniles who had been institutionalized in a judicial institution or drug treatment centre (institutionalized respondents: IR) (18 boys; 10 girls) and 10 juveniles who had never been institutionalized in such institutions, encountered at a recreational youth centre (non-IR) (four boys and six girls).

Content analysis of interviews (Bardin, 1977; L'Écuyer, 1990) and, more specifically, thematic analysis (Ghiglione and Matalon, 1978) were the principal means employed to reduce the material. First, researchers proceeded vertically, conducting a within-case analysis of each of the interviews; then they proceeded transversally, attempting to identify points on which narratives converged or diverged.

Furthermore, a sequential analysis of events and their effects on the youth, according to his (her) own view, was conducted. For this sequential analysis, three biographical lines illustrating respectively general history (social trajectory), drug use and delinquency at different ages were drawn and graphically produced for each respondent in order to be linked with each other.

PORTRAIT OF RESPONDENTS

Most of the young people in both groups (IR and non-IR) came from families with two or more children. In the majority of the cases, the parents had separated during the youth's childhood. As well, almost half of IR and non-IR respondents mentioned that at least one of their parents had used illegal drugs for many years, or was an alcoholic. The majority of IR and non-IR respondents, whether girls or boys, admitted to having been physically or sexually abused on one or more occasions.

Delinquency preceded drug use on the majority of young IR respondents' trajectories (n = 17). Other IR youths stated that they had begun their use of illegal drugs before their involvement in petty crime (n = 10), while a minority had begun both deviant behaviours at the same age (n = 3). The non-IR youths present a different portrait. First, only four out of 10 youths admitted to having engaged in both delinquent acts and illegal drug use[6] (dual problem). Two of the four stated that their delinquency had begun before their drug use, while the other two stated the opposite.[7] Essentially, with only three exceptions (Anouk, Quincy and Samuel), the non-IR respondents generally described a less deviant lifestyle than the IR youths in our sample.

THE EVOLUTION OF DEVIANT LIFESTYLES

Prior to the deviant lifestyle: childhood

To understand how juveniles have come to adopt a deviant lifestyle, it is important to begin by examining the meanings and emotions that the young people associate with the circumstances surrounding their childhood, circumstances which preceded their first delinquent and drug experiences. While various studies have provided information concerning the nature and number of risk factors confronting juveniles (Clayton, 1992; Hawkins *et al.*, 1992; Vitaro *et al.*, 1994; Yoshikawa, 1994; Petraitis *et al.*, 1995; Garnier and Stein, 1998; Lloyd, 1998), few have consulted juveniles to verify how the latter experience and interpret these risk factors or life experiences, which is what we propose to do here.

Negative feelings in institutionalized youths

Several IR youths, in particular, stated that they had experienced and occasionally still did experience negative feelings – rejection, guilt and contempt – in connection with events that had occurred during their childhood, before their involvement in deviant activities. Their statements reveal a certain degree of 'touchiness', leading them to 'take personally' situations they find disagreeable and in which they may be directly or indirectly involved.

For example, Arianne, an IR juvenile, tells of the feeling of rejection she experienced in connection with her parents' separation and, more specifically, with her father's subsequent attitude towards her sister and herself:

> It's like, after he left us, he didn't want to see us anymore. We moved, and he said: 'We're separated now. We'll see each other once every two weeks', then it was once every three weeks, then once every two months... I felt rejected. He's your father, he's the one who created you, and then he leaves right afterwards. It seems to me that we were his responsibility. If he didn't want to take care of us, he could have not brought us into the world.

Another IR juvenile, Isabelle, feels she is responsible or guilty for the arguments that led to her parents' separation:

> I feel as if I'm the one who caused the separation. I feel guilty. I feel guilty about my entire childhood. I feel guilty about my parents' divorce... My parents were always fighting and arguing ...

Non-IR youths like Anouk, on the contrary, do not seem to have felt rejected by their parents after their parents' separation:

> My parents always loved me the same. I know that. It's just that they don't love each other anymore, so they got separated.

The non-IR youth Victor dissociates himself from the circumstances surrounding his parents' arguments of the past:

> I let them go at it, I told myself: 'they can solve their problems themselves'. So I didn't pay attention to it. I thought it was stupid because, say I fought with my sister, they'd tell me to stop fighting and everything, but then, after that, they'd fight... But I think it's funny, you know, it doesn't bother me especially, you know, it's just that I find it stupid or I dunno, you know.

Thus several IR youths in the sample expressed feelings of rejection, guilt or contempt when recounting events from their childhood that concerned the family as a whole. This is consistent with Cloutier *et al.*'s (1994) finding that adolescent youth centre (centre jeunesse) institutionalized youths are more negative about their lives, particularly with regard to feelings of personal well-being and anxiety, than young students (or, in the current study, non-IR recreational youth centre respondents). Non-IR respondents seemed to experience fewer negative feelings in connection with their childhood context even though, from an objective viewpoint, many of the childhood situations they had experienced were similar to those experienced by IR youth (parental separation, drug-addicted or alcoholic parents, victimization experiences). Similarly, Born *et al.* (1997) affirm that resilience (here associated with the lifestyle of non-IR youths) is more closely tied to personal, intra-individual variables (for example, maturity, adjustment potential) than to objective familial factors (for example, delinquent family members, broken home). The current study focuses more specifically on the personal variables of meanings and emotions associated with experiences, with IR youths reporting greater dissatisfaction with their childhood context than non-IR adolescents who had undergone many similar experiences.

Adoption of a deviant lifestyle

In this study, the adoption of a deviant lifestyle stage is understood to consist of initiation into and initial involvement in the deviant behaviour of illegal drug consumption or that of delinquency, or both. Many IR and non-IR youths associate positive meanings and emotions with their adoption of a deviant lifestyle.

Pleasure

Several authors have previously shown the importance of pleasure in the genesis of delinquency (Cusson, 1989; Gottfredson and Hirshi, 1990; Le Blanc, 1996) and drug use (Therrien, 1994; Glauser, 1995; Collison, 1996). Indeed, pleasure was the initial motivation for drug use and delinquency most frequently mentioned by the young people interviewed for this study. Thus, Nathan and Antoine (IR youths) tell of the positive light in which they viewed their experiences with drugs during the initial stage of their drug use:

> At first, it was just for fun, see. (Antoine)

> All I saw was that it was 'cool' and I liked the high. In the beginning, just five bucks of hash makes you laugh like crazy, like crazy, man ... (Nathan)

It was somewhat different for some non-IR youths, who cite curiosity as being at the root of their first deviant experiences:

> Well, like the first time I tried it, it was to see what it was like ... (Tania)

> Pot smelled good, so we tried it... Acid was a 'trip' I wanted to try. (Quincy)

Anouk states that she and her best friend have engaged in various forms of experimentation, largely through curiosity:

> ... I think that it was more out of curiosity like, with my best friend... For three years, we've done almost everything together, we've tried almost everything together ... We wanted to know what it was like.

Authors such as Fagan and Chin (1990) and Erickson and Weber (1994) have already shown that initiation into deviant behaviours often occurs in a context of curiosity or solidarity. The accounts of IR and non-IR youths seem to support this finding, expressing it in the young people's own words. Moreover, in their discourse, the juveniles explicitly associate the beginning of their deviant lifestyle with playful motivations (pleasure). More specifically, for them, pleasure, laughter, sensation seeking, curiosity and solidarity constitute the playful motivations that they associate with their first misdemeanours and incidents of illegal drug use.

Positive self-esteem

It is generally accepted that deviant behaviours, particularly delinquency and drug use, play an important role in the development of self-esteem for those who engage in such behaviours (Kaplan, 1995; Glauser, 1995; Warner *et al.*, 1999). Many youths who neither felt appreciated nor liked themselves very much at other times, IRs in particular, stated that delinquency and drug use gave them greater self-esteem. The account of Louis (an IR youth) is particularly eloquent in this regard:

> And you know, I didn't have very high self-esteem then, you know. The only way I found to feel more important was to show the others that I had balls, and that I wasn't scared. So I started doing little crimes, little things you know. And I started doing drugs around that time too. You know, you had to prove who was toughest. And, little by little, that's how I started to feel better about myself, and say, like, I'm tough. Like, I smoke dope, I steal and everything, Louis's no wimp, you know. That's how it all started.

According to Louis, the feeling of self-worth his deviance gave him explains why he adopted a deviant lifestyle. Referring to the thefts and drugs, he clearly states: 'That's how it all started.'

On somewhat similar lines, non-IR juveniles, like Sandra, explain that they became involved with illicit drugs or delinquency out of a desire to fit in, to reinforce their sense of belonging and identity:

> It was harder to adapt when I got back to Canada than when I arrived there [in Africa]... I was used to the Grade 7s here, and then, there you are in Grade 9 [after two years away]: 'okay, what do I do now?' I didn't know how to deal with them. That's why I said to myself: 'okay, I'm going to do what everyone else does. I'm going to drink, I'm going to take drugs, I'm going to smoke and everything.' I wanted to be like everyone else.

The dimension of positive self-esteem, which bears a certain similarity to the dimension of pleasure mentioned earlier, specifically in terms of their shared agreeable nature, is associated primarily, in the young people's discourse, with a state of dissatisfaction or a feeling of inadequacy which disappears (temporarily) with perceived appreciation of their deviant behaviours by their peers.

Thus, for both IR and non-IR youths, the processes of initiation into deviance generally appear to grow out of 'commonplace' factors (Bouhnik, 1996); here, the 'commonplace' factors are pleasurable motivations and increased self-worth. Certain authors believe that the juveniles who adopt the most deviant and persistent trajectories differ from the others through heightened egocentricity and hedonism, and increased sensation seeking and so on (Fréchette and Le Blanc, 1987, Cusson, 1989; Martin and Robbins, 1995; Wood *et al.*, 1995; Loeber *et al.*, 1998). According to our study, this distinction does not seem to apply at the beginning of the deviant trajectory. There seems to be no difference between IR and non-IR youths (the latter having a less deviant lifestyle) in our sample with regard to the motivations for their first misdemeanours and initial incidents of illegal drug use. In their accounts, the young people described the adoption of a deviant lifestyle stage in terms of feelings of pleasure, sensation seeking, self-worth, sense of belonging and identity, curiosity and solidarity.

Progression of the deviant lifestyle

For most youths, the intensification of their deviant lifestyle seems linked to their interpretation of the events they have experienced, and the meaning they attribute to the latter.

Amnesic functions of drugs

Dina (IR juvenile) was sexually assaulted by her stepfather. At first, she did not want to believe it or to make a connection between the aggression and her deviant behaviour, but later, she said that she had felt very ashamed of the situation, which had caused her to take more drugs in an effort to forget:

> It {the sexual abuse] lasted a month, and at first I didn't believe it; afterwards, I got deeper into drugs, so that I could cut myself off and hide from everything.

For her part, Pamela (another IR juvenile) associates the difficult relationship she had with her father during a particular period in her life with the concurrent intensification of her deviant lifestyle:

> My father associated me with what happened between him and my mother, so I went maybe three years without seeing him, and saying as little as possible to him. And during that time, I'd take what I needed to escape and not think about anything. And then I started doing lots of mescaline... It was like, as long as I'm good and high...: it was as if I wasn't really there anymore, I didn't feel what was going on, it hurt too much.

These two excerpts highlight the amnesic function of drugs associated with a desire to escape one's problems. This motivation for drug use was mentioned by the young people in our sample on numerous occasions. Other authors have shown that drugs in particular can fulfil the role of permitting a subject to forget his or her problems or anaesthetizing suffering at certain times, especially as deviant behaviours become an increasingly important part of the youth's lifestyle (Tremblay and Wener, 1991; Cormier, 1993; Glauser, 1995; Bouhnik, 1996; Brunelle *et al.*, 1998). In the cases mentioned above, analysis of the young people's comments, in which they associate perceptions and feelings with certain life events and with their subsequent reactions, indicates a connection established by the young people themselves between their own perception of the events and their adoption of deviant behaviours.

Marking events: turning points

It would appear that, for many juveniles, certain events represented turning points which resulted in a more deviant lifestyle with more pronounced, lasting involvement in drug abuse and delinquency, in terms of either frequency, quantity or intensity/seriousness. The discourse of many of the youths, in particularly of the IR youths, is built around an important event which may be read as a turning point in their progression towards a more deviant lifestyle (Brunelle *et al.*, 1997a, 1997b). The young respondents construct their life histories around this event, which represents far more than a temporal reference point in their discourse: almost everything in their account is defined as occurring either before or after or in relation to this turning point.

The impact of these events depends, of course, on their nature, but also on when they occur and, above all, on how they are interpreted by the young people. The interpretation brings together both the juvenile's feelings and the event's relationship to other situations the young person has experienced, giving a meaning to his or her life experience as a whole (Brunelle *et al.*, 1998).

Thus it is clear to Lilianne (an IR juvenile) that the moment her mother admitted to her that she was homosexual, Lilianne's life underwent an abrupt change of direction. This event is very important to her because she believes it to be the cause of several painful situations: her parents' separation, early and intense questioning of her own sexuality and the termination of a romantic relationship (her mother having fallen in love with her boyfriend's mother, the relationship between the two young people became impossible). Variations in Lilianne's drug use tend to be linked to the issue of her mother's lesbian relationships, which provides the key element around which Lilianne organizes her own life history:

I've moved at least five or six times...I went to live in the country near Rivière-du-Loup. My mother had been with the same woman for a year. I thought it was absolutely disgusting... Then she tells me: 'Come home, Lilianne. I got back together with your father a week ago.' I was super happy. I started to go back like I used to be, stopped doing drugs, stopped drinking... And then I came back, and two days later she went back to the other one. After that, I went back to using even more, all the time. I was always stoned, always.

As for Louis, an IR youth, he had been shifted from child care institution to foster home to group home before finally finding a family with whom he felt happy. Virtually overnight, the Child Protection Agency (DPJ) decided to remove the foster family's accreditation, which meant that Louis could no longer stay with them. Then, as for now, the event elicited a slew of emotions for Louis. He says that initially he experienced a great deal of anger:

And then I felt like, you know, I felt incredibly powerless. And then I began to raise my voice and became more aggressive [with the DPJ representative when she told him of the removal of the foster family's accreditation]. I said: 'Hey, now, you can't do that like that. You have no right, you know.' I said: 'Christ, we do have rights, you know...' Anyway, just thinking about it makes me mad.

Then, he says, he felt completely discouraged about his life:

That was like the last straw, when you say that your life never goes anywhere, and every time you begin to feel a bit better, when you've just about got your head above water when, bang, something happens to push you right back down where you started from. It's always like that, you know, I felt like my life was going around in circles, you know, and that it did no good, you know...

Louis associates this event with his low self-esteem, which he clearly expresses throughout his account:

And uh, my self-esteem wasn't very high either, you know... I said to myself, 'Whatever'... you don't tell yourself you deserve it but you act that way anyway, unconsciously. You feel like that, you feel like a piece of shit... It's like you experience it and you take it a little as if you deserved it somehow, you know. You feel guilty for tons of things that basically you shouldn't, you know.

The conclusion Louis draws from the different events he has experienced, particularly this key event in his story, is clear: 'You wind up thinking you deserved it, that you're a piece of shit.' This is how he came to believe that he had nothing to lose in turning to petty crime and especially in taking drugs:

And uh, the biggest problem, it's not really the crimes, it's more the dope, you know. And uh, a little what happened was, you know, it was like I didn't have much to lose so, uh, go for it, you know? Instead of basically sitting in a corner all depressed, and thinking of suicide all the time, and everything, you know. It wasn't really my style, you know, suicide.

Kaplan (1995) has suggested that drug use may be linked to loss of motivation to conform to dominant values, and that one may be tempted to deviate from such values when one has had humiliating experiences with 'conformists'. Louis' case seems to corroborate this: the DPJ's removal of the foster family's accreditation was, in a sense, the final straw that convinced him that he was worthless, simultaneously destroying what little self-esteem he still possessed.

As the stories of Lilianne and Louis demonstrate, it is not necessarily the events themselves that constitute turning points in the young person's life, it is the young person's interpretation of them, the importance the young person attributes to them and the emotions generated by them. To understand young people's evolution, it is not enough to itemize potentially disturbing events that have occurred in their lives. In order to truly appreciate the consequences of events, one must be able to understand the meanings juveniles have attributed to them, the importance they give them. It so happens that these meanings and emotions can only be revealed by the young people themselves in an interview context in which they are allowed to speak as freely as possible.

Taking into account not only the presence of certain elements contained in the young people's accounts, but the structure of the accounts as well, one observes, for example, that for many IR juveniles, during the periods of progression on their deviant trajectories, the playful dimension present at the time of the adoption of the deviant lifestyle fades somewhat or entirely. Indeed, in their accounts, the juveniles associate these periods of progression with situations they found difficult. Thus their motivations evolve. Among the non-IR youths in the sample, the lifestyle described above as less deviant seems to have remained at the same level or diminished. Tania (a non-IR juvenile) explains how she maintained her drug use at the same level without increasing it, as the result of a deviant incident which she experienced negatively and a feeling of powerlessness (loss of control) she associated with the incident:

> But it depends; I don't like to go too far, for example. I don't like to completely lose control. Like ... I've never been sick, but there was this one time when I really didn't feel good, I was freaking. I was sitting on the couch and, you know, I felt as if I was constantly falling back and back and back. I was screaming, I was totally freaking out. I really didn't like it, you know.

Unlike the IR youths' case continuation of involvement in deviant behaviour is more a matter of purely playful motivations for non-IR youths, as if their motivations did not evolve after their adoption of the deviant lifestyle. For Victor, a non-IR youth, pleasure continues to be his principle, if not sole, motivation for drug use, and pleasure is made possible in a party context with his friends:

> But me, I do drugs more at a party with friends, just for fun.

The preceding examples imply that the continuation – or progression – of IR youths' involvement in deviant behaviour is tied to a desire to escape from one's problems, an increasingly 'amnesic' pleasure, while that of non-IR adolescents' deviant involvement generally continues to be driven by playful motivations. Thus, for many youths, the quest for pleasure, either playful or amnesic, is always present throughout the course of their deviant trajectory. It is important that youths be asked to elaborate further when they say that they take drugs or commit crimes for 'fun'. Analysis of the life histories of the youths in our study indicates that the type of 'fun' that is sought after in an effort to forget the reality of one's life is more closely tied to the progression of a deviant lifestyle than is the purely playful type of 'fun', and that it is most commonly mentioned by IR youths.

Regression of deviant lifestyles

The deviant lifestyle trajectories of the young people we encountered are scattered with periods when involvement in delinquency or drug use temporarily or 'permanently' declined. Qualitative studies which treat the decline of deviant lifestyles more or less directly tend to be more specifically concerned with social rehabilitation of homeless or drug-addicted adults (Castel *et al.*, 1992; Racine and Mercier, 1995), and young delinquents and drug addicts are underrepresented in them.

Furthermore, most studies (quantitative and qualitative) which examine the decline of deviant lifestyles are concerned with the more general reduction in delinquency that comes with age, particularly at the end of adolescence and after the age of 30 (Gauss curve) (Hirshi and Gottfredson, 1983; Le Blanc, 1994a). Their focus is on a more long-term regression (decrease), generally observable in adulthood. For our part, we are as interested in the temporary periods of regression in deviant lifestyles on young respondents' trajectories as in the more durable ones.

The inventoried reasons linked to this decrease in involvement in delinquency or drug use are many and varied depending on the individual, whether it be a question of maturation, values, employment, life events or something else. (Ouimet and Le Blanc, 1993; Sampson and Laub, 1993; Brochu, 1995; Grapendaal *et al.*, 1995; Kelley *et al.*, 1997; Vaughn and Long, 1999). Here, we will examine the young people's point of view with regard to the reasons which led them to decrease their involvement in deviant behaviour at certain times.

Positive influence of peers

According to some young respondents, a period during which they associated with friends or a girlfriend or boyfriend whose lifestyle was characterized by little or no deviance would be linked to an interruption or decrease in their own involvement in deviant behaviour. For example, Isabelle (IR juvenile) stated that she temporarily stopped taking illegal drugs and committing certain delinquent acts during a period when she spent a lot of time with what she calls 'normal people':

> I have some good friends who helped me stop doing drugs two years ago. I stopped assaulting people, doing stupid things. I stopped hanging out with my gang. I'd changed friends. They were normal people, like you and me, people like that.

For Quincy, a non-IR youth, dating a girl who did not take illegal drugs and who did not like it when he took them, influenced his decision to diminish and then cease his use of cannabis:

> Since I've been going out with my girlfriend, well you know, before that, my friend and I would do blotters almost every day. But since I've been going out with her you know... In the beginning when I started dating her, I'd do a blotter once a month. After that, I stopped. I'd smoke up but now I don't anymore. It's been about four months since I last smoked a joint. It's rare now. Well, I knew she didn't like it... And then she started to freak out. So then I cut back and I stopped.

Like Isabelle and Quincy, certain young people in both of the sample's subgroups (IR and non-IR) mentioned experiencing a 'temporary' sense of belonging to a conformist group, or to what one might call a conformist identity, in explanation of a period of regression in their deviant lifestyle. The role played by conformist peers in the abandonment of deviance has been pointed out by Esbensen and Elliot (1994). As illustrated by the following excerpt from Nathan's account, the young respondents in our study generally mentioned these periods as being a positive part of their lives:

> One of my friends started getting on my tail to stop doing drugs. Those guys, my old childhood buddies, they hadn't dropped me. They didn't drop me during that whole period. So that's it, they had stopped doing drugs, and then they started working out, and getting jobs and you know, a normal life. And that's it, they wanted to talk me into doing the same. That's when I realized a lot of things that, that I was fed up with that sort of life,

that I was better, that I liked myself more when I didn't do drugs. That I felt good when I didn't do drugs, that I was somebody, that I was a man, you know...

Our study highlights the positive view the young people hold of periods of regression in their deviant lifestyle associated with the positive influence of conformist peers. This dimension is certainly encouraging from an intervention perspective.

Social representations

For Pamela and Arianne (IR juveniles), a period of reduced deviance followed a psychoactive substance transition (from cannabis and chemical drugs to cocaine), a transition which prompted them to request treatment:

> Then, in the end, it had really gotten to the point like, you know, like I started doing white stuff and then I said to myself: 'No, I don't want to start selling my ass down on Sainte Catherine's', I didn't feel good anymore, I was really unhappy... (Pamela)

> I didn't do coke for long because I went into [voluntary] treatment not long afterwards. Because coke, you know, I didn't want to go there. But even my other friends, they weren't doing good at all, you know, I'd look at them and I was like: 'Fuck, I'm becoming just like them.' They were practically on the street. I didn't want to be on the street. Things were bad with my mom, things were bad with my dad, things were bad with my boyfriend. (Arianne)

In Pamela's and Arianne's minds, they had reached the 'critical limit': for them, cocaine use represented prostitution and homelessness. The social image they had of it made them realize that they did not want to go that far, that they had become too unhappy and that cocaine use would make them even more so. Thus the actions of these IR juveniles are guided by their values, beliefs and feelings.

Concerning adult drug addicts, studies have shown that beliefs, feelings or social representations could explain at least temporarily cessation of drug use (Erickson and Weber, 1994; Mercier and Alarie, 2001). A clear example of this is the belief that injecting drugs represents a too dangerous and addictive mode of drug use (Erickson and Weber, 1994) or that heroin consumption causes all kinds of troubles (Duprez and Kokoreff, 2000). Here we see that fear of experiencing a situation which one represents to oneself as being extremely negative can cause young drug users and delinquents who feel unhappy to put a halt to their deviant lifestyle at certain points along their trajectory. It should be remembered that these young people 'developed' this social representation of cocaine use based on their own and other people's perception, and their experience of society in general (Blumer, 1969).

Feeling of having too much to lose or nothing to gain

The fear of losing living conditions judged to be relatively satisfactory was cited in the non-IR group in a somewhat similar fashion to the notion of a critical threshold discussed above, to explain decreased involvement in deviant activity. What distinguishes this group of juveniles from Pamela and Arianne, the IR juveniles quoted above, besides the question of institution, is the non-IR juveniles' perception of their living conditions and feeling of general well-being. In effect, Pamela and

Arianne describe themselves as being initially dissatisfied with their living conditions, while the young people in the following examples describe relatively satisfactory perceptions of initial well-being.

Anouk (a non-IR juvenile) states that she is aware that her delinquency could further compromise her relationship with her mother. Anouk lives with her mother and, while her relationship with the latter is growing more acrimonious, she is scared of having to go and live with her father whom she finds too severe. She has therefore stopped shoplifting:

> I don't do it anymore, I calmed down because I said to myself that if I get caught again ... It's not that I mind getting caught or that I feel bad, it's just that they call my mom. Like, I don't want her to be angry with me. And it's a bit much, I already cause her enough headaches. After all, I want to continue living there; if I didn't live there, where would I live? I don't want to go live with my dad, it's hell living with him. He's way too strict.

The risk of seeing one's living conditions affected (represented here by a possible change in residence) certainly has a less dissuasive effect when the youth does not consider existing conditions to be satisfactory.

Samuel (a non-IR youth) explains, for his part, that his use of psychoactive drugs diminished significantly as a result of, on the one hand, the fear that his parents, with whom he has a good relationship, would find out he was taking drugs and, on the other hand, the feeling that he had nothing to gain from what had developed into drug abuse:

> And then, at a certain point, I had two really intense weeks, and I got like fed up. I said to myself: 'Why? What does it change?' It's mainly, you know, that my parents didn't know. Every time I'd go home, I never knew if my parents would figure out what was going on, every time, you know. And then, at a certain point, I got fed up with being afraid, and I realized that I wasn't gaining anything by it. So you know, why be afraid of something that does nothing for you? ... And like 'No more, I'm going to stop.'

Thus, for non-IR juveniles like Anouk and Samuel, the sense of having too much to lose or nothing to gain creates the impression of having reached a limit, which can provide an explanation for the abandonment of their deviant activities either in whole or in part. For the IR youths in our study, this limit or threshold comes at the end of a much more advanced continuum of deviance frequency and seriousness than for the non-IR youths, and seems to be more closely tied to social representations than to the fear of compromising either relationships or relatively satisfying living conditions. The feeling of having a great deal to lose on both interpersonal and social levels is also apparent in explanations provided by the non-IR youths for choosing not to become involved at all or more deeply involved in deviant behaviour. Conversely, many IR youths use the argument of having nothing to lose in becoming involved in delinquency and psychotropic drug use to justify the continuation and progression of their deviant activities (Brunelle, Cousineau and Brochu, 2002).

It seems that attachment to parents and their values, and scholastic involvement play a potentially dissuasive role for the youths in our sample who have never been institutionalized (non-IR). The dimensions of attachment and involvement with regard to primary institutions of socialization such as the family and school, as well as the potential of such institutions for informal social control have been discussed many times by different authors (Hirshi, 1969; Sampson and Laub, 1993; Benda, 1999). Smith and Brame (1994) state that, while social control theory is able to explain why youths do or do not become involved in a deviant activity, it does not explain why the youths' involvement in such a lifestyle continues or progresses. Without confirming the applicability of social control theory as a whole to the origins of involvement in deviance, our results seem to support the notion of a relationship in adolescents having adopted a less deviant lifestyle (non-IR) between the specific dimension of familial attachment and periods of decreased delinquency and illicit drug use.

CONCLUSION

Several authors have treated deviant trajectories in terms of initiation (risk factors), persistence, intensification (frequency, seriousness), progression and abandonment of behaviours, but none, to our knowledge, has examined trajectory evolution from the point of view of young people and especially in connection with the meanings juveniles attribute to their experiences and the feelings provoked by these experiences. In order to shed a different, phenomenological, light on the deviant trajectories of adolescents, we have focused on the meanings and feelings associated by the young people in their discourse with periods of adoption, progression and regression in their deviant lifestyle.

Our study is thus unique in that, instead of focusing on behaviours, factual elements and sequences, it concentrates on young people's own personal logic concerning the trajectory they follow in connection with a deviant lifestyle. Autobiographical accounts allow respondents to make connections between the different situations they have experienced, and to express their feelings vis-à-vis these situations. Only the respondents themselves can explain the importance specific experiences may hold in their lives, and the connections the experiences may have with their deviant lifestyles.

From the point of view of the juveniles (IR and non-IR alike), the processes involved in the adoption of a deviant lifestyle were primarily a result of playful motivations or a desire to enhance one's self-worth, while processes leading to the progression of a deviant lifestyle, which affected IR youths to a greater extent, involved negative feelings instead: shame, guilt, rejection, contempt, negative self-esteem, as well as a desire to forget one's problems. It seems that, for IR youths, marking events formed turning points resulting in a still more deviant lifestyle; the importance these events held for the youths was determined by the young people's own interpretation of the events and negative feelings concerning them. More precisely, it seems that IR youths experienced more negative feelings in connection with their past or present life context than did non-IR adolescents, and that there was a connection between this growing dissatisfaction and the periods of progression in their deviant lifestyle.

The young IR and non-IR respondents disclosed that their deviant lifestyle regressed during periods which involved: (a) positive feelings associated with a more conformist identity – resulting from associations which were, themselves, of a more conformist nature, (b) negative social representations associated with cocaine use, homelessness and prostitution and (c) restoration of a degree of well-being judged satisfactory by the young person, or avoidance of the deterioration of a state of well-being. The sense of having too much to lose or nothing to gain by continuing deviant involvement is more specifically associated by non-IR youths with a temporary or more permanent decrease in deviance.

Thus, in the context of youth delinquency or drug abuse rehabilitation, it seems desirable to ask juveniles to describe their trajectory, and to identify periods of regression in their deviant lifestyle and, above all, what they associate with these periods, so as to work from the elements that they themselves will have identified. This way of working with young people seems more positive and constructive than focusing exclusively on relapse or recidivism factors, for example. The positive impact which the young people attributed to periods during which they associated with conformist peers is puzzling in light of the current 'trend' to isolate 'problem' youths so as to avoid their being in contact with other young people and 'contaminating' the latter, or to provide them with specific or 'adapted' services. Perhaps, instead, we should stimulate and provoke interaction between these different young people. Also our results seem to indicate that we should give greater encouragement to the establishment of adolescent peer helper groups. As can be observed in certain drug-abuse prevention programmes, for example, this involves training older adolescents so that they are able to listen to, help and support younger adolescents. It seems that conformist adolescents (who have perhaps not always been so) may enjoy greater credibility in the eyes of youths who have adopted a deviant lifestyle than conformist adults.

In light of these results, it seems to us that certain elements of the deviant lifestyle trajectory evade purely factual, risk factor-type analyses. Elements related to meanings and feelings deepen our understanding of the trajectory or rather of the different possible trajectories (Brunelle, Cousineau and Brochu 2002). Thus it would appear that the motivations and reasons associated with the adoption and evolution of a deviant lifestyle may consist of risk and protection factors already identified, and may be linked to the situational or more immediate context of the experience, but they are primarily associated with a 'state of mind' related to the youths' perceptions and feelings in connection with past or current situations or events. In short, the idea is to neglect neither aspect of the analysis of the deviant trajectories of young people, and probably of adults as well. Instead of being satisfied with the obvious, we must dig deeper, exploring the situational context of experiences and, above all, taking into account the point of view of the concerned party for, in the final analysis, it is the subject's own point of view which explains his behaviour and, hence, his trajectory. It is necessary to have access to the social actor's personal logic to fully understand the trajectory he has followed in a deviant lifestyle; we believe that our study takes one more step in this direction.

NOTES

1   Meaning an increase in deviant behaviours.
2   Meaning a decrease in deviant behaviours.

3   The studies on protection factors are more recent, and not as well known or developed as those on risk factors.
4   Few studies on risk or protection factors manage to explain more than 50 per cent of the total variance, which would seem to indicate that a different or additional approach would be better suited to understanding the phenomenon as a whole.
5   See Brunelle (2001) for a discussion on the choice of the term 'trajectory' over the terms 'career' and 'pathway'.
6   Juveniles who had committed a single offence during their childhood, or who had tried an illegal substance once or twice, were not considered to have adopted those two forms of deviant behaviour.
7   Subsequent drug/crime links on the pathways of IR and non-IR youths are discussed in another article (Brunelle, Cousineau and Brochu, 2002).

REFERENCES

Alexander, L.B. (1996), 'Women with co-occuring addictive and mental disorders: an emerging profile of vulnerability', *American Journal of Orthopsychiatry*, **66** (1), 61–70.

Bardin, L. (1977), *L'analyse de contenu*, Paris: Presses universitaires de France.

Benda, B.B. (1999), 'Theoretical model with reciprocal effects of youthful crime and drug use', *Journal of Social Service Research*, **25** (1/2), 77–107.

Billson, J.M. (1996), *Pathways to Manhood: Young Black Males Struggle for Identity*, New Brunswick: Transaction Publishers.

Binet, L. and Sherif, T. (1992), 'Les récits de vie, mode d'emploi', *Revue canadienne de service social*, **9** (2), 183–200.

Blumer, H. (1969), *Symbolic Interactionism: Perspective and Method*, Englewood Cliffs: Prentice-Hall.

Born, M., Chevalier, V. and Humblet, I. (1997), 'Resilience, desistance and delinquent career of adolescent offenders', *Journal of Adolescence*, **20**, 679–94.

Bouhnik, P. (1996), 'Système de vie et trajectoires des consommateurs d'héroïne en milieu urbain défavorisé,' *Communications*, **62**, 241–56.

Brochu, S. (1995), *Drogue et criminalité: une relation complexe*, Collection perspectives criminologiques, Montreal: Presses de l'Université de Montréal.

Brochu, S. and Brunelle, N. (1997), 'Toxicomanie et délinquance: une question de style de vie?', *Psychotropes*, **3** (4), 107–25.

Brochu, S., Morissette, P., Larkin, J.G. and Chayer, L. (1997), '*Toxicomanies et prévention au Québec et en Amérique du Nord*', paper presented at Journées de formation et d'études de l'ANPASE, Aix-les-Bains, 1997.

Brownfield, D. and Thompson, K. (1991), 'Attachment to peers and delinquent behavior', *Canadian Journal of Criminology*, **33** (1), 45–60.

Brunelle, N. (2001), 'Trajectoires déviantes à l'adolescence', unpublished PhD thesis, University of Montreal.

Brunelle, N., Brochu, S. and Cousineau, M.-M. (1998), 'Des cheminements vers un style de vie déviant: adolescents des centres jeunesse et des centres pour toxicomanes', Cahiers de recherches criminologiques (no. 27), Montréal, Centre international de criminologie comparée, Université de Montréal.

Brunelle, N., Cousineau, M.-M. and Brochu, S. (1997a), 'Cheminement vers un style de vie déviant: pré-expérimentation', Montréal, Centre international de Criminologie comparée, Université de Montréal.

Brunelle, N., Cousineau, M.-M. and Brochu, S. (1997b), 'Comprendu le jeune déliquante à travers son Listoire de vie', *Psychologie*, **14** (3), 19–22.

Brunelle, N., Cousineau, M.-M. and Brochu, S. (2002), 'Trajectoires types de la déviance juvénile: un regard qualitatif', *Revue canadienne de criminologie*, **44** (1), 1–31.

Byqvist, S. and Olsson, B. (1998), 'Male drug abuse, criminality and subcultural affiliation in a career perspective', *Journal of Psychoactive Drugs*, **30** (1), 53–68.

Castel, R., Benard-Pellen, M., Bonnemain, C., Boullenger, N., Coppel, A., Leclerc, G., Ogien, A. and Weinberg, M. (1992), *Les sorties de la toxicomanie; types, trajectoires, tonalités*, Paris: Groupe de recherche et d'analyse du social et de la sociabilité.

Clayton, R.R. (1992), 'Transitions in Drug Use: Risk and Protective Factors', in M. Glantz, and R. Pickens (eds), *Vulnerability to Drug Abuse*, Washington: American Psychological Association, pp.15–51.

Cloutier, R. (1996), *Psychologie de l'adolescence*, 2nd edn, Boucherville: Gaëtan Morin.

Cloutier, R., Champoux, L., Jacques and C., Lancop, C. (1994), '"Nos ados et les autres": étude comparative des adolescents des Centres jeunesse du Québec et des élèves du secondaire', Sainte-Foy : Centre de recherche sur les services communautaires, Université Laval.

Collison, M. (1996), 'In search of the high life', *British Journal of Criminology*, **36** (3), 428–44.

Cormier, D. (1993), *Toxicomanies: styles de vie*, Montreal: Méridien.

Cousineau, M.-M. and Hamel, S. (in preparation), 'Conducting trajectory analysis of the gang phenomenon in order to understand or to normalize: Distinct approaches resulting in distinct conclusions'.

Cusson, M. (1989), *Délinquants pourquoi?*, Montreal: Bibliothèque québécoise.

Debuyst, C. (1989), *Acteur social et délinquance*, Brussels: Pierre Mardaga.

Dembo, R., Pacheco, K., Scmeidler, J., Fisher, L. and Cooper, S. (1997), 'Drug use and delinquent behavior among high risk youths', *Journal of Child and Adolescent Substance Abuse*, **6** (2), 1–25.

Dembo, R., Williams, L., Wothke, W., Schmeidler, J. and Brown, C.H. (1992a), 'The role of family factors, physical abuse, and sexual victimization experiences in high-risk youth's alcohol and other drug use and delinquency: a longitudinal model', *Violence and Victims*, **7** (3), 245–66.

Dembo, R., Williams, L., Schmeidler, J., Berry, E., Wothke, W., Getreu, A., Wish, E.D. and Christensen, C. (1992b), 'A structural model examining the relationship between physical child abuse, sexual victimization, and marijuana/hashish use in delinquent youth: a longitudinal study', *Violence and Victims*, **7** (1), 41–62.

Desmarais, D. and Grell, P. (1986), *Les récits de vie; théorie, méthode et trajectoires types*, Montreal: Éditions Saint-Martin.

Duprez, D. and Kokoreff, M. (2000), 'Usages et trafics de drogues en milieux populaires', *Déviance et Société*, **24** (2), 143–66.

Erickson, P. and Weber, T.R. (1994), 'Cocaine careers, control and consequences: results from a canadian study', *Addiction Research*, **2** (1), 37–50.

Esbensen, F.A. and Elliot, D.S. (1994), 'Continuity and discontinuity in illicit drug use: patterns and antecedents', *The Journal of Drug Issues*, **24** (1), 75–97.

Fagan, J. and Chin, K.L. (1990), 'Violence as Regulation and Social Control in the Distribution of Crack', *NIDA Research Monograph Series, Drugs and violence: Causes, Correlates and Consequences*, Rockville, MD, National Institute on Drug Abuse, **103**, 8–43.

Farrington, D.P. (1994), 'Interactions Between Individual and Contextual Factors in the Development of Offending', in R.K. Silbereisen and E. Todt (eds), *Adolescence in Context: The Interplay of Family, School, Peers and Work in Adjustment*, New York: Springer-Verlag, pp.366–89.

Fréchette, M. and Le Blanc, M. (1987), *Délinquances et délinquants*, Boucherville: Gaëtan Morin.

Garnier, H.E. and Stein, J.A. (1998), 'Values and the family, risk and protective factors for adolescent problem behaviors', *Youth and Society*, **30** (1), 89–120.

Ghiglione, R. and Matalon, B. (1978), *Les enquêtes sociologiques: théories et pratiques*, Paris: A. Colin.

Glauser, A.S. (1995), 'Cocaine use: Glimpses of heaven', *Journal of Mental Health Counselling*, **12** (2), 230–37.

Gottfredson, M.R. and Hirshi, T. (1990), *A General Theory of Crime*, Stanford: Stanford University Press.

Grapendaal, M., Leuw, E. and Nelen, H. (1995), *A World of Opportunities: Lifestyle and Economic Behavior of Heroin Addicts in Amsterdam*, Albany: State University of New York Press.

Guyon, L. and Landry, M. (1993), 'Analyse descriptive de la population en traitement de Domrémy-Montréal à partir de l'IGT 1991–1992', RISQ, Montreal.

Hammersley, R., Forsyth, A. and Lavelle T. (1990), 'The criminality of new drug users in Glasgow', *British Journal of Addiction*, **85** (12), 1583–94.

Hawkins, J.-D., Catalano, R.F. and Miller, J.Y. (1992), 'Risk and protective factors for alcohol and other drug problems in adolescence and early adulthood: implications for substance abuse prevention', *Psychological Bulletin*, **112** (1), 64–105.

Hirshi, T. (1969), *Causes of Delinquency*, Berkeley: University of California Press.

Hirshi, T. and Gottfredson, M. (1983), 'Age and the explanation of crime', *American Journal of Sociology*, **89**, 552–84.

Horney, J., Osgood, D.W. and Marshall, I.H. (1995), 'Criminal careers in the short-term: intraindividual variability in crime', *American Sociological Review*, **60** (5), 655–73.

Hubbard, R.L., Mardsen, M.E., Rachal, J.V., Harwood, H.J., Cavanaugh, E.R. and Ginzburg, E.R. (1989), *Drug Abuse Treatment – A National Study of Effectiveness*, Chapel Hill: The University of North California Press.

Kaplan, H.B. (1995), 'Drugs, Crime, and Other Deviant Adaptations', in H.B. Kaplan, *Drugs, Crime, and Other Deviant Adaptations Longitudinal Studies*, New York: Plenum Press, pp.3–48

Kelley, B.T., Loeber, R., Keenan, K. and DeLamatre, M. (1997), 'Developmental pathways in boys' disruptive delinquent behavior', *Juvenile Justice Bulletin*, **12**.

Lanctôt, N. and Le Blanc, M. (2000), 'Les trajectoires marginales chez les adolescentes judiciarisées: continuité et changement', *Revue internationale de criminologie et de police technique*, **53** (1), pp.46–68.

Le Blanc, M. (1994a), 'La conduite délinquante des adolescents et ses facteurs explicatifs', in D. Szabo, M. Le Blanc, M (eds), *Traité de criminologie empirique 2nd edn*, Montreal: Presses de l'Université de Montréal, pp.44–89.

Le Blanc, M. (1996), 'Changing patterns in the perpetration of offences over time: trajectories from early adolescence to the early 30's', *Studies on Crime and Crime Prevention*, **5** (2), 151–65.

Le Blanc, M. and Kaspi, N. (1998), 'Trajectories of delinquency and problem behavior: comparison of social and personal control characteristics of adjudicated boys on synchronous and nonsynchronous paths', *Journal of Quantitative Criminology*, **14** (2), 181–214.

L'Écuyer, R. (1990), *Méthodologie de l'analyse développementale de contenu: méthode GPS et concept de soi*, Sillery: Presses de l'Université du Québec.

Lloyd, C. (1998), 'Risk factors for problem drug use: identifying vulnerable groups', *Drugs: Education, Prevention and Policy*, **5** (3), 217–32.

Loeber, R. and Farrington, D.P. (1998), 'Never too early, never too late: risk factors and successful interventions for serious and violent juvenile offenders', *Studies on Crime and Crime Prevention*, **7** (1), 7–30.

Loeber, R., Farrington, D.P., Southamer-Loeber, M., Moffitt, T.E. and Caspi, A. (1998), 'The development of male offending: key findings from the first decade of the Pittsburgh youth study', *Studies on Crime and Crime Prevention*, **7** (2), 141–71.

Martin, S.S. and Robbins, C.A. (1995), 'Personality, Social Control, and Drug Use in Early Adolescence', in H.B. Kaplan (eds), *Drugs, Crime and Other Deviant Adaptations: Longitudinal Studies*, New York: Plenum Press, pp.145–61.

McCord, J. (1995), 'Relationship Between Alcohol and Crime Over the Life Course', in H.B. Kaplan, *Drugs, Crime and Other Deviant Adaptations: Longitudinal Studies*, New York: Plenum Press, pp.129–41,

Mercier, C. and Alarie, S. (2001), 'Pathways out of deviance: Implications for program evaluation', in S. Brochu, C. da Agra and M.M. Cousineau (eds), *Drug and Crime Deviant Pathways*, Aldershot: Ashgate Publishing.

Miller, B.A. and Downs, W.R. (1995), 'Violent Victimization among Women with Alcohol Problems', in M. Galanter (ed.), *Recent Developments in Alcoholism; Alcoholism and Women*, vol.12, New York: Plenum Press, pp.81–101.

Nagin, D.S., Farrington, D.P. and Moffitt, T.E. (1995), 'Life-course trajectories of different types of offenders', *Criminology*, **33** (1), 111–39.

Normand, N. and Brochu, S. (1993), 'Adolescents, psychotropes, activité criminelle, contexte environnemental', Centre international de criminologie comparée, Université de Montréal.

Ouimet, M. and Le Blanc, M. (1993), 'Événements de vie et continuation de la carrière criminelle au cours de la jeunesse', *Revue internationale de criminologie et de police technique*, **3**, 321–44.

Patterson, G.R., Forgatch, M.S., Yoerger, K.I. and Stoolmiller, M. (1998), 'Variables that initiate and maintain an early-onset trajectory for juvenile offending', *Development and Psychopathology*, 10, 531–47.

Petraitis, J., Flay, B.R. and Miller, T.Q. (1995), 'Reviewing theories of adolescent substance use: organizing pieces in the puzzle', *Psychological Bulletin*, **117** (1), 67–86.

Pirès, A.P. (1997), 'Échantillonnage et recherche qualitative: essai théorique et méthodologique', in J. Poupart, J.-P. Deslauriers, L.-H. Groulx, A. Laperrière, R. Mayer and A.P. Pirès (eds), *La recherche qualitative: enjeux épistémologiques et méthodologiques*, Montreal: Gaëtan Morin, pp.113–69.

Piron, F. (1993), 'Être jeune, devenir adulte: analyses et témoignages d'adolescents et adolescentes de Québec', *Nouvelles pratiques sociales*, **6** (2), 107–24.

Piron, F. (1996), 'Répondre de soi: réflexivité et individuation dans le récit de soi d'une jeune Québécoise', *Sociologie et sociétés*, XXVIII (1), 119–34.

Racine, G. and Mercier, C. (1995), 'Histoire(s) de s'en sortir; propos de personnes toxicomanes sans abris', *Psychotropes*, **1**, 21–44.

Sampson, R.J. and Laub, J.H. (1993), *Crime in the Making: Pathways and Turning Points Through Life*, Cambridge, MA: Harvard University Press.

Schutz, A. (1987), *Le chercheur et le quotidien: phénoménologie des sciences sociales*, Paris: Méridiens Klincksieck.

Simons, R.L., Wu, C.I., Conger, R.D. and Lorenz, F.O. (1994), 'Two routes to delinquency: differences between early and late starters in the impact of parenting and deviant peers', *Criminology*, **32** (2), 247–75.

Smith, D.A. and Brame, R. (1994), 'On the initiation and continuation of delinquency', *Criminology*, **32** (4), 607–27.

Therrien, A. (1994), *Quand le plaisir fait souffrir: la gestion expérientielle*, Quebec: Trécarré.

Tremblay, R. and Wener, A. (1991), '*Guide du formateur: programme de formation des intervenants de première ligne*', Ministère de la Santé et du Bien-être social et Centre de réadaptation Alternatives, Quebec.

Tremblay, R.E., Masse, B., Perron, D., Le Blanc, M. and Ledingham, J.E. (1992), 'Early disruptive behavior, poor school achievement, delinquent behavior, and delinquent personality: longitudinal analyses', *Journal of Consulting and Clinical Psychology*, **60** (1), 64–72.

Tubman, J.G. (1993), 'Family risk factors, parental alcohol use, and problem behaviors among school-age children', *Family Relations*, **42** (1), 81–6.

Vaughn, C. and Long, W. (1999), 'Surrender to win: how adolescent drug and alcohol users change their lives', *Adolescence*, **34** (133), 9–24.

Vitaro, F., Dobkin, P.L., Gagnon, C. and Le Blanc, M. (1994), *Les problèmes d'adaptation psychosociale chez l'enfant et l'adolescent: prévalence, déterminants et prévention*, Quebec: Presses de l'Université du Québec.

Warner, J., Room, R. and Adlaf, E.M. (1999), 'Rules and limits in the use of marijuana among high-school students: The results of a qualitative study in Ontario', *Journal of Youth Studies*, **2** (1), 59–76.

Way, N. (1998), *Everyday Courage: The Lives and Stories of Urban Teenagers*, New York: New York University Press.

White, J.L., Moffit, T.E., Earls, F., Robins, L. and Silva, P.A. (1990), 'How early can we tell?: Predictors of childhood conduct disorder and adolescent delinquency', *Criminology*, **28**, 507–27.

Windle, M.A. (1990), 'Longitudinal study of antisocial behaviors in early adolescence as predictors of late adolescent substance use: gender and ethnic group differences', *Journal of Abnormal Psychology*, **99** (1), 86–91.

Wood, P.B., Cochran, J.K., Pfefferbaum, B. and Arneckley, B.J. (1995), 'Sensations-seeking and delinquency substance use: an extension of learning theory', *Journal of Drug Issues*, **25** (1), 173–93.

Yoshikawa, H. (1994), 'Prevention as cumulative protection: effects of early family support and education on chronic delinquency and its risks', *Psychological Bulletin*, **115** (1), 28–54.

Part III
ADULT, DRUG
AND CRIME PATHWAYS

Chapter 8

Drug/Crime Pathways
Among Cocaine Users

Isabelle Parent and Serge Brochu

A pattern that is rather popular these days positions drug consumption as a precursor to crime. This analysis perceives a causal relation between the consumption of psychoactive substances that induce a (physiological or psychological) dependency and are relatively expensive and one's involvement in money-oriented crime (Ball *et al.*, 1983). This conceptualization perceives drug dependency and the high costs of such products as insightful elements leading to crime. In one example illustrating this relation, Johnson *et al.* (1985), in a seminal study, indicate that daily heroin users have monthly spending patterns of, on average, $17 282 (US). Results obtained by Collins *et al.* (1985) indicate similar figures for cocaine users. Various studies indicate a number of illicit actions that are often turned to as means for obtaining and meeting the needs of the financial imperatives of heavy drug use: prostitution (Lecavalier, 1992; Anglin and Hser, 1987), drug trafficking (Faupel and Klockars, 1987; Hunt, 1991) or various forms of stealing (Faupel, 1991; Dobinson and Ward, 1986).

This linear conceptualization of the drug/crime relation incorporates some limits. This model has its origins in theories that perceive drug use as a sickness (Grapendaal *et al.*, 1995; Peele, 1989) that renders users choiceless: they must turn to crime in order to respond to their constant need for drugs. The personal or social meaning of the individual's actual actions is therefore ignored, discredited or denied (Grapendaal *et al.*, 1995; Peele, 1989). It seems, therefore, that this reductionist construction of reality does not take into consideration all the available information. It omits, in this sense, those drug using episodes that follow long periods of low drug availability and that result in a reduction and even an abstinence from consumption (Faupel, 1991; Wilson and Hernstein, 1985). It also deliberately ignores those persons that are able to control their consumption (Zinberg, 1984). Since such persons are not generally the object of services offered by treatment centres and do not usually find themselves in jails or prisons, they are more than often neglected by researchers. One cannot restrict one's understanding of the phenomenon to those elements that are the most likely observed. Furthermore, this conceptualization does not consider that, for a large number of young offenders, petty crime appears well before consumption of hard drugs and even more before the first signs of dependency (Brochu and Douyon, 1990; Elliott and Morse, 1989; Sarnecki, 1989).

An analysis of the scientific research leads us to argue, along with Hunt (1991), that involvement in crime by users of strongly prohibited drugs is a function of (a) the income of the user in relation to the price of the product in question; (b) the frequency of use, as well as the consumer's lifestyle; and (c) one's criminal antecedents. In light of this, the economic-compulsive model would apply to only those persons with limited incomes in responding to their drug consumption patterns and who are strongly dependent on expensive drugs. In addition, this model seems more fitting to consumers who are already implicated in a criminal trajectory.

Recently, clinical and empirical studies have placed us in an epistemological break with positivist conceptualizations of the drug/crime relation and have resulted in the development of a new conceptual model framing this relation between drug use and crime (Brochu, 1995). It consists of a social–psychological model that places the consumption of illicit drugs and crime within a larger schema of social deviance: as an adoption of a deviant lifestyle (we borrow the notion of deviance as it appears in the work of da Agra, 1986). According to this integrative model, an ensemble of factors placing an individual at risk of adopting a deviant lifestyle are found at the foundation of the consumption of illicit drugs and criminal behaviour. These risk factors are situated along a continuum. Depending on the case, the pressures from risk factors exercised on individuals may be weak, moderate or high. These factors may come from sociodemographic characteristics of the environment in which the individual evolves (socioeconomic level, place of residence and so on) (Tremblay *et al.*, 1991a), the influence of deviant peers (Agnew, 1991; Kumpfer and Turner, 1991), a distance taken from classical institutions of socialization (family, school and so on) (Tremblay *et al.*, 1988; White *et al.*, 1987) or from social norms (religious and normative values) (Bennett, 1990; Fagan *et al.*, 1990). These risk factors may also be attenuated by personal protective factors (self-esteem, solid bonds with institutions of socialization) (Tremblay *et al.*, 1991b). The impact of such factors is moderated or intensified by the meaning that social actors attribute to them.

This conceptual model assumes that some people follow a drug user's trajectory. This trajectory is not unidimensional and may be abandoned by the person at any moment. For analytical purposes, this trajectory may be highlighted by three stages: (1) the onset stage, (2) the stage of mutual reinforcement (between deviant or criminal behaviours that are adopted) and (3) the economic-compulsive stage (during which drug dependency imposes an important financial burden). The onset stage is characterized by an experimental or irregular consumption. The majority of consumers do not go beyond this stage. For others, consumption becomes more than an experimentation (for those with whom risk factors are higher). Drug use and crime may influence each other in that a higher level of revenue permits one to consume more and, in turn, a higher consumption habit renders one more likely to increase the level of money-oriented criminal activities. Involvement in small traffic with friends or relatives is common at this stage. Traffic activities, while yielding a considerable level of revenue, will also facilitate one's personal access to drugs and could lead to more drug consumption. Most users, once again, do not proceed beyond this stage of the trajectory (Zinberg, 1984; Faupel, 1991). For others, however, this regular pace of drug consumption is transformed into (physical or psychological) dependency that necessitates a regular financial income of increasingly higher yields. At this stage, the user is a victim of his/her consumption and cannot carry on without involvement in crime. They therefore proceed into the economic–compulsive stage. Those following the trajectory into this stage are generally individuals who have chosen to take a deviant route.

The model elaborated throughout past studies questions the causal determinism that represented more traditional models. Strategies extending from the actual battle against drug use have been based on such traditional models. We therefore suggest a transition from a deterministic criminology to the study of pathways. The aim, here, is to further accentuate an understanding of the deviant trajectory taken by regular cocaine users, particularly by analysing the process embracing the passage from one stage of consumption to the next. We therefore focus on the three stages of the drug-user trajectory observed in past research in order to better understand the drug/crime relation throughout each of these phases.

METHOD

The study aims at understanding the drug/crime relation amongst adults. Considering that a large number of adolescents that are drug users or who manifest delinquent behaviours cease their deviant trajectories on their entrance into adulthood, it was decided that, rather than follow a wide sample of adolescents in order to obtain a reasonably large number of eventual adult drug users, the study would focus specifically and directly on adult respondents.

The sample is made up exclusively of men. It is well known in drug addiction research as well as in the crime and delinquency field that male and female patterns remain considerably distinct. It is therefore important that the respective dynamics marking each gender are not intertwined. Hence it was decided that the study's aim would be restricted to the cocaine–crime relation amongst men only. We remain aware, at the same time, that it will be impossible to generalize the study's findings to women. A concurrent study focusing exclusively on female respondents has progressed independently of the present research. Since cocaine is the most popular and expensive illicit drug in Quebec, the study is concerned only with regular consumers (three times or more per week) of this drug. Finally, a preliminary selection was based on respondents' primary sources of income. In order to distinguish the level of involvement in a deviant lifestyle, the majority of a respondent's earnings had to come from (a) work, (b) drug dealing or (c) other illegal activities (hence representing three distinct levels of immersion in a deviant lifestyle).

Three recruitment strategies were used in constituting the sample. These different strategies had a common aim of attaining a representative sample of the cocaine-user population. Since an objective of the study was to encounter a small number of cocaine users that would be interviewed in greater depth, the search for persons susceptible to participating in the study could not follow the traditional statistical methods of attaining a representative sample based on an established population. This sample, made up of 42 respondents, is therefore not representative of either the cocaine-using or larger drug-using population. However, the recruitment and selection of participants for the study did remain consistent with representative characteristics of the cocaine-using population in Montreal.

The first recruitment method consisted of meeting those cocaine users who were under treatment for their drug addiction and who volunteered to participate in the study (see Table 8.1). Fourteen (33.3 per cent) of the 42 respondents were located at and recruited from six different treatment and detoxification facilities in Quebec. Other respondents were recruited from prisons. Eight (19 per cent) of the 42 participants were inmates at the time of the interview. Finally, a series of respondents were recruited through a snowball sampling method that consisted of asking key informants (drug users) to put us into contact with friends and acquaintances from their own milieus who were also regular consumers of cocaine. This method allowed us to reach a population of users that would not have been identified in the judicial system or in any treatment centre. In using several sources to initiate snowball sampling processes, we were also able to avoid interviews being restricted only to a small circle of friends. Snowball samples were initiated by seven different sources and led to 36 additional references, 16 of which were excluded because they failed to meet all selection criteria (adult, male, regular user of cocaine). Hence the majority of respondents were recruited via this snowball sampling method (20 of the 42, or 47.6 per cent).

Table 8.1 Three sample recruitment strategies by deviant lifestyle type

	Work	Drug dealing/trafficking	Other crime	Total
Snowball	9	7	4	20
Treatment	5	4	5	14
Prison	0	3	5	8
Total	14	14	14	42

The study's participants were seen individually for a period of three to four hours during which interviews were taped. Semi-directive interviews were conducted with an objective of understanding the principal life events and factors associated with the actual lifestyles of the interviewees. Interviews began with respondents being asked to describe what they judged as significant in their lives. While the interviewer purposely limited the number of intrusions into the respondents' accounts, some direction was deemed necessary in some cases, most notably for respondents who were never in treatment or in detention and who had no experience of describing their lives. Also, during the interviews, the interviewer asked some additional questions in order to clarify, to situate events described in the person's trajectory, to reformulate various statements or to lead the respondent to talk in regard to a major theme that had yet to be raised spontaneously. The interviewer also systematically asked respondents, in concluding the interview (if the case was deemed pertinent) if they thought there was a link between their drug use and their involvement in crime.

Verbatims were recorded from taped interviews and analysed individually with a codification form by two research assistants. A transversal analysis of the interviews was subsequently conducted with the help of the NUD*IST qualitative software package.

RESULTS

The onset stage

At the onset stage, drug use is a function of contacts with other users as well as the amount of money available. Two situations may be observed: onset linked to opportunity (work) and onset linked to petty crime.

Onset linked to opportunities (work)

For a minority of our sample's respondents, money needed for occasional consumption of psychoactive substances (characteristic of the onset period) comes from work or other legitimate forms of income. This covers the situation of individuals who were, in their pasts, exposed to few risk factors and who presented, at the time of the interview, minimal involvement in crime. Onset linked to legitimate income opportunities assumes a late initiation with psychoactive substances because few young adolescents work and possess enough revenue to support an experimental level of consumption. In fact, onset linked to legitimate opportunities has been minimally identified in the trajectories of respondents participating in this study.

Onset linked to petty crime

For most of the interviewees, delinquency appeared before first drug use. However, some of the delinquent acts may be in relation to drug/alcohol consumption:

> We were getting together at night to plan our next prank. You know, like leaving a bag of shit at a door and putting it on fire. We did all that. All the things that little troublemakers do, we did – you know, like stealing beer and getting together later to drink the beer. (Daniel)

Many of these pranks yielded small sums of money. Money made from such acts would subsequently be used for different expenditures, among them the consumption of psychoactive substances.

> (I: What were you doing to pay for the brandy and other liquors?) Well, I was selling. I was also stealing. I was already stealing from my parents – that started when I was in seventh grade. (I: Stealing from your parents?) Ah, after that it was like, oups, take a brown bill – it didn't show that much, it didn't show much. But it did show at one point, but, that was it, I didn't have any problems from that, or the trouble that I did get from that was usually forgotten, you know. I was missing money. Hum, hum, what do you want, you know? That was it. At first, that's the way it is. I was stealing because I needed money to play video games. I needed something to be comfortable in the world – to buy drugs, to smoke a small joint. (Robert)

At this stage, delinquency, although providing the necessary money for consumption, may not be committed with this goal in mind:

Drugs were for partying and I didn't really feel a need for money. The time that I stole from my brother, I didn't really need that money – it was just to trip more. (Yan)

In a similar sense, the following excerpt demonstrates how money from crime may be spent on drugs.

We were meeting to decide where we would steal and to see if everything was all right. And, I was always the first one to arrive and I was the one who was opening the door or breaking the windows. That was me. When we had finished, we would go out and buy a case of beer and return to the park and party. We were making fires, telling each other stories. We were fooling around, you know. (Éric)

At the onset stage, the social context takes on a crucial importance. Petty crimes and irregular consumption sometimes serves the same needs of adolescents: to be part of a social group.

No, it started that way, but it was like I said, it was because of the others I was hanging around with, they were into committing crimes and everything and they were the ones who would smoke-up and everything. (Chris)

In brief, onset is characterized by irregular consumption that usually depends on legitimate and illegal incomes. Initiation to crime generally preceded first experiences with drugs. Since adolescents did not habitually have legitimate jobs or other sources of revenue, it was observed that drug use was mainly financed though petty crimes or delinquent activities. However, delinquency, in general, turned out to be minimally necessary to pay for one's drug use at this stage. This was so for several reasons, among them that first drug consumption experiences were often paid for by those who facilitated the initial experience with drugs and that drug use, at this stage, is low in financial costs. Although criminal acts were not necessarily committed with a money-for-drugs motive, acquiring money through criminal routes often proved useful when confronting the costs of psychoactive substances. At this stage, delinquency and consumption both represent activities that permit adolescents to meet the crucial need of belonging to a group of peers. It is within such groups that the contacts and necessary opportunities leading to initiation in delinquency and drug use are supplied.

The mutual reinforcement stage

Mutual reinforcement between drug consumption and criminal activities appears when drug use becomes regular. At this stage, the relation between crime and the consumption of psychoactive substances becomes bidirectional: the use of drugs facilitates criminal activities and the latter help to support the costs of the former.

At the mutual reinforcement stage, available money constitutes, once again, the most important factor explaining consumption. Money from crime is not always a necessity. Indeed, some yield excellent incomes from their legitimate jobs and others work hard in order to reach the necessary incomes to support their expensive consumption. The following examples illustrate this situation rather clearly:

I was named director of a large firm on a Caribbean island. I was really excited, but I didn't know that this was the island of all the vices. Everything is wild on this island. You come in and out like in a church. The goods are the same. There are no laws, no rules... So, that's it, I was there and there was a lot of cocaine, lots of alcohol, many women – it was the island with all the vices. So, I hit bottom many times. I had many high times as well. I made tons of money. I bought a house. Finally, I renovated a house right on the beach. I had my boat right in front, a car, a motorcycle. I had it all. It was really the American dream. I would get high with class, as we say. (...) I was making between 10 000 and 20 000 dollars or more per month. That was a huge salary and I was travelling every weekend... (Richard)

(I: Did you always pay for your drug use with your salaries?) Always with my salaries, all the time. I would work like crazy – twelve and fifteen and twenty hours per day. I was working from Monday morning to Friday night without any sleep... (Georges)

At this stage, however, most consumers have already turned towards money-oriented crime in order to support at least some of the costs of their consumption. Some individuals would not have been involved in crime if they had not entered into a regular consumption of illicit drugs.

Using drugs equals crime, that's sure and certain. Because you want to keep on being all right – well to keep on using – you have to hang around in places where it's being sold. So you go to bars, houses – places like that. People who sell dope are all criminals. Because they're all criminals, you get into that yourself and automatically become a criminal too. If you don't consume, well good for you. You have to change your world, that's for sure. You have to get away from that type of life, you know. (Bill)

In fact, drug use facilitates involvement in crime in many ways. For example, the effects of psychoactive substances may contribute in neutralizing hesitations to commit illegal acts and give courage to go through with a crime.

Well, it's clear that when I was using I was more willing to steal. I was... [short silence] (I: When you would steal, you would consume before?) Not all the time. Not all the time. There were some crimes that I was doing straight. (I: Did you feel less willing for those crimes?) Well, more nervous, not less willing – but more nervous. (Alain)

It is for this reason that some state that drug use facilitates an increased involvement in crime. Some individuals do mention that they would have still committed a certain number of crimes even without the use of any psychoactive substances, but this would be at a less frequent pace.

It's evident – if I wasn't using I would have probably still been a criminal, but much less. (I: You're saying that it would be much less, but you would be the same?) Well, yeah, I say yes because it was a thrill when I was young. Maybe I wouldn't have gone as far as I did, but I would have always been a little bit criminal. (Serge)

Furthermore, the social milieu that engulfs an illicit drug user also contributes in facilitating involvement in crime. The following examples demonstrate how the social milieus of consumers of psychoactive substances supply criminal opportunities as well as values that ease such involvement in crime.

> For me, it started when I started using. When you use, you live with others who use, and for those who use, they all do it ... when I was younger ... they all did small crimes. So if it's done in your environment, it's not that bad ... it's part of life, you know... then everything gets mixed up ... it starts everything. It's not like if you were at home with your family doing only good things, and some guy comes and see you and says: 'Do you want to steal a bike with me?' Or ... : 'Do you want to pull a fast one ...?' There, you see, it's like, aie aie aie, now that's a crime. But when you're ... it's a transition that brought me there ... that brings you to crime in my case anyway, in the way that it happened. It's like, you're in a circle of users and in a circle of users well ... even if you're young, there's always some who will be into committing small crimes. Stealing there, ripping that off there, selling some drugs to support their own needs. And it's acceptable, it's like it's social ... in the social, in your social, these things are acceptable. Now, sure if the guy comes up to me and says: 'C'mon, we're going to kill him ...' 'What are you crazy', that's not right. Or: 'Get a gun, we're going to rob that lady ...' 'Are you sick?' It wasn't that. It started with small stupid things happening around. The guy would tell me: 'Do you feel like coming?' 'Yeah sure, we'll come, we'll come and help.' But you don't see that as a crime, you know. It wasn't seen ... It didn't feel like a crime for me because no one was getting hurt. Well it doesn't hurt anyone. Well, if the dummy is stupid enough to take the check, he'll still get over it, ha ha ha [pretends to laugh]. And you're stoned and it's fun and ... Well that's the transition that explains how you take off ... that using brings you to crime without you realizing that it was crime. (...) So with me, they weren't crimes, they were small things, you know ... Like we say – small white lies – and that's what you justify the whole thing with. But you're in an environment. You're the excuse if you ... if you think ... if you give an opinion that: 'you shouldn't pass a check'. Or, you know, the grocery store belongs to someone – that these people work hard. Everyone would laugh at you. It would have ... so if everyone is to laugh at you, and this is everyone that you hang around with, the 10–15 people that you hang around with, well, you say, 'well shit, these guys got something, you know, it's not ... it's not all that bad.' Because it does that inside of me ... anywhere in society, when you're the only one who thinks in a certain way, well, you question yourself. (Léon)

In another sense, financial incomes coming from crime facilitated the possibility for regular drug consumption. In fact, without money from crimes, it would be difficult for most to support the costs of psychoactive substances. As a result, there are many who are actively involved in crime.

> (I: And when you returned to Montreal and you got back into contact with the others, did your cocaine consumption increase?) Yes. (I: And you didn't have any more money?) Yes. (I: And that's why you were consuming more?) Well, I was still living pretty well. I was using like crazy – enormously. I was always dressed really sharp, everything, the more money you have, the more you spend. There was nothing to it – just take a good dose and away you go. (Alex)

Thus crime permits one to acquire the money necessary to keep up an expensive lifestyle consisting of frequent outings, diverse excesses and the consumption of psychoactive substances.

It was only dope. Sometimes I was bored at home – I didn't care – I was grabbing a piece and then doing a hold-up and then I would be able to go out at night. (I: More because of boredom?) Yeah, I was saying: 'I'm going out tonight. I'm not staying home, it's boring. I'm going out to the clubs.' It goes together – drugs, booze, it's all the same crap. (Alex)

It is for such reasons that, even though some yield high revenues from crime, most of the study's respondents were able to economize only small sums of money. Many consumers acquire a habit of luxury and the power that money brings them. These advantages acquired through money also constitute further reinforcement to pursue a criminal path as well as the possibility of consuming drugs.

It's income, the big life, traveling, taking drugs. We were making a lot of money – a thousand dollars a month. I was still using as much as I always did – it was regular, every day. I would wake up in the morning, go to work – I was sniffing to wake myself up. After that, right after we finished, we were selling our stuff and we were buying some dope. We were getting high every night. That's the way it was every day. (André)

At this stage, several possibilities, aside from crime, exist that permit the individual to acquire money. In addition, the individual is not yet completely dependent on the psychoactive substances and the type of crimes committed is selected in accordance with one's values. At the reinforcement stage, drug users are not yet at the point of doing just anything for money.

To pay my dope, I was selling drugs. I was making exchanges, you know – like with the stuff that I had. I sold the things that I had. I was working with things that I had bought – let's say that I had bought a gold chain and well, at the end of a night, there was some coke missing – like a gram was missing – for a gram, you know, I would exchange my chain for a gram. Stealing money or stealing in general? I never did any break-ins in any private house and I never picked anybody's pockets. (Claude)

The dealing and traffic of drugs represents one of the most frequent criminal activities at this stage. This involvement permits one to obtain money to support one's use, reduce the costs linked to buying the substance, while acquiring more of an ease in obtaining the desired drug. One does not get involved in dealing in order to support the needs extending from drug dependency. Instead, one seeks an opportunity facilitating regular consumption.

When I started dealing, I was already using. I was offered to deal. When I got the offer, what went through my head? It was like: 'I wouldn't have to pay the full price anymore, you know.' For me, I was becoming their best client, you know – in some ways, you know. But it's obvious that I wasn't the best client because with the quantity that I was selling, you know, I wouldn't have been able to consume as much as I was selling, you know. It's obvious that that's why I started dealing. Because for me, it was all connected. To use, well, you have to sell, you know. (William)

This facility in obtaining psychoactive substances may, however, produce a perverse effect: an increase in consumption that precipitates an eventual dependency on the psychoactive product.

(I: How do you see the relation between selling and using dope?) It's a proportional relation that follows dealing. The more you sell, the more you take. The more you sell, the more you run, the more money you make, the more you take. (...) That's for sure. All the money that I made dealing, that was all money that I ended up spending. (Marc)

At this stage, some decrease their dealing pace in order to better control their consumption.

No, I always stayed pretty much at the same level. Of course I would have liked to have gone higher and sold more, but it wouldn't have meant much because what I was selling, like I said, was for my own consumption. The more I would have had, the more I would have taken. And there would have come a time when I wouldn't have been able to sell any more and I would have been using too much. I preferred staying at the minimum and sell to support what I was taking, you know, but I wasn't making any money like that. In the end, like I said, I did make some, but I wouldn't make any money with that. You know, all that I sold – the profits from that – went back to my own use. (Chris)

Hence drug dealing may lead to an increase in drug use. This progression in drug use may, in turn, result in an increase in criminal involvement, in that revenues coming from crime diminish rapidly with a higher pace of consumption.

In this sense, some become dishonest in their drug transactions in order to make more money and subsequently consume more.

Yes, to pay my own consumption, I was dealing for a guy. He was giving me so much per gram [he laughs] – I hope that he doesn't hear about this. He was giving me so much per gram and I was cuttingh the gram myself [he laughs]. (Claude)

This involvement in the drug business may also lead to crimes inherent in the distribution of illicit products.

I was continuing sniffing, continuing sniffing and, at one point, oups, I started smoking, freebasing, smoking. (...) I was taking care of my clients and as soon as I had a couple of minutes free, I was getting totally blasted. As soon as I had one minute, that's the way it was. And, everyone owed me money, I was starting to collect from them and I was getting really charged, you know. When you get to the point that you have to wake up a guy from bed and start punching him in the face because it's been a month that he owes you $400... (Luc)

Aside from an involvement in the dealing of drugs, a second type of crime frequently committed at this mutual reinforcement stage is that linked to one's work environment. Some commit frauds, steal or commit other crimes that are found in the set of opportunities rendered possible in the workplace. This was a situation that was observed rather frequently with the subgroup of the sample for which the principal source of income was legitimate work.

I started using a lot more and I found myself in a black hole in society because I went through all my personal reserves – my bank account. So I had to use the firm to respond to my consumption and my personal lifestyle. So I started laundering money. I realized that the investors from different firms and even the owners were doing it. So why couldn't I do it too? (...) Finally, both sides found out. When they came to me to tell me that they knew that I was laundering money, I told them that I knew that they were doing the same thing. So I threatened them. We shook hands, said goodbye, and everything was okay. (Richard)

Drugs become both the cause and the consequence of crime. The following excerpt illustrates this circular relation between drugs and crime.

Crime pushed me to consume and my consumption made me stay in crime. That pretty well sums it all up, eh? (Daniel)

This stage involves a bidirectional relation between the consumption of psychoactive substances and criminal involvement in which each behaviour reinforces and facilitates the other in a way in which a lifestyle is created that keeps these two deviant behaviours tightly linked. For some, this relation is held in place until dependency sets in.

The economic–compulsive stage

The economic–compulsive stage of the drug/crime relation takes place as the drug addiction trajectory is well advanced. The individual reveals problems of dependency on a substance that, because of its high costs, keeps financial needs high as well. Crimes committed at this stage are essentially lucrative. The drug addicts that were encountered during this study clearly expressed, in their own words, this drug/crime relation:

It started at the car wash, then, after that, it went to hold-ups because I needed more money – you know, it becomes more expensive. I was injecting. (Robin)

The following excerpt illustrates how crime is intensified to support the financial needs linked to drugs and the graduation of criminal acts during this stage.

That's when the crimes started. I started stealing, frauding. I was stealing checks, printing checks. I was frauding and, through all that, I got to know the people in that milieu – you know, those people who are more or less credible, but they were very useful for me at that time because they were allowing me to consume. So I started selling, stealing, stealing. The first people that I stole from were my own parents. I robbed my parents many times – many times for several thousand dollars. I was taking advantage – coke takes you down really low because I was able to profit from my mother's weaknesses. She was in the middle of a divorce with my father and she really needed me, you know. She needed me to be there. I lied, I took advantage of her weakness by taking money and manipulating her quite a bit. In about four months, my mother had probably given me about $100 000. Fake investments, all kinds of... I had a big, I had a very big imagination and it served me quite well... I was stealing to consume. I was really happy in those moments when I had my stash of coke. I was all right, everything was all right. When the stash of coke was finished, then I was always backing down to the same point, but always with something else – you know, always with another problem to add on to everything. I had a lot of problems. At one point, I did a robbery because nothing was working right, so I tried another way. I did a robbery and I ended up in prison. I wasn't arrested at the time of the robbery. I got the money and I used up all the coke. (Nicolas)

Those crimes committed often become less thought out and prepared during this stage. The importance is to have money rapidly, no matter what the consequences may be.

You don't really think it over. It pretty much happens right on the moment. No matter what, I would get to want some, and I wouldn't have any left, I would go out and I would get what I wanted. A car, eh ... anything, eh ... a nice lady walking down the street – for that one, I regretted it afterwards. I still feel guilty for that today. You see, me, I love my mother a lot, eh? And, if anyone would try to jump my mother to take her purse, I'm telling you that I would be really pissed off with the guy, you know. So, now I tell myself that I did exactly that, you know. I did the same mistake. But I never did it again. I could even tell you that it's not all right to do that – not all right at all, you know. For sure, when we talk about the secondary effects ... of consuming, well, it could turn into things like that, you know. (William)

The swindling of individuals who are part of the drug user and/or criminal milieu also increases at this stage.

Yeah, when you're out of money, you get a tendency to find illegal ways of getting some more. There's one time I remember that I won't even tell you about. Of course when you're missing money and you're in need of some stuff ... Well, I'll tell you about the last time that happened. I already did something bad because of that. I have my reasons not to talk about it. The last time that I consumed, I knew the delivery guy pretty well. So when he came that night, I had no money, you know. I only had about ten dollars. So I told him that I wanted a gram and he gave me a gram. So he asks me if I'm going to pay and I tell him no – I tell him that I'd pay him on Wednesday. And, then he starts – and I know about how much these guys make in a night – about 70 bucks. He would make about 100 bucks a night, you know. I didn't even ask any permission, you know. This guy's a courier, you know. I needed some – I was really desperate. And, he thought that the guy that was with me had a gun, so nothing really happened, you know. He was really pissed off, you know. And, I had a knife near my bag, you know – he thought that I was ready to use that knife, you know. I told him that I wouldn't hurt anyone for a gram, you know. He said, you fucker, you're going to pay for it the next time that I see you. I couldn't care less. Ten minutes later, I told myself that, shit, that he had a gang behind him and ... So I called the boss. I said, hey big guy, I just made a really bad mistake. He said that he knew all about it and that he was thinking of what he should do with me. I told him that he knew that it wasn't really me that was responsible for all that – that I was desperate. I told him that I would pay him the moment I received my pay next week – that there wasn't any problem, you know. He told me that I should have called him first. Yeah, but, I told him, you know how things are when you're high, when you're desperate. I told him that I thought of everything the moment that it happened and it just happened – Bing bang, and now it's been about ten minutes since and I'm pretty pissed off with myself. I said that getting beaten up, I don't need. He said that he was about to send someone over for that. I said, listen, I don't need to get beaten up, that I was able to understand, and that I always paid – that I was a very good client. I asked him if he understood. He told me yes, as long as I paid, that there would be no problems. At that moment, there were two gangs waiting for me outside – I was really scared. It woke me up. It made me realize that I was at the end of the line. I knew that I was at the end and if I would continue doing coke, I would get myself really hurt – I was afraid of getting hurt. (Philippe)

While the drug/crime relation becomes economic–compulsive, it is evident that crime intensifies because of the individual's desire to have money. In contrast, however, we sometimes forget that it is not only crime that increases, but that all possible means of getting money are turned to. For example, some may work more intensively at a legitimate job, sell their goods, and use their imagination to acquire money in more or less legitimate ways.

I had two, three jobs. I was working in a garage, I worked in car washes, I was selling a little. All my money went into consuming so I never had anything. I wasn't paying anything – no transportation, no clothes, no food, nothing. I had no place to live. All I was paying was my dope. Even for booze, I wouldn't pay – I would steal it. Montreal is free – it's free. It was like, well, it was enough – everyone was afraid of me, I was getting worse and worse – I was almost going crazy. It got to the point that I was shoplifting with a piece on me. If someone would try to arrest me, I would tell them to mind their business, you know. With this fuckin' gun, I wasn't going to put them just in the street, you know – I would tell them to mind their own business, you know. It was like it was getting too heavy, you know. (Robin)

At this stage, two phenomena linked to economic–compulsive crime arise and render the relation between crime and drug use even more complex. First, intensification in criminal involvement, with a main objective being the supply of money necessary to consume drugs, may create a psychological dependency on crime. In this sense, crime becomes almost compulsive.

The moment I started using again, oops, the cut becomes too expensive. So, then, I would start doing more, you know. Instead of doing a half-gram, I was up to a gram. Then two grams. Oh boy, that was about 200, 300 bucks a day. Yeah, you can't make it anymore, okay. You start getting into things, you start doing a few houses. It all starts over again. It's a feeling that comes over you. If you would tell me that there was no way I would be able to get into a house, you know, I would still do it and an hour later I'd be at the bank. It's probably like, how do we call it, a kind of sickness. (Bill)

Second, those criminal acts committed may lead to a strong feeling of guilt for many drug users. Many drug addicts attempt to forget this feeling by consuming, which leads to the creation of a vicious circle. The individual therefore commits crimes to support the financial needs that extend from drug dependency, but seeks to forget this involvement in crime by consuming more and further immersing himself in addiction, which, in turn, requires a return to an intensified pursuit of money through crime. This sad situation repeats itself constantly and implants the individual in a deviance that is ever more difficult to escape from.

Well, after a couple of years, I was starting to steal. It was really to get some money to buy dope, you know. I didn't like that too much, you know. I didn't like stealing and consuming – it's just that I was really desperate. At that point, the need was physical – more physical than mental. The mental part of you tells you that it's not all right and you know it, so every time that you do something that was against your values, you do it, but you have to hit yourself on the head three times harder so that you could forget it all. You have to get stoned, but because you have to get stoned to forget, you start all over and get into another act, which, for you, is not at all in your value system, you do it anyway and it starts all over again, you know – a vicious cycle. (Jean)

SYNTHESIS

Once started, the career of a cocaine user is therefore characterized by a number of twists and turns. The behaviour of the market sometimes governs consumption. Abstinence is often replaced by a relapse. Arrests also accentuate the trajectory. Nevertheless, it is possible to distinguish, throughout this evolution, a transformation within the drug/crime relationship. The drug, which was at the onset a source of pleasure that satisfied a young consumer in his search for strong sensations or for celebrating his criminal successes, leads the regular user towards crime linked to the distribution of the illicit product (crime permits a sufficient financial income to purchase more drugs, but, in return, the drug permits the expansion of one's criminal activities), and the dependent consumer towards lucrative crime accentuated by the need for drugs and the fear of severance. At the end of the evolution of the drug addict's career and the criminal trajectory exists a link that intertwines these two deviant behaviours ever more tightly. The more one proceeds into the trajectory, the harder it becomes to distinguish the two behaviours. Drug addiction therefore manifests itself deceitfully. First it appears in the guise of an evidently costly habit, but one which is easily satisfied by the proceeds from crime. For some, it metamorphisizes gradually and transforms into demanding a constant financial need that is much more considerable than for regular consumers. It serves to increase the intensification of a criminal trajectory that is already well under way. However, one must understand that not all consumers reach the end of this trajectory; a considerable number quit along the way. One must therefore not perceive this trajectory as an unavoidable linear course.

REFERENCES

Agnew, R. (1991), 'The interactive effects of peer variables on delinquency', *Criminology*, **29** (1), 47–72.

Anglin, M.D. and Hser, Y.I. (1987), 'Addicted women and crime', *Criminology*, **25** (2), 359–97.

Ball, J.C., Shaffer, J.W. and Nurco, D.N. (1983), 'The day to day criminality of heroin addicts in Baltimore – a study in the continuity of offence rates', *Drug and Alcohol Dependence*, **12** (2), 119–42.

Bennett, T. (1990), 'Links between drug misuse and crime', *British Journal of Addiction*, **85** (7), 833–35.

Brochu, S. (1995), *Drogues et criminalité: une relation complexe*, Montreal: Presses de l'Université de Montréal/Brussels: De Boeck-Wesmael.

Brochu, S. and Douyon, A. (1990), 'Prévalence de la consommation de psychotropes chez les jeunes en centre d'accueil', paper presented at the Conférence midi de la Cité des Prairies, March.

Collins, J.J., Hubbard, R. and Rachal, V. (1985), 'Expensive drug use and illegal income: a test of explanatory hypotheses', *Criminology*, **23** (4), 743–64.

da Agra, C. (1986), *Science, maladie mentale et disposilts de l'enfance: du paradigme biologique au paradigme systimique*, Lisbonne, Instituto Nacional de Investigacao Ci entifica.

Dobinson, I. and Ward, P. (1986), 'Heroin and property crime: an Australian perspective', *Journal of Drug Issues*, **16** (2), 249–62.

Elliott, D.S. and Morse, B.J. (1989), 'Delinquency and drug use as risk factors in teenage sexual activity', *Youth and Society*, **21** (1), 32–60.

Fagan, J., Weis, J.G. and Cheng, Y.T. (1990), 'Delinquency and substance use among inner-city students', *Journal of Drug Issues*, **20** (3), 351–402.

Faupel, C.E. (1991), *Shooting Dope: Career Pattern of Hard-Core Heroin Users*, Gainesville, FL: University of Florida Press.

Faupel, C.E. and Klockars, C.B. (1987), 'Drugs crime connections: elaborations from life histories of hard core heroin addicts', *Social Problems*, **34** (1), 54–68.

Grapendaal, M., Leuw, E. and Nelen, H. (1995), *A World of Opportunities: Lifestyle and Economic Behavior of Heroin Addicts in Amsterdam*. Albany: State University of New York Press.

Hunt, D.E. (1991), 'Stealing and Dealing: Cocaine and Property Crimes', NIDA Research Monograph Series. The Epidemiology of Cocaine Use and Abuse, Rockville, MD: National Institute on Drug Abuse, **110**, 139–50.

Johnson, B.D., Goldstein, P.J., Preble, E., Schmiedler, J., Lipton, D.S., Spunt, B. and Miller, T. (1985), *Taking Care of Business: The Economics of Crime by Heroin Abusers*, Toronto: Lexington.

Kumpfer, K.L. and Turner, C.W. (1991), 'The social ecology model of adolescent substance abuse: Implications for prevention', *The International Journal of the Addictions*, **25** (4a), 435–63.

Lecavalier, M. (1992), 'L'abus de drogues licites et de cocaïne chez les femmes en traitement: Les différences et similitudes dans les stratégies d'approvisionnement et dans les conséquences qui s'y rattachent ainsi que dans les antécédents personnels', unpublished MSc thesis, Université de Montréal.

Peele, S. (1989), *Diseasing of America: Addiction Treatment Out of Control*, Lexington, MA: Lexington Books.

Sarnecki, J. (1989), 'Rapports entre l'abus de drogue et la délinquance', in *Renaissance urbaine en Europe: Vol. 35, Stratégies locales pour la réduction de l'insécurité urbaine en Europe*, Strasbourg: Conseil de l'Europe, pp.327–35.

Tremblay, R.E., LeBlanc, M. and Schwartzman, A.E. (1988), 'The predictive power of first-grade peer and teacher ratings of behavior: sex differences in antisocial behavior and personality at adolescence', *Journal of Abnormal Child Psychology*, **16** (5), 571–83.

Tremblay, R.E., Loeber, R., Gagnon, C., Charlebois, P., Larivée, S. and LeBlanc, M. (1991a), 'Disruptive boys with stable and unstable high fighting behavior patterns during junior elementary school', *Journal of Abnormal Child Psychology*, **19** (3), 285–300.

Tremblay, R.E., McCord, J., Boileau, H., Charlebois, P., Gagnon, C., LeBlanc, M. and Larivée, S. (1991b), 'Can disruptive boys be helped to become competent?', *Psychiatry*, **54**, 148–61.

White, H.R., Pandina, R.J. and LaGrange, R.L. (1987), 'Longitudinal predictors of serious substance use and delinquency', *Criminology*, **25** (3), 715–40.

Wilson, J.Q. and Hernstein, R.J. (1985), *Crime and Human Nature*, New York: Touchstone.

Zinberg, N.E. (1984), *Drug, Set and Setting: The Basis of Controlled Intoxicant Use*, New Haven: Yale University Press.

Chapter 9

Flexing Crack in Toronto: a Deviant Pathway for Poor, Homeless Drug Users

Patricia G. Erickson, Jennifer Butters and Beric German

Illegal drug markets are shadowy, subterranean enterprises that are not readily accessible to law abiding citizens, researchers or the police. The higher the echelons of the trade, the more secrecy is protected. The profits are enormous, with the global illicit drug market estimated to be worth $500 billion annually, or as much as 8 per cent of the world's total trade (NAPHP, 1999). Not surprisingly, little is known in most countries about these illicit economic structures and how they may vary according to the drug involved, the location and the major players. A common and visible feature, however, is the expression of the drug trade in open drug scenes on the streets of larger cities in North America, Europe and Australia. Here the addicted users who lack conventional social support, including those who sell, barter or exchange drugs to provide their own supply, are found (Reuter and MacCoun, 1992). Because of their visibility, their dealing activities and their often disruptive public presence, crack users/sellers are among the most despised elements of society. 'Crack head' has become an even more pejorative label than the 'heroin junkie' or 'dope fiend' of previous moral drug panics (Goode and Ben-Yehuda, 1994). In Toronto, the middlemen of the crack trade are known as 'flexers'.

In Canada, the introduction of crack in the late 1980s, as in the USA, generated an insidious form of illegal drug market characterized by low entry costs, a cheap, short-acting product and rapid recruitment from the ranks of those lacking other economic alternatives (Reinarman and Levine, 1997; Erickson *et al.*, 1994). Crack use and distribution have been shown to be strongly associated with poverty, unemployment and social disorganization, lodged among the most vulnerable members of the population (Erickson and Cheung, 1999). Crack users who are engaged in the street drug markets are at the bottom of the drug distribution chain (Waldorf *et al.*, 1991). These users run the biggest risks of violence, their health is the most compromised, and they are the easiest for the police to catch (Fagin and Chin, 1991; Erickson, 1998). Without them, many regular consumers are not served and no profits can flow upward to the elusive 'Mr Bigs'.[1] The thriving crack market in a downtown Toronto neighbourhood in the 1990s has thrown up a particular expression of this niche position of user-seller, the 'flexers', as they are locally known.[2]

METHODOLOGY

This chapter presents the results of interviews with 17 male flexers in a Toronto locale with an active street drug market. All the interviews were conducted by the first author, in 1995, by arrangement through a trusted intermediary (the third author) working in the area. Many different aspects of the flexers' lives are examined – their drug use, other crime, previous and current family ties and work history, perspective on rehabilitation and their assessment of alternatives – in order to provide a picture of how they end up in their present situation. Open- and closed-ended questions were used; answers were recorded by hand, not taped. Also considered is some assessment as to whether the direction of their deviant involvements is upward, downward or stable, and whether exits are possible in some circumstances. What is revealed in their stories is how many different pathways have led to the common denominator of crack market involvement on the streets of Toronto and, once there, how difficult it is to leave this high-risk role. We suggest that the concept of 'cumulative disadvantage' (Hagan and Parker, 1999) best describes this deviant spiral.

WHAT DOES THIS CRACK MARKET LOOK LIKE?

To someone passing through this section of the city, with its lovely park, its mix of hostels, well maintained old housing, new condominiums, small businesses and bustling sidewalk life, the drug related activities would not be too obvious. It is an old neighbourhood, encompassing the city's original 'skid row', prostitution strip and the largest concentration of social welfare and support services in Toronto for its homeless, poor and underhoused population (Erickson *et al.*, 1997). Nevertheless, in the vicinity of the crossroads where we recruited participants for this study, on any given day an estimated several hundred regular crack users, from 50 to 100 flexers, and five to 10 dealers could be found, collectively producing on the order of several thousand drug transactions. Also part of the scene are the 'drive throughs', the customers who come in cars or taxis to the area to purchase crack or 'rock'. The supply of crack, according to respondents, is transported to the area from the suburbs to the key dealers on 'the corner'.

The dealer, also a lower-echelon player in the drug distribution hierarchy, is differentiated from the flexers by being a non-user. Flexers perceive the dealers as the front men for the higher ups, those who 'drive the BMWs and have houses', as one respondent comments. Motivated primarily by profit not addiction, the street corner dealer or 'main man' is someone who receives the 'quarters' (quarter-ounce) but never holds drugs for long, who collects the money and passes it back up the chain. The key to the street distribution scene is the flexer. As this flexer describes his relationship to the dealer: 'My guy has the stash [hidden somewhere]; I get a few pieces, people come up who I know or in taxis. I take it to them, get more; they [dealers] are safe – I do the dirty work.'

The flexer rejects the title of 'dealer' or 'drug seller'. Rather, he insists on terms such as go-between, intermediary or middleman to describe his role. As one respondent summarizes his job: 'I get a piece off the dealer and a piece off the buyer, and get free rock.' Flexers consider themselves working on commission, and take their pay in drugs. In a high demand environment, flexers sometimes present a rather benign view of their role: 'I treat people, I drop it [crack] on them, I share.' A succinct description is this: 'I sell and I smoke.' Flexers either buy a piece of crack outright and break it up for further distribution to users, or take the more risky option of 'fronting' the drug. This involves getting a piece of crack as a loan, breaking it up to sell at a marked up price, and paying back the dealer after they have sold some of it to cover the original cost. If they smoke it all instead, they have to find the money quickly or risk physical punishment. The largest unit most would ever handle is an '8 ball' (an eighth of an ounce or three and a half grams) worth about $160–180 (reportedly a decline from about $250 the year before). Usually flexers handle smaller amounts; in descending order, the units are half-ball, then $50– $20– $10– $5 pieces. Some work hard 'middling' all night for several consecutive days, and save up all their crack 'profits' for a binge, while others alternate between flexing and using dozens of times each day. While hundreds of dollars worth of crack cocaine routinely pass through their hands on any given day, the flexers' reward is measured in terms of minutes or hours high, and success in terms of 'breaking even' by covering their drug costs.

WHO ARE THE FLEXERS?

The 17 male respondents in this study volunteered for the interview and were paid $10 for their time. The only criterion was that they had been flexing in the area in the past year or longer. All but two were active flexers at the time of the interview. Although there is no way to know how representative this group is of all male flexers operating in this particular drug market scene, the insider knowledge of the intermediary, and the considerable time spent by project staff in the area, give us confidence that those recruited are quite typical. It should also be mentioned that many women are involved in crack use and flexing as well in this location, with many linked to the sex trade. Results of these studies are reported elsewhere (Butters *et al.*, 1997).

Flexers are not a young group. Four respondents were in their late 20s, seven were in their 30s, and five in their 40s; only one person was over 50. Twelve were white and five non-white. Virtually all were Canadian born and raised, though some came from outside Ontario. They were all poor, unemployed, living on a small fixed or no income. Several were receiving disability payments for physical or mental health conditions. While some had marginal housing in nearby hotels or apartments, most were homeless and living in shelters or hostels in the area. The average time living locally was nearly 10 years, the range from two years to 'my whole life'. Physically, the collective impression the flexers made was of being small, thin and unhealthy, much older in appearance than in chronological age, with a number displaying visible facial scars, limps or other types of disabilities. Even the younger and stronger-looking ones often relayed accounts of fairly serious beatings they had experienced, or health problems such as an infected heart valve or a 'blown lung', that had compromised their physical activities.

The flexers' work and family histories showed that their lives had not always been like this. Most had had regular jobs at one time, some involving training and professional qualifications such as chef, computer programmer, insurance salesman or engineer, while others mentioned being a carpenter, roofer, driver or bouncer. Several had been married and still saw or supported their children. Some described the failure of a business or the breakdown of their marriages as when everything 'started to fall apart'. Loss of employment, or the inability to sustain regular employment, was a common thread in their more distant past.

The participants were also asked about their drug use and criminal histories, though the various events tended to be intertwined. It was to be expected that, as current crack users, this would be a highly drug exposed group. People very rarely take crack without a substantial prior history of taking other illicit drugs, as well as alcohol, and the flexers are no exception (Erickson *et al.*, 1994). Alcohol and canna-bis have been used by all at some time, as well as currently by most. At least half admit ever using heroin, though as many have only tried and not liked it as have been regular injectors. Other drugs tried by less than half were LSD, speed and PCP; however, most of these are not used currently. When asked about being addicted to drugs in the past, 14 indicated they were, and identified alcohol (six individuals), heroin (three), barbiturates (two) and powder cocaine (two) as the primary drug of abuse; one who described himself as an 'addictive personality' said food and sex addiction preceded his crack experience.

Their criminal histories involved both drugs and other types of offences. All but one respondent admitted prior arrest, over half of them several times, but most of these arrests occurred before the past year. The most common past offences were assault, receiving stolen property, theft and drug possession, although a small number admitted to serious offences such as armed robbery or higher level drug trafficking. A history of trafficking in heroin or cannabis was more common than cocaine trafficking. Only one respondent had been a non-using crack dealer (on the corner) until his arrest on an unrelated matter led to a prison term, 'losing everything', and only then, crack use and flexing. Again, nearly all of the participants had done some jail time, though this varied from 30 days to five years at a stretch.

The initial impression, then, is that, for these flexers, their journey into deviance commenced some time previously, connected to other life changes and growing involvements with illicit drugs and crime. As these events accumulated, the crack scene was emerging. Crack addiction appears more likely to have reinforced or intensified, rather than launched, their deviant trajectory. Flexing was closer to an end than a beginning.

WHAT IS THE DEVIANT LIFESTYLE OF THE FLEXER?

Let us now consider in more detail some aspects of their current lives. Spending their time on the streets of downtown Toronto, how do flexers survive? How do they perceive the risks and rewards of their lifestyle, how much criminal involvement do they have, how central is crack use to understanding this pattern? With the main exceptions of Percodan (a codeine derivative) or Valium (a tranquillizer), by far the dominant drug handled by the flexers is crack, and the crack market rhythm dictates the pace of their days. Most have a routine when they are on the street, some rigorously sticking to seven days per week, with the same hours of the day (or night), others working in three- or four-day stretches before taking a break. Virtually any place in the neighbourhood can be used for a deal – park, bar, doughnut shop, taxi, store, washrooms, laneways – and is, but they stress it is important to keep on the move and 'keep your wits about you'. Some illustrations of the ways in which a small piece of crack is handed over to the consumer are as follows: the change slot of a payphone, in a cereal box in a store, or in a cigarette package. The few flexers who have their own rooms also are 'pieced off': provided with some crack as the price of admission to other users who want a more private place to get high. This is also where some of the 'sex for crack' transactions occur with the prostitutes in the area.

While most flexers indicate they prefer to work alone and not be responsible for anyone else, a few prefer to have a partner 'to watch my back'. The main image they project is of the loner: 'I'm connected for myself.' Being opportunistic, as one comments, is important, 'I am always working; all my hours ... I'm paying attention. You do deals everywhere anyone is hanging out – there is activity where street people are.' Familiarity with the local scene is a given: 'everyone knows who is using and who wants'. Of the dozens of daily contacts they make with eager customers, most are described as people they know in the neighbourhood, their 'regulars', or someone new who is vouched for. Only a few flexers who do the all-night shift sell to people in cars, again whom they usually know as prior customers, whereas other areas of the city are said to be more noted for drive-through deals. Most say they avoid taking chances with strangers, unless 'desperate', fearing a set-up by the police. One flexer speaks of the importance of providing a good product: 'I got to make you happy, it's my business.' The participants agree that the demand is so great that 'there is enough business for everyone', and 'it's an open corner – no one controls it'. Some of the turf battles that have been documented in the American inner city crack scene are not apparent in this Toronto setting (Goldstein *et al.*, 1989).

Even without a highly competitive atmosphere, illegal drug markets are not noted for their peace and harmony, and this Toronto scene is no exception (Goldstein, 1985; Erickson *et al.*, 1997). 'Violence is an everyday thing in this area,' as one flexer notes. Another remarks, 'more drugs – more violence'. All of the respondents acknowledge that there are dangers involved in their activities, and take steps to avoid or minimize them. At the street level, the main source of violence is related to 'vicing', that is, users who are cheated – victimized – by being sold poor-quality or non-existent crack. Apparently, slivered almonds and wax make good imitation crack. Vicing also occurs when the seller takes money but does not return with the drugs – said to be a more common occurrence with strangers or those who are suspected of being undercover police officers. Everyone at some time has witnessed someone else being hurt over drug activities, with examples ranging from beating, stabbing, shooting, death threats, leaving town or knee caps broken to actually witnessing a killing. About half of the respondents themselves have also personally experienced violence in relation to their drug market involvements. When these interviews were done, in 1995, there had been one murder over crack in the past two years, involving someone, known locally as a very violent individual, who stabbed another user over a $20 rock (several respondents volunteered this story, verified by the local contacts). The weapons of choice tend to be knives, baseball bats or juice bottles, not guns, because 'the dealers don't want the heat' (that is, the police attention), according to respondents.

While most participants do not directly acknowledge hurting others, in the course of drug exchanges, the four who did so indicate that it happened either for revenge or in self defence. One person describes how he took a gun from someone he wanted to buy crack from, and who then tried to rob him, 'I didn't realize he had the gun till after I took him down – I'll sell it today, but not in the area.' Two flexers are explicitly non-violent in these replies: 'I don't believe in violence; it doesn't make sense', and 'I don't carry weapons, not even a knife'. Some of the more non-committal responses are: 'you have to take your own measures – it's dog eat dog' and 'I run alone, so I have to do a bit of scrapping to show I'm not an easy target.' Other participants refer to having people 'watch out for me', or say, 'you have to have back-up', indicating a sense of preparedness for possible interference. As a warning, another describes how he 'always carries a knife or screwdriver – they see it and leave me alone'. But another respondent comments, 'I feel safe down here ... I know a lot of people.' For most the possibility of violence is a constant backdrop to their street activities.

The flexers perceive the risks of serious injury to themselves as more remote than those expressed by dealers in US studies (Reuter *et al.*, 1990) perhaps reflecting a smaller likelihood of lethal violence and the relative lack of handguns at this level. Flexers volunteer that the guns are carried by the (real) dealers, those higher up in the network. The flexers' accounts suggest that the risk of violence may be diminished on the streets by having a reputation as fair, as someone who delivers the real goods, and also by presenting oneself as ready to defend yourself if necessary, or by having someone available as back-up. These strategies appear to be an essential aspect of the flexers' role, in order to cope with the constant tension on the street and the omnipresent threat of violence. Image and presentation of self are important survival skills.

What about their other income-generating activities, particularly the non-drug criminality that coexists with the street drug market in this area? When presented with a list of possible non-drug crimes that they might do to get money currently, flexers appear to be engaged in very few other illegal activities. Most concentrate on flexing, collecting welfare or disability benefits and 'stemming' (begging or panhandling). One participant says that he likes to ask for hand-outs near bank machines, on nights where hockey games attract many fans. Another individual, while asserting what he will not do, 'I don't sell myself [that is, prostitution] and I don't steal', shows the interviewer a bag of t-shirts with a bank logo, which he says he will go off and sell when they are finished, and presents her with one, saying 'Take it; they're not stolen.' Several other respondents also volunteer: 'People get me to sell stuff' or 'If someone wants something, I know how to get it.' Whether the property is actively stolen or has 'fallen off a truck', poor neighbourhoods have always been prone to this kind of informal redistribution of wealth.

Many respondents indicate that being a drug middleman is all that is necessary to keep them supplied with crack, and even that their other crimes had diminished: 'Before I flexed I used to break into cars; I have enough money now.' Another who had a long criminal history and incarceration record is cautious about doing anything more serious than flexing because 'I'd face a lot of prison time if I was caught.' A few admit to concurrent stealing, mainly breaking into cars, shoplifting and intercepting cheques. Flexers are an opportunistic, street-wise group, most of whom continue to engage in petty criminality, but are mostly focused on crack transactions. This initiative sets them apart from the more numerous crack users in the area who do not flex. Why do flexers take such big risks – of arrest, of violence, of ill health and of being stigmatized as 'crack dealers' in the public eye?

Central to an understanding of their embeddedness in a deviant lifestyle is their sense of addiction to crack cocaine. As mentioned earlier, most acknowledged a prior addiction, as in this comment: 'When I wasn't using dope, I was a big-time drunk; now I choose the rocks.' This theme, that taking crack had supplanted previous favoured forms of drug taking, came up repeatedly: 'I was addicted immediately – it's a good high.' The flexer group would by most behavioural definitions, including their own, be considered addicts. They describe almost a love-hate relationship with their current drug of choice, liking the high, resenting the dependence: 'Crack is the only drug man invented that acts for such a short time – you're sure to be back'; 'Crack is a greedy, anti-social drug'; and 'It's the worst drug I ever used in my life – you never get enough.' One flexer provides a practical description of the difference between use and addiction: 'I would like to think of myself as a user, but I guess I'm an addict since I think of what I'm going to do to get high when I get up [every] morning.' Several qualify their response about addiction to crack in these ways: one says he does not know if he is addicted, because he had stopped for nine months (but is using again now); another says, 'I would rather drink and smoke marijuana, I stopped crack for two years, then went back; it's a phase.' Another participant makes the distinction between physical addiction (with withdrawal symptoms) to alcohol and heroin which he acknowledges experiencing, and crack with its short-term high. Even among addicts, there is a scale of degradation, the bottom being the 'Joneser' who crawls around on the floor looking for crumbs of unsmoked crack, and 'some people will pick up kitty litter and smoke it'. One respondent mentions a 'turning point' when he was prepared to prostitute himself to get money for crack; this led him to cut back his crack consumption and become a more intermittent user.

Nevertheless, despite heavy, continuing crack consumption, its apparent priority in users' lives, and the numerous adverse consequences associated with using and obtaining crack, the behaviour of so called 'addicts' cannot be understood simply as the drug controlling them (Reinarman and Levine, 1997). Compared to poor, homeless crack users, middle class users have many other activities and demands competing with drug use and often choose them over drugs (Erickson *et al.*, 1994). Within the constraints of their impoverished lives, flexers are individuals who analyse their situations quite dispassionately and also make choices. They can articulate a number of positive features of their way of life. It takes a lot of skills to survive in the street life, and some respondents show pride in their prowess at 'keeping afloat', having enough money and drugs for their needs and avoiding arrest. Most flexers are busy, on the move every day, and some thrive on the action: 'I'm good at what I do and I get a thrill out of it' and 'Even if I'm not using, I have to run around, be doing something.' Using crack must be seen in this context of a street life otherwise lacking in legitimate employment and conventional family and social ties. Time is very empty: 'I don't want to give it [crack] up; it fills my nights and days.' Crack flexing provides some structure and purposeful activity, and some sense of 'success' within the parameters of the street culture. At least half of the flexers interviewed present as unapologetic, even upbeat, make no excuses and express little desire or expectation for their situation to change. The remainder appear less resigned, more tired and have generally vague notions of needing alternatives. Given the extent to which their lives are circumscribed by poverty, homelessness, criminal records and unemployment, how likely is it that flexers would seek an exit? And, if they do, what are their prospects?

ARE THERE ROUTES OUT OF THE FLEXER WAY OF LIFE?

One place to start getting out is treatment, to do something about the addiction. When asked if they had ever sought treatment, about half answer 'yes', but report mixed experiences. Only one says he was helped to quit crack as a result of being in a three month residential programme where 'you work all day'. Others respond that they have gained new insights, even if they continue crack use: 'I know what the problem is but not what to do about it'; 'I know why I do it but I don't care', another mentions receiving practical help: 'I learned a lot – how to stay away from diseases.' Some consider treatment a temporary respite from the life of the streets: 'a chance to rest and dry out'. Similarly, periods in jail or detoxification centres are described as 'rehab.' (rehabilitation) and respondents often mention weight loss as a concern that prompts the need for this kind of 'time out'. Indeed, some flexers consciously alternate periods on the street with periods 'away', at such a facility or at a family refuge (if there is one) 'to relax and restart'.

Those who have not sought treatment say unequivocally they are not interested in quitting: 'What would I want treatment for?', 'I do not want to give it up', and 'Treatment would not tip the scale in either direction. My mind is my mind.' One person who recently stopped using crack describes how he stopped on his own: 'I woke up one morning, said to myself I'm getting old, I'm tired of going to jail, and I left the area.' He is back living in this area now, where he was raised, but says he is clean, the police know he is and leave him alone, and 'When I wake up, there is a light at the end of my tunnel.' He is the exception.

Another aspect of getting out of the flexer life is to find alternative work. Both of those who stopped crack use and are no longer flexing want to get into the labour force but have been unsuccessful and express a lot of concern about their prospects. One says it is 'touch and go', though he has a seasonal job which will get him off the corner. The other had been in a car accident the year before (and was visibly not very mobile) which he said limited his options and 'there's no pension' for a flexer. One active flexer who expresses an interest in taking job training and finding another way to make a living, recognizes the economic lure: 'I used to wash dishes before I got into dealing; there's a lot more money in crack.' Those with somewhat vague ideas of wanting to 'better myself' do not see a clear way to go about it.

Finally, their response when asked how they foresee their lives in the years ahead produced mostly pessimistic, though perhaps realistic, assessments: 'Just to wait to die'; 'I am just trying to stay alive – I've had two heart attacks'; 'I don't look that far ahead'; 'I'm tired, I've been everywhere, I'll stay here'; 'You don't see people much past 45 in my lifestyle'; and, most briefly, 'Nothing.' Two flexers mention the importance of female partners in their short-term decisions. One was hoping a former girlfriend would come back, they would both quit and then they would leave the area; the other person's girlfriend had died from an overdose four months previously, and he describes himself as 'messed up' and having to get away. A small number of the flexers mentioned family that they would see at Christmas, or visit occasionally, but for most their ties with previous lives seem to be severed. On the other hand, as one noted, 'You can't starve to death in Toronto', and the availability of free meals and hostels in the area, for those who know how to gain access to services, provides a minimal subsistence living. Most seem to accept these limits and focus on survival and drugs, one day at a time.

CONCLUSION

This chapter has depicted the lives of flexers, crack addicts who act as middlemen to provide their own supply, in the context of an active street drug scene in Toronto. They are found to occupy a unique position in the drug market hierarchy, between users and dealers. While in the eyes of the law, and to most of the public, flexers warrant the highly stigmatized label of 'crack dealer', they do not consider themselves dealers. They reserve that title for those above them in the distribution chain who profit financially from drug sales. Flexers view themselves as providing a useful service to both dealers and the multitudes of users, for which they run a daily risk of arrest and violence, and are rewarded with crack. For many, the busy life on the street, along with some petty crime and other hustles, occupies their days and provides some satisfaction; however, most also recognize the stress and hardship of surviving without jobs, very little money and no secure housing. Few see a future that can or will be very different.

Their routes into the role of flexer are individualistic, but also reflect an accumulation of negative life events: lengthy prior histories of unemployment, lack of family ties, injuries and poor health, crime, alcohol and other drug use and previous addictions. Most had already fallen off the ladder of conventional society before crack swept into this neighbourhood in the early 1990s. Already leading marginal lives, and getting by as they could, they found that crack provided them with both an attractive high and a way of keeping afloat. Therefore crack should be seen as an extension, or another layer, on the core of their deviant status. In a broader sense, flexers have lost their social capital (defined as their ability to gain access to legitimate resources in mainstream institutions) and have acquired criminal capital (defined as connections to various illegal activities and networks that provide criminal opportunities); this transition has paved the way for the crack exchange role (Erickson and Cheung, 1999).

While it is tempting to adopt simplistic mechanistic explanations of crack 'causing this downfall', we favour a more voluntaristic explanation (Erickson *et al.*, 1994). Rather than seeing the relentless pursuit of crack as a loss of control, it may be more accurate to view flexers as people whose current situations offer little beyond the pleasure of the high and the demands of survival on the street. With nothing to compete with crack, it is hardly surprising that middle-class routes out of addiction – treatment, rehabilitation, education, jobs, family support – have little relevance to these men. Flexers are ignored or arrested, neither of which events addresses their drug use or their lifestyle, but rather serves to amplify their deviance through further stigmatization and criminalization. Most of these respondents have achieved a kind of stability and are 'getting by'. If crack disappeared tomorrow, their lives would likely remain mired in deviance. In this sense, they reflect a broader challenge to legal and social policies.

NOTES

1   Although of course, separate markets exist to serve middle class users and are quite different; see Waldorf *et al.* (1994).
2   Another example of the middleman role is found in Lesieur's (1976) ethnography of the compulsive gambler and the combination of ever-increasing risk with declining opportunity. We thank Dr Andrew Hathaway for drawing our attention to this parallel.

REFERENCES

Butters, J., Hallgren, A. and McGillicuddy, P. (1997), *Poor Women and Crack in Downtown Toronto*, Toronto: Street Health and Addiction Research Foundation.
Erickson, P.G. (1998), 'Drugs, violence and public health: what does the harm reduction approach have to offer?', paper presented at the Fraser Institute Conference, 'Sensible Solutions to the Urban Drug Problem', Vancouver, British Columbia, 21 April.
Erickson, P.G. and Cheung, Y.W. (1999), 'Harm reduction among cocaine users: reflections on individual intervention and community social capital', *International Journal of Drug Policy*, **10**, 235–46.
Erickson, P.G., Adlaf, E.M., Smart, R.G. and Murray, G.F. (1994), *The Steel Drug: Cocaine and Crack in Perspective*, 2nd edn, New York: Lexington Books.
Erickson, P.G., Butters, J., Fischer, B., Fehrman, E., Haans, D. and Poland, B. (1997), 'Exploring drug market violence in a more peaceable society', Appendix G in the Draft Report of the Drugs–Violence Task Force, US Sentencing Commission, Washington, DC.
Fagan, J. and Chin, K. (1991), 'Violence as Regulation and Social Control in the Distribution of Crack', in M. De La Rosa, E. Lambert and B. Gropper (eds), *Drugs and Violence*, Rockville, MD: National Institute on Drug Abuse, pp.8–43.
Goldstein, P. (1985), 'The drugs/violence nexus: A tripartite conceptual framework', *Journal of Drug Issues*, **21**, 345–67.
Goldstein, P., Brownstein, H., Ryan, P. and Belucci, P. (1989), 'Crack and homicide in New York City: a conceptually based event analysis', *Contemporary Drug Problems*, **16**, 651–87.
Goode, E. and Ben-Yehuda, N. (1994), *Moral Panics: The Social Construction of Deviance*, Oxford: Blackwell.
Hagan, J. and Parker, P. (1999), 'Rebellion beyond the classroom: a life-course capitalization theory of the intergenerational causes of delinquency', *Theoretical Criminology*, **3**, 259–85.
Lesieur, H.R. (1976), *The Chase: Career of the Compulsive Gambler*, Garden City, New York: Doubleday.
NAPHP (National Association for Public Health Policy) (1999), 'A public health approach to mitigating the negative consequences of illicit drug abuse', *Journal of Public Health Policy*, **20** (3), 268–81.
Reinarman, C. and Levine, H.G. (eds) (1997), *Crack in America: Demon Drugs and Social Justice*, Berkeley: University of California Press.

Reuter, P. and MacCoun, R. (1992), 'Street drug markets in inner-city neighbourhoods', in J.B. Steinberg, D.W. Lyon and M.E. Vaiana (eds), *Urban America: Policy Choices for Los Angeles and the Nation*, Santa Monica, CA: RAND, pp.227–51.

Reuter, P., MacCoun, R. and Murphy, P. (1990), *Money from Crime*, Santa Monica, CA: RAND.

Waldorf, D., Murphy, S. and Lauderback, D. (1994), 'Middle class cocaine sellers: Self reported reasons for stopping sales', *Addiction Research*, **2**, 109–26.

Waldorf, D., Reinarman, C. and Murphy, S. (1991), *Cocaine Changes: The Experience of Using and Quitting*, Philadelphia: Temple University Press.

Chapter 10

Black Women's Pathways to Involvement in Illicit Drug Distribution and Sales: an Exploratory Ethnographic Analysis

Lisa Maher, Eloise Dunlap and Bruce D. Johnson

What factors in black women's backgrounds lead them towards crack (and other drug) sales as a primary economic activity in adulthood? This chapter is an exploratory analysis designed to identify common factors (called 'pathways') during adolescence and early adult years reported by African–American women involved as crack and other drug distributors. The pathways identified below show how the impact of structural and cultural disinvestment constrained the family backgrounds and labour market opportunities of these women so as to effectively exclude them from the formal economy. At the neighbourhood level, an early investment in street life and continuing exposure to informal sector activity, including criminality, meant that drug selling was one of the limited economic options available to these women.

BACKGROUND

Drug research has rarely depicted women as economic agents, actively involved in the purchase, sale and consumption of illicit substances. Rather, the literature has been primarily focused upon prescription drug use, prostitution and female sexuality, and the effects of illicit drug use on women's reproductive functioning. Studies also suggest that women's initial experiences of illicit drug use, and heroin use in particular, are strongly mediated by males (Rosenbaum, 1981a; Blom and van den Berg, 1989; Stephens, 1991).[1] Heroin use results in a 'narrowing of options' for women (Rosenbaum, 1981a; Maher and Curtis, 1992) whereby women generate income through sex work and other gendered forms of lawbreaking such as shoplifting and fraud and are only rarely involved in violent interpersonal crimes such as robbery or the distribution and sale of illicit drugs (for example, Adler, 1985; Johnson et al., 1985; Williams, 1989; Maher and Curtis, 1992). Within the heroin economy, women appeared confined to low-status, passive and peripheral roles such as 'bag followers' and 'holders' (Goldstein, 1979).

However, by the 1990s research highlighted the salience of crack distribution and sales as a source of income generation among drug users in the inner city (for example, Bourgois, 1989, 1995; Hamid, 1990, 1991a, 1991b; Mieczkowski, 1990). During this period, crack was clearly the most lucrative and frequently sold drug in street-level markets in New York City and even drug users active in other forms of lawbreaking were unable to generate income from these activities which rivalled that received from crack sales (Johnson *et al.*, 1994). While little was known about the participation of women, early studies pointed to new opportunities in the wake of the crack-propelled expansion in street-level drug markets. In a study of women crack users in Miami, Inciardi *et al.* (1993) found that drug business offences represented a much greater proportion of total crime (94 per cent) than that found among two earlier cohorts of female heroin users (28 per cent and 34 per cent respectively) and women were less likely to engage in prostitution than the female heroin users studied previously. In New York City, Fagan (1994) found 36 per cent of women drug users reported having sold drugs more than 50 times, concluding that,

> the size and seemingly frantic activity of the current drug markets has made possible for women new ways to participate in street networks. Their involvement in drug selling at high income levels defies the gendered norms and roles of the past, where drug dealing was an incidental income source often mediated by domestic partnerships ... The expansion of drug markets in the cocaine economy has provided new ways for women to escape their limited roles, statuses and incomes in previous eras. (Fagan, 1994: 210)

Similarly, 'The high incidence of incarceration and homicide among young, inner-city minority males, in the wake of the expanded demand for drugs, has provided an opportunity structure for female entry into the informal drug economy' (Baskin *et al.*, 1993: 410–11; Mieczkowski, 1994). However, ethnographic research cautions that while crack has prompted shifts in the gender patterns of crime, these shifts have not necessarily strengthened the position of women (Bourgois and Dunlap, 1993; Maher and Daly, 1996; Maher 1997). Where women are involved in crack distribution, they tend to be concentrated in secondary roles and/or low-level distribution activities (Dunlap, 1992, 1995; Dunlap *et al.*, 1997; Inciardi *et al.*, 1993; Fagan, 1994: 202). 'Life in criminal subcultures is dynamic, and much suggests that, with the ascendancy of crack, the lot of black women who engage in deviant activity has taken a turn for the worse' (Austin, 1992: 1794).

THE PATHWAYS APPROACH

Feminist research has highlighted the importance of several factors identified as pathways to criminal activity for women. This approach is perhaps best represented by Miller's (1986) pioneering study of Milwaukee 'street women'. Miller suggests three analytically distinct pathways that characterize women's entry to 'deviant street networks' and participation in criminal activity: drug use, membership of domestic networks, and running away from or being 'pushed out' of home.

While the drug use 'causes' crime hypothesis remains one of the 'highly cherished beliefs' (Inciardi and Pottieger, 1986: 101) of drug research, a growing body of literature suggests that involvement in lawbreaking may precede regular drug use (for example, Anglin and Speckart, 1988; Anglin and Hser, 1987; Chaiken and Chaiken, 1990). Inciardi and Pottieger found that 'criminal activity emerged concomitant with drug experimentation, and regular use of heroin and other narcotics began only several years after the onset of crime (1986: 104; see also Inciardi *et al.*, 1993, on female crack users).

Similarly, Miller (1986: 108) found 'The overwhelming majority of women with serious substance abuse problems developed them *after* they were already immersed in the fast life.' Substance abuse served as a pathway for only 10 out of a sample of 64 women (Miller, 1986: 109).[2] Miller argues that young black women are more likely to be recruited to 'street life' and criminal activity via the interface between black domestic networks comprised of kin, non-kin and pseudo-kin, and deviant street networks. Compared to white and Hispanic women, for whom household *disorganization* (expressed by conflict between young women and their caretakers) propels recruitment into deviant street networks as a result of running away and drug use, 'It is the *organization* of households among poor blacks into domestic networks that promotes the recruitment of young black women directly to deviant street networks' (ibid.: 117; emphasis in original).

Cultural practices within the black community, such as othermothering and involvement of the extended kin network in the caring and rearing of children, are also implicated in this process:

> the very system that may be responsible for household survival then, may promote the initiation of young adults into a generally disapproved way of life simply by exposing them to more possible recruiters to deviant street networks. A very striking example of this has to do with the cultural pattern of 'child-keeping' ... On the one hand, this pattern clearly promotes the care and nurturing of children in an environment of scarce and uncertain resources ... On the other hand, this pattern may maximize exposure to deviant networks. (ibid.: 79)

Miller's work calls attention to the organization of domestic networks (which were primarily law-abiding in Milwaukee in the early 1980s) and to running away from home as female pathways to deviant street networks. Miller (1986) found that running away served as a pathway to involvement in deviant street networks and criminal activity for young women regardless of race/ethnicity and social class. The sexual victimization of young women is believed to play a prominent part in this process.

> [Sexual abuse] is a much more important factor in patterns of running away and drug use and, thus, in recruitment to deviant street networks than is generally acknowledged. It is also my belief that the experience of emotional distancing during sexual contact that incest victims often describe is too like the psychological state described by prostitutes when they are servicing a trick for one not to be a sort of rehearsal for the other. In those cases, sexual exploitation on the street seems but an extension of sexual exploitation in the family. (ibid.: 115)

Indeed, much feminist research has explored the apparent links between childhood victimization and abuse and adult female lawbreaking (for example, Widom, 1989, 1990; Gilfus, 1992). As Chesney-Lind and Rodriguez (1983: 62) have argued, 'young girls faced with violence and/or sexual abuse at home ... became criminalized by their efforts to save themselves (by running away) from the abuse'. Similarly, in a study of 50 black women imprisoned in New York City,

Arnold (1990) proposes a trajectory from gender victimization to imprisonment in accounting for Black women's criminalization. Drug use plays a prominent role in this process whereby young Black women respond to or resist their victimization, both in terms of 'dulling the pain' and in providing a 'pseudo-family' (ibid.). Daly has constructed a composite of women's pathways to involvement in lawbreaking which she terms the 'street woman scenario':

> Whether they were pushed out or ran away from abusive homes, or became part of a deviant milieux, young women begin to engage in petty hustles or prostitution. Life on the streets leads to drug use and addiction, which in turn leads to more frequent lawbreaking to support a drug habit. Meanwhile, young women drop out of school because of pregnancy, boredom or disinterest in school or both. Their paid employment record is negligible because they lack interest to work in low-paid or unskilled jobs. Having a child may facilitate entry into adult women's networks and allow a woman to support herself in part by state aid. A woman may continue lawbreaking as a result of relationships with men who may also be involved in crime. (Daly, 1992: 14)

This chapter examines Black women's pathways to involvement in drug distribution in light of recent feminist research and theorizing which strongly implicates the 'street woman scenario' in women's lawbreaking and participation in the criminal economy. Utilizing ethnographic data from a small sample of women engaged in street-level drug distribution, it provides insights into the lives of a 'hidden' group of women participating in what has historically been regarded as a male-dominated labour market. By exploring the role of domestic networks and neighbourhood contexts, women's experiences of the formal sector workforce, drug use and 'street life' itself, the chapter attempts to identify key factors shaping black women's involvements in the drug economy.

RELATED FINDINGS FROM THIS STUDY AND THE UNIQUE CONTRIBUTION OF THIS CHAPTER

This chapter is one of several publications emerging from a major federally-funded project on crack selling (see below) and has a focus designed to illuminate the complex of forces influencing inner-city African–American women's involvement in crack selling. Dunlap and Johnson (1992a) summarize approximately 20 major 'macro forces' (for example, declines in manufacturing, high housing costs, reduced value of welfare benefits, and so on) in the American social and economic system. These macro forces have affected most severely households and minority families living in American inner cities, and especially in New York City (Kasarda, 1992) and have had 'micro consequences' (see Dunlap 1992, 1995).

In a related paper, Dunlap *et al.* (1997) document the specific (usually low-level) roles in crack distribution activities in which several of the women (also quoted below) engaged. That paper documents their activities when selling crack, how they selected or were selected for various crack distribution roles, how they worked with or for male sellers, how they entered, left and re-entered distribution positions, negotiated their relationship as sellers with men and routinely adjusted their behaviours to a variety of gendered differences in power and economic dependence/independence in the crack-selling business (see also Maher and Daly, 1996; Dunlap, 1995; Dunlap and Johnson, 1992b, 1996; Dunlap, Johnson and Rath, 1996).

The unique contribution of this chapter is to 'bridge' the analytic gap between women's exposure to the macro forces/micro consequences in their households of orientation during childhood/adolescence and their adult participation as crack sellers. The analysis below documents the pathways (or factors noted in the literature review above) as they were experienced by these crack-selling women. Moreover, the analyses below represent the *most common* pathways and patterns reported by African-American women from the inner city who have become crack sellers as adults (see Fagan, 1994, for quantitative data supporting this position). Women like Debbie (with a high school degree and some extended experience in legal work) or Rachael (next paragraph) are a distinct minority among the larger pool of African–American women working at the lower levels of street crack markets, many of whom are also without regular places to live (see Maher *et al.*, 1996; Maher 1997).

The case history of Rachael (summarized in this paragraph only) provides a direct contrast to the more common pathways and selling patterns documented later in this chapter. Rachael was a successful crack-selling, African–American woman living in Harlem. With no arrests for any crime, her success depended primarily upon selling crack to a small number of working/middle class people who were older cocaine and crack users from her apartment; she avoided sales to street crack users (Dunlap, Johnson and Manwai, 1996). Rachel also experienced a very different pathway into crack selling (Dunlap and Johnson, 1996) than the pathways documented below for the more typical African–American female crack sellers. Her career path to, and success as, a crack seller was primarily due to the importance of Rachel's powerful grandmother (despite an alcoholic mother) who provided Rachel with many critical skills in household and interpersonal management; Rachel made critical choices to limit her drug consumption and business operations that effectively prevented her from becoming enmeshed as a street-level seller or sex worker.

This chapter will specifically focus on understanding the complex and subtle factors which emerged during ethnographic fieldwork and data analysis – factors which are not captured by even the most sophisticated quantitative studies. The analysis here allows women to explain in their own words how they thought and framed their lives and paths to their current crack-selling activities.

METHODOLOGY

The data presented here are derived from a NIDA-funded study, 'The Natural History of Crack Distribution/Abuse'. This research consists of an ethnographic study of the structure, functioning and economics of cocaine and crack distribution in low-income, minority communities in New York City. The data set generated for this project constitutes one of the richest in this field, containing several thousand pages of transcribed recorded material and drawing on the insights of a variety of informants and a multidisciplinary team of ethnographic researchers. The study includes a healthy representation of dealers from a range of economic statuses including street corner crack sellers and cocaine/crack weight distributors. More than 300 crack distributors, both male and female, were contacted and observed during the course of the research and their activities recorded in the form of detailed field notes. Approximately 250 males and 107 females provided in-depth tape-recorded interviews from which the quotations below were derived. Close relations and rapport were established and maintained with many of the dealers and their families over a period of three to five years. Staff have extensively documented the details of the study methodology, including gaining access to sellers (Dunlap and Johnson, 1994), recruiting and interviewing procedures (Dunlap *et al.*, 1990; Lewis *et al.*, 1992), ensuring the confidentiality and personal safety of subjects and ethnographers (Williams *et al.*, 1992), and retrieving and analysing textual data from transcripts for ethnographic analysis (Manwar *et al.*, 1994).

A total of 87 African–Americans, 15 Latinas and five white women from different neighbourhoods in New York City participated in the study. The analyses below are confined to African–American women in the study.[3] All participants completed a tape-recorded in-depth interview which covered familial and personal histories and how they became involved in crack sales and distribution activity. Women provided information reflecting a range of experiences and factors associated with their entry into drug use and crack selling. These experiences were very similar to the those of the African–American crack sellers studied, so the following analysis represents the most common factors and pathways to crack selling among this sample.

Women tended to be concentrated at the lower levels of drug distribution. In most cases, women either acquired their supply from male distributors and/or worked for males. The women in this sample were ethnic minority women of either African–American or Afro-Caribbean ethnicity, and all were engaged in the sale and distribution of crack cocaine at the time of interview. They were all current daily or near-daily consumers of crack and, in some instances, other drugs as well. Consistent with the findings of previous research (Fagan and Chin, 1989, 1991; Golub and Johnson 1992, 1994a, 1994b, 1994c; Fagan 1994; Inciardi *et al.*, 1993), the women in this sample were not drug neophytes; most had extensive histories of drug use prior to the introduction of crack to their consumption repertoires and many had sold marijuana, cocaine powder or heroin prior to their crack-selling career.

These women are part of a 'hidden' population about which little is known. The ethnomethodological, ethnographic mode of inquiry provides a means of clarifying common patterns among people who are 'outliers' (that is, rare among general populations) and of understanding aspects of their lives that are rarely illuminated through strictly quantitative analysis. While the women studied here constitute a non-representative sample, and findings should not be generalized beyond Black women in the inner-city context, their experiences of drug use and sales are consistent with findings about crack-using women provided by quantitative studies (Fagan, 1992, 1994; Fagan and Chin, 1989, 1991; Johnson *et al.*, 1994). By drawing on ethnographic data in the form of observations and interviews, this research contributes to a small body of research designed to chart the natural history of and the relatively typical women's 'careers' in drug distribution (Dunlap *et al.*, 1990; Dunlap and Johnson, 1992a, 1992b, 1994). Several key aspects of these womens' pathways to crack selling are presented: deviant networks and neighbourhood contexts, limited formal labour force participation, drug use/sale and non-drug users' criminality, and street life.

DOMESTIC NETWORKS AND NEIGHBOURHOOD CONTEXTS

Low-income urban communities in the United States have a long history of reliance on the informal sector (Whyte, 1943; Liebow, 1967; Stack, 1974; Valentine, 1978). These informal trading and exchange systems, based on social and kin networks, serve to meet the survival needs of the urban poor (Susser, 1982; Sharff, 1987). Within such communities, the informal economy provides opportunities for income generation and access to goods and services for populations that are denied access to formal sector mechanisms because of the inadequate division of labour in advanced industrial economies (Pahl, 1980). In addition to providing an alternative market for jobs, goods and services, these activities may also serve as a kind of 'glue' which gives both 'form and stability to social life' (Ferman, 1985; Folb, 1980). Within many inner-city 'ghetto' neighbourhoods, 'everyone beyond early childhood has knowledge of or at least indirect contact with "hustling" as a possible alternative source of income' (Valentine 1978: 23). All women in this study grew up in impoverished inner-city minority communities characterized by the presence of a strong informal economy, including the drug trade. Drug distribution and sales activity were an institutionalized aspect of the local economy, providing opportunities for income generation and redistribution of the limited wealth.

Queen Bee is a 35-year-old African–American woman, born in the south and raised in New York City. Queen Bee's recollections of her childhood indicate that both her domestic network and the wider community in which she grew up were deeply involved in the pursuit of income through informal opportunities. Queen Bee was raised by an aunt from the age of nine months. Queen Bee's aunt worked in a restaurant. Although she received a small supplement for Queen Bee through the foster care administration, formal sector income was inadequate to ensure the economic survival of the household. In order to make ends meet, Queen Bee's aunt sold food (dinners and sandwiches) and hosted card games or 'parties' in her apartment, during which she also sold liquor.

As a child, Queen Bee held mixed feelings about these ventures. Aware of the struggle to survive from an early age, she did not view them as iniquitous. However, her aunt's negative teachings against her mother and father prompted Queen Bee to develop a degree of animosity towards her aunt. As an adolescent, Queen Bee's desire for interaction with her peers and certain social activities were curtailed by her aunt's insistence that she help out with these enterprises. She began to view her aunt as greedy and as having too many parties. As she put it, her aunt took advantage of 'a good thing' (her free labour).

Today, what Queen Bee remembers most about her aunt is her entrepreneurial abilities and her constant efforts to generate income through card games, illicit liquor sales, home-cooked food and other informal sector activities. Queen Bee's aunt clearly provided an important role model for the adolescent girl, instilling in her a desire for economic independence and teaching her to think in business terms. Talking about her aunt's dinners and parties Queen Bee recalled,

> we used to sell food outside, right in front of the store – fried chicken, uh, rice and beans, macaroni and cheese, cakes, and dinners on the weekend ... We made money. It wasn't like a waste of time. Yeah, we sold food and liquor. We made money. We made what you cut out you double it and you triple it.

While Queen Bee's family of orientation illustrates how inadequate wages forced many minority women to look for other sources of income to support their families, it also suggests that such involvements extend beyond domestic networks into the community. Indeed, individual or household participation is only made possible by the availability of such options at the neighbourhood level. Queen Bee's experiences of the informal economy clearly extended beyond her domestic or kinship network, serving to reinforce the role of the informal economy, and the drug industry in particular, as a source of alternative institutions for the fulfilment of community needs (see also Hamid, 1991a, 1991b). Growing up, Queen Bee remembers 'number runners' and 'drug dealers' serving as a banking system for the community. Because many people could not go to a bank and expect to receive a formal loan, alternative institutions arose to provide this service. As she explained,

> Well, at the time like that around there, the people from the number hole and the block were wrapped so together if I, I had a pair of sneakers, and I had holes in them, then, you know she [Queen Bee's aunt] went to – in there, and he gave her the money. But no strings attached to it, because she plays her numbers there.

Nor was it necessary to be a drug user or a numbers customer in order to get a loan from these sources.

> Even if, they didn't use drugs – and they went to one of those drug dealers for food money, for food, or whatever, they have one of they workers to go shoppin' and bring you food. I'm tellin' you what I know for a fact. All right. I remember Nicky Barnes bought my outfit for school. Because we had had a fire in the building. And it was around school time, you know for school to start back in September? ... And a lotta, uh, you know, my clothes and stuff got messed up. And he gave my mother some money, and they just throw us some money, and we still went to school on that first day like we would usually do.

The local-level informal economy played an important role in Queen Bee's childhood and had a profound effect on her. Her experience indicates how larger social structures and economic conditions, in addition to prompting individual adaptations, served to promote the development of alternative institutions in impoverished inner-city communities. Although their activities were illegal, 'number runners' and 'drug dealers' performed valuable economic and social functions for this community.

> They used to give us bus rides, in the summer time they went to block parties. Even the drug dealers. They had free bus rides. They made sure it was enough buses so that all the kids could go free – babies on up. And if it wasn't enough buses, they order another bus, or they cars would take you. Yes, those are the days that I'll never – it's just a fact, they have to do it, but they kept that money in their community.

Denied access to legal avenues and formal institutions, inner-city residents were forced to rely on the informal sector. For children like Queen Bee, illegal activities, especially number games and drug dealing, were cast in a positive light at an early age.

Similarly, Sha, a 32-year-old African–American woman, grew up in an adjacent community with a long history of informal economic institutions. Although her family of origin was engaged in a wide variety of informal-sector activity, Sha's kinship network was also heavily immersed in drug distribution and sales.

> My people didn't do nothing. All my people know about is drugs, eatin' and livin', that's all they know about. They didn't never get involved [in my schooling]. The only time my mother came up to the school if I got a call from the teacher and then she'd be there – you know what I'm sayin' – Church? shoot. I'm a Baptist, man. My moms didn't know nothin' about no church.

Nor is participation in the informal sector confined to single-parent families. Sha's family of origin indicates the bind that many two-parent black families are caught in when the man is unable to earn enough to support the household. Despite the presence of a husband, Sha's mother, like Queen Bee's aunt, was an active participant in the informal economy, hosting card games most Friday nights and selling liquor on the side.

> She'd sell drinks at the card games to keep the people, you know keep the money goin' ... I guess she was doin' it for a while until my father got a promotion and enough money to, you know. She did it for a while.

Even though this was a two-parent household, Sha's family of orientation struggled to survive. In the wake of regional economic restructuring in the 1970s (Kasarda, 1992), blue collar workers like Sha's father were rendered increasingly marginal to the formal labour force. Denied access to the growing service sector and confronted with the prospect of severe impoverishment, Sha remembers her mother and father as increasingly willing to do anything that would enable the family to survive. This included participation in drug selling.

> My uncles, they stay in drugs, you know, I was in that type of situation all my life ... they drug dealers and stuff like that. And I was around, my mother was around at that time so it affected my family too. My mother too at that time cause we was in there, you know, cause I guess that they was the only people that she could turn to at the time when she had us, so we was there involved with this and I was there seein' it.

During Sha's adolescence, her parent's gradual immersion in drug dealing prompted considerable residential instability and a series of short-term accommodations, including stays in abandoned buildings and, at one stage, relocation to Florida:

> you know we couldn't stay in one apartment too long ... like they made a certain amount of money and we had to move outta there before they get busted for some old wild shit. But I knew I was movin' so everywhere I went it was home.

Sha's life history suggests how the labour market marginality of her father reinforced the lure of alternative opportunities for income generation offered by the drug industry. However, as Preble and Casey (1969: 19) noted more than 30 years ago, the drug economy existed to service the needs of a broader community beyond drug users and those unwilling, unable or denied access to formal labour market participation. Heroin users, in particular, have long been regarded as 'important figure[s] in the economic life of the slums' and have typically received support for their income-generating activities in return for providing a supply of cheap goods. Crime – as a form of redistribution – produces 'complex chains of interaction resulting in local tolerance and shelter ... for illegal activities' (Sullivan, 1986: 386, 1989). In many low-income inner-city neighbourhoods, the drug economy is firmly embedded in a local context whereby a range of illegal activities are both possible and 'tolerated' because of the functions they perform in providing alternative economic institutions and redistributing scarce resources.

The expansion of the drug economy and, in particular, the rapid growth in street-level crack markets must be viewed in the broader context of a long history of informalization, exacerbated by recent processes of economic restructuring and the increasing polarization of economic and social life in the inner city (Wilson, 1987, 1991; Bailey and Waldinger, 1991; Mollenkopf and Castells, 1991). The simultaneous expansion of the informal sector and, in particular, the crack economy in large urban centres, created significant opportunities for participation in illegal work. However, there is almost no evidence to suggest that the street drug economy has attracted many well-educated or skilled participants from the formal economy; rather, most crack sellers have been drawn from the underemployed and unemployed, earning low wages and/or with histories of participation in drug use and sales (Fagan, 1992, 1994). In the context of distressed inner-city minority neighbourhoods where persistent poverty, structural unemployment and urban dispossession already supported a thriving informal sector, this combination provided many minority women with increased opportunities and motivation for participation in the informal economy (Sassen-Koob, 1989; Sassen, 1991).

LIMITED FORMAL LABOUR FORCE PARTICIPATION

Previous studies of heroin users indicated that Black women were more likely to be unemployed than white women (Covington, 1988). More recently, ethnographic research conducted among women crack users in New York City found that minority women were less likely than European–American women to have experience of the formal sector workforce (Maher, 1997).

Debbie was a 27-year-old African–American woman. Born and raised in New York City of a Panaman mother and an African–American father, Debbie was the youngest in a family of four children. Although she had begun to smoke and sell marijuana while still in high school, peer pressure in the form of her friends 'studying and doing their homework' prompted Debbie to stop and concentrate on her studies. Upon high school graduation however, she resumed selling marijuana until she acquired a legal job as a detective in a department store, which she held for a few years. Her brief and unsatisfactory work experience demonstrated the ways in which racism shaped the formal labour market experiences of many black women. In Debbie's case, doing the job she was hired to do resulted in her being fired.

> I lost the job in [department store] – they sent me out to Wildlife. I was the youngest so, and I made a bust out there on some employee. And it seemed like the employee was a, uh, some big time people. I was all the way out in, uh, Far Rockaway. They was sellin',

uh, it was records. And the girl had rang up 88 cents on about – it was at least $300 worth of records. And I was in there dancing. They didn't know who the hell I was cause I used to come in to work bummy and stuff. And that's what they sent me out there for to watch the record shop. And I caught them – I caught it. Three people got fired, yup. Three White people got fired. Uh, a week later they told me they had to let me go cause, uh, somethin' was wrong with they, uh, it was a silly – it was a lie anyway. Yeah. I didn't get no pink slip. I was there for a while and never got an appointment or anything. I found out afterwards that I had busted some of the top people.

Without a job and lacking a good reference, the subsequent legal work experience of this bright young woman was confined to menial labour such as door-to-door sales and waitressing. Exploited by a magazine company who gathered crews of young people and took them throughout America selling magazines, Debbie was eventually forced to get money from her family to return to New York. Back in New York, she worked as a waitress in various after-hour clubs where she became entrenched in drug consumption/sales.

Unlike most women in this study, Debbie acquired a high school education and had several years of legal employment. However, her experiences suggest that the attainment of formal qualifications did little to enhance her labour market opportunities. Her high school education was no longer sufficient in the job market. Debbie's job as a store detective was a low-wage entry-level position with few prospects of advancement; her experience illustrated the additional obstacles minorities faced in the workplace. Debbie's desire to work and the lack of opportunities for minority women were evident in her willingness to take the below minimum wage magazine-selling job which took her thousands of miles away from her home and family, as well as in her subsequent waitressing positions. Her experience attested to the considerable motivation and persistent efforts expended by many minority women in attempting to penetrate the legal employment sector, albeit with limited or no success.

For other women, however, the effects of macro forces (Dunlap and Johnson, 1992a) of structural and cultural disinvestment, and the lack of viable economic alternatives in the formal sector, led most to conclude that the informal economy had more to offer. For a small group of women, participation in the drug economy clearly represented a crude cultural adaptation to their poor job prospects. Not unlike the minority males described by Bourgois (1989, 1995), Sullivan (1989), Moore (1991) and others, these women decided at a young age to substitute investment in the informal economy for allegiance to the dominant culture and the prospect of minimum wage jobs and workplace racism.

Although Mena, a 39-year-old African–American woman, did not complete high school, her labour market position was similar to that of Debbie in that they both faced a lack of economic opportunities. While Mena perhaps realistically saw her choices as being between drug dealing and menial labour, her mother remained convinced that a high school education would provide her daughter with the opportunities she herself had been denied. Indeed, Mena's mother resorted to drastic measures to encourage Mena to complete high school education; Mena recalls having been 'beat' by her mother and forced to attend school. Mena's mother struggled to keep her daughter at school and 'off the streets' demonstrating the enormous task faced by many Black women in their roles as economic providers and female heads of households. Despite her mother's best efforts, Mena dropped out of school in the tenth grade.

Upon leaving school, she held a short-lived succession of legal jobs – in the garment industry, the parks department and as a messenger – before deciding that she could earn more money in the drug industry. As her drug consumption increased and her options narrowed, the viability of a distribution career was confirmed. As she put it, 'I could see myself dealing more with selling drugs rather than somebody else selling my body.'

For many of the families of orientation in this study, the combination of economic marginality and low social status meant that they were unable to pass on much in the way of cultural capital to their children. These women's parents' employment histories revealed that, while they had been relegated to low-paying menial jobs (Dunlap, 1995; Dunlap and Johnson, 1992b, 1996; Dunlap, Johnson and Manwai, 1996; Dunlap, Johnson and Rath, 1996), most had at least been able to find and hold legal employment. Many of their children, however, were unable to find any employment at all. The rapid expansion of the drug industry in the 1970s and 1980s meant that illegal work offered not only alternative opportunities for income generation, but in some cases provided the only 'work' opportunities. As Sha indicated, given the disjuncture between her aspirations and the options open to her, participation in the drug economy was a rational choice.

> I like a lot of things. I like to travel. That's what I told you. I like to get that fast money, and I don't like the white man tellin' me what to do all the time, breathin' and holdin' over my neck. So this is the way I do it.

Although all the women were engaged in crack selling to support their consumption, some women were not drug users when they began selling drugs. Moreover, even those women who entered the market as consumers reported motivations that extended beyond simply supporting their consumption. For many of these women, then, drug selling was a profession which, in addition to income, provided them with a sense of security and self-esteem (Dunlap *et al.*, 1997). For some, it was the only profession they had ever had. Being able to sell large quantities of drugs made them feel they could do something well. Many of the women in this study were proud of their ability to sell and considered themselves excellent saleswomen. As Sha noted,

> It gave me a whole lot of self-esteem. I felt good about myself. I had everything I had on was brand new. I could do whatever I want, eat whatever I want ... it felt damn good.

Just as importantly, being a good seller also allowed women to differentiate themselves from other crack consumers. Women user/sellers often sought to distinguish themselves from other users insofar as they perceived that, while they 'could hold down a job', they still had control over at least one aspect of their lives. This may be particularly significant for women who have lost or are at risk of losing their children and are often estranged from their families of orientation or procreation (ibid.). The feelings of independence and self-assurance that involvement in drug distribution brought some of these women provided them with a rare opportunity to feel that they were in control of at least one aspect of their lives.

DRUGS AND CRIME

While women's attitudes and experiences of the informal sector were influenced by family and community participation, as young adults their exposure to experiences of racism and sexism in the formal sector workplace served to confirm their own labour market marginality. For many women, this realization encouraged them to utilize alternative avenues of income generation. For most young women growing up in impoverished inner-city neighbourhoods, this may simply mean participation in the kinds of relatively innocuous 'off-the-books' informal sector activities their mothers and female kin before them had done, such as selling food, hosting card games and babysitting. For other young women, their own drug use was an intervening variable which structured informal sector participation of a more serious, criminal nature.

Both the drug use and criminal careers of these women typically started in their early and mid-teens, usually while they were still in school. However, while all of the women were able to recount clearly, and in some instances vividly, their initial drug use experiences, most did not view their first forays into lawbreaking as significant and in fact, many could not even remember their first 'crime'. Moreover, it is important to note that the majority of the women maintained that drug sales, typically crack sales, were the most serious offences they had committed.

Their initial foray into drug selling was typically linked with a recognition of their social marginality (for example, no legal job/legal income, no clear options), their growing drug consumption, and participation in informal networks of drug sellers. A key linkage was direct interaction with specific persons from whom they bought drugs. It was often not clear that a woman's initial involvement in a drug sales role occurred because the woman 'sought out' or 'asked for' some role in drug selling, or whether it was 'suggested' or 'offered' as an opportunity by a supplier (a seller). The informal give-and-take between sellers and customers, and especially steady customers who wanted 'free' (for example, no cash payment) drugs, often led a woman to do 'favours' for a seller, by transporting drugs or money (but rarely both at the same time) to a buyer or to other sellers, or by acting as a lookout for a seller, or by providing other services (see Dunlap *et al.*, 1997, for details of various drug distribution roles).

Debbie (who lost legal employment – see above) recognized the importance of her marginality as instrumental in seeking employment with sellers, but she was initially confronted by one crack seller who at first resisted employing women.

Interviewer: What made you take your first hit?

Debbie: I ain't had nothing better to do. I was homeless. [Laughs] She just drops it off; and, she goes and I call her when I am finished.

Interviewer: She drops it off. Who drops it off?

Debbie: Me. Anyway um ... I use to just run around the corner. I use to run around the corner and cop. From the same guy I am selling for right now. And there was some other guys who had a spot upstairs that was Thomas. That had that spot upstairs and I use to go up there and buy.

So one day Gregory sat right in front of the spot in a chair. And started selling capsules [crack vials] right in front the spot. So I asked Gregory could I sell for him?

He told me, 'No Mama.' 'We don't want no women work for me.' He didn't want me to work for him. So I asked Tuffy could I sell. Tuffy said, 'Do you think you could sell?' 'Because if you can't sell my things, don't tell me you can sell my things if you can't sell my things.'

I said, 'Yeah, Man, I could sell. I could sell. So they gave it a little while. It took me about a month before I ... they would even trust me to sell something for them. They use to tell me go upstairs and get the money from who ever they had up there selling.

Interviewer: You were kind of a runner?

Debbie: Yeah. I use to be like um ... I use to drop off the stuff [drugs] and come back and pick up the money. You know. I'd use to accept a lot of money from them; it was just little chicken fee... I was still smoking it [crack]. They knew I was smoking that shit.

Once Debbie established her value as a reliable go-between and seller Gregory (who was supplying Tuffy) relented and set her up with 'too much' crack.

Debbie: They said, 'Deb, we can't even deal with it. You going to have to stay up there and sell it'. I started juggling for the both of them. As matter of fact, I started working for Tuffy... It wasn't Gregory I was working for because Gregory kept insisting I couldn't ...

But after he saw ... that I was making so much good money for a, for Tuffy, he started getting jealous and saying how I worked for him first. And he is the one who took Tuffy upstairs and it was a whole big scene with us ... with this.

Tuffy said, 'I can't get you to work for me no more, you got to work for Gregory.' I said, 'No. I could work for the both of you.'

You know. The first package Gregory gave me I thought I was going to shit myself. He gave me a thousand dollars' worth of coke, crack vials. Yeah. You know how much crack, that's two hundred capsules... When I thought he said two hundred... I thought he meant two hundred dollars. He gave me two hundred capsules. And I am like. You should of seen I was like in a panic man. I flew home. [laughs] Flew home with them. Dug I dug a hole in my mother's yard. [laughs] And put, put a certain amount down there. Took a certain amount in the house so that I could just come in the house and snatch it up ...

Interviewer: How long did it take you to sell that?

Debbie: Not long, after the clientele started getting really big. It took us a while to get in, in the money. But I'd say about no more than a month for business to really start rolling.

Interviewer: You were selling how much a day?

Debbie: I was selling like sometime five, six hundred a day.

Interviewer: Six hundred capsules a day or six hundred dollars a day?

Debbie: A day ... Capsules. I mean dollars.

Interviewer: Six hundred dollars a day?

Debbie: Six hundred dollars a day that's for only one person. I was working for two people .... See it was easy to keep track of Gregory's money because Gregory would only give you like five hundred or a thousand at a time. You know. I told him never bring me two hundred capsules again ... please.

Although Debbie was selling about 200 vials each day, she did not wish to be in possession of so many vials at one time.[4] Almost all the other women experienced similar 'trial' periods where they functioned in and demonstrated reliability and competence in performing various low-level distribution roles (Johnson *et al.*, 1991) prior to engaging in direct sales, as street sellers, or in upper level roles (Dunlap *et al.*, 1997). However, for the women in this study, drug use neither initiated nor served to 'drive' their participation in criminal activities (also see Elliott *et al.*, 1983, Waterston 1993). For these women, drug distribution was much more than a means to an end and, as noted in the previous section, women felt that it offered them control over their economic lives and additional benefits beyond supporting personal consumption. Experimental drug use and criminal activities occurred almost simultaneously during adolescence and well prior to problematic use (Inciardi and Pottieger, 1986; Inciardi *et al.*, 1993).

Nonetheless, like heroin, crack use appeared to amplify women's lawbreaking to incorporate not only income generating activities such as drug distribution and prostitution, but involvement in violence (see also Anglin and Hser, 1987; Fagan, 1994; Johnson *et al.*, 1995). For example, Mena began drug consumption earlier than many of these women. At age 12 she began to smoke marijuana and use alcohol. At 15 she sniffed glue, at the age of 16 she went to a friend's house where she received her first shot of heroin. She continued to shoot heroin for over 20 years. At 20 she started shooting cocaine, sampling angel dust (which she did not like) at the age of 34. Mena added crack to her drug consumption when she was 38 years old, and was a current crack user and seller in her early 40s.

Mena was well versed in street life and in addition to her current crack selling activities, she had participated in various types of lawbreaking, including robbery (in which her friend was killed when they tried to rob a store to get money for heroin) and drug-related burglaries. Mena's drug career also prompted involvement in violent incidents including one occasion where she stabbed a man in the chest as he attempted to rob her and again during a bar quarrel where a man attempted to cut her throat. Mena carried the scars from the many stitches she received following these episodes. Crack use, then, while not functioning as a pathway to lawbreaking *per se*, exacerbated involvement in and commitment to the drug economy, bringing women into situations not only where they were at risk of more serious offending, but which increased their likelihood of violent victimization.

The relationship between drug use and crime is clearly complex. The interactive nature of this relationship over time was mediated by the social and economic environments in which both drug use and criminal activity occurred. While most of the women had a history of concomitant minor lawbreaking/illicit drug consumption, our research revealed that, for the women in this sample, participation in the crack economy as adults was strongly preceded by an active street life in adolescence.

STREET LIFE

In the inner city, the 'street' is not normally conceived of as 'something we walk or drive along, or that chickens cross' (Connell, 1987: 132). For drug users and inner-city residents in large urban centres, the notion of the 'street' encapsulates a complex of meanings. In the Black vernacular, the 'street' functions as a 'source of practical experience and knowledge necessary for survival' (Folb, 1980: 256). Immersion in street life, or being 'out there', includes elements of risk and excitement not always present in everyday life. Within this context, street life provided some women with 'opportunities to feel a sense of mastery, independence, individual accomplishment, and immediate reward' (Miller, 1986: 140).

An important element of street life was 'partyin', (ibid.: 139). For the women in this study, 'partyin', meant 'good times'. Kiki's story emphasizes the pull of street life – the fast pace and 'good times' that it appeared, at least initially, to offer young women (Gilfus, 1992). After dropping out of school and getting married at the age of 16, Kiki began street life by 'partyin" during her husband's extended work-related absences.

> I remember very good, the first day that I had to myself in the house, I partied, didn't I call all the brothers over, we had our drinks, we had our liquor. You see we had a room under my apartment, that my husband painted the ceiling black and with what you call the colors the bright colors that go on the light ... and all the flat paint and then he used the ultra violet colors and there was the stars and the moon, there was Jupiter shooting across, you know.

Kiki's account emphasizes the 'partying' and the 'good times' that many women perceived enticed them into street life. Street life proceeded at a fast pace involving a constant round of parties, drug consumption, sexual experimentation and an influx of new friends and acquaintances. This was a lifestyle that kept women busy and some women enjoyed the 'fast money'[5] and frantic pace of life on the street and clearly felt that they were too young to stop participating. However, while many women were clearly ambivalent about traditional gender roles and expectations, most simultaneously dreamed of a future which involved settling down in a stable residence.

> I would consider a good life, like settlin' down, gettin' out of the streets, you know. I'm still kind of young now, so basically I still want to run around, and have fun. You know ... I guess when I get older, I'll, you know, have to settle down – you get old you have to slow down, to like think about life, what you're gonna do when you get to senior citizen age. You know, stuff like that.

However the downside, as related by Mena, was that before they realized it, women had nowhere else to go. Immersion in street life had a high cost in terms of forgone opportunities for participation in mainstream social and economic life. Even if initially acquired, the social and economic skills necessary to compete in the legitimate job market were soon obsolete. While women were busily acquiring much-needed knowledge and skills in street life and the drug economy, they were simultaneously reducing or eliminating their chances of finding even the most menial of employment in the legitimate job market. As Mena noted,

> See it's just mainly the environment down this road, you know. Like you say it's nothing to do with, I am bored, and it's other people around that's doing it [drugs and partying], you know ... so that's what make me just say chuck it in, just go along with the program, you know.

Similarly, Renee, a 26-year-old woman, who retailed crack out of the apartment she shared with her female partner, dropped out of school in the 12th grade and began 'hangin' out in the street'. Looking back on her adolescence, Renee related that,

> I started hangin' out with the wrong group, got into drugs, and now I regret it cause I had so much. My family gave me and I really regret it. I was doin' cocaine, I was doin' crack, I was smokin' reefer, drinkin' and now I realize this is the wrong mother fuckin' move.

Renee's involvement in street life and 'partyin', led her further and further into drug consumption. Although she managed to acquire an apartment in the projects for herself and her daughter and was working in a security job and collecting welfare, Renee found that her income was increasingly being expended on drugs. She eventually lost her apartment and became homeless. Indeed, it was in the city shelter system that Renee met her present girlfriend, also a crack user. Like Mena and Renee, most women crack users realized that the 'partyin', was rapidly replaced by the 'mission' – the intense, constant and never-ending search for crack. So, although it might offer a 'good life' initially, as crack consumption increased and resources were depleted, street life also functioned (more predictably) as a route to chronic impoverishment, homelessness and despair.

Ironically, vigorous participation in street life was an occupational prerequisite for women who wished to become involved in street-level drug distribution. A dynamic street life provided women with contacts and customers as well as street knowledge or 'smarts', and a broad range of skills crucial to occupational health and safety in this hazardous workplace. Most of these women had large networks of acquaintances and associates. An early exposure to street life and the subsequent development and fine tuning of survival skills combined with a pool of existing and potential customers to provide the women in this sample with access to drug distribution careers. As Dee noted, watching others make money through drug distribution, she began to think about 'earning some money'.

> People I used to go to school with and I was hangin' around with them. I had nothing else to do, so I was like, let me get a package ... let me start ... I asked for a package and they told me the guy they was gettin' it from and they let me start sellin'... there was other people around me, it was all girls ... a all girl crew, about ten of us, you know ... I saw the fast money ... the money made me interested, you know.

Similarly, Ninety-Nine, 30-years-old, grew up in a large inner-city housing project. Most of the people she grew up with were involved in street life and her own network expanded rapidly as she herself began to participate during adolescence. Like the other female dealers presented here, Ninety-Nine knew most of the people in her area. These were essential credentials in street life for both men and women. Likewise, Queen Bee, in talking about her freelance dealing career – how she developed her contacts, learnt to make certain drugs, found out about where to get equipment – summarized the significance of an active street life.

> You gonna find somebody that know something that you wanna know ... well I can't explain it no further than that but in the street you'll find somebody that, you know, whatever you lookin' for they help you.

However, street life can only be participated in to its full extent when one does not accept one's responsibilities for conventional adult roles. Most of these women had children in their teens and twenties. Their children were being (or had been) raised by kin or fictive kin or had been placed in foster care. For the majority of these female dealers, family responsibilities were secondary to participation in a vigorous street life which provided opportunities for income generation and crack consumption. Indeed, crack consumption encouraged them to act from a stance of immediate gratification. Although these women repeatedly expressed their love for their children, and some vowed that they intended to quit street life and drug use because their children were getting older, street life was hard to leave because such participation further narrowed the options available to women drug users (see Dunlap *et al.*, 1997; Maher *et al.*, 1996).

DISCUSSION

As noted by Miller in relation to her analysis of Milwaukee street women, 'The separate consideration of each route is not meant to suggest that in every case one can say without hesitation which particular path was followed ... there may be more overlap in the behaviors actually exhibited and the structural conditions that appear to have promoted them than the separate treatments offered here suggest' (Miller, 1986: 116). Indeed, the factors identified here – positive exposure to the local level informal economy during childhood, the historical positioning of Black women as producers and consumers within the informal sector, the impact of structural and cultural disinvestment, drug use and importantly, early recruitment to and extensive participation in street life – point to the difficulties in isolating any one 'causally dominant route' (ibid.).

However, while these women's pathways to involvement in drug distribution exhibit considerable overlap, this analysis indicates the critical importance of structural conditions in shaping the nature and extent of Black female participation in the drug economy (Dunlap and Johnson, 1992a). In doing so, it points to the need for research which explore the impact of structural and cultural disinvestment (reduced governmental and private spending on education, job development, placement and other investments primarily benefiting inner-city low-income Americans) on the lives of Black women and, in particular, how this relates to women's involvement in lawbreaking and female participation in the drug economy.

All of the women in this sample grew up in impoverished inner-city communities characterized by the presence of a strong informal economy and a history of institutionalized drug distribution and sales. Within these communities, existing disincentives to formal labour force participation were exacerbated during the 1970s and 1980s. Regional economic restructuring (primarily a striking decline in stable low-wage manufacturing jobs, declining purchasing power of welfare grants, and deterioration and escalating cost of rental housing for low income persons) and the resultant social and economic dislocation combined with the rapid expansion of the drug economy in the late 1980s to provide powerful incentives for participation in drug distribution and sales by large numbers of inner-city residents. However, for the most part these opportunities were created by and utilized among young minority males who, by virtue of their spatial and skill mismatches, have been excluded from formal sector opportunities for income generation (Bourgois, 1989, 1995; Williams, 1989, 1992; Fagan, 1992).

Although minority women have a long history of informal-sector participation, historically relatively few women participated directly in drug distribution and sales activities. Almost all of the women in this study began drug consumption at an early age. Their decisions to initiate drug use took a variety of different forms, occurred in a number of different settings and took place in the context of varied relationships – although almost all women first used illicit drugs in the presence of an older experienced user. Some women initiated drug use in concert with males, some with another female, others in a group, and still others alone (Maher, 1995).

Both kinship networks and community level opportunity structures also exerted considerable influence over women's attitudes towards drug use and distribution activities. All of the women grew up in neighbourhoods where participation in the formal economy was limited and the informal economy provided a crucial and well-recognized means of income generation and survival. These women's lives and communities were steeped in participation in the informal economy long before they themselves actually engaged in drug use or selling activity.

However, this research has also suggested that, while the individual career trajectories of the female dealers presented here exhibited considerable variation, all acquired an early start in street life and an early introduction to ways of making 'fast' money. For these women, street life presents as a critical variable, mediating their involvement in drug distribution. Rather than exposure to deviant domestic networks or a history of serious criminality, the women in this study evinced extensive involvement in street life during adolescence which may or may not have involved lawbreaking, but which brought women into situations and circumstances wherein they acquired the various skills and networks of associates that enabled them, not only to generate income, but also to survive in hostile and often dangerous environments.

Over time, participation in 'partyin' and street life enabled these women to amass a significant amount of social capital in the neighbourhood street networks. In addition to cultivating extensive street knowledge, broad social networks and a variety of potential distribution channels, most of these women developed a 'rep' for, among other things, toughness or a certain amount of 'juice', and a capacity for diffusing potentially dangerous situations. In addition, a vigorous street life provided women with important information and opportunities for the sale and exchange of drugs and stolen goods. Perhaps just as significant, street life and, in particular, the element of 'partyin', while promoting and legitimizing both drug use and lawbreaking, also provided women with a social organization that enabled them to alleviate the strain, frustration and boredom of being poor, black and female in the inner-city context.

This study found little evidence to support Miller's (1986: 109) claim that 'The social world of deviant street activity and the social world of the addict are to a certain extent distinct and incompatible. The chaos that can pervade the lives of addicts, at least episodically, precludes their ever being more than peripheral members of deviant street networks.' (While that statement may have been true when Miller conducted her research in Milwaukee during the early 1980s, it was not true in New York, as Johnson *et al.* (1985) documented in their study of the central role of addicts in street life during the same time period.) In the context of crack selling in New York, at least, street life, drug use and drug selling have become so intertwined as to be nearly impossible to disentangle.

For a minority of women in the present study, family life was also characterized by intergenerational and intragenerational drug use and participation in the drug economy (Dunlap, 1992, 1995; Dunlap and Johnson, 1992b, 1996; Dunlap, Johnson and Rath, 1996). Using Miller's (1986) terminology, the 'domestic' networks (households and kin) of many inner-city women in the 1980s and 1990s consisted of several (often interchangeable) adults whose primary economic activities included heroin, crack or other drug sales and/or non-drug users' criminality. Few household adults were employed or had a legal income other than welfare. Rather, in such households, the 'street' and 'deviant' networks have effectively been incorporated into the 'domestic' networks. Girls (and boys) growing up in such households in the 1990s learned about street culture within their households, from their parents, guardians and kin networks,[6] but had limited opportunities to learn conventional living patterns. Indeed, many adolescent girls no longer need to 'run away' from home to engage in street life, as they grow up in households permeated by 'street people' (often their relatives) seeking respite from street life, but who also bring street behaviours into the household (Dunlap, 1995; Dunlap *et al.*, 1997).

Examining these women's street lives also extends the picture of female participation in drug dealing beyond that of simply being adjuncts to males. While the results of this examination were consistent with other studies indicating that drug use leads women into dealing (for example, Rosenbaum, 1981a; Anglin and Hser, 1987; Hunt, 1990), these women demonstrated considerable agency in the negotiation of pathways into the drug industry. Their participation extended beyond either pharmacological enslavement or connectedness to some male. Indeed, for most of these women, the decision to engage in drug distribution can be seen as rational and intelligible, given their lack of social capital, limited options for formal-sector participation and the increasing constraints of their personal consumption.

CONCLUSION

The structural and economic contexts in which women's involvement in drug use and distribution are situated have altered significantly since the mid-1970s. In contrast to the research literature prior to the 1990s, this study highlights the declining significance of intimate involvement with males in facilitating women's pathways to drug use and distribution. Nor was there evidence to suggest that these women had run away from home to begin their drug consumption and dealing careers. While drug use was a crucial variable in determining their subsequent involvements in distribution activities, our research indicates that most women sellers were engaged in lawbreaking prior to commencing regular involvement in illicit drug use.

These women's experiences also reveal the inadequacy of explanations which depict female lawbreaking through a single gendered lens. Sex/gender clearly does not operate in a vacuum isolated from race and social class and their effects on women's lives. These results suggest that black female participation in drug distribution and other forms of lawbreaking is closely related to structural forces and that the antecedents of Black female criminality may be located within a different set of experiences and contexts than that of either white females or other women of colour. Raised in low-income inner-city communities, these women gained early exposure to an opportunity structure which implicitly sanctioned the use of criminal means to achieve not only culturally approved goals, but perhaps more importantly, day-to-day survival. While they were all disadvantaged in relation to education, vocational training and opportunities for legitimate work, for many women, prospects of legal employment were further compromised at a young age by the existence of racism, sexism and criminal records.

However, unlike Miller's (1986) findings, these women's accounts strongly suggest that it was not domestic networks *per se* which served as conduits to the street for young Black women. Rather, the concept of 'domestic networks' may be somewhat misleading in this context. Focusing on individual household units and kinship groupings such as domestic networks serves to deflect attention away from the broader macro-level structural forces which constrain participation in legal labour markets and the role of the institutionalized informal economic activities at the neighbourhood level. Within such contexts, individual women's domestic networks can only be understood by reference to the enduring structural features of the global and regional economies which ensure the maintenance of alternative economic institutions at the local level.

These women's experiences strongly suggested that it was not merely the involvement of the domestic network or kinship group in extra-legal and illegal activities but, rather, the lack of social and economic infrastructure and the absence of legitimate opportunity structures and employment at the neighbourhood level, that prompted women to seek alternative avenues of income generation. For many minority women, this meant utilizing the opportunities they had grown up with and had always known were there. As Edin's (1989) multi-ethnic research on women in receipt of AFDC (Aid to Families with Dependent Children) benefits in Chicago found, women's involvement in unreportable (illegal) income generation was conditioned by an opportunity structure which included the neighbourhood milieu, as well as a woman's family and friends, and individual variations in human capital. For the women in this study, an early investment in street life yielded social capital which was valuable, but only within street networks and drug markets. Their experiences suggest that, despite the concomitant risk of problematic drug use, this capital was put to opportunistic use in gaining access to a male-dominated labour market. Cognizant of the fact that the dominant culture had failed to make sufficient investment in their futures, these women generated their own social capital by cultivating an active and vigorous street life.

Finally, these women's accounts indicate that experiences within the drug economy, while clearly gendered in important respects (Maher, 1997) are diverse and cannot be captured by a singular perspective. As in the legitimate world, a combination of life events and experiences, including what had been identified here as significant social capital accruing from participation in street life, facilitated the entrée of a small number of women into a male-dominated enclave. Theirs was, above all, a participation rooted in, and made possible by, the social and economic structure of the neighbourhood and the interrelation of gender, race and class at the local level. While their experiences attest to the fact that the drug economy cannot simply be characterized as patriarchy writ large, the overwhelming concentration of women at the lowest levels of the distribution hierarchy is hardly suggestive of an equal opportunity marketplace. Moreover, there are indications that the halcyon days of the street-level crack market may be a thing of the past (Golub and Johnson, 1994c). While the rapid expansion of street-level drug markets in the previous decade may have provided limited opportunities for participation by women drug users, the current declining market and shrinking pool of consumers suggests that as street-level markets consolidate, women drug users, among the last hired, will surely be the first to go.

NOTES

1   Research on the contexts surrounding women's initiation to heroin, cocaine HCL and smokeable cocaine/crack use, however, suggested that male involvement may be mediated both by drug of initiation and by race/ethnicity. In this particular sample, although 56 per cent of women initiated use within the context of a male-female dyad, only 38 per cent were introduced by a husband or boyfriend. Latinos and European–American women were more likely than African–American women to be introduced by husbands and boyfriends with 69 per cent of African–American women initiating drug use with either one or more female companions. Heroin and cocaine HCL initiates were more likely than smokeable cocaine initiates to experience first use in the context of a male, compared to 57 per cent of smokeable cocaine initiates who first used with other women (Maher, 1995).

2   Other studies of women drug users support the notion that drug use may serve as a pathway to criminal activity. In particular, the notion of drug use as precipitating female involvement in lawbreaking resonates strongly with feminist concerns to place women's experiences of crime and deviance within the context of their subordinate status in society and their status as victims (for example, see Arnold, 1990; Gilfus, 1992).

3   Many similarities in the personal histories were also found for Latinas and white women crack sellers, but these are not analysed here. The pathways to crack selling among the more numerous male crack sellers were also similar to those analysed here for women. Moreover, project staff observed and informally discussed the factors associated with crack selling, but did not conduct in-depth interviews with well over 100 additional African–American women crack sellers. This study was not designed to interview 'comparison' women (for example, women exposed to similar familial, socioeconomic deprivations and inner-city communities but who were not crack sellers). Such comparative research is being conducted by co-author Dunlap in a related research project (see note 6).

4   If Debbie had been arrested possessing 200 vials of crack, and if the aggregate weight was over five grams, and she was prosecuted in the federal court system, she would likely have received a mandatory minimum sentence of five or more years (despite the absence of a prior arrest record).
5   As Miller noted, 'fast money', in addition to denoting the rapid acquisition of cash, also means 'money made in a "fast" (exciting as opposed to boring) way' (1986: 139–40).
6   Eloise Dunlap has a NIDA-funded project, 'Family Violence among Crack Selling Households' to document the organization/disorganization of family/household systems of crack sellers and their families in much greater detail. This study will document high levels of violence within such households, early sexual experience – often with adult men, and socialization of children and adolescents for careers as prostitutes, sex workers, drug sellers and criminals.

BIBLIOGRAPHY

Adler, P.A. (1985), *Wheeling and Dealing: An Ethnography of an Upper-Level Drug Dealing and Smuggling Community*, New York: Columbia University Press.
Anglin, M.D. and Hser, Y. (1987), 'Addicted women and crime', *Criminology*, **25** (2), 359–97.
Anglin, M.D. and Speckart, G. (1988), 'Narcotics use and crime: a multisample multimethod analysis', *Criminology*, **26** (4),197–234.
Arnold, R.A. (1990), 'Processes of victimization and criminalization of Black women', *Social Justice*, **17** (3), 153–66.
Austin, R. (1992), 'The Black community, its lawbreakers and a politics of identification', *Southern California Law Review*, **65**, 1769–1817.
Bailey, V.T. and Waldinger, R. (1991), 'The Changing Ethnic/Racial Division of Labor', in J.H. Mollenkopf and M. Castells (eds), *Dual City: Restructuring New York*, New York: Russell Sage Foundation, pp. 43–78.
Baskin, D., Sommers, I. and Fagan, J.A. (1993), 'The political economy of violent female street crime', *Fordham Urban Law Journal*, **20**, 401–7.
Blom, M. and van den Berg, T. (1989), 'A Topology of the Life and Work Styles of "Heroin Prostitutes": From a Male Career Model to a Feminized Career Model', in M. Cain (ed.), *Growing up Good: Policing the Behavior of Girls in Europe*, Newbury Park, CA: Sage, pp.55–69.
Bourgois, P. (1989), 'In search of Horatio Alger: culture and ideology in the crack economy', *Contemporary Drug Problems*, **16** (4), 619–49.
Bourgois, P. (1995), *In Search of Respect: Selling Crack in El Barrio*, New York: Cambridge University Press.
Bourgois, P. and Dunlap, E. (1993), 'Exorcising Sex-for-Crack: An Ethnographic Perspective from Harlem', in M.S. Ratner (ed.), *Crack Pipe as Pimp: An Ethnographic Investigation of Sex-for-Crack Exchanges*, New York: Lexington Books, pp.97–132.
Chaiken, J. and M.R. Chaiken (1990), 'Drugs and Predatory Crime', in M. Tonry, J.Q. Wilson (eds.), Drugs and Crime, *Crime and Justice*, Chicago: University of Chicago Press, **13**, 203–40.
Chesney-Lind, M. and Rodriguez, N. (1983), 'Women under lock and key: a view from the inside', *The Prison Journal*, **63**, 47–65.
Chesney-Lind, M. and Sheldon, R. (1992), *Girls, Delinquency and Juvenile Justice*, Pacific Grove, CA: Brooks/Cole Publishing.
Connell, R.W. (1987), *Gender and Power*, Stanford, CA: Stanford University Press.
Covington, J. (1985), 'Gender differences in criminality among heroin users', *Journal of Research in Crime and Delinquency*, **22** (4), 329–54.

Covington, J. (1988), 'Crime and heroin: The effects of race and gender', *Journal of Black Studies*, 18, 486–506.

Daly, K. (1992), 'Women's pathways to felony court: Feminist theories of lawbreaking and problems of representation', *Southern California Review of Law and Women's Studies*, **2** (1), 11–52.

Dunlap, E. (1992), 'Impact of Drugs on Family Life and Kin Networks in Inner-city African–American Single Parent Households', in A. Harrell and G. Peterson (eds), *Drugs, Crime and Social Isolation: Barriers to Urban Opportunity*, Washington, DC: Urban Institute Press, pp.181–207.

Dunlap, E. (1995), 'Inner-City Crisis and Drug Dealing: Portrait of a Drug Dealer and His Household', in S. MacGregor and A. Lipow (eds), *The Other City: People and Politics in New York and London*, Atlantic Island, NJ: Humanities Press, pp.114–31.

Dunlap, E. and Johnson, B.D. (1992a), 'The setting for the crack era: macro forces, micro consequences (1960–1992)', *Journal of Psychoactive Drugs*, **24** (3), 307–21.

Dunlap, E. and Johnson, B.D. (1992b), 'Structural and economic changes: an examination of female crack dealers in New York City and their family life', paper presented at the Annual Meeting of the American Society of Criminology, New Orleans, November.

Dunlap, E. and Johnson, B.D. (1994), 'Gaining access for conducting ethnographic research among drug dealer/sellers', paper presented at Society for Applied Anthropology, Cancun, Mexico.

Dunlap, E. and Johnson, B.D. (1996), 'Family/resources in the development of a female crack-seller career: case study of a hidden population', *Journal of Drug Issues*, **26** (1), 177–200.

Dunlap, E., Johnson, B.D. and Maher L.E. (1997), 'Female crack dealers in New York City: who they are and what they do', *Women and Criminal Justice*, **8** (4), 25–55.

Dunlap, E., Johnson, B.D. and Manwar, A. (1996), 'A successful female crack dealer: case study of a deviant career', *Deviant Behavior*, **15**, 1–25.

Dunlap, E., Johnson, B.D. and Rath, J. (1996). 'Aggression and violence in households of crack sellers/abusers', *Applied Behavioral Science Review*, **4** (2), 191–217.

Dunlap, E., Johnson, B.D., Sanabria, H., Holliday, E., Lipsey, V., Barnett, M., Hopkins, W., Sobel, I., Randolph, D. and Chin, K. (1990), 'Studying crack users and their criminal careers: the scientific and artistic aspects of locating hard-to-reach subjects and interviewing them about sensitive topics', *Contemporary Drug Problems*, **17** (1), 121–44.

Edin, K.J. (1989), 'There's a lot of month left at the end of the money: how welfare recipients in Chicago make ends meet', unpublished PhD thesis, Northwestern University.

Elliot, D.S., Ageton., S.S., Huizinga, D., Knowles, B.A. and Canter, R.J. (1983), 'The prevalence and incidence of delinquent behavior: 1976–1980', *The National Youth Survey Project Report No. 26*, Boulder, Colorado: Behavioral Research Institute.

Fagan, J.A. (1992), 'Drug Selling and Licit Income in Distressed Neighborhoods: The Economic Lives of Street-level Drug Users and Dealers', in A. Harrell and G. Petersen (eds), *Drugs, Crime and Social Isolation: Barriers to Urban Opportunity*, Washington, DC: Urban Institute Press.

Fagan, J.A. (1994), 'Women and drugs revisited: female participation in the cocaine economy', *Journal of Drug Issues*, **24** (2), 179–225.

Fagan, J.A. and Chin, K. (1989), 'Initiation into crack and cocaine: a tale of two epidemics', *Contemporary Drug Problems*, **16** (4), 579–617.

Fagan, J.A. and Chin, K. (1991), 'Social processes of initiation into crack', *Journal of Drug Issues*, **21** (2), 313–43.

Ferman, L.A. (1985), 'The Role of the Informal Economy in the Economic Development of Low Income Neighborhoods', unpublished Monograph, The Institute of Labor and Industrial Relations, The University of Michigan, Ann Arbor.

Folb, E.A. (1980), *Runnin' Down Some Lines*, Cambridge, Ms: Harvard University Press.

Gilfus, M.E. (1992), 'From victims to survivors to offenders: Women's routes of entry and immersion into street crime', *Women and Criminal Justice*, **4** (1), 63–88.

Goldstein, P.J. (1979), *Prostitution and Drugs*, Lexington, MA: Lexington Books.

Golub, A. and Johnson, B.D. (1992), 'Crack and the developmental progression of substance abuse', paper presented at the Annual Meeting of the American Society of Criminology, New Orleans, LA, November.

Golub, A. and Johnson, B.D. (1994a), 'The shifting importance of alcohol and marijuana as gateway substances among serious drug abusers', *Journal of Alcohol Studies*, **55** (5), 607–14.

Golub, A. and Johnson, B.D. (1994b), 'Cohort differences in drug use pathways to crack among current crack abusers in New York City', *Criminal Justice and Behavior*, **21** (4), 403–22.

Golub, A. and Johnson, B.D. (1994c), 'A recent decline in cocaine use among youthful arrestees in Manhattan (1987–1993)', *American Journal of Public Health*, **84** (8), 1250–54.

Hamid, A. (1990), 'The political economy of crack-related violence', *Contemporary Drug Problems*, **17** (1), 31–78.

Hamid, A. (1991a), 'From ganja to crack: Caribbean participation in the underground economy in Brooklyn, 1976–1986, Part 1, Establishment of the marijuana economy', *International Journal of the Addictions*, **26** (6), 615–28.

Hamid, A. (1991b), 'From ganja to crack: Caribbean participation in the underground economy in Brooklyn, 1976–1986, Part 2, Establishment of the cocaine (and crack) economy', *International Journal of the Addictions*, **26** (7), 729–38.

Hunt, D. (1990), 'Drugs and Consensual Crimes: Drug Dealing and Prostitution', in M. Tonry and J.Q. Wilson (eds), Drugs and Crime, *Crime and Justice*, Chicago: University of Chicago Press, **13**, 159–202.

Inciardi, J.A. and Pottieger, A.E. (1986), 'Drug use and crime among two cohorts of women narcotics users: an empirical assessment', *Journal of Drug Issues*, 16, 91–106.

Inciardi, J.A., Lockwood, D. and Pottieger, A.E. (1993), *Women and Crack Cocaine*, New York: Macmillan.

Johnson, B.D., Golub, A. and Fagan, J.A. (1995), 'Careers in crack, drug-use distribution and non-drug criminality', *Crime and Delinquency*, **34** (3), 251–79.

Johnson, B.D., Hamid, A. and Sanabria, H. (1991), 'Emerging Models of Crack Distribution', in T. Mieczkowksi, (ed.), *Drugs and Crime: A Reader*, Boston: Allyn-Bacon, pp.56–78.

Johnson, B.D., Natarajan, M., Dunlap, E. and Elmoghazy, E. (1994), 'Crack abusers and noncrack abusers: profiles of drug use, drug sales and nondrug criminality', *Journal of Drug Issues*, **24** (1), 117–41.

Johnson, B.D., Goldstein, P.J., Preble, E., Schmeidler, J., Lipton, D.S., Spunt, B. and Miller, T. (1985), *Taking Care of Business: The Economics of Crime by Heroin Abusers*, Lexington, MA.: Lexington Books, D.C. Heath.

Kasarda, J. (1992), 'The Severely Distressed in Economically Transforming Cities', in A. Harrell and G. Peterson (eds), *Drugs, Crime and Social Isolation: Barriers to Urban Opportunity*, Washington, DC: Urban Institute Press, pp.45–98.

Lewis, C., Johnson, B.D., Golub, A. and Dunlap, E. (1992), 'Studying crack abusers: strategies for recruiting the right tail of an ill-defined population', *Journal of Psychoactive Drugs*, **24** (4), 323–36.

Liebow, E. (1967), *Tally's Corner: A Story of Streetcorner Men*, Boston: Little, Brown and Company.

Maher, L. (1995), 'In the name of love: women and initiation to illicit drugs', in R.E. Dobash, R.P. Dobash and L. Noaks (ed.), *Gender and crime*, Cardiff: University of Wales Press, pp.132–66.

Maher, L. (1996), 'Hidden in the light: discrimination and occupational norms among crack using street-level sexworkers', *Journal of Drug Issues*, **26** (1), 145–75.

Maher, L. (1997), *Sexed work: Gender, race and resistance in a Brooklyn drug market*, Oxford: Oxford University Press.

Maher, L. and Curtis, R. (1992), 'Women on the edge of crime: crack cocaine and the changing contexts of street-level sex work in New York City', *Crime, Law and Social Change*, **18** (3), 221–58.

Maher, L. and Daly, K. (1996), 'Women in the street-level drug economy: continuity or change?', *Criminology*, **34** (4), 465–91.

Maher, L., Dunlap, E., Johnson, B.D. and Hamid, A. (1996), 'Gender, power and alternative living arrangements in the inner-city crack culture', *Journal of Research on Crime and Delinquency*, **33** (2), 181–205.

Manwar, A., Johnson, B.D. and Dunlap, E. (1994), 'Qualitative data analysis with hypertext: a case of New York City crack dealers', *Qualitative Sociology*, **17** (3), 283–92.

Mieczkowski, T. (1990), 'Crack dealing on the street: an exploration of the YBI hypothesis and the Detroit crack trade', paper presented at the Annual Meeting of the American Society of Criminology, Baltimore, November.

Mieczkowski, T. (1994), 'The experiences of women who sell crack: some descriptive data from the Detroit crack ethnography project', *Journal of Drug Issues*, **24** (2), 227–48.

Miller, E. (1986), *Street Woman*, Philadelphia: Temple University Press.

Miller, J. (1993), 'Gender and power on the streets: the ecology of street prostitution in an era of crack cocaine', unpublished paper.

Mollenkopf, J.H. and Castells, M. (eds) (1991), *Dual City: Restructuring New York*, New York: Russell Sage Foundation.

Moore, J.W. (1991), *Going Down to the Barrio: Homeboys and Homegirls in Change*, Philadelphia, PA: Temple University Press.

Pahl, R.E. (1980), 'Employment, work and the domestic division of labor', *International Journal of Urban and Regional Research*, **4**, 1–20.

Preble, E. and Casey, J. (1969), 'Taking care of business: the heroin user's life on the street', *International Journal of the Addictions*, **4**, 1–24.

Rosenbaum, M. (1981a), *Women on Heroin*, New Brunswick, NJ: Rutgers University Press.

Rosenbaum, M. (1981b), 'Sex roles among deviants: The woman addict', *International Journal of the Addictions*, **16** (5), 859–77.

Sassen-Koob, S. (1989), 'New York City's Informal Economy', in A. Portes, M. Castells and L.A. Benton (eds), *The Informal Economy: Studies in Advanced and Less Developed Countries*, Baltimore, MD.: The John Hopkins University Press, pp.60–77.

Sassen, S. (1991), 'The Informal Economy', in J.H. Mollenkopf and M. Castells (eds), *Dual City: Restructuring New York*, New York: Russell Sage Foundation, pp.79–101.

Sharff, J.W. (1987), 'The Underground Economy of a Poor Neighborhood', in L. Mullings (ed.), *Cities of the United States: Studies in Urban Anthropology*, New York: Columbia University Press, pp.19–50.

Stack, C.B. (1974), *All Our Kin: Strategies for Survival in a Black Community*, New York: Harper & Row.

Stephens, R.C. (1991), *The Street Addict Role: A Theory of Heroin Addiction*, Albany: University of New York Press.

Sullivan, M.L. (1986), 'Getting over: economy, culture and youth crime in three urban neighborhoods', unpublished PhD thesis, Columbia University, New York.

Sullivan, M.L. (1989), *Getting Paid: Youth Crime and Work in the Inner City*, Ithaca, New York: Cornell University Press.

Susser, I. (1982), *Norman Street: Poverty and Politics in an Urban Neighborhood*, New York: Oxford University Press.

Valentine, B. (1978), *Hustling and Other Hard Work: Life Styles in the Ghetto*, New York: Free Press.

Waldorf, D. (1973), *Careers in Dope*, Englewood Cliffs, NJ: Prentice Hall.

Waterston, A. (1993), *Street Addicts in the Political Economy*, Philadelphia, PA: Temple University Press.

Whyte, W.F. (1943), *Street Corner Society*, Chicago: University of Chicago Press.

Widom, C.S. (1989), 'Child abuse, neglect and violent criminal behavior', *Criminology*, **27**, 251–71.

Widom, C.S. (1990), *The Cycle of Violence*, National Institute of Justice Research in Brief, Washington, DC: U.S. Department of Justice.

Williams, T. (1989), *The Cocaine Kids*, Reading, MA: Addison-Wesley.

Williams, T. (1992), *Crackhouse: Notes From the End of the Line*, New York: Addison-Wesley.

Williams, T., Dunlap, E., Johnson, B.D. and Hamid, A. (1992), 'Personal safety in dangerous places', *Journal of Contemporary Ethnography*, **21** (2), 343–74.

Wilson, W.J. (1987), *The Truly Disadvantaged*, Chicago: University of Chicago Press.

Wilson, W.J. (1991), 'Studying inner-city social dislocation: the challenge of public agenda research', *American Sociological Review*, **56** (1), 1–14.

Part IV
WAYS OUT

Chapter 11

The Background of Illegal Drug Abuse: a German View

Helmut Kury, Joachim Obergfell-Fuchs and Theodore Ferdinand

In recent years the problem of illegal drugs/drug abuse has become a key issue, especially drug abuse among youths and young adults. McKenna and Smith (1998: 301) properly point out that the drug problem has become an international problem: 'The use of addictive opiates and cocaine continues to increase globally despite intense international efforts to reduce drug supply through interdiction and enforcement.'

The main German office against illegal drugs and its problems, the Deutsche Hauptstelle gegen die Suchtgefahren (DHS), estimates (1999) on the basis of treatment statistics, population surveys and police activity that in Germany at the beginning of 1999 (82 million inhabitants), there were about 2.5 million alcoholics, 1.4 million people with a medicine dependency, 150 000 with a dependency on hard drugs, 300 000 consumers of amphetamines, 2 million consumers of marijuana, 5 to 6 million female nicotine addicts and 8 to 9 million male smokers who need treatment. The number of people who regularly use hard drugs with a high risk of disease (that is, intravenous use) comes to 100 000–150 000, almost exclusively heroin consumers. This figure no doubt reflects the level of the problem, but it also depends to some extent upon police policy as well (ibid.).

The federal Drugs and Trafficking Office (see Bundesministerium für Gesundheit, 1999) reports that first-time consumers of hard drugs came to 20 943 in 1998, which was an increase of 1.7 per cent over the previous year. In comparison with others, juveniles were most often checked for drugs, and the proportion of drug users among those arrested aged 12 to 25 years old was 22 per cent. At the end of the 1980s the level was about 17 per cent. Since 1993, drug use has gone much higher especially among female juveniles and among teenagers (12 to 17 years old).

In many countries, including Germany, drug policy has shifted more and more from a purely repressive policy to a policy of treatment and 'harm reduction'. Increasingly, we have seen that the problem of drug abuse cannot be remedied via a single-minded repressive policy. In Germany, as in many other countries, such as the United States with its 'war on drugs', drugs have been regulated with criminal sanctions, which means in turn a considerable increase in the imprisonment of drug offenders. The differences in punishments imposed by different countries on drug offenders are interesting. In Switzerland, the consumption and possession of illegal drugs is severely punished (imprisonment is possible) and the same is true in Sweden. In France, consumption is punishable, in Spain consumption and possession is punished only with a police fine, in Italy, consumption, possession and selling for consumption are not punished, though unpleasant administrative measures can be taken by the police. In Germany and Denmark consumption is not punishable *de jure* though *de facto* it is, since possession can be punished. In the Netherlands, Great Britain and Austria consumption as a rule is not punished, and in Belgium only common use is punishable. In contrast with consumption, the trafficker is punishable with prison in all European countries (Estermann, 1997).

The basis of this diversity as well as press confusions lies in the fact that in Europe there is a growing drug problem and a pressing need to mobilize its regulation. In Germany, the discussion of what must be done has swung between increasing repressive measures and expanding therapeutic measures (ibid.). Therefore, in the drugs and addiction report of the federal government (Bundesministerium für Gesundheit, 1999), the 'new policy towards drugs and addiction' takes a supportive form more than heretofore for addicts. 'The aim here is to enable those who are dependent on drugs to again lead independent lives.' The offer of help will hereafter involve contact in convenient locations with minimal questions, the possibility of substituting methadone prescriptions along with experimental methods for treating heroin dependency, special help for women, families and children, and for foreign addicts, and programmes supporting work and business. According to a report issued by the DHS (1999) there are currently in Germany 1219 conference/treatment walk-in offices for basic care of addicts of which 800 care for addicts independently of other addiction programmes. About 150 are devoted exclusively to working with drug users. Thus a broad range of help is available, especially in densely populated areas. They offer non-intrusive help via walk-in facilities, live-in care, advice and treatment, private consumption areas, as well as qualified antidote, adjustment and aftercare services. In 1997, Germany treated 25 000 heroin-dependent users with methadone, and there were 5230 live-in places for drug-dependent users. In 1996, there were 8529 approved requests for non-live-in drug-dependency treatment in west Germany, but in east Germany only 76, which suggests a sharp difference between the two regions.

In the following overview we examine the fundamental issues regarding illegal drug use in Germany. It is necessary to note that living conditions changed fundamentally in European countries after the dramatic political changes around 1990, especially in the former Soviet bloc. The opening of frontiers and the easing of travel restrictions invited a broad migration from the poor eastern countries into wealthy western lands. This same phenomenon certainly took place in Germany after reunification and brought with it many changes in living conditions, especially for the east Germans. These changes included a clear increase in the crime problem in Germany's new eastern states (see Kury *et al.*, 1996, 2000), an increase in poverty and increases in the use of drugs and in drug dependency. In the former German Democratic Republic illegal drugs were practically non-existent, but, as expected, all that changed after reunification (see below).

The collapse of the socialist regime in East Germany as in the other eastern European states brought far-reaching changes including a greater responsiveness to the people. The new German states received after reunification not only financial help but also west German experts and technicians, while other eastern bloc countries were left more or less on their own. Despite support for eastern Germany, however, the upheaval was deeply unsettling for the people. The opening of the borders, not only with West Germany but also with eastern Europe (Poland, Hungary and Russia) brought with it a sizeable migration and, among other things, a clear increase in criminality in the entire area. The official crime rate in the former GDR was about 10 per cent that in West Germany before reunification.

Just as individual groups showed sharp increases in criminality in Germany, so too did police arrests overall, as well as prison sentences for drug and foreign offenders. The number of drug offenders in 1977 (the first year they were distinguished in police statistics from other offenders) was 64 per 100 000 inhabitants, but by 1996 this figure had increased nearly fourfold to 228 per 100 000, and the increase was especially sharp after 1994. After 1977, drug offenders displayed an enormous increase, which contributed to the rise in criminality as a whole and probably to violent criminality as well. As a result of arrests among young adults (18 to 21-year-olds), the number of arrests of drug offenders began to rise sharply after 1990, and accordingly the number of imprisoned drug offenders has also risen dramatically. Thus both the rate of police registrations and the rate of imprisonment for drug offences have moved upward significantly since 1977. Regarding foreign offenders, police statistics show that imprisoned foreign offenders, next to drug offenders, have shown the sharpest increases since 1995. This fact reflects especially recent migrations of young people predominantly from the former eastern bloc and the Balkan countries in crisis.

THE CAUSES OF DRUG-ABUSING BEHAVIOUR

The origins of drug abuse and criminality will often be found in the same factors. According to Kreuzer (1999: 37) 'a relationship between drug abuse, drug dependency, and delinquency is a central question in criminological research'. He suggests that a possible link among cases with similarities might be found in similar origins, and along these same lines he proposes that the probable relationship between criminality and drug abuse need not be causal; that is, drugs do not necessarily cause crime. The link between drugs and a criminal career is not inevitable and can be interrupted. The path from extremity to normality is unexplored, criminal careers are not inevitable, and in the extreme criminal group without drug dependency all possible combinations are found. Thus Kreuzer (1999) sees the relationship between drug involvement and delinquency as stemming from factors within an individual's life course: the personality of those who become dependent on drugs; socialization experiences leading up to and accompanying dependency; precursors of delinquency; age and social context at the start of a drug abuse; the dynamic underlying drug dependency; the particular dependency of reference groups; and the intensifying and preventive effects of drug policy.

In connection with the causes of crime and drug abuse, we should also discuss basic socialization in the family, school and peer group, the reintegration of punished offenders into society as well as such factors as poverty, anomic situation in the society, and the meaning of illegal drug use.

FAMILY

The family as the primary means of socialization certainly exercises considerable influence over individual development and therefore also shapes social deviance, drug abuse and criminal behaviour. The concept of the family as a basic factor in socialization was developed initially in psychoanalytic theory at the turn of the century (Freud 1969), but it has since been grounded in socialization research so that the family's role in shaping the individual's personality is no longer questioned.

Since the 1960s, Germany, along with the rest of the industrial world, has confronted a crisis in marriage and the family that manifests itself in various ways. For example, the number of marriages per 1000 inhabitants has fallen considerably since 1965. In 1965, the rate was 8.3, in 1980 it was 5.9, in 1990 it was 6.6, and in 1995 it was only 5.7. At the same time the birth rate has dropped. The number of live births per 1000 inhabitants in 1965 was 17.7; by 1980 it had fallen to 10.1; it climbed slightly in 1990, to 11.5 but in 1995 it fell again to 10.3. During this same period the number of divorces climbed considerably, from 39.2 per 10 000 inhabitants in 1965 to 61.3 in 1980, to 81.0 in 1990, and to 91.0 in 1990 (see Peuckert, 1997). Given the dramatic growth in divorces, it should come as no surprise that the number of single parents (usually mothers) raising children has also shown a remarkable increase. The proportion of single parent families rose from 8 per cent in 1975 to nearly 20 per cent in 1997 and, as expected, the number of children raised by single parents has also risen sharply.

The 'dissolution of the family' (ibid.: 305ff) frequently accompanies individualization in modern industrial society, and the emancipation of women has itself resulted in considerable change. Peukert (1997) describes three areas in which women have been pressing for change: inequality in the home, unequal opportunity in the world of work, and the combination of two major responsibilities in work and in the home.

A growing insecurity in social relationships in our individualized society works itself out negatively as far as childcare is concerned. Along with this decline in childcare, other crises have made themselves felt, especially among the weakest members of the family, the children, for example, growing long-term unemployment has implications for child rearing. According to several relevant studies, unemployment encourages family arguments and family violence. The unemployment rate in western Germany – especially since the beginning of the 1980s – has climbed considerably. It moved lower towards the end of the 1980s but it has since risen to 10 per cent and more in the 1990s.

In the last few years a decline in the official unemployment rate has occurred throughout Germany, but in the east German states unemployment is still nearly double that in west Germany, even though in East Germany under socialism there was little unemployment. In the midst of long-term unemployment, more and more families slide inexorably into poverty, and it is thus that children are afflicted in their development. It should be noted, however, that those in poverty in one of the richest countries of the world are supported by the state at a level that enables only a simple existence. In the 1970s, poverty was found mainly in Germany among marginal peoples, and in the 1980s it became a serious concern in the midst of rising unemployment. Persistent unemployment during times of prosperity has provoked an inquiry into the economic basis of such a contradiction. By 1987, those who received social welfare came to 4.4 per cent of the population, surpassing even the level reached in the 1950s.[1] According to Schott-Winterer (1990), who has reviewed welfare surveys in the Federal Republic of Germany from 1978 to 1988, the situation of the lower strata has deteriorated, so that the social contrast between the rich and the poor has sharpened and the impact of the poor on the mean standard of living in Germany has become greater. Between 1970 and 1991, the number of those receiving social welfare more than doubled, and poverty is viewed as a disability that prevents full participation in normal social life. Recently, by way of contrast, the number of households with high or very high incomes has sharply increased in Germany (see Geissler, 1992: 51). Reports of illegal schemes of enrichment among the rich and upper strata not only in Germany but internationally as well have become common and no doubt help to undermine the public's confidence in society's value system as a whole. From public surveys we learn that the basis of poverty or 'inequality in our society' is often seen as personal bad luck, laziness or a lack of willpower (Bös and Glatzer, 1992: 207).

Groups that are especially vulnerable to unemployment and poverty include foreign workers, the working class, the undereducated, those raised in single-parent homes, the homeless and children. The underprivileged condition of these vulnerable groups can be relieved, but they are worsened by bad housing and health conditions and poor education, along with social isolation and stigmatization (see Buhr *et al.*, 1991). Children – the weakest group in society that is brought into poverty and deprivation with very little power to correct their condition – are seen as the main, undeserving sufferers. Walper (1995) evaluated international research on the effects of poverty on children and found that a spectrum of deficiencies that stretched from language, intellectual development and health problems, to performance failures stemming from anxiety, low esteem, and aggressiveness (see also Brinkmann, 1994; Sünker, 1991). Friedrichs (1997) emphasized in this connection that 'inequality and its results, not poverty, are the origins of criminality – at least in mature industrial societies'. Thus relative deprivation is the problem and those who are deprived perceive that they have no just share in the bounty of society. Under such conditions it is also likely that the poor will search for scapegoats among foreigners who compete with them in the workforce.

Broekman (2000) reports that the number of children in Germany growing up in poverty in recent years has increased. Defining families in poverty as those who receive less than 50 per cent of the mean income in Germany, in 1990 15.1 per cent of the children under 15 in Germany were growing up in poverty (west Germany 16.7 per cent, and east Germany 5.1 per cent).[2] In 1995 there were 21.4 per cent of such children, with 21.8 per cent in west Germany and 19.7 per cent in east Germany. Thus, including children and parents the number touched by poverty rises to more than 40 per cent. Moreover, with decreasing household income, this figure could easily increase.

The anomic situation in German society will only increase on the basis of profound changes in politics and the economy following reunification. Durkheim's concept of anomie is the foundation upon which growing criminality arises, and it has been shown in Germany (see Kury *et al.*, 1996) that, indeed, different regions evidence different types of anomie. In a nationwide survey in 1992, the German people were asked about their opinions and lifestyle. The results indicate a considerably degree of individual anomia (see Friedrichs, 1997). A very large majority (70.8 per cent) expected a worsening of conditions for the people; 33.7 per cent felt that it is no longer reasonable to believe in the future or to bring children into this world; 79.1 per cent believe that politicians are uninterested in the people; and 76.5 per cent believe that most people in the last analysis are uninterested in their fellow-man.

Numerous studies have clearly pointed out the connections between pathological families, that is, parental handling, and drug abuse among children. Kraus and Bauernfeind (1998) for example, pointed to the connection between parental experience with legal and illegal drugs and particularly abuse of drugs with deviant behaviour among the children. This connection, especially that regarding drug abuse and alcoholism, may reflect both genetic and psychosocial links. It is evident that children with drug dependent parents have themselves a more difficult problem from the outset than children with parents who are not addicted. Viewed in this way it comes as no surprise that children from such families show a much greater risk of addiction (see Maier, 1995). Kraus and Bauernfeind (1998) found that 25 per cent of drug consumers interviewed, who according to DSM-IV (the Diagnostic and Statistical Manual of Mental Disorders, 4th edition, published by the American Psychiatric Association, Washington D.C., 1994) were diagnosed as drug abusers or addicts, had fathers who were also abusers, in comparison with only 13 per cent of those who were also drug users but were not diagnosed as abusers or addicts, and with only 6 per cent of the probationers who were not drug users. Similarly, mothers, though less often drug abusers than fathers, were more commonly drug abusers among those probationers who were classified by DSM-IV as abusers or addicts (12 per cent, as against 4 per cent and 4 per cent, respectively). When grandparents were examined, 41 per cent of drug consumers with a diagnosis from DSM-IV as abusers or addicts had early family problems, but only 24 per cent of consumers and 11 per cent of the control group. The likelihood of family problems among those with severe drug problems was nearly four times that found among non-consumers. Kraus and Bauernfeind also looked at family problems that ended in divorce and found that these problems had very detrimental effects upon children aged under 10 years: 29 per cent of the consumers of drugs with a diagnosis of severe drug abuser or addict came from parents who later separated or divorced, whereas only 17 per cent of drug users not diagnosed as above, and only 9 per cent of non-consumers came from such families. Similarly, Leppin (2000: 68) concluded that parents 'doubtless were a decisive influence' upon juvenile drug abusers. At the same time, he stressed that alcoholic problem behaviour is also intensified among juveniles from low-status, underprivileged families.

Kury *et al.* (1996: 381) organized in 1991 a large, representative survey of 5000 east Germans and 2000 west Germans that asked questions of juveniles at least 14 years old. The interview contained 12 prepared answers to the question, 'What do you think is the reason for some people using drugs?' In west Germany, the answer 'because friends and acquaintances also do it, and one could then talk over the experience' was endorsed by 77.5 per cent of the west Germans, but in east Germany only 59 per cent did. As many as 81.2 per cent of the 14 to 29-year-olds in west Germany agreed with this same answer (in east Germany, 73.9 per cent). These differences, 18.5 per cent and 7.3 per cent, were both significant, at beyond the 5 per cent level. It could be that the 'drug culture' had not penetrated eastern Germany's peer culture by 1991/2, at least among young adults. The use of 'drug highs' to flee from a problematic reality along with those who simply wanted to try them out, were also common motives, especially among juveniles. These response levels were the highest for all items in both regions.

With other items the differences between the regions were small. The largest arose with the alternative 'in order to forget problems'. While between 50.4 per cent and 54.8 per cent of respondents in the three west German cities selected this answer, the proportion of east German respondents in Jena and Kahla agreeing with it was 53 to 55.6 per cent. These differences though small, suggest that the strongest motive in east Germany for using drugs was to avoid everyday problems.

Regarding the other alternatives the three west German cities were generally in agreement. Thus, from 38.1 per cent to 44.4 per cent selected 'in order to talk about the experience'. Some of the other answers in west German cities were 'in order not to be regarded as an outsider'(from 34.4 to 38.5 per cent) and 'to experience an indescribably good feeling' (32.6 to 35.5 per cent).

It is interesting that, in the smallest village, Löffingen, 33 per cent of the respondents answered that it 'was simple to find drugs here' but in larger cities, Emmendingen (29.7 per cent) and Freiburg (23.8 per cent), the level of agreement was much less. This suggests that attitudes toward drugs are sometimes shaped by rumour and gossip, because the drug market is indeed very small in the village of Löffingen, and from that we can conclude that the estimate provided by its residents is primarily an assumption regarding the drug market in larger German cities.

The remaining prepared answers were selected rarely as reasons for using drugs in west Germany. Only 15.9 to 17.9 per cent picked 'because idols and role models do it', and 'because it is the "in" thing to do' was selected by only 19.1 per cent to 22.2 per cent.

In both eastern cities the answer 'because I want to forget a problem' was most common, while in west Germany it was 'because friends do it and talk over their experience'. In the east the 'appeal of doing something forbidden' (31.8 to 33.7 per cent) was in second place, in third, rather different from west Germany, was 'out of a pure sense of adventure' (26.7 to 33.2 per cent) and in fourth was 'to experience an indescribably good feeling' (26.3 to 27.3 per cent). These are reasons that seem to deal with inner feelings and intuitions rather than the 'social' reactions found among west Germans. East Germans, perhaps, are more inner-directed than west Germans.

East–west comparisons are also interesting in the response 'because it is simple to find drugs here'. In west Germany, between 24 and 33 per cent selected this response, but in the east only 12.8 and 15.2 per cent, about half that in the west. This reflects the still limited penetration of drug culture into the east by 1991/92. In the last ten years this may have changed considerably.

This study also sought to determine the extent to which the respondents themselves had used drugs at least once. We can not be sure that all respondents replied truthfully, but the results seem reasonable. In west Germany, in Freiburg, 14.8 per cent, about twice as many respondents, had tried drugs as in the smaller towns. In both east German communities, the figure is much smaller: 1.7 per cent. The fact that in Jena drug experimentation was one-tenth that in Freiburg shows how irrelevant the drug problem was in east Germany in 1991/92.

This study also underlines the influence of anomie upon drug use. At the appropriate time local studies may look at the extent to which insecurity, aimlessness and anti-foreign sentiments are linked with drug use; that is, how much effect these variables have upon the presumed motives for drug use. Here an anomie scale, such as Srole's scale (1956), might be useful. In this regard our results show that Freiburg respondents who felt that people used drugs because they were easily obtained also displayed a heightened degree of anomie. It is certainly plausible and even expected that those who think that it is easy to get drugs also see their neighbourhood as disorganized. From east German (Jena) respondents, additional evidence may clarify this question. Those who gave as the reason for taking drugs 'to forget a problem' also showed a heightened level of anomie, suggesting that subjective beliefs (in this case, aimlessness) can also be a factor. Still, one must be sure that such beliefs are not isolated, that those who chose this response out of aimlessness do indeed represent a valid category of 'anomic' probationers. Interestingly, those who regarded drugs as simple to obtain and gave as a reason for drug use 'a quest for adventure' displayed a significantly lower level of anomie. The relationship between drug consumption and anomie requires further research. It is surprising, and perhaps important, that in Freiburg those who have already tried illegal drugs showed less anomie than those who have not, but in Jena there did not seem to be a clear difference between the two, even though the results pointed weakly in that direction. It should be pointed out that drug use here embraces a broad spectrum from hashish and marijuana to designer drugs and opiates, and that these results suggest as well a link between illegal drug use and a subculture or lifestyle, for example, the techno- and rave cultures where the drug, ecstasy, is a key part of the scene. In such situations, anomie theory as a discrepancy between norm and goal will have little application. Along these lines, Kreuzer (1999) found that delinquency and drug dependency were both associated with early socialization and violent episodes in childhood and adolescence. The harsher the socialization, that is, with strict or rejecting parents, the greater the delinquency problem among drug users. Violent experiences during childhood and adolescence are followed by violent crime and drug dependency in adulthood. Many in Kreuzer's study who found themselves in the drug scene and prone to violent crime were in childhood victims of violence.

PEER GROUPS

Groups of a similar age, peer groups, are of special importance to the socialization of youth, and certainly this is true as regards youthful deviant behaviour. Leppin (2000) emphasizes that, even though parents are crucial in the development of their children during the early years, their youngsters' attitudes during adolescence depend more and more on their peers. If one wishes to grasp the problems and opinions of youth from a time-limited perspective, it would be wise to consult such studies as the 12th Youth study 'Jugend 97' by the Jugendwerk of the Deutsche Shell (1997). The focal points of their study were the opinions of youth regarding the future, their adjustment to society and their political orientation. Using standardized interview schedules 2102 juveniles and young adults between the ages of 12 and 24 years were questioned, and the questionnaires were supplemented by qualitative interviews and 19 biographical portraits. The studies revealed clearly that youth were distinctly individualistic in their attitudes (Fischer and Münchmeier, 1997).

One of their main concerns was the possibility of future unemployment and its consequences. About half of the juveniles in east and west Germany regarded the future with mixed feelings, and this is especially the case for young women (65.2 per cent) in the new east German states. The political detachment of many young people was also evident. Politics was of little interest and political concerns and obligations were given little heed. They favoured political parties based on citizen initiative that protect the environment. The study concluded that the boundary between different youth cultures is difficult to grasp exactly. Youth culture will become increasingly non-political and even include elements of antisocial groups as well. Young people, however, avoid long-term commitments to their groups and resist well established rules. They prefer short-term groups with narrowly defined goals. On the whole, 'the violence potential of youth is slight, and activities that imply or lead directly to violence are strictly rejected' (Fischer and Münchmeier, 1997: 19; Kury *et al.*, 1999 discuss the problems with punks, hooligans and right-wing extremism among the youth).

Certainly, peers play a big role in drug dependency in adolescence, especially where doing drugs is a group activity. Such groups often provide juveniles with their first experience with drugs. Kraus and Bauernfeind (1998) indicate that the first drug experience among juveniles is usually in a social setting with peers. Approximately three-quarters of their respondents tried drugs for the first time with friends and acquaintances. Only about 10 per cent of those who took opiates did so alone. About 30–40 per cent were offered drugs for the first time, and the rest had to ask for them (about 40–50 per cent). According to Kraus and Bauernfeind, direct pressure from peers was relatively rare: at most, about 6 per cent tried opiates under pressure and only 3 per cent used cannabis for the first time under direct peer pressure. Peer suggestion however, obviously plays a big role in introducing youngsters to drugs. Furthermore, Kreuzer (1999: 40) reports that 'those who used alcohol and cigarettes early in life, especially when they had models in their immediate groups (family and friends) were less hesitant later to try illegal drugs'. And along these same lines Leppin (2000: 70) found that peers are consistently a factor in the initiation and continuing use of alcohol by young people.

School violence

According to Kaiser (1996), since the 1980s the problem of school violence has received growing attention in Germany (see also Holtappels and Hornberg, 1997). One of the early studies of juvenile delinquency is the Tübinger Juvenile Comparative Study (Tübinger-Jungtäter-Vergleichsuntersuchung) in which troublesome, incarcerated juveniles and young adults were compared with a free population in the same geographical area. In this fashion those in school who were 'at risk of delinquency' were also identified. The results showed that youths in the institution included many who were very rebellious in school and that only 47 per cent of the inmates had graduated from school. Of the free population, 91 per cent had graduated. Moreover, young offenders played truant from school much more frequently. A study of both eastern and western Germany (Schubarth, 1995) shows that violence among school children was not unknown, especially in schools for the disabled (Förderschulen), while theft was more common in preparatory high schools (Gymnasia). Over the five years of the study, there was an increase in deviance in east German schools but in west German schools deviance declined. In general, however, the large majority of the students suffered very little from violence, and the headmasters, when asked about preventive measures, pointed out that in addition to in-school measures, suggestions were under way for outside school.

Schwind *et al.* (1995) has also published a comprehensive study of violence in the schools in Bochum (see also Schwind, 1995, 1996). In this study not only were 934 students surveyed via standardized questionnaires but so also were 123 headmasters, 208 teachers who were available, and 26 secretaries and janitors. They reported that serious, violent fights were infrequent. To be sure, numerous headmasters reported that fights among students occurred regularly during the week, but student questionnaires revealed that these consisted mainly of relatively harmless tests of strength. Verbal aggression by the students was common in this study, and according to both the students and the headmasters, up to one-third of the students engaged in violent fights with weapons; about one-quarter of the older students had at least once carried a weapon for protection 'because the others do it', though its use was rare. Altogether, Schwind's study showed that secondary, basic and special schools experienced aggressive confrontations dominated by verbal accusations more often than Gymnasia did. According to headmasters and teachers, the level of violent behaviour by male students has escalated since 1995, and the behaviour has become more serious.

To look at the possible causes of violence in school it is necessary to consider the adults who mentioned the influence of the home (especially lack of time with the children and socioeconomic difficulties), media influences and school internal conditions (for example, inattention to the school's socializing mission, or a neglect of order and structure). Students specifically list the search for recognition as a major factor in school violence. To summarize, Schwind *et al.* (1995) established that violence is a problem in many German schools, even though as a whole the media focus mainly on dramatic incidents and ignore ordinary violence. Little attention is given to solving the violence problem, and studies and recommendations regarding possible preventive measures are not considered, even though many of the studies mention these measures (see Schwind *et al.*, 1995). Thus school vacations and the coming and going of students should be examined more closely as occasions for violence, and the rare repetitive offender should be systematically followed, instead of more impulsive, single-event reactions being made. Similarly, class and school 'atmosphere' could be improved by strengthening the students' feeling of belonging, and more attention should be given to clear behavioural guidelines. Verbal aggression could be regulated, for example, as in soccer, when misbehaviour is signalled with yellow or red cards. Student complaints against school routines and professional complaints by the teachers must be considered seriously with appropriate support and help provided.

The Anti-Violence Commission (Schwind *et al.*, 1990), in its report, squarely confronts the issue of school violence. Three central recommendations for the prevention of school violence are made by the Commission (Schwind *et al.*, 1990: 150ff): (1) encouraging responsibility by promoting student participation, by strengthening the sense of belongingness in school, and by building schools and creating structures that facilitate supervision so that good deeds as well as harm can be reported by the students; (2) the correction of achievement problems through extra help and by counselling, making clear the availability of emergency help as well as psychological and social efforts to compensate for structural deficits and the feeling of being rejected by the school; and (3) a return to the school's educational purposes by re-emphasizing the contribution of teachers to the learning process and to a violence-free and fair school. The conclusions of the Commission must be personally transplanted to the school with the norm of a violence-free school at the centre. The teachers and students deserve no less.

Violence and criminality in schools go together with heavy drug abuse among the students. Kreuzer (1999: 41) found relationships between drug activity and a variety of deviant behaviour – thoughts of suicide and unexplained absences from home and school – by children and juveniles. 'People who are inclined to such behaviour are also drawn to conflict and unpleasant situations.' Violence and drug abuse are especially common in schools at lower educational levels. Kolip (2000: 30) established that public schools at a low educational level tend to have a larger proportion of their students who smoke and use alcohol, and accordingly more smokers are found in high school (Hauptschule) than in preparatory school (Gymnasium). 'The nature of the school however, has less to do with it than broader social milieus that themselves play decisive roles in the use of such substances.' Müller (2000) investigated drug use among the new east German states and uncovered extensive abuse going back to socialist times. He noted that the psychosocial burden among school children in the 1990s has clearly increased and probably encouraged the students' alcohol consumption. Thus there are multiple relationships between student anxieties and climbing alcohol consumption (see also Müller and Kersch, 1996).

Criminalization/decriminalization of drug abuse

Kurze (1994: 17) maintains that the 'regulation of social drug behaviour [has become] on the international level a heavily discussed issue. The state seems to have outreached its grasp with the paradigm of controlling drugs through law'. But recently many questions have been raised. 'The United States and Europe are facing the limits of their respective policies to either repress or tolerate drug use' (McKenna and Smith, 1998: 301). There is currently in Germany under the label of community crime prevention a reluctance on the part of the police to supervise drug dependency, in favour of a strong turn towards the 'clinical paradigm'. By viewing drug dependency as a sickness we can justify, for example, a wider use of methadone substitution (Schneider, 1997: 233). The 'get tough' policy towards illegal drugs is regarded by more and more scientists and scholars as a failure. 'Neither a repressive policy nor one based on a prevention strategy can reduce the use of drugs, discourage new users, dissipate the illegal drug market, or even effectively help the users' (ibid.: 237). As soon as abuse and, certainly dependency develop, we see laws condemning illegal drug abuse and trafficking just as fraud and theft to finance drugs appear (Küfner *et al.*, 1999).

Insofar as drug abuse leads to further punishable behaviour, a broad legalization of drugs would avoid these difficulties (see Gebhardt, 1998; and, critically,

Bühringer *et al.*, 1993). After a broad literature review of deviance, criminal behaviour, and drug abuse Rautenberg (1998) comes to the conclusion that we cannot hold drug abuse responsible for delinquency. It would be better to presume that a deviant lifestyle in childhood and adolescence is a central factor in drug abuse as well as in criminal behaviour. Egg and Rautenberg (1999) assert that a search for a causal link between drug dependency and criminality leads only to contradictory results (see also Tappan, 1960, Mischkowitz *et al.*, 1996). The current situation seems to be 'a dependency upon a surfeit of factors. Does drug abuse accompany delinquency; are the two conditioned by changing factors; are they reinforcing or simply parallel to one another; or even does delinquency lead to drug abuse' (Egg and Rautenberg, 1999: 146). Finally, Egg and Rautenberg suggest that 'drug abuse and delinquency do not fall into a recognizable causal relationship, but more likely both are facets of a deviant lifestyle. Socioeconomic variables and the immediate family and peer groups are the basic conditioning variables for both forms of deviant behaviour'. Though it is clearly mistaken, social workers have fostered the view that criminality is merely an outgrowth of drug dependency and, as a result, it will disappear more or less automatically as dependency is gradually conquered (ibid.: 148). At the same time, Kraus and Bauernfeind (1998) maintain that deviance as a special form of delinquent behaviour in childhood and adolescence plays a larger role in the development of abuse of illegal substances than has been appreciated up to now. Still, this conclusion should not be oversimplified by suggesting that a deviant past always foreshadows drug abuse. Recent research has uncovered a series of predictive factors – for example, genetic disturbances, ways of raising children, models in family and reference groups, or peer supports – that play a considerable role in the course of drug abuse. We should give more attention to the deviant lifestyle as a stronger risk factor than we have in the recent past (ibid.).

Studies also suggest that the risk and preventive factors in the development of deviant or delinquent behaviour, as with the development of drug abuse, are at least partly comparable. Kreuzer *et al.* (1999) found in his own research that 91 per cent of his respondents became delinquents before their drug career began. It would appear that delinquency results from more than just drug abuse. In an international, comparative, study of Germany, the United States and Australia, Kreuzer *et al.* (1991) reported that drug users were more numerous than delinquents in all three countries. In Germany minor and moderately severe crimes predominated (warehouse theft, theft from a motor vehicle), but in Australia and the United States more severe crimes dominated (robbery, residential burglary). Estermann (1997: 82) emphasizes that, in countries with strict punishments for drug users, the prevalence is not significantly reduced from its earlier level: 'Thus the hypothesis must be accepted as valid that punitiveness has minimal influence on the number of consumers and new users.' The 'war on drugs' in Europe in the 1960s and 1970s has produced, according to Samui (1997: 159), at least 30 000 dead victims, who were mostly under 30 years of age. Schultz (1997: 95), himself a law professor, maintains that 'it is not the job of the penal law and those who are trusted with its effectiveness to struggle against the use of drug paraphernalia. There are other more suitable ways of accomplishing that'. Punishment is not the appropriate reaction to drugs. And Kreuzer (1999: 48) maintains that penalizing getting or possessing illegal drugs for consumption is a 'dubious affair'. A better solution would be to reduce cannabis possession to a city ordnance violation. He points to epidemiological studies in Germany and the Netherlands that show that the rate of activity in illegal drugs in the two neighbouring countries is very similar, even though the Dutch follow a very liberal drug policy and in Germany the policy is more repressive. 'The current drug policy has only minimal influence on the actual course of events. If, however, the former repressive policy is less effective than a moderate one, should we not push for a careful, cautious amendment of the penal law regarding drug use?' (ibid.).

The German Federal Supreme Court in its 'Cannabis Decision' of 1994 found a constitutional basis for a penalty against cannabis use even in small amounts. The Court, however, limited the application of the law so as to avoid an overly severe penalty for minor offences. The penal law against marijuana does not apply when it is prepared in small amounts for one's own consumption and poses no threat to the public. 'This decision is a first step towards reconsidering and easing the penal law prohibiting drugs. The current law regarding illegal drugs should be changed so that getting and possessing small amounts of drugs can no longer be punishable by imprisonment' (ibid.: 49). This is above all necessary because the penal prosecution of drug laws in each state in Germany is very distinctive.

Kreuzer (1999) asked 465 members of the anti-drug force (Rauschgiftfahnder) in Bayern, Baden-Württemburg, Hessen and Nordrhein-Westfalen what they would do if they came upon an intravenous drug user who had a needle but no drugs. In both Bayern (68 per cent) and Baden-Württemburg (63 per cent) a majority said they would register an arrest, but in Hesse (39 per cent) and in Nordrhein-Westfalen (34 per cent) only a minority said they would: that is, about half the number of their colleagues in southern Germany. The actions ranged from a simple 'watch him' (a de facto decriminalization) to a preventive arrest with the goal of penal prosecution. Kreuzer came to a conclusion (1999: 51) that the 'state's struggle against the preparation of drugs has taken us down a dead-end'.

At the same time, total freedom to use any drugs would not be responsible either. We must find a middle way, and the penal law must take that path, but neither extreme. The penal law must not be like a 'broadband antibiotic threatening every social and legally disapproved behaviour'. The penal law should instead stand in the middle between criminalization and decriminalization. It should urge a gradual decriminalization of consumption and dependency by way of reducing further damage to those who need treatment (harm reduction), relieving the effects of struggle and therapy as well as their offshoots.

Pies (1997) emphasizes that not only is suppression of the heroin market impossible but in the attempt we often create other problems. The goal of prohibiting heroin has probably increased its use. Two reactions are possible: strengthen the punishments ('more of the same'), which a broad segment of the German population and the conservative parties favour, or, under the goal 'harm reduction', evolve a new policy that an increasing number of scientists favour. Prohibition of heroin use has, in addition to its ineffectiveness, numerous disadvantages. First, many consumers are pushed into illegal occupations that result in their criminalization, and secondly, these consumers do not have the usual protections which guard against overdose and other problems. Heckmann (1993) found in an investigation into the deaths of 427 drug users that 72 per cent died as a result of inadvertent overdoses. Third, heroin consumers live in a subculture with open channels in which heroin is given to first-time users at a very cheap price or even free. With that technique the drug scene is expanded enormously. In surveys of dependent heroin users, 93 per cent received their drugs for the first time from relatives or acquaintances, and 70 per cent said that the first time they paid nothing for the drugs (Kreuzer *et al.*, 1991; Reuband, 1992).

Pies (1997) and many other authors plead for a legal treatment of heroin users with legal prescriptions of heroin. Such an innovation is favoured in open-minded political circles, but nevertheless this solution is greeted by massive criticism from conservatives. Schneider (2000), a major opponent of prosecution and penal policy regarding drug dependency wants to end the dramatization of the drug scene, and a clearer and more accurate description of regulated substances. The suppression of drugs is also a giant measure to create work for the unemployed (ibid.: 25). 'All groups that undertake to offer services to drug users owe their existence to the social creation of a dramaturgy of the "drugs problem", to the clientelizing and pathologizing of drug consumers, and to official authorities and their facts in support of policy (our city must become more beautiful!).' The dream of a drug-free society is of course legitimate, but it is also an illusion and therefore dangerous. 'The mission for a drug-free society is the surest way to an absolutistic, totalitarian society' (Wolf, 1992: 555). According to Marzahn (1991), it is not our purpose to prosecute and punish, but to advance drug education and responsible drug behaviour. The prohibition against drugs prevents the socialization of the drug users.

In Germany today about 30 000 people are compulsive drug users who suffer severe, chronic illnesses from their drug use. According to Chapters 35ff of the German Drug Law (BtmG), punishments can be withdrawn if the dependent user agrees freely to participate in a treatment programme that may end his dependency. About two-thirds of the participants, however, break off their treatment programme during the first four months (see akzept NRW e.V., 1997).

Since drug suppression and severe punishments have been shown to be ineffective, many cities in Germany have turned to a substitution treatment policy. Hamburg and Frankfurt have organized especially progressive programmes, and up to now evaluation studies have mostly shown that a programme of substituting methadone, for example, for heroin, produces a reduction of the problem (Gerlach and Schneider, 1994; Zenker and Lang, 1995; Raschke *et al.*, 1996; Kalke, 1997; Sells, 1983). A punitive policy, which has been followed in Germany up to now, results in immense costs in dealing with drug offenders and especially in prison construction. But even with imprisonment complete control is not possible because drugs are often available, especially in big prisons. Drug dependency results as a rule, as with other offenders, from disturbed families and social relationships, though through prosecution offenders are plagued with additional problems and forced underground, which limits or even eliminates their willingness to use treatment programmes.

DISCUSSION

Since the end of the 1980s, punitiveness has gathered support in Germany. A growing criminality was clearly the basis for a cry for harsher sanctions, and in west Germany the crime rate has climbed steadily since the 1950s. 'Globally, west

Germany's climbing crime rate has become virtually its trademark' (Albrecht, 1997: 542). Germany's experience however, is similar to that elsewhere, so that, relatively speaking, western industrial nations have followed much the same path. However, the public responds to the dramatic influence of the press, and as a result the public becomes a 'partner in a game in which the suppression of threatening criminality is driven by reactionary public officials' (ibid.).

But criminal policy has clearly changed despite a steadily growing crime rate in the last 40 years. People in the 1970s regarded treatment programmes as very important for offenders, and resocialization as a goal was recommended in the newly reformulated German penal law. As the difficulty of resocializing prisoners in prison became apparent, and as foreign criminologists especially in the United States, pushed for more diversion programmes, alternatives to imprisonment also became more common. Thus, despite growing criminality, imprisonment became less common and the number of prisoners declined. The political climate in the 1970s and 1980s in west Germany was optimistic and a growing prosperity was supportive of a liberal penal policy. Thus, in the early 1990s, a growing crime rate did not inhibit the development of a clear, rational crime policy.

Based on the unification of Germany, a fleeting feeling of euphoria took hold, but growing economic problems in both parts of Germany and notorious socioeconomic difficulties soon rose to the surface. An unemployment problem became especially severe in the new, eastern states and growing numbers of families and single persons slowly slid into poverty. As a result, in the new east German states the crime rate grew enormously, doubling and tripling its level in the former German Democratic Republic. These negative changes were presented and to some extent dramatized by the press, all of which led to a growing sense of insecurity among the German people generally, which was often regarded as a broad anxiety and not just an isolated fear of offenders. In the midst of this fear, then, isolated offences were highlighted and featured by the press as a pattern of rightist riots by juveniles in the eastern states or as sexual crimes against children. Finally, under pressure from the public the 'Law Against Sexual Crimes and other Dangerous Offences' was revised in 1998 by making penalties harsher especially for sex offenders, and by reducing the possibility of an early discharge as well as requiring a thorough examination by psychiatric and psychological experts regarding the potential for further offending in the community. On this basis, the number of prisoners will probably increase in the future, even if the crime problem is reduced.

But criminological knowledge and expertise seems to indicate otherwise. Albrecht (ibid.), for example, reminds us that focusing public attention on criminality will result in other problems being ignored: crime is only one of a cluster of linked problems (such as poverty, psychological alienation, structural disadvantages or ethnic discrimination) and 'the struggle against crime ought not to be driven narrowly simply by its importance'. Increasing sanctions against wrongdoing is not the best way to reduce social deficiency or criminal behaviour. In an analysis of anomie as an explanation for several German problems, Albrecht (ibid.: 543) emphasizes that 'if we really believe that anomie is an important factor in criminality, we cannot solve it [that is, anomie] via the penal law. We need instead other programmes that focus on and rectify the sources of anomie' to remove an underlying source of society's problems. On this basis primary prevention is frequently advanced, even by German criminological political authorities, who then in practice return to the age-old remedy – sharper sanctions, 'the favourite instrument of the penal law' (ibid.: 544). Today, on the basis of international research, we know a great deal regarding 'deviant pathways', how they begin and end, what works and what does not, for example, and we ought to intervene at the source of social problems not only to be effective but also to be cost-efficient. With deviant pathways, it is most important to think about support programmes for families and children from broken families.

To be sure, in Germany for many years attention has been paid to families in need, with support programmes to avoid, among other things, later offending by children from these families. The federal government in Germany, however, could not guarantee continuous support to families with children, and accordingly the federal Supreme Court under the German Constitution ordered the federal government to issue no later than 1 January, 2000 a new rule regarding tax relief for families with children, and to fashion no later than 1 January, 2002 a guarantee to relieve household financial burdens. Meanwhile the financial support for families increased. These measures go a long way to lifting the financial burdens of families with children. The German Supreme Court endorsed the idea that the nation must adjust 'taxable income even to the extent of making it tax-free to set in society a minimum standard of living in accord with human dignity. This minimum standard is the basis upon which the lower limit of income taxation is fixed'. Thus the difficulty policy makers have in translating their promises into policies shows us that, ultimately, the Supreme Court must resort to constitutional authority to gain an equitable family policy from policy makers.

In the 1990s, programmes for community criminal prevention in Germany enjoyed powerful support, and upwards of 5000 distinct initiatives have been launched, many of which concentrated on child and juvenile offenders and on drug abuse. These initiatives exhibit an extraordinary breadth (Babl and Bässmann, 1998; Innenministerium Baden-Württemberg, 1996, 1998, 1999; Obergfell-Fuchs, 2000). Admittedly, in small programmes, often little thought is given to concrete measures, and the programmes are often half-hearted in confronting the problem. A careful evaluation and companion study does not usually result, so that a systematic, objective interpretation of the results can hardly be expected. But this kind of information is a solid basis for finding the best and most effective programmes.

Further advances in Germany, through its unification with other European countries and the accompanying globalization, are difficult to foretell. Prognoses are regularly revealed as false. Social scientists, and especially criminologists, are somewhat discouraged. Friedrichs (1994) for example, regards a steady decline in social norms to an indisputable basic core as essentially an argument for the notion that one must follow relevant norms even if they are controversial. This is especially true of adolescents. According to Sander and Heitmeyer (1997: 481) the risk of cultural conflict grows 'especially if welfare programmes are fragmented along ethnic lines and fear of conflict mounts. Little by little, the "collective conscience" dissolves and the way opens up for intercultural conflict. In this fashion the foundations for socially destructive violence are set in place'. Heitmeyer (1997) sees similar dangers that could lead to increasingly urgent social problems including crime: a growing habituation to violence, a declining opportunity for minorities to voice their concerns, a decline in civility, a growth in the culture of violence, and growing ethnic conflict. And, of course, ethnic conflicts have already become quite public in the eastern German states. Friedrich *et al.* (1991) surveyed 2794 high school students, apprentices, college students and young workers in a two-part study and found that hostility towards foreigners after reunification had grown sharply among young people in east Germany. The attitude of juveniles towards foreigners and their problems, moreover, was hostile, unfriendly, cool and was hard to change. The authors' view was that the opinions of east German youth towards foreigners could only be understood in light of their living situation. A growing insecurity, voiced by the Socialist Party, a feeling of having been cheated, has developed on the basis of disappointed hopes for rapid development and a fear that the future will bring something even worse.

The plight of those who are drug-dependent highlights the dubious nature of penal-based solutions to the drug problem (Schneider, 2000). Pies (1997) rightly suggests that the policy of suppressing drug use has already failed in concept since it only brings disadvantages, if we only look ahead and see that it only creates places for the penal apparatus and the therapeutic apparatus. Prohibition creates, organizes and offers drug dealers a lucrative market, but it makes users' lives unnecessarily hard, in contrast to the alcoholics who are much more numerous. Routine protections are unavailable to users because normal warnings and dosage guidelines, as used with legal medicines, are not available to drug users, for obvious reasons. On this basis, Schneider supports a decriminalization of less risky drugs such as marijuana and ecstasy and a medically controlled release of new drugs if necessary.

Discussion in Germany focuses increasingly on providing heroin to opiate-dependent users. According to Schneider (2000), drugs are not intrinsically dangerous, but they become dangerous through their social condemnation, that is, through the criminalization of drug abuse. According to Quensel (1991: 68), criminalizing drug use prevents full clarification of the drug situation. 'An effective and humane clarification should above all arrange for tolerance for drug users; it should then organize a practical approach to the problem in which people understand the real problems and dangers as well as the blissful side of these drugs. It should also promote a drug culture in which the rules, ingredients, situations and scenes is as free as risk awareness permits and the social environment can accept.'

Research results must make one thing clear: a repressive policy towards dependency on illegal drugs can go no further. Here help is needed more than punishment. At the same time, the meaning of preventive measures for families and schools should also be clarified by research. In the future we must make available to policy makers our knowledge about 'deviant pathways' which in the end favours changes in social policy that provide help for underprivileged social groups. Nearly 100 years ago, the German legal scholar Franz von Liszt (1905) suggested that in the future we must ensure that a good social policy is also the best criminal policy. He was right.

NOTES

1   It should be noted that the growing numbers of social welfare recipients does not stem simply from more generous contributions from the state as the German economy has strengthened.

2   The German Democratic Republic (East Germany) provided much stronger support for impoverished families than did the Federal Republic of Germany (West Germany).

BIBLIOGRAPHY

akzept NRW e.V. (1997), 'Drogenpolitisches Positionspapier für Nordrhein-Westfalen (NRW) (A Position Paper on Drug Politics in Nordrhein-Westfalen) (NRW)', in J. Estermann (ed.), *Auswirkungen der Drogenrepression* (The Effectiveness of Drug Repression), Berlin: Verlag für Wissenschaft und Bildung, pp.207–15.

Albrecht, G. (1997), 'Anomie oder Hysterie – oder beides? Die bundesrepublikanische Gesellschaft und ihre Kriminalitätsentwicklung (Anomie or Hysteria – or Both? German Society and its Criminal Development)', in W. Heitmeyer (ed.), *Was treibt die Gesellschaft auseinander?* (What Drives Society Asunder?), Frankfurt/M.: Suhrkamp, pp.506–54.

Babl, S. and Bässmann, J. (1998), *Kriminalprävention in Deutschland und Europa – Akteure, Modelle und Projekte* (Criminal Prevention in Germany and Europe – Actors, Models and Projects), Wiesbaden: Bundeskriminalamt.

Böss, M. and Glatzer, W. (1992), 'Trends subjektiven Wohlbefindens (Trends in Feeling Healthy)', in Hradil (ed.), *Zwischen Bewußtsein und Sein. Die Vermittlung 'objektiver' Lebensbedingungen und 'subjektiver' Lebenweisen* (Between Being Conscious and Existing. Mediating between 'objective' living conditions and subjective lifestyle), Opladen: Leske + Budrich, pp.197–221.

Brinkmann, W. (1994), 'Reiches Land und arme Kinder. Zur Armutspolitik und ihren Folgen für die Kinder in Deutschland (A Rich Land and Poor Children. The Politics of Poverty and Its Consequences for Children in Germany)', in P. Kürner and R. Nafrath (eds), *Die vergessenen Kinder. Vernachlässigung und Armut in Deutschland* (The Lost Children. Neglect and Poverty in Germany), Cologne: PapyRossa-Verlag, pp.21–30.

Broekman, A. (2000), 'Präventive Sucht- und Drogenpolitik für von Armut betroffene Kinder und Jugendliche', in B. Schmidt and K. Hurrelmann (eds), *Präventive Sucht- und Drogenpolitik. Ein Handbuch*, Opladen: Leske u. Budrich, pp.193–223.

Buhr, P., Leisering, L., Ludwig, M. and Zwick, M. (1991), 'Armutspolitik und Sozialhilfe in vier Jahrzehnten (Policy on Poverty and Social Welfare over Forty Years)', in B. Blanke and H. Wollmann (eds), *Die alte Bundesrepublik – Kontinuität und Wandel* (The Old German Federal Republic – Continuity and Change), Opladex: Westduetschen, Verlag, Leviathan 12, pp.502–46.

Bühringer, G., Künzel-Böhmer, J., Lehnitzk, C., Jürgensmeyer, S. and Schumann, J. (1993), 'Expertise zur Liberalisierung des Umgangs mit illegalen Drogen', *IFT-Berichte*, vol. 65, Munich.

Bundesministerium für Gesundheit (1999), *Drogen- und Suchtbericht 1998 der Drogenbeauftragten der Bundesregierung* (Drugs and Addiction Report 1998 of the Drug Commission of the Federal Government), Bonn: Bundesministerium für Gesundheit.

Deutsche Hauptstelle gegen die Suchtgefahren (1999), *Suchtkranke in Deutschland* (Addiction in Germany), Hamm: DHS.

Egg, R. and Rautenberg, M. (1999), 'Drogenmißbrauch und Kriminalität. Ergebnisse einer vergleichenden Literaturanalyse', in R. Egg (ed.), *Drogenmißbrauch und Delinquenz*, Wiesbaden: Eigenverlag der Kriminologischen Zentralstelle, pp.139–51.

Estermann, J. (1997), 'Die Verfolgung von Drogendelikten (The Prosecution of Drug Offenders)', in J. Estermann (ed.), *Auswirkungen der Drogenrepression* (The Effects of Drug Repression), Berlin: Verlag für Wissenschaft und Bildung, pp.75–82.

Fischer, A. and Münchmeier, R. (1997), 'Die gesellschaftliche Krise hat die Jugend erreicht (The Societal Crisis has Reached the Juvenile)', in Jugendwerk der Deutschen Shell (ed.), *Jugend '97. Zukunftsperspektiven, Gesellschaftliches Engagement, Politische Orientierungen* (Youth '97. Perspectives on the Future, Societal Engagement and Political Orientation), Opladen: Leske + Budrich, pp.11–23.

Freud, S. (1969), *Gesammelte Werke* (Collected Works), 5th edn London: Imago Publishers.

Friedrich, W., Netzker, W. and Schubarth, W. (1991), *Jugend in den neuen Bundesländern. Ihr Verhältnis zu Ausländern und zu einigen aktuellen politischen Problemen* (Youth in the East German States. Their Attitudes towards Foreigners and towards some Current Political Problems), Weinheim: Freudenberg-Stiftung.

Friedrichs, J. (1994), *Anomietendenzen und soziale Integration – Schleswig-Holstein im Vergleich. Gutachten* (Anomie Tendencies and Social Integration – Schleswig-Holstein in Comparison. Testimony), Cologna: Universität Köln.

Friedrichs, J. (1997), 'Normenpluralität und abweichendes Verhalten. Eine theoretische und empirische Analyse (Norm plurality and Deviant Behaviour: A theoretical and empirical analysis)', in W. Heitmeyer (ed.), *Was treibt die Gesellschaft auseinander?* (What Drives Society Asunder?), Frankfurt/M: Suhrkamp, pp.473–505.

Funk, W. (1995a), 'Gewalt an Schulen: Ergebnisse aus dem Nürnberger Schüler Survey (Violence at School: Results of the Nuremberg School Survey)', in S. Lamnek (ed.), *Jugend und Gewalt* (Youth and Violence), Opladen: Leske + Budrich, pp.119–38).

Funk, W. (ed.) (1995b), *Nürnberger Schüler-Studie 1994* (The Nuremberg School Study 1994), Regensburg: Roderer Verlag.

Gebhardt, C. (1998), 'No 9. Drogenpolitik', in A. Kreuzer (ed.), *Handbuch des Betäubungsmittelstrafrechts*, Munich: C.H. Beck, pp.583–650.

Geissler, R. (1992), *Die Sozialstruktur Deutschlands. Ein Studienbuch zur Entwicklung im geteilten und vereinten Deutschland* (The Social Structure of Germany. A Handbook on Development in Divided and United Germany), Opladen: Leske + Budrich.

Gerlach, R. and Schneider, W. (1994), *Methadon- und Codeinsubstitution* (Methadone and Codeine Substitution), Berlin: Verlag für Wissenschaft und Bildung.

Heckmann, W. (1993), *Drogennot und Todesfälle. Eine differentielle Untersuchung der Prävalenz und Ätiologie der Drogenkriminalität* (Drug Problems and Death: A Differential Investigation into the Prevalence and Etiology of Drug Crimes), Schriftenreihe des Bundesministeriums für Gesundheit, Bd. 28, Baden-Baden: Nomos.

Heitmeyer, W. (1997), 'Gesellschaftliche Integration, Anomie und ethnisch-kulturelle Konflikte (Social Integration, Anomie and Ethnic Cultural Conflict)', in W. Heitmeyer (ed.), *Was treibt die Gesellschaft auseinander?* (What Drives Society Asunder?), Frankfurt/M.: Suhrkamp, pp.629–53.

Holtappels, H.G. and Hornberg, S. (1997), 'Schulische Desorganisation und Devianz (School Disorganization and Deviance)', in W. Heitmeyer (ed.), *Was treibt die Gesellschaft auseinander?* (What Drives Society Asunder?), Frankfurt/M.: Suhrkamp, pp.328–67.

Innenministerium Baden-Württemberg (ed.) (1996), *Kommunale Kriminalprävention* (Community Criminal Prevention), Stuttgart: Landeskriminalamt Baden-Württemberg.

Innenministerium Baden-Württemberg (ed.) (1998), *Kommunale Kriminalprävention – Projekte* (Community Criminal Prevention – Projects), Stuttgart: Landeskriminalamt Baden-Württemberg.

Innenministerium Baden-Württemberg (ed.) (1999), *Kommunale Kriminalprävention – Fachkongreß 21.7.1998* (Community Criminal Prevention – Specialist Congress 7/21/1998), Stuttgart: Landeskriminalamt Baden-Württemberg.

Jugendwerk der Deutschen Shell (ed.) (1997), *Jugend '97. Zukunftsperspektiven, Gesellschaftliches Engagement, Politische Orientierungen* (Youth '97. Perspective on the Future, Social Engagement and Political Orientation), Opladen: Leske + Budrich.

Kaiser, G. (1996), *Kriminologie* (Criminology) 3rd edn., Heidelberg: C.F. Müller Verlag.

Kalke, J. (1997), 'Methadonpolitik in der Bundesrepublik Deutschland – Rückblick (NRW) und Perspektiven (Methadone Policy in Germany – A Look Back and a Perspectives)', in akzept e.V. (ed.), *Drogen Visionen* (Some Views of Drugs), Berlin: Verlag für Wissenschaft und Bildung, pp.289–300.

Kolip, P. (2000), 'Tabak- und Alkoholkonsum bei Jugendlichen: Entwicklungstrends, Prävalenzen und Konsummuster in den alten Bundesländern', in A. Leppin, K. Hurrelmann and H. Petermann (eds), *Jugendliche und Alltagsdrogen. Konsum und Perspektiven der Prävention*, Neuwied, Kriftel, Berlin: Luchterhand, pp.24–44.

Kraus, L. and Bauernfeind, R. (1998), 'Repräsentativerhebung zum Gebrauch psychoaktiver Substanzen bei Erwachsenen in Deutschland 1997', Sucht 44, Sonderheft 1.

Kreuzer, A. (1999), 'Delinquenzbelastung von Drogenkonsumenten', in R. Egg (ed.), *Drogenmißbrauch und Delinquenz*, Wiesbaden: Eigenverlag der Kriminogischen Zentralstelle, pp.37–55.

Kreuzer, A., Römer-Klees, R. and Schneider, H. (1991), *Beschaffungskriminalität Drogenabhängiger* (Fostering Criminality though Drug Dependency), Wiesbaden: Bundeskriminalamt.

Küfner, H., Bühringer, G., Schumann, J. and Duwe, A. (1999), 'Die Rolle der Devianz und Delinquenz bei der Entwicklung und Aufrechterhaltung des Drogenmißbrauchs', in R. Egg (ed.), *Drogenmißbrauch und Delinquenz*, Wiesbaden: pp.9–36.

Kury, H. (1979), *Sozialstatistik der Zugänge im Jugendvollzug Baden-Württemberg für das Jahr 1978* (Social Statistics on Admissions in Youth Prisons in Baden-Württemberg in 1978), Freiburg: Max-Planck-Institut.

Kury, H., Obergfell-Fuchs, J. and Ferdinand, T. (1999), 'Criminal behavior', *Comparative Law Review*, 33 (2), 19–85.

Kury, H., Obergfell-Fuchs, J. and Würger, M. (2000), *Gemeinde und Kriminalität – eine Untersuchung in Ost- und Westdeutschland*, Freiburg: edition iuscrim.

Kury, H., Dörmann, U., Richter and H., Würger, M. (1996), *Opfererfahrungen und Meinungen zur Inneren Sicherheit in Deutschland*. (Victims' Experiences and Attitudes on Security in Germany), 2nd edn., Wiesbaden: Bundeskriminalamt.

Kurze, M. (1994), *Strafrechtspraxis und Drogentherapie. Eine Implementationsstudie zu den Therapieregelungen des Betäubungsmittelrechts*, 2nd edn., Wiesbaden: Eigenverlag der Kriminogischen Zentralstelle.

Leppin, A. (2000), 'Alkoholkonsum und Alkoholmißbrauch bei Jugendlichen: Entwicklungsprozesse und Determinanten', in A. Leppin, K. Hurrelmann and H. Petermann (eds), *Jugendliche und Alltagsdrogen. Konsum und Perspektiven der Prävention*, Neuwied, Kriften, Berlin: Luchterhand, pp.64–94.

Liszt, F. von (1905), 'Der Zweckgedanke im Strafrecht, 1882 (The Idea of Purpose in Penal Law, 1882)', in F. von Liszt (ed.), *Strafrechtliche Aufsätze und Vorträge, Bd. 1* (Penal Essays and Lectures, Vol. 1), Berlin: J. Guttenberg, pp.126–79.

Maier, W. (1995), 'Mechanismen der familiären Übertragung von Alkoholabhängigkeit und Alkoholabusus', *Zeitschrift für Klinische Psychologie*, 24, 147–58.

Marzahn, C. (1991), 'Drogen und Lebensqualität – Suchtprävention als Drogenkultur', in Ministerium für Arbeit, Gesundheit und Soziales des Landes Nordrhein-Westfalen (ed.), *Prävention zwischen Genuß und Sucht*, Düsseldorf: Mags, 127–39.

McKenna, B. and Smith, M. (1998), 'A Harm Reduction Approach to the Depenalization of Drug Crime Via Community Based Outpatient Treatment', in J. Boros, I. Münnich and M. Szegedi (eds), *Psychology and Criminal Justice. International Review of Theory and Practice*, Berlin: Walter de Gruyter, pp.301–9.

Mischkowitz, R., Möller, M.R. and Hartung, M. (1996), *Gefährdung durch Drogen*, Wiesbaden: Bundeskriminalamt.

Müller, H. (2000), 'Zum Drogenkonsum bei der Schuljugend in den neuen Bundesländern', in A. Leppin, K. Hurrelmann and H. Petermann (eds), *Jugendliche und Alltagsdrogen. Konsum und Perspektiven der Prävention*, Neuwied, Kriften, Berlin: Luchterhand, pp.45–61.

Müller, H. and Kersch, B. (1996), 'Problembelastungen – Drogengebrauch – Prävention', in R. Möller, A.G., Neubauer and K. Traumann (eds), *Kindheit, Familie und Jugend: Ergebnisse empirischer Forschung*, Münster u.a.: Waxmann, pp.130–41.

Obergfell-Fuchs, J. (2000), *Ansätze und Strategien Kommunaler Kriminalprävention – Begleitforschung im Pilotprojekt Kommunale Kriminalprävention in Baden-Württemberg anhand der Stadt Freiburg im Breisgau* (Concepts and strategies of community crime prevention – research in the pilot project 'community crime prevention in Baden-Württemberg' in Freiburg in Breisgau), Freiburg: edition iuscrim.

Peuckert, R. (1997), 'Die Destabilisierung der Familie (Destabilization in the Family)', in W. Heitmeyer (ed.), *Was treibt die Gesellschaft auseinander?* (What Drives Society Asunder?), Frankfurt/M.: Suhrkamp, pp.287–327.

Pies, J. (1997), 'Drogenpolitik aus ökonomischer Sicht (Drug Policy: the Economics Point of View)', in J. Estermann (ed.), *Auswirkungen der Drogenrepression* (The Effects of Drugs Repression), Berlin: Verlag fürWissenschaft und Bildung, pp.195–204.

Quensel, S. (1991), 'Aufklärung über Prävention', in R. Ludwig and J. Neumeyer (eds), *Die narkotisieste Gesellschaft*, Marburg, Schüfen pp.59–68.

Raschke, P., Vertheim, U. and Kalke, J. (1996), *Substitution in Hamburg. Methadonbehandlung Opiatabhängiger 1990 bis 1995.* Bericht der Begleitforschung (Substitution in Hamburg. Methadone Treatment with Opiate Dependency from 1990 to 1995. A Report on Cooperative Research), Hamburg: Freiburg Lambertees.

Rautenberg, M. (1998), *Zusammenhänge zwischen Devianzbereitschaft, kriminellem Verhalten und Drogenmißbrauch*, Baden-Baden: Nomos.

Reuband, K.-H. (1992), *Drogenkonsum und Drogenpolitik. Deutschland und die Niederlande im Vergleich* (Drug Use and Drug Policy. A Comparison of Germany and the Netherlands), Opladen: Leske + Budrich.

Samui, M. (1997), 'Repression im Alltag (Repression in Everyday Life)', in J. Estermann (ed.), *Auswirkungen der Drogenrepression* (The Effects of Drugs Repression), Berlin: Verlag für Wissenschaft und Bildung, pp.148–60.

Sander, U. and Heitmeyer, W. (1997), 'Was leisten Integrationsmodi? (What Works with Integrative Methods?)' in W. Heitmeyer (ed.), *Was hält die Gesellschaft zusammen?* (What Holds Society Together?), Frankfurt/M.: Suhrkamp, pp.447–82.

Schneider, W. (1997), 'Neue Wege in der Suchtprävention: Sachgerechte Substanzaufklärung als Verbraucherberatung (New Ways of Preventing Addiction: Specific Descriptions of Substances in User Counselling)', in J. Estermann (ed.), *Auswirkungen der Drogenrepression* (The Effects of Drugs Repression), Berlin: Verlag für Wissenschaft und Bildung, pp.233–45.

Schneider, W. (2000), 'Drogenmythen. Zur sozialen Konstruktion von Drogenbildern' in *Drogenhilfe, Drogenforschung und Drogenpolitik*, Berlin: VWB – Verlag für Wissenschaft und Bildung.

Schott-Winterer, A. (1990), 'Wohlfahrtsdefizite und Unterversorgung (Welfare Shortcomings and Falling Short in Care-giving)', in D. Döring, W. Hanesch and E.U. Huster (eds), *Armut und Wohlstand* (Poverty and Prosperity), Frankfurt/M.: Suhrkamp, pp.56–78.

Schubarth, W. (1995), 'Gewalt an Schulen im Spiegel aktueller Schulstudien (Violence among students as presented in current school studies)', in S. Lamnek (ed.), *Jugend und Gewalt* (Youth and Violence), Opladen: Leske + Budrich, pp.139–54.

Schultz, H. (1997), 'Die strafrechtliche Behandlung der Betäubungsmittel (Penal Law and Drug Paraphernalia)', in J. Estermann (ed.), *Auswirkungen der Drogenrepression* (The Effects of Drugs Repression), Berlin: Verlag für Wissenschaft und Bildung, pp.83–96.

Schwind, H.-D. (1995), 'Gewalt in der Schule – am Beispiel von Bochum (Violence in the School – the Example of Bochum)', in S. Lamnek (ed.), *Jugend und Gewalt* (Youth and Violence), Opladen: Leske + Budrich, pp. 99–118.

Schwind, H.-D. (1996), 'Gewalt in der Schule. Geschichte – Phänomene – Ursachen – Prävention (Violence in the School. Stories, Phenomena, Causes, and Prevention)', in J.-M. Jehle (ed.), *Kriminalprävention und Strafjustiz* (Crime Prevention and Penal Justice), Wiesbaden: Eigenverlag Kriminologische Zentralstelle e.V, pp.155–75.

Schwind, H.-D., Baumann, J., Schneider, U. and Winter, M. (1990), 'Gewalt in der Bundesrepublik Deutschland. Endgutachten (Violence in the Federal German Republic. A Final Report)', in H.-D. Schwind, J. Baumann, F. Lösel, H. Remschmidt, R. Eckert, H.-J. Kerner, A. Stümper, R. Wassermann, H. Otto, W. Rudolf, F. Berckhauer, M. Steinhilper, E. Kube and W. Steffen (eds), *Ursachen, Prävention und Kontrolle von Gewalt* (The Sources, Prevention and Control of Violence), Berlin: Duncker & Humblot, pp.1–85.

Schwind, H.-D., Roitsch, K., Ahlborn, W. and Gielen, B. (eds) (1995), *Gewalt in der Schule* (Violence in School), Mainz: Weisser Ring.

Sells, S.B. (1983) 'Drugs and Crime: Treatment and Rehabilitation', in S.H. Kalish (ed.), *Encyclopedia of Crime and Justice. Vol. 2*, New York: The Free Press, pp.258–92.

Srole, L. (1956), 'Social integration and certain corollaries: an exploratory study', *American Sociological Review*, **21**, 709–16.

Sünker, H. (1991), 'Kinder und Armut (Children and Poverty)', *Neue Praxis* (New Praxis), **21** (4), 316–24.

Tappan, P. (1960), *Crime, Justice and Corrections*, New York: The Haddon Craftsman.

Walper, P.P. (1995), 'Kinder und Jugendliche in Armut (Children and Youth in Poverty)', in K.J. Bieback and H. Milz (eds), *Neue Armut* (New Poverty), Frankfurt/M.: Suhrkamp, pp.181–219.

Wolf, J.C. (1992), 'Recht auf Rausch oder Pflicht zur Mäßigung?', *Universitas*, **82** (9), 551–63.

Zenker, C. and Lang, P. (1995), *Methadon-Substitution in Bremen (Methadone Substitution in Bremen)*, Bremen: Bremer Institut für Präventionsforschung und Sozialmedizin.

Chapter 12

Deviant Pathways of Alcoholic and Drug-addicted Patients

Françoise Facy, Myriam Rabaud and Daniel Ruffin

In France, since the introduction of the 31 December, 1970 law, social and health responses to the consequences of addiction behaviours have been divided between law enforcement and health services. Specialized care for addicted persons in France has been separated into alcohol and drug addiction treatment, primarily in the form of specialized centres since 1975. This includes treatment of incarcerated patients, as the end of the 1980s saw the experimental creation of specialized treatment units in prison settings, while regional psychological health care services in penitentiaries have, since 1995, assumed responsibility for testing and following alcohol or drug addicted subjects during their incarceration.

Indeed, several surveys have demonstrated that these addictions affect an important segment of prison populations, with 15 per cent of inmates being addicted to drugs, and 40 per cent to alcohol, but with significant regional differences. The surveys conducted by the Institut national de la santé et de la recherche médicale (INSERM) since the creation of the prison units have also revealed specific characteristics which differentiate incarcerated drug addicts from addicts seeking treatment at centres in free settings (disproportionately high numbers of men, lower mean age, tendency to multiple addictions and difficulties). They also show that the offences responsible for subjects' incarcerations are not always drug-related, and that the study of dependent inmates' health needs should not therefore be restricted by the use of such criteria.

In the 1992 study conducted by the Observatoire Régional de la Santé de Provence–Alpes–Côte d'Azur (Rotily *et al.*, 1994, 1998; Report of the European Network on HIV/AIDS, 1998) of 432 inmates in Marseille, 20 per cent of the inmates interviewed admitted to intravenous drug (primarily heroin) use over the course of their lifetime, while half of this group admitted to having shared needles. In 1996, of 574 inmates interviewed in the same establishment, 23 per cent mentioned previous intravenous drug use. Slightly more than one third of the active drug injectors professed to having shared a needle over the course of the previous three months.

In a 1997–8 European survey, 43 per cent of 1212 inmates interviewed admitted to having consumed (smoked, sniffed or swallowed) illegal substances such as cocaine, cannabis/hashish and benzodiazepines during the 12 months prior to incarceration. Twelve per cent of all inmates stated that they had injected drugs intravenously over the course of their lifetime, and 9 per cent had done so during the 12 months preceding incarceration. The principal substances mentioned by the intravenous drug users were heroin (62 per cent), cocaine (42 per cent) and benzodiazepines (37 per cent).

One incoming inmate in three professed to regular, extended drug use during the year preceding incarceration, while 25 per cent mentioned regular, extended use of cannabis, 14 per cent of opiates, 9 per cent of cocaine or crack, 9 per cent of prescription drugs used as intoxicants, 3 per cent of other drugs (LSD, ecstasy, glue, solvents and so on). Fifteen per cent of incoming inmates mentioned the use of more than one substance, 6 per cent would take part in a drug replacement programme using Subutex, and less than 1 per cent in one using methadone.

With regard to other psychoactive substances, 10 per cent of incoming inmates drank regularly (at least five glasses of alcohol a day) and 33 per cent drank regularly or excessively (at least five consecutive glasses at least once a month). Fourteen per cent combined alcohol and drugs, the most common form of multiple-drug use. Four per cent of hard-drug users had excessive alcohol consumption and 30 per cent smoked more than 20 cigarettes a day. Four out of every five arriving inmates smoked, with one of the four smoking more than 20 cigarettes a day. One incoming inmate in five spoke of undergoing treatment using psychotropic drugs, primarily anxiolytics or hypnotics.

The different studies demonstrated that incarcerated females accounted for only 5 per cent of incoming addicts. The female addicts were less likely to consume cannabis or tobacco, and much less likely to use alcohol, but they had a greater tendency to use heroin, and roughly the same likelihood as their male counterparts to use cocaine and crack (3 per cent of females as opposed to 4 per cent of males). Many of them entered drug replacement programmes upon arrival in prison, and they took psychotropic medication more often than the men. It also seems that drug addiction was more frequently the cause of the incarceration of the women than that of the men, with some judges even mentioning the 'protective' role of the prison environment.

In recent prison studies, minors (16–17-year-olds) represented slightly less than 5 per cent of incoming inmates. Their drug-use profile was very similar to that of the other subjects: cannabis (24 per cent), opiates (5 per cent), smokers of six to 20 cigarettes a day (59 per cent), occasional alcohol consumption (12 per cent) (five consecutive glasses at least once a month).

METHODOLOGY

Research on the deviant trajectories of addicted persons (alcoholics or drug addicts) has focused on legal problems, particularly incarceration. Several epidemiological surveys conducted by INSERM in specialized drug and alcohol treatment centres have made it possible to describe addicted patients, establish the frequency and location of incarcerations on addicts' calender lines, and to compare subjects having undergone periods of incarceration with others who have not in order to identify the characteristics which differentiate the two groups.

Four types of settings were retained for observation,[1] the first *prison environments*, the other three in health care environments.

1 *Drug addiction units:* description of the 3733 drug addicts detected at the time of their incarceration between 1996 and 1998.

2   *Specialized drug treatment centres:* description upon arrival of 4115 drug
    addicts between 1996 and 1998.
3   *Methadone substitution programmes:* description upon admission into the
    programme of 2635 drug addicts between 1997 and 1998.
4   *Specialized alcohol treatment centres:* 29 557 new patients in 1996 and 1997,
    of which a subgroup of 435 patients was examined in prison.

Indicators drawn from the epidemiological surveys were used to differentiate
statistically subgroups exemplifying various trajectories.

Individuals admitting to addictions of 12 years or more[2] were selected from the
various surveys to determine the existence of trajectories. Several different
trajectories were identified. One subgroup was composed of subjects undergoing
treatment in the prison units who had undergone previous health care treatment
(contact with a specialized drug treatment centre, detoxification in a health care
institution), whereas another included patients in the health care sector with
previous prison experience. Some trajectories remained exclusively within a given
sphere (the specialized drug addiction health care sector, the law enforcement
sector), while others showed cross-over.

The different stages in deviant trajectories were defined with reference to clinical
criteria used to differentiate among patients encountered in treatment centres. The
indicators used in this study relate to delinquency. Other possible indicators include
treatment procedures, whether court-ordered or personally initiated at treatment centres.

ANALYSIS AND RESULTS

Sociodemographic characteristics of the populations under study

The drug addicts

There are differences between the demographic characteristics of the population
observed in prison drug addiction treatment units and those of health sector
populations. Men were overrepresented in the prison units (95 per cent). In drug
treatment centres, as in methadone programmes, male overrepresentation was less
pronounced, but the proportion of men in the subgroups having previous prison
experience remained high (drug treatment centres: 81 per cent of the subgroup
versus 64 per cent of the remaining treatment centre population; methadone
substitution programmes: 81 per cent versus 66 per cent). A similar trend was
observed with respect to nationality, as foreigners were highly overrepresented in
the prison units (30 per cent), as well as in health sector populations with previous
prison experience (drug treatment centres: 12 per cent versus 5 per cent of those
with no previous prison experience; methadone substitution programmes: 8 per cent
versus 5 per cent). In terms of age, the patterns of overrepresentation were different:
the population of the prison units was younger (26 per cent were under 25 years of
age, 39 per cent were 30 or above), while in the health care sector it was the patients
with previous prison experience who were oldest (proportion of patients 30 and
older: in drug treatment centres, 51 per cent of those with previous prison

experience versus 37 per cent of those with no previous prison experience; in methadone substitution programmes: 68 per cent versus 55 per cent). This result is explained by the youth of the prison population, and the fact that in the health care sector the 'previous prison experience' criterion tended to select a sample with a longer average period of addiction, and consequently a higher mean age.

In the health care setting, the group with no history of incarceration included a higher proportion of patients with *baccalaureate* level education (university entrance level) or higher (drug treatment centres: 22 per cent versus 13 per cent; methadone substitution programmes: 28 per cent versus 14 per cent) and signs of good socioprofessional integration (personal lodgings, continuous employment).

In the health care setting (specialized drug treatment centres), patients with previous prison experience were more prone to abuse different substances (heroin, codeine and opiates, prescription drugs, cocaine), reflecting a greater degree of multiple addictions. By comparison, in the prison units, the proportion of cocaine and prescription drugs addicts was higher, and that of heroin addicts was lower. The differences in drug abuse profiles are largely explained by the age and gender characteristics of the prison population, but also by the loyalty of health care facility clientele to types of treatment.

The alcoholics

At the alcohol treatment centres, 15 per cent of new patients were seen by an alcoholism treatment team at the request of prison officials. Over nine in 10 patients referred for treatment by the prison administration were men, and 91 per cent were of French nationality. Their mean age at the time of the consultation was 35, with 52 per cent being younger than 35. Twenty-eight per cent lived alone and 39 per cent in reconstituted families; 60 per cent were parents.

Thirty-six per cent had primary school level education and 49 per cent had obtained BEPC or CAP high-school technical diplomas. Forty-eight per cent were blue-collar workers. At the time of the consultation, 22 per cent were unemployed and 16 per cent were receiving the *revenu minimum d'insertion* (RMI: minimum integration revenue).

Trajectories of the patients

Deviant trajectories among the drug addict population

Three model trajectories were identified for drug addiction in subjects having at least 12 years of addiction: (a) incarcerated drug addicts not having undergone treatment, (b) drug addicts with no history of incarceration having undergone treatment, and (c) methadone patients with a history of incarceration. Each of the sub-groups was then compared to a complementary group in the same survey.

Observed sociodemographic differences A correlation was found between gender and previous prison experience in patients currently undergoing treatment for addiction (methadone substitution programmes: 81 per cent of subjects with previous prison experience were male, versus 67 per cent of subjects with no previous prison experience; drug treatment centres: 87 per cent versus 73 per cent). Owing to the initial selection criterion (long period of addiction), there was no observable age difference. In both studies, a correlation was found between nationality and previous prison experience (methadone substitution programmes: 9 per cent of those with previous prison experience were foreigners, versus 4 per cent of those with no previous prison experience; drug treatment centres: 13 per cent versus 5 per cent).

In the prison units, there were no significant differences between men and women with regard to previous treatment for addiction. However, there were significant differences between age groups: a greater proportion of patients age 40 or older stated that they had never come into contact with the health care sector. Analogous results were found for nationality: inmates of foreign nationalities were less likely to have come into contact with the health care sector.

Similar socioprofessional differences were noted in both the treatment centres and the methadone programmes: patients with no previous prison experience had a higher level of formal education (proportion having baccalaureate level or higher: drug treatment centres: 20 per cent of patients without previous prison experience versus 13 per cent – methadone substitution programmes: 43 per cent versus 25 per cent). Patients with no previous prison experience were more likely to occupy personal lodgings (drug treatment centres: 69 per cent versus 49 per cent – methadone substitution programmes: 63 per cent versus 50 per cent), with members of the group having previous prison experience tending more frequently towards collective housing arrangements (group homes, hotels and so on). The percentage of patients with regular employment was higher in the group with no previous prison experience (drug treatment centres: 33 per cent versus 18 per cent; methadone substitution programmes: 30 per cent versus 13 per cent); the group with prison experience included more patients who had never worked, worked irregularly or on a contractual basis, or experienced long periods of inactivity.

In the prison units, there were no significant differences linked to these variables. The group that had undergone previous treatment for addiction and the group that had not were comparable in terms of professional qualifications, lodgings and occupation, with both groups being generally disadvantaged in all these areas. On the other hand, the proportion of RMI (minimum revenue) recipients was higher among incarcerated subjects having undergone previous treatment.

Observed differences in drug use A correlation was established in the prison units between previous health care intervention and current use of heroin, various opiates and past or present intravenous drug use. Cannabis users mentioned fewer health care interventions.

In the specialized drug treatment centres, a greater proportion of heroin, cocaine and prescription drug users and a smaller proportion of cannabis users had previous prison experience. Current intravenous drug use also occurred more frequently in patients with previous prison experience.

The more severe forms of drug abuse (heroin, intravenous drug use) corresponded to a combination of law enforcement and health care responses. For patients taking methadone, which is indicated in the specific context of opiate dependency, the differences in drug use concerned prescription drug abuse: 26 per cent of those who had been incarcerated were currently using such drugs, as opposed to 19 per cent of those with no previous prison experience.

Observed differences in physical and mental health In prison units, the percentage of subjects admitting to previous suicide attempts was higher among those having had prior contact with health care establishments (28 per cent versus 18 per cent), as was the percentage of those having overdosed (40 per cent versus 17 per cent). There does not seem to be a significant link between this overrepresentation and prior difficulties with drug addiction. This result is confirmed by other mental health indicators: among incarcerated subjects, there were more instances of psychiatric intervention in cases with past health care experience (41 per cent having undergone hospitalization versus 19 per cent; 59 per cent having undergone psychiatric consultations versus 29 per cent), but the differences in the numbers of hospitalizations and psychiatric consultations prior to drug addiction were not significant.

Conversely, in drug treatment centres, more of the patients with no history of incarceration mentioned having attempted suicide (27 per cent versus 13 per cent), an indicator of psychological difficulties prior to the addiction; there is less correlation between this comorbidity and a stay in prison. In the same vein, the psychiatric dimension of care provided by the drug treatment centres was greater with patients having no history of incarceration or court-ordered treatment, whereas there were no differences between these patients and the others as far as other types of care were concerned (psychosocial follow-up, somatic treatment, or medical or hospital follow-up).

In terms of physical health, more HIV-seropositive subjects were found among cases with mixed trajectories (current inmates with past histories of health care addiction treatment, current drug treatment centre or methadone treatment patients with past incarceration experience). The same was true of subjects with hepatitis.

Examples of deviant alcoholic trajectories

To examine the profiles of patients entering treatment at the instigation of prison authorities, the group was compared to other groups of patients entering treatment through other referral procedures:

- treatment on referral by the court,
- treatment on referral by social services,
- treatment on referral by medical specialists,
- treatment following previous hospital detoxification,
- treatment following prior psychiatric care,
- patients having undertaken no other steps prior to treatment.

As for the drug addicts, the comparisons here concern subjects with alcohol dependencies of at least 12 years. No matter which of these subgroups was compared to the patients entering treatment at the instigation of prison authorities, the differences were always along the same lines. On a sociodemographic scale, these subjects were younger, and the percentage of men was always significantly higher, as was the percentage of foreigners. More of these subjects had no schooling or only primary school-level education, and more of them were blue-collar workers. They had a greater tendency to ask for help with difficulties with the court system.

In terms of drug use, the patients seen in prison had a greater tendency to smoke tobacco and cannabis (with the exception of patients over 35 years of age). More drank alcohol on a weekly basis (but fewer did so daily), consuming a wider variety of drinks at a wider variety of locations. The mean age at which alcohol abuse began was always lower than in other groups, the percentage of patients having begun to abuse alcohol before the age of 20 being consistently higher. It should be noted that there was a significant percentage of abstainers in the 'prison' subgroup, though it was nonetheless lower than that found in the 'hospital detoxification' subgroup.

Indicators of stages in deviant trajectories of incarcerated drug addicts

With respect to certain clinical situations, incarcerated drug addicts may be studied in the light of three criteria: recidivism, previous recourse to specialized drug treatment centres and court-ordered treatment.

Recidivism

In cases of recidivism, certain judicial situations are overrepresented: convictions (61 per cent of repeat offenders versus 35 per cent of first-time inmates), offences other than violations of narcotics legislation (ILS[3]) (64 per cent versus 34 per cent), non drug-related offences (25 per cent versus 14 per cent), and offences that are indirectly related to drugs (25 per cent versus 16 per cent). As compared with the other repeat offenders, those whose first prison term preceded the drug addiction were first incarcerated at a younger age (19 versus 20 years old) and had a greater total number of incarcerations (five versus four): thus prison experience prior to addiction was a factor in earlier prison experience, although it did not cause the current criminal profile to differ.

On a sociodemographic level, there was an even greater overrepresentation of males among repeat offenders (97 per cent versus 91 per cent), and of foreigners (31 per cent versus 27 per cent). The mean age of recidivists was higher (29.5 years old versus 26.5). They more frequently stated that they had children (42 per cent versus 33 per cent). The family environment was more highly affected by a partner's drug addiction (85 per cent versus 79 per cent), and siblings' drug addictions (19 per cent versus 9 per cent) and alcoholism (7 per cent versus 3 per cent). Fewer repeat offenders stated that they had regular professional employment (9 per cent versus 23 per cent), professional qualifications or diplomas (39 per cent versus 51 per cent) or personal lodgings (39 per cent versus 44 per cent). A quarter of them were RMI recipients (24 per cent versus 13 per cent of first-time inmates).

In terms of drug addictions, there were more past or present intravenous drug users among repeat offenders (56 per cent versus 33 per cent), and fewer non-drinkers at the time of the study (66 per cent versus 57 per cent). As compared to first-time inmates, their current drug use tended to consist more of heroin (69 per cent versus 53 per cent), prescription drugs (44 per cent versus 24 per cent) and alcohol (27 per cent versus 18 per cent), and less of cannabis (52 per cent versus 64 per cent). A greater percentage of recidivists had previously had recourse to specialized treatment (contact with a drug treatment centre: 42 per cent versus 22 per cent and institutional detoxification: 27 per cent versus 15 per cent).

Repeat offenders' state of health was not as good as that of the first-time inmates; the former had much higher rates of HIV (9 per cent versus 1 per cent), hepatitis (29 per cent versus 10 per cent) and sexually transmitted diseases. On a mental health level, repeat offenders had been hospitalized in psychiatric wards more often (26 per cent versus 13 per cent). While more of them stated that they had attempted suicide (21 per cent versus 13 per cent), suicide attempts prior to the development of the addiction were less common than among first-time inmates (24 per cent versus 37 per cent). Repeat offenders whose first incarceration preceded the development of the addiction were more likely to have a history of psychiatric hospitalizations (25 per cent versus 17 per cent) and psychiatric or psychological consultations (32 per cent versus 19 per cent), and twice as likely to have a past history of attempted suicide (39 per cent versus 19 per cent) as repeat offenders whose first incarceration followed the development of the addiction. The chronology of these events in the individual's story seems to be a determining factor in recidivism.

Prior recourse to specialized drug treatment centres

Incarcerated drug addicts mentioning prior medical treatment for the addiction (prior involvement with a drug treatment centre, institutional detoxification or count-ordered treatment) were compared to those mentioning no such prior treatment. It should be noted that 31 per cent of subjects who had been in contact with the specialized treatment sector mentioned currently being monitored within the structure of this sector.

The legal status of the two groups of subjects were different: in the group with previous health care treatment, there were more convictions (59 per cent versus 48 per cent), more non-ILS offences (65 per cent versus 47 per cent) and more indirectly or non drug-related offences (48 per cent versus 40 per cent). The percentage of recidivists was higher (80 per cent versus 66 per cent).

In sociodemographic terms, the population with previous specialized health care sector experience had a slightly higher feminine component (6 per cent versus 4 per cent) and more substantial French component (78 per cent versus 63 per cent). In addition, the numbers of unemployed subjects registered with the French employment centre (ANPE) and of RMI recipients were higher.

In terms of drug use, there was more use of heroin, the other opiates, prescription drugs and alcohol. Sixty-five per cent of the subjects having had contact with the specialized health care sector had experimented with intravenous drug use (versus 31 per cent). Also the partners and siblings of these subjects were more likely to be drug addicts, and the rates of HIV and hepatitis infection were higher.

Court-ordered treatment

In cases of court-ordered treatment, that is for subjects who end up in prison and for whom one could therefore qualify the treatment alternative as a relative failure, the contrasts between the groups were of different degrees.

In terms of drug addiction, there was a disproportionately high number of heroin addicts (60 per cent versus 52 per cent) and intravenous drug users (58 per cent versus 46 per cent), and greater use of the specialized health care system. There were relatively more non-drinkers (37 per cent versus 24 per cent), and the offence responsible for the current incarceration was less often drug-related (29 per cent versus 41 per cent[3]).

In terms of mental health, there was a greater number of instances of psychiatric hospitalization or consultations and of suicide attempts.

In sociodemographic terms, the group having undergone court-ordered treatment contained more French nationals (79 per cent versus 68 per cent), women (7 per cent versus 4 per cent) and subjects with diplomas or professional training (58 per cent versus 50 per cent). This group also included more unemployed subjects registered with the ANPE (43 per cent versus 36 per cent) and recipients of the RMI (27 per cent versus 19 per cent). The use of court-ordered treatment varies greatly among magistrates, and the social and health benefits for subjects who agree to it are difficult to measure.

CONCLUSION

Regardless of the setting (prison or health care) in which drug addict trajectories are observed, a large number of the subjects experience overwhelming judicial difficulties, although this is less often true for alcoholics.

Although the trajectories of subjects with longer periods of addiction are marked by repeated judicial interventions, there are a variety of profiles. Thus some subjects are multiple repeat offenders, whereas others receive only health care interventions. For the first group, the main risk factors appear to be early onset of substance abuse and belonging to disadvantaged sectors of society. For the second group, psychiatric comorbidity would seem to be an important factor in some cases, especially the presence of suicide attempts.

In the health care setting, those of the patients with at least 12 years of addiction who have been in contact with the courts during their trajectory are more often male, of foreign nationality, with a low level of education, and without regular professional employment or personal lodgings. Alcoholics seen in specialized treatment centres at the request of prison authorities are also differentiated from the others on the basis of most of these characteristics (sex, nationality, diplomas and so on). A correlation exists in prison settings between nationality and previous health care intervention.

Regardless of the setting, more 'simple' trajectories are encountered in cases of cannabis use (fewer instances of previous health care intervention among incarcerated subjects, fewer instances of previous incarcerations among drug treatment centre patients). Conversely, mixed trajectories are more common in cases of heroin and intravenous drug use (past history of incarceration when observed in a health care setting, past health care experience when observed in a judicial setting). As for cocaine and prescription drug use, a significant difference is only observable in the health care sector.

The effects of selection of treatment programmes (especially methadone) are particularly evident for trajectories with the most cross-over between drug addiction and delinquency. The role of teams of specialists working in prisons is demonstrated by the different levels of needs of addicted persons: (a) diagnosis of addiction and comorbidities, (b) initial treatment of addiction, and (c) prevention of relapses. The differences in interventions due to the particular client populations may be determined, not only through qualitative studies of different subgroups, but also through evaluations of the subjects' evolution by type of intervention.

NOTES

1   The surveys of drug addicts drew on a partial pool of resources, as they relied exclusively on the collaboration of voluntarily participating centres. On the other hand, all specialized alcohol treatment centres participated in the surveys.
2   Length of addiction to the primary substance is calculated as being the difference in the subject's age from when the individual began using the primary substance to when the interview leading to the present intervention was conducted.
3   Violation to Narcotics Legislation.

BIBLIOGRAPHY

Facy, F. (1997), *Toxicomanes incarcérés. Etude épidémiologique auprès des antennes 1992–1995*, Paris: Éditions Médicales et Scientifiques.
Facy, F. (1999), *Toxicomanes et prescription de méthadone*, Paris: Éditions Médicales et Scientifiques.
Facy, F. and Rabaud, M. (1999), 'Gestes suicidaires et conduites de dépendance (alcool, héroïne)', *Annales médicales de psychiatrie*, **157** (8), 537–43.
Facy, F., Brochu, S. and Simon, F. (1996), 'Injonction thérapeutique à l'égard des toxicomanes: comparaison des systèmes français et québécois', *Criminologie*, **29** (2), 115–40.
'Report of the European Network on HIV/AIDS and Hepatitis Prevention in Prisons', paper submitted to the European Commission, June 1998.
Rotily, M., Galinier-Pujol, A., Escaffre, N., Delorme, C. and Obadia, Y. (1998), 'Survey of French prisons found that injecting drug use and tattooing occurred', *British Medical Journal*, **316**, (7133), 777.Rotily, M., Toubiana, P., Vernay-Vaisse, C., Galinier-Pujol, A., Gastaut, J.A. and Obadia, Y. (1994), 'Le VIH en milieu carcéral. Une enquête en région Provence–Alpes–Côte d'Azur (PACA)', *B.E.H.*, **24**, 107–8.

Chapter 13

Pathways out of Deviance: Implications for Programme Evaluation

Céline Mercier and Sophie Alarie

Although the majority of research has focused on the pathways towards deviance, the study reported in this chapter was concerned with progression outside deviance. One of its purposes was to identify 'progress' indicators as reported by individuals who perceived themselves as being in the process of getting out of deviance. The interest for such a study was twofold: (a) to verify to what extent these indicators were comparable to those usually referred to in specialized literature on services outcomes and; (b) to consider whether these indicators could be used as outcome indicators for the evaluation of services aiming at social reintegration.

Outcome studies are confronted with the problem of identifying relevant indicators and progress/success criteria. When addressing a clientele with multiple and severe problems in which rehabilitation is extended over many years, there is a growing interest in qualitative and quantitative indicators that are more gradual or related to the attainment of intermediate objectives. The assumption underlying this study was, that if we knew more about how individuals with multiple problems (in this case, substance abuse and homelessness) change their habits and rebuild their lives, we should have access to indicators that are more refined that would eventually be more pertinent. The strategy was then to ask people directly what made them consider that they were 'doing better'.

Up to now, the research on the social reintegration of marginalized populations has been mainly conceptualized from the point of view of services. The domains of interest are then related to the services objectives and areas of intervention. Thus, in order to evaluate the success of rehabilitation services for the homeless or the substance abusers, emphasis is put on consumption, objective living conditions (housing, financial situation, employment, legal status, and social relationships), on physical and mental health, and on the use of services (Mercier *et al.*, 1992).

A limitation of this predominance of services and providers perspective is that it cannot be assumed that these outcomes correspond to those held by the individuals themselves in the evaluation of their progress. Little is known about what constitutes a successful attainment of one's goal ('a success'), from the individual's point of view. This situation could result in the providers and the services evaluators not recognizing the potential signs that could indicate the individuals are overcoming their problems and are reaching the fulfilment of their goals, if these signs do not correspond to the usual outcome criteria they use. In response to these concerns, a study was conducted in Montreal on 'The reintegration process in the homeless alcoholic and drug addict population' (Mercier *et al.*, 1999) with two main goals: to document the rehabilitation process as described by individuals who actually experienced it, and to identify progress and stabilization indicators from the services users' perspective.

METHOD

Population of interest and selection of participants

Two series of interviews were conducted with a nine-month interval, with clients of a rehabilitation centre offering non-medical detoxification services, rehabilitation and community follow-up to the homeless, alcoholics and drug addicts. The 15 men and 15 women who participated in the research had to be considered by the referring care provider as individuals whose condition was improving or whose situation had stabilized significantly in the past three months; and had to be registered at the participating rehabilitation centre, so that a case manager could be available for the complementary interview.

In order to attain the objective of 30 individuals, 34 were solicited for the study: two refused to participate and two experienced a relapse at the point at which the recruitment or the interview was being done. The follow-up interview was completed with 24 of the 30 respondents who were met initially for the first interview, a response rate of 80 per cent.

Interview process

The interviews were of a semi-structured nature and lasted for approximately two hours. Both the initial and follow-up interviews were structured according to the following themes: (1) the development of the individual from the point at which he/she had the sense that he/she was improving up to the time of the interview; (2) the indicators that signified for the individual that the situation had improved, was continuing to get better, or was deteriorating; (3) what constituted an accomplishment of one's goal (a 'success'), at a level that was considered satisfactory for the individual; (5) the individual's perceptions of their actual situation; (6) the systematic exploration of different aspects of the actual situation.

The second interview (which took place nine months later) sought for the following: (1) to examine how the individual judged his/her current situation; (2) to study the rehabilitation process over a shorter length of time; (3) to verify, elaborate or complete elements from the first interview. All analyses were transcribed, with the participants' consent.

Data analysis

The analyses were conducted using the data-processing NUD.IST, version 3.0 (Richards and Richards, 1991). With this software, categories may be modified during the course of the coding and analysis process and a wide variety of cross-category logical operations may be performed to construct new categories, to cluster them to form higher-level categories or to establish links between categories. This software is therefore particularly appropriate for research of an exploratory nature aimed at generating new propositions. Exhaustive coding of all textual units (sentences) and the use of software allowing more than one code to be assigned to each unit also favours an analysis that is grounded in the original text rather than imposing a predefined categorization scheme.

After completion of the coding phase, data were analysed by participants, but also by comparing and contrasting the initial and the follow up interviews, the clients' and the case managers' interviews.

Description of the sample

The sample consisted of an equal number of males and females with an average age of 44 years for males and 36 years for females. A large proportion of the sample were single (73 per cent) particularly for females (93 per cent). The primary source of income for the majority of respondents was welfare (87 per cent).

A small proportion of the respondents had never been homeless (14 per cent). The female participants were less often on the streets for a month or more at a time (47 per cent versus 86 per cent). Although Fournier (1991) reported that approximately a quarter of the homeless in Montreal were homeless for a year and more; this is the case for 40 per cent or the respondents in this study. Thus our sample was made up of a subgroup that was more deeply rooted to the homeless population. The majority of participants in the study were drug users (46 per cent) and poly-drug users (31 per cent). In accordance with the present trend, alcoholics represented less than a quarter (23 per cent) of the sample.

RESULTS

The results will be presented along the dimensions usually referred to in outcome studies. Each of these dimensions will be examined and discussed with the intention of understanding the manner in which the respondents employ them as outcome indicators.

Consumption

The individuals met described in detail the long process they underwent in order to be able to come to the conclusion that they had overcome or were in the process of overcoming their substance abuse problem. Among these accounts, every change in the type, the frequency or the quantity of drugs consumed constituted a sign of movement towards success. However, paradoxically, the relapses characteristics represented the most frequently named indicators in the evaluation of progress with respect to consumption. In order to mark an improvement, relapses have one or another (generally all three) of these characteristics: they are shorter, less frequent and their repercussions are less serious. We can almost make reference to 'controlled' relapses:

> Relapses are less frequent. I relapsed three times in the last five months. Three small binges in five months, one-day, two-day binges. Usually, that was the reverse: two or three days 'dry'. Just enough time to recover a bit.

> Even if I relapsed on April 1st, I didn't demolish everything. I didn't get disorganized at all.

Indicators related to relapses were also recognized by care providers:

> Shorter, less quantity... then she was less deteriorated physically and mentally.

Housing

Emphasis on maintaining one's dwelling represents a first line outcome indicator for homeless individuals. This indicator is usually measured following the time spent in one's place of residence. From the perspective of both the clients and their providers this criterion appears too simple: the mere fact of having a place to live does not represent an indicator of success. Above all, what is of importance is the 'symbolic' appropriation of the dwelling. The relationship with the place of residence was cited most often as an indicator of change, rather than the simple fact of being established in a residence. A user spoke of his home in terms of 'sanctuary'. The individuals encountered felt at ease in their homes. They enjoyed making purchases and no longer sold their belongings to find themselves left with nothing. Their relationship towards their dwelling had changed. They did their housecleaning and maintenance, bought food, and even stored some for later when possible. In short, they had settled down in their homes, and considered a long-term occupancy:

> Before, I rented furnished, heated, lighted flats, and it did not matter. Everything was there. I was looking for the cheaper rent and in inner city neighbourhoods where no one would matter about my consumption. Now, it is the reverse, I am looking for dwelling places where there is no consumption.

Some providers highlighted the importance of investing in one's residence in order to create a link, a feeling of ownership. Investing in a home involves putting a part of oneself into it, while leaving involves losing a part of the self. However, this relationship with one's dwelling develops gradually:

> When I arrive at his home, he offers me a coffee and tells me: 'Look I painted. Look I got this and this.' He has decorated, he has put a part of himself in his apartment. Colors may be weird... but that's his choice. He has invested himself. He tells me: 'Before, I would never have done that.'

Financial situation

One of the outcomes researched by the programmes helping homeless substance abusers is their access to social security, and the adequate handling of the funds received. For users, financial autonomy is also an important indicator of change. Actually, the administration of their budget allows for a certain level of autonomy with respect to their resources and allows them to organize themselves. For both clients and providers the act of taking control over their money represents a very significant outcome:

> I don't sell my belongings anymore.

> Now, I have a budget and I hold to it. I set priorities: the rent, the food, my tobacco and a small reserve for unforeseen circumstances. I have much more discipline at that than before.

Financial autonomy could be a long-term indicator of success. Respondents considered that, once they are in the position to administer their budget without assistance, they will have overcome their problem and could be independent from the services.

Social relationships

In specialized literature on programme evaluation, the following indicators have received a lot of attention: frequency of family and social relationships and activities; and extent of social support and social network. Clients have noticed improvements of this sort as well:

> The relationships with my children are much better, the relationships with my family have improved, with my friend, it is much better, much better...

But the most significant changes were noticed in the area of communication. The respondents explained how changes in their way of being were related to more satisfying social relationships. They made changes in their behaviour and their attitudes, were able to express themselves more effectively, to control their aggressive behaviour, and became more tolerant of others:

> Now, I can talk about my own concerns.

> When I am angry, I can verbalize it, instead of keeping it for myself.

> I am more refined, that's true, more patient. I did not change 100 per cent, for sure, but I can see I am changing.

> I am more tolerant, less aggressive.

Which is also confirmed by the care providers:

> He will tell things in a more appropriate way.

He is less impatient. I see he is more able to deal with frustrations.

Respondents will also refer to more adequate social behaviours:

Now, I will be in a group and I will listen. When someone expresses an idea I find good, I am able to say that's a good idea. When it is not so good an idea, I can discuss it. Before, I would have discarded or discredited the idea without any comment, just saying; 'It's crazy, what you think, that does not make any sense, you are a nut.'

I am more patient, I listen more. Before, I could not stop talking. When I was somewhere I used to take all the place. I was a 'talking machine'.

I am ... less stubborn and less aggressive. (...) I don't whine as much.

Now, I can apologize.

The users also modified or worked on inadequate behaviours such as aggression and violence. Some admitted having to adjust to society to 'avoid' rejection. Their case managers observed that they no longer accumulate frustrations, and that they are concerned with the ways they solve their conflicts:

Regarding the inadequate behaviors, when I was referring to her aggressiveness, now, she can detect her behavior and modify it at once.

These changes that occurred with respect to behaviours, attitudes and appearances were socially reinforced: the individuals noticed that others were more drawn to them. They felt more liked, better appreciated, proud of themselves and closer to others:

I am proud of myself and I feel that people like me more. When I talk with people, I feel that they listen to me.

Now, people recognize me for who I am.

There are many people who really like me, and it is not because I deal coke.

Citizenship

The respondents introduced another dimension related to the regaining of a social status. It was mentioned by some that a better control of their consumption was related to changes in their relationship with society:

I am not a shame for the society anymore. I am not living anymore on the society, giving back nothing. There was a time when my name did not appear on any computer, even not on social security database, or electoral lists, or income taxes .. Anonymous, completely anonymous ... I did not want to be part of the society, of the system ... And now, my name is on many files, I even voted, I quitted anonymity (...). Now, I have a bank book, my name is in the telephone book.

For this respondent, it is so important to have a place in the society.

Mental health

The respondents made no references to mental health indicators in the manner in which they are usually used in programme evaluation, in the form either of diagnosis categories or of scales measuring levels of psychological well-being or distress. However, indicators proposed by the sample such as 'the way of looking at life' or 'the discovery of the self' pertained to the area of positive mental health.

The vision of life

The users encountered clearly dealt with changes in connection with their way of looking at life and in their perception of the world. In the past, their lives were marked by difficult events which they reacted to negatively. These attitudes gave them a negative self-image which they would have preferred to ignore. By modifying their perceptions of these events and by choosing to view them differently, they modified their self-image:

> It is my way of being that changed, my way of seeing life. The fact that I see things differently has changed my life. That changed me. Life is much less difficult if you look at events in a different way, not with only one perspective, but with many perspectives.

This new way of viewing life takes different forms: rebuilding one's life, forgetting death; rediscovering the pleasures of life; discovering one's self.

Rebuilding one's life, forgetting death

The users rediscovered the desire to live, to 'live fully', to build a life, to quote their expressions. Several amongst them believe that it is not too late. They affirm that they still have the hope to rebuild their lives, while others speak of succeeding at life:

> I have a taste to build myself a life, and it is what I do: I build a life for myself.

Similarly, the idea of death, which constituted a central theme in many of the interviews, was abandoned. Having chosen life, the respondents think less of death and suicide. They give themselves a chance to live, they try life:

> It was the death. I was running after the death. Today I don't think of that anymore.

Rediscovering the pleasures of life

These users have rediscovered the 'love of themselves' and, consequently, they give themselves pleasure, they care for themselves. From now on, they benefit from the little pleasures. They invest in themselves and give themselves chances to appreciate life.

If I did not want to succeed, in the first place, I would not try so hard to offer myself some little pieces of good time.

They have discovered or rediscovered beautiful things such as art, museums and nature. Many are having new experiences and discovering new areas of interest. They expand their horizons. In short, they give themselves all possible chances to appreciate and succeed at building a life that is not 'not too boring', that is 'normal':

Now, things have changed, because when I see a show, after, I am very happy, I am more happy than I was when I was taking drugs.

The care providers also appreciate changes on the basis of these indicators:

I will observe that he is doing better, in the sense that he is living better, that he will be more in touch and in harmony with himself.

Discovering one's self

Both clients and their providers consider the capacity to be aware of their strengths and of their worth, but also of their weaknesses and limitations, as a significant indicator of progress. To know oneself 'as an individual' allows one to have greater sense of self-confidence and more self-assurance regarding one's potential:

When I compare with who I was before, I think that I have been able to admit my limitations, but also my strengths and my values. I also modified my expectations regarding people, things, events...

Now, I am very much myself, instead of trying to give an image.

DISCUSSION

New indicators for usual dimensions

The respondents made reference to several areas generally used in evaluative research: consumption, residential and financial stability, social relationships and mental health. Nevertheless, they had the tendency to suggest new indicators with respect to these dimensions. With respect to consumption, the users and their providers invited a re-examination of the relapse, which should not always be considered as a sign of failure, but rather evaluated in comparison with characteristics of previous relapses. What is significant is a modification in the relapse pattern. Less frequent and shorter relapses in a given period of time with limited consequences represented an indicator of progress. Clients as well as their therapists agreed on this criterion and stressed its importance.

The fact of occupying a dwelling place for a certain period of time constitutes a positive indicator in the specialized literature. The care providers used it to assess and rate the progress of their clients. For the latter, a stable residence does not as such constitute an indicator of a positive evolution. To be significant, the occupation of a residence must be accompanied by an investment in their residence, an investment demonstrated in the care (maintenance or decoration) or in the resources (purchases) they put into it.

Financial stability is often associated with residential stability, as a fixed address makes it easier to obtain access to social security. Services providing trust allow for strengthening of financial stability in such a way that it is evaluated positively, when people maintain their trust. For these clients, these criteria for financial stability are too great. From their perspective, they will have attained financial stability at the moment they will be able to administer their budget in an autonomous manner. However, the fact of controlling their expenses and of respecting their budget was perceived by the clients as an intermediate outcome indicator.

The area of interpersonal social relationships forms a fourth area for the evaluation of outcomes. In fact, the clients observed numerous changes in their interpersonal relationships. These changes were no longer uniquely quantitative (more contacts with the family members or a more extensive social network) but also qualitative: richness of exchange, authenticity and profoundness of relationships. The users attributed these changes at work to the incredible improvements in their attitudes (for example, less distrust or suspicion, less intolerance and more patience) and their behaviour (less verbal and physical aggressiveness, more listening).

The respondents did not make allusions to indicators in the area of mental health in the evocation of their progress indicators, in the way that they are normally used in evaluation programmes, either in terms of diagnostic categories or at the level of psychological distress. On the other hand, two of their proposed indicators, 'way of seeing life' and 'the discovery of the self', stemmed from the area of positive mental health. According to the interviews, these indicators were related to the notions of hedonism, self-esteem, autonomy and affirmation of the self. They were also linked to the diversity of interests and to emotional investments. It was also observed that these changes took place during subsequent stages of the reintegration process.

Missing dimensions

The respondents spoke little of their physical health with respect to the outcome of intervention. When they did make reference to it, it was for more serious irreparable situations (such as HIV) or crisis situations (such as assault or suicide attempts). Evidently, general health is not an object of immediate preoccupation of users and their providers, even if their medical history places them as individuals at high risk for numerous illnesses (Raynault, 1996).

Work was the object of a fair number of commentaries from users, but not in terms of expected outcomes from the rehabilitation process. The fact that employment was not considered as an outcome indicator can be explained in two ways. First, some individuals exhibited a certain amount of ambivalence towards work. They found the idea of working desirable, yet they feared that work-related stress would launch them into a relapse. Therefore they wanted to wait to be ready before committing themselves to an active search for employment. The second reason is that few people worked or maintained a significant activity other than mutual aid groups. For those for whom this was the case, this activity had a determining effect on the course of their development. Regarding the productive or social activities (volunteer or paid work) they were more often considered as means than as objectives.

The legal situation was not mentioned, except in rare cases and never with respect to an outcome. It is possible that the majority of respondents had resolved their legal situations at the time of the interview and that this dimension was no longer an indication of change.

References to the use of services were extremely rare in the corpus. The eventual effects on the number or type of services used were never referred to. With respect to services, some clients noted that there was a change in their personal levels of involvement in follow-up programmes or therapies. With respect to the care providers, they noted an increased capacity to maintain engagements and a greater compliance:

> He is compliant with his appointments, he can follow all the steps to find an apartment by himself, he went to verify his inscription at the social security. Our disorganized clients just can't do that, can't respect that. He did not miss any of his medical appointments.

> This is what she has really acquired, I think, her commitment to the AA meetings that she maintained all the way. And she was also able to involve herself in a love relationship.

> She has learned to fulfill her commitments, to maintain her decisions... This was really demanding for her, that was the most difficult part.

Two new dimensions

The participants involved in the investigation proposed a group of original indicators related to changes in their communication behaviours, and attitudes. As regards behaviour, references were made to improved control of aggression, to more suitable social behaviours, to the capability to express one's emotions and limitations and to listen to others. With respect to attitudes, the changes that are considered as indicators are mainly related to tolerance with respect to frustration and differences. These indicators could represent a new dimension 'communication', or be related to the already existing dimensions of 'functional level/ behaviour' or 'social relationships'.

Similarly, the respondents made reference to another original outcome indicator in the social sphere, that of the rediscovery of a social status, if not citizenship itself. Some individuals mentioned that an end to consumption goes hand in hand with changes in their participation in society. They wanted to rebuild their lives, and be through with being anonymous. The acts of opening a bank account, of receiving mail, of having an interest in current events, of voting or of registering in governmental programmes (health insurance, social security) represented indications of their return to civil society. It is worthy of interest that this indicator corresponds to the emerging movements towards empowerment and social participation. Given its importance and specific character, access to citizenship could be a distinct dimension, apart from social relationships.

CONCLUSION

Throughout the interview process, the respondents made reference to most of the dimensions which are usually examined in the evaluation of rehabilitation services for homeless individuals with substance abuse problems. With respect to consumption, housing and financial situation, however, the users and their care providers brought forth several more refined meanings which prompt us to see usual indicators for a new perspective. In the social sphere, they proposed the reclaiming of a social status and of citizenship, as a potentially new dimension, while remaining insistent on the qualitative aspects of social relationships. The users and their care providers cited changes in communication, behaviours and attitudes, changes that until now were not considered in outcome studies. Regarding mental health, clients' and care providers' indicators were of a completely different nature from those that are usually referred to in the literature on evaluation. Rather than making reference to mental health problems or psychological distress, they mentioned elements of emotional well-being or positive mental health. Finally, respondents made few references, or failed to make reference, to physical health, employment status or legal situation. Better compliance and personal involvement were the indicators used in the area of services utilization.

An emerging issue from the interviews was that the indicators could be related to a certain extent to phases of the rehabilitation process. They could have a specific meaning and relevance if an individual is at the beginning of the process or has already established a certain amount of stability in different areas of life. This type of observation leads to the possibility of introducing a dynamic dimension in outcome studies and of modifying the choices of indicators or of the interpretation of information according to the phase of the process the individual being evaluated has reached. Further research should explore this hypothesis, with the objective of focusing on elements that are of great importance for both clients and their care providers. Programme evaluators would then be more able to take the objectives pursued by clients and their providers into consideration by following the stages of the clients' reintegration process.

REFERENCES

Fournier, L. (1991), *Itinérance et santé mentale à Montréal. Étude descriptive de la clientèle des missions et refuges*, Verdun: Centre de recherche de l'hôpital Douglas.

Mercier, C., Corin, E. and Alarie, S. (1999), *Les parcours de réinsertion chez des personnes sans abri, alcooliques et toxicomanes*, Verdun: Centre de recherche de l'Hôpital Douglas.

Mercier, C., Péladeau N. and Fournier, L. (1992), 'Program evaluation of services to the homeless: Challenges and strategies', *Evaluation and Program Planning*, 15 (4), 417–26.

Raynault, M.F. (1996), 'Santé physique', in L. Fournier and C. Mercier (eds), *Sans domicile fixe. Au-delà du stéréotype*, Montreal: Médirien, pp.89–117.

Richards, L. and Richards, T.J. (1991), 'The Transformation of Qualitative Method: Computational Paradigms and Research Processes', in N.G. Fielding and R.M. Lee (eds), *Using Computers in Qualitative Research*, Newbury Park, CA: Sage Publications, pp.38–53.

Conclusion

Marie-Marthe Cousineau, Candido da Agra and Serge Brochu

When deciding upon the formula to adopt for the expert seminars which led to the preparation of this volume, it was agreed from the outset to attempt to obtain the broadest possible representation of research into the question of deviant pathways, without favouring any particular approaches, theories or methods. Indeed, the texts contained in this volume reflect the wide variety of approaches, theories and methods used to achieve a single objective, that of gaining a better understanding of the issue at hand.

In attempting to synthesize the mass of information gathered during the seminars and included in this volume, we faced the challenge of performing a transversal analysis of the material included in all the chapters with the objective of presenting a somehow integrated theory of the drug/crime relationship marking individual deviant pathways. We were rapidly confronted not only by the complexity of the task, but much more fundamentally by the complexity of the reality under study. The different angles explored by all the researchers, the different methodologies and instruments employed and the numerous aims pursued, certainly contributed to the enrichment of our comprehension in many ways. But, at the same time, they showed more than ever how far we have to go and how many dimensions and considerations should be taken into account when trying to understand a human reality.

Many of the studies conducted by the experts who attended the seminars were derived from preliminary quantitative observations of the prevalence of so-called 'deviant behaviours' such as drug use, on the one hand, and delinquent or criminal activities, on the other hand, and the frequent co-occurrence of the two behaviours concerning the same individual. Epidemiological studies permit such observations, leading to more specific questions such as when, where and why certain behaviours would take place, who would be more inclined to adopt these behaviours and in what circumstances. The research by Facy *et al.* contained in this collection (Chapter 12), represents a good example of work conducted in this fashion, revealing how such an approach could lead to more than a simple description of a reality. Many studies cited by Kury *et al.* (Chapter 11) also rely on an epidemiological approach making it possible to establish the prevalence and importance of drugs, crime and drug/crime links.

Also based on quantitative data, gathered this time using a longitudinal approach, the studies by Carbonneau (Chapter 5) and Born and Gavray (Chapter 6) permit us to discover some factors that explain the adoption of deviant pathways, namely drug use and delinquent activities, more specifically by teenagers. In both cases, the authors describe the development of deviant behaviour patterns and identify variables that best explain the emergence of such behaviours, with the ultimate goal of predicting the behaviour being studied. As a result, some individual factors (aggressive or antisocial personality, impulsivity, anxiety) and environmental elements (family disruptiveness or aggressiveness, academic difficulties, association with deviant peers) prove to be linked to the adoption of deviant behaviours such as the consumption of psychoactive substances and delinquency, both behaviours often being present simultaneously in one individual pathway. For Carbonneau, relying on his more recent studies concerning young boys, 'individual characteristics, especially externalizing problems – disruptiveness, hyperactivity and aggression, in particular – represent an early step in the development of later antisocial behaviour'. But, more importantly, the stability of externalizing problems across elementary school appears to be the best predictor of a delinquent career. For Born and Gavray, predictors of persistent delinquency and drug use career rely more on environmental factors: lack of family ties, school drifting, association with deviant peers and valuing a deviant lifestyle.

It has to be said that, in the course of these quantitative, generally longitudinal, studies not only risk factors but also protective factors (close ties to parents, ample time spent as a family, academic and social competence, adoption of social norms and values, positive self esteem) have been recognized. These are seen as enabling young people to resist the influence of risk factors leading notably to delinquency and drug abuse. Carbonneau and Born and Gavray state that protective factors have to be taken into account when seeking to predict the development of persistent deviant pathways.

Other researchers have espoused qualitative methods to understand why and how individuals come to adopt drug-related addictive and/or delinquent behaviours, and to trace the subsequent evolution of subjects' pathways. The focus here is on the individuals' own accounts of their experience. Deviant pathways revealed by way of in-depth interviews with young people or adults adopting such a route are shown to be rarely linear. They tend instead to wind back and forth, at times veering towards more highly deviant behaviour, at others becoming more conformist. This holds true particularly during the adoption of a deviant lifestyle, which is often a gradual process (Brunelle *et al.*, Chapter 7), as well as during the abandonment of a deviant pathway, frequently marked by periods during which the subject goes back and forth (Mercier and Alarie, Chapter 13). The development of certain stages on pathways may even be circular, as Parent and Brochu point out in Chapter 8, in their representation of the mutual reinforcement stage: 'the relationship between crime and the consumption of psychoactive substances becomes bidirectional, meaning that the use of drugs facilitates criminal activities and that the latter help to support the costs of the former'. At this stage, the authors state, drugs become both the cause and the consequence of crime.

The authors would agree that we must find a way to take into account the nonlinearity of the pattern in pathway analysis. In their view, it is not enough to take two (or three or even four) points in time and observe a progression, or regression, in the pathway so as to complete analysis confirming movement in one direction or another. A path, which may appear to trace a linear course in one direction (progression) or the other (regression), will sometimes prove, when examined in light of the account provided by the individual in question, to be dotted with movements back and forth and turning points, reversals of direction which at times may only be short-lived, and at other times may play a decisive role in determining the pathway's course (Brunelle *et al.*, Erickson *et al.*, Chapter 9). Abandonment pathways appear to be more particularly characterized by this sort of back-and-forth movement, often making it difficult to confirm the success of such pathways and, consequently, of the means of intervention used. Mercier and Alarie point out how professionals, confronted by deviant clienteles exhibiting compound problems (drugs and criminality, for example), have observed the development of 'a growing interest in qualitative and quantitative indicators that are more gradual or related to the attainment of intermediate objectives'. In the search for such indicators it becomes essential to understand what factors, in the eyes of those principally concerned, makes them consider that they are doing better. The task of modelling and then getting a better understanding of these non-linear routes appeared to be eased by the use of an instrument specifically designed for the task, such as the *biogram*, presented by Manita and da Agra in Chapter 2. This way, the life history of a single individual could be seen in its temporal and historical course, two dimensions that add to the understanding of the pathway being studied.

It also appears that pathways take on a different meaning, depending on the drug/crime relationship studied. Thus it is important to differentiate user pathways from those of flexers (user–dealers) or traffickers. In all cases, it is essential that the study of pathways take into account the setting in which the pathway occurs. For its part, the path adopted by drug traffickers is considered more in terms of a career than of a simple pathway. Kokoreff and Faugeron begin Chapter 3 explicitly with this discussion of the preference for one reading (in terms of pathways) over another (in terms of a career). The title of their contribution: 'Drug Addiction and Drug Dealing – from Trajectories to Careers', introduces an interesting line of thought: according to the two researchers, while users would seem to adopt more or less deviant pathways, the activities of dealers, flexers and traffickers may be read in terms of delinquent careers. Thus the paths of the participants in the study by Erickson *et al.* and the one by Maher *et al.* (Chapter 10) could be read in terms of careers which occur in a given environment that present a limited number of legitimate opportunities, in direct contrast to the ease of access to illegitimate opportunities, a consideration also mentioned in the studies by Kokoreff and Faugeron, and by Fernandez and Neves (Chapter 4).

Chapters 10 and 4, both of which are based on ethnographic approaches, stress the role played by the environment and the opportunities provided by the individual's living environment or acquaintances in determining the careers of dealers, flexers or traffickers (male and female). In the authors' opinion, a context combining, on the one hand, the absence of legitimate opportunities permitting the individual to achieve a 'meaningful life for him or for her' through the adoption of a conformist lifestyle, and, on the other hand, the presence of illegitimate opportunities leading to the realization of this goal of a meaningful life, creates an environment favourable for the adoption of deviant behaviours. Referring to Dunlap and Johnson's reflection (1992a), Maher *et al.* show how the presence of 'macro forces' of structural and cultural disinvestments and the lack of viable economic alternatives in the formal sector led most women in their study to conclude that the informal economy (linked to the drug market) had more to offer them. It is recognized that the drug/crime pathway is consistent with the adoption of a broader deviant lifestyle, a notion introduced by Brochu (1995) and da Agra (1997).

Regardless of the level of involvement – personal user pathway or dealer, flexer or trafficker career, several authors stress the fact that the individual is, at least to a certain extent, 'master of his destiny'. Maher *et al.*, for example, clearly state:

'deviant pathways are adopted by individuals who analyse their situations quite dispassionately and make choices'. Similarly, Brunelle *et al.* stress the importance of taking into consideration the role played by young people in determining their own pathway and of seeing them, 'not as victims of a psychoactive substance, or of imposed circumstances, but, instead, as interacting with their personal and social environment and organizing their lives according to their own point of view'.

Nevertheless, in Chapter 9, Erickson *et al.* insist on the idea that choices are, at least in part, a question of opportunities, and that those opportunities vary in relation to the environment surrounding the individual. This is where the notion of social and cultural capital introduced in Maher *et al.*'s analysis comes into play. The authors would say of the women in their study, devoid of social and cultural capital recognized by the dominant class, that their 'participation in partying and street life enabled them to amass a significant amount of social capital in the neighbourhood street networks, permitting, for one thing, drug dealing'. Similarly, Erickson *et al.* specify that, in the case of flexers, one can affirm that they 'have lost their social capital (defined as their ability to gain access to legitimate resources in mainstream institutions) and have acquired a criminal capital (defined as connections to various illegal activities and networks that provide criminal opportunities)'.

One can clearly see from the above the many dimensions implied when addressing such an issue as the drug/crime deviant pathways. In this view, would it seem possible to achieve an integrated theory that would take into account all the dimensions potentially involved? Could the autopoiesis theory suggested at the very beginning of this volume be at least part of the answer to this question? Undoubtedly, further discussions are needed.

In closing, we deliberately chose to favour an open approach in this book. In our view, this wide perspective has undoubtedly enriched our understanding of the reality being studied. Indeed, it would appear that, far from contradicting one another, the different approaches used to account for and understand all the various facets of the phenomenon most often tie in with and complement one another in some way. They do not, however, necessarily form an integrated whole. To use a well-known metaphor: each contribution is another building block to be used in the erection of a structure which is still under construction. Many more bricks will be required before we will at last be able to obtain a clear understanding of the drug/crime relationship and especially of drug/crime pathways. This project definitely calls for multidisciplinary cooperation that should take place the very first moment a research initiative is envisioned. The Portuguese research programme presented in da Agra's specific contribution to this collection (Chapter 1) could be taken as an example. Expert group meetings, such as the ones we held, represent another way to attain the goal of sharing ideas and knowledge. But the exchange should not be limited to a few precious moments of discussion, however intense those discussions might be. They should materialize in common, not only comparative, research projects where every contribution has an added value and the result is an integrated scientific explanation taking every pertinent dimension into account: should those dimensions be linked to the individual, the contextual or the structural levels, should the analytical level be macroscopic, mesoscopic, or microscopic. A combination of perspectives, theories, methods and instruments should be favoured. In our view, a multiangled approach could only lead to a better understanding of deviant pathways.

REFERENCES

Brochu, S. (1995), *Drogue et criminalité: une relation complexe*, Montreal: Presses de l'Université de Montréal/Brussels: De Boeck.

da Agra, C. (1997), 'A Experiência Portuguesa: Programmea de Estudos e Resultados', in C. da Agra (ed.), Projecto Droga e Crime: Estudos Interdisciplinares, vol. I, Lisbon: G.P.C.C.D– Ministério da Justiça.

Index

Page numbers in *italics* refer to tables.